MILD COGNITIVE IMPAIRMENT

OXFORD WORKSHOP SERIES

AMERICAN ACADEMY OF CLINICAL NEUROPSYCHOLOGY

Series Editors

Susan McPherson, *Editor-in-Chief*
Ida Sue Baron
Richard Kaplan
Sandra Koffler
Greg Lamberty
Jerry Sweet

Volumes in the Series

Mild Cognitive Impairment and Dementia
Glenn E. Smith, Mark W. Bondi

Neuropsychology of Epilepsy and Epilepsy Surgery
Gregory P. Lee

The Business of Neuropsychology
Mark T. Barisa

Adult Learning Disabilities and ADHD
Robert L. Mapou

Board Certification in Clinical Neuropsychology
Kira E. Armstrong, Dean W. Beebe, Robin C. Hilsabeck,
Michael W. Kirkwood

Understanding Somatization in the Practice of Clinical Neuropsychology
Greg J. Lamberty

Mild Traumatic Brain Injury and Postconcussion Syndrome
Michael A. McCrea

Ethical Decision Making in Clinical Neuropsychology
Shane S. Bush

American Academy of Clinical Neuropsychology

MILD COGNITIVE IMPAIRMENT AND DEMENTIA
Definitions, Diagnosis, and Treatment

Glenn E. Smith
Mark W. Bondi

OXFORD WORKSHOP SERIES

OXFORD
UNIVERSITY PRESS

UNIVERSITY PRESS

Oxford University Press is a department of the University of Oxford.
It furthers the University's objective of excellence in research, scholarship,
and education by publishing worldwide.

Oxford   New York
Auckland   Cape Town   Dar es Salaam   Hong Kong   Karachi
Kuala Lumpur   Madrid   Melbourne   Mexico City   Nairobi
New Delhi   Shanghai   Taipei   Toronto

With offices in
Argentina   Austria   Brazil   Chile   Czech Republic   France   Greece
Guatemala   Hungary   Italy   Japan Poland   Portugal   Singapore
South Korea   Switzerland   Thailand   Turkey   Ukraine   Vietnam

Oxford is a registered trademark of Oxford University Press in the UK and
in certain other countries

Published in the United States of America by
Oxford University Press
198 Madison Avenue, New York, NY 10016

Library of Congress Cataloging-in-Publication Data
Smith, Glenn E.
  Mild cognitive impairment and dementia : definitions, diagnosis,
  and treatment / Glenn E. Smith, Mark W. Bondi.
  p. cm.
  Includes bibliographical references and index.
  ISBN 978-0-19-976418-1
  1. Dementia–Treatment.   2. Mild cognitive impairment.   3. Cognition disorders–
  Diagnosis.   4. Cognition disorders–Treatment.
  I. Bondi, Mark W.   II. Title.
  RC521.S592 2013
  616.8'1–dc23
  2012030247

ISBN 978-0-19-976418-1

9 8 7 6 5 4 3
Printed in the United States of America
on acid-free paper

To Bob and Kay, who taught me how to work
To Brad, Anna, Myles and Mimi, who remind me how to play
To Jennifer, who shows me how to love

GES

To my mother, Barbara, who instilled the value of education and familial left-handedness,
To my father, Frank, my little league coach and ardent dugout supporter through life,
To my children, Conor, Taylor, Keira, and Siena, who've taught the most cherished of life's moments involve but time and togetherness,
To my wife, Karen, my loving companion, best friend, and constant inspiration

MWB

And to the countless families who've suffered at the hands of dementia, this book is humbly dedicated

GES & MWB

Contents

Preface

It might not be the ideal time to release this book. During the period in which this book was drafted the American Psychiatric Association proposed new criteria for major and minor neurocognitive disorders (the entities previously known as dementia and mild cognitive impairment, respectively) for public comment. Field trials of these criteria are now underway, including a site at the Mayo Clinic being led by one of the authors (GES). Within weeks of the American Psychiatric Association's posting, the joint National Institute on Aging and Alzheimer's Association task forces released their proposed new criteria for Alzheimer's disease diagnosis. These proposals include revisions to the 28-year-old National Institute of Communicative Disorders and Stroke (NINCDS-ADRDA) criteria for Alzheimer's diagnosis, add criteria for diagnosis of mild cognitive impairment (MCI) due to Alzheimer's disease, and add a focus on research criteria for the identification of preclinical Alzheimer's disease. This past year also saw the release of a statement from the American Stroke Association and American Heart Association on the vascular contributions to cognitive impairment and dementia, updating some of the decades-old work on defining vascular dementia. So, too, has the American Psychological Association issued an updated version of its guidelines for the assessment of cognitive aging and dementia. At the same time advances in imaging and genetics are generating new schemes for classifying the frontotemporal dementias. The challenge of understanding the spectrum of Lewy Body pathology in everything from Parkinson's disease and multisystem atrophy to Alzheimer's disease persists.

So it may be folly or hubris, or both, to publish a book on MCI and the dementias at a time of such uncertainty and revision in the area. However, perhaps the time is ripe to summarize and integrate these recent efforts in a single source and offer suggestions for neuropsychologists in their daily work with older adults. Clearly the number of patients that can be helped by neuropsychologists is only increasing. The baby-boomer wave is entering the age of risk for dementia right now. We really have no choice but to try to keep up and to offer our unique neuropsychological perspectives to this vast array of diagnostic nosology. So we offer this book with humility and the recognition that by the time the book is released some if not much of the content of the book may be dated and ripe for revision.

Ideally the book is a culmination, aggregation, and hopefully a synthesis of information we have garnered in our professional experiences to date. In that regard, not all of the ideas, figures, tables, or words presented herein are new or novel. We have drawn heavily on past collaborative and separate works in preparing this book. For example Chapter 2 draws heavily from GES's plenary presentation at the 2010 International Congress on Alzheimer's Disease that was subsequently expanded for a review publication in *Nature Neurology Reviews* by Julie Fields, Tanis Ferman, Brad Boeve, and GES (2011). Many of the chapters drew from a prior piece by MWB, David Salmon, and Al Kaszniak on the neuropsychological assessment of dementia in *Neuropsychological Assessment of Neuropsychiatric Disorders*, with Igor Grant and Ken Adams as editors, and from a 2009 chapter by David Salmon and MWB in the *Annual Review of Psychology*. Chapter 9 includes updates to concepts originally reflected in a 2001 *Mayo Clinic Proceedings* paper published by Bruce Sutor, Teri Rummans, and GES. In addition this book reflects concepts and ideas reported in prior chapters by GES and MWB, and by GES, Bob Ivnik, and John Lucas, respectively, in the *Textbook of Clinical Neuropsychology* edited in 2008 by Joel Morgan and Joe Ricker. The focus in Chapter 6 on vascular dementia was aided by the concepts and directions put forward from a few sources, including a chapter by David Libon and colleagues (Seidel, Giovannetti, & Libon, 2012) for the *Behavioral Neurobiology of Aging* volume, coedited by Marie-Christine Pardon and MWB; the landmark 2007 article published in *Brain* by Bruce Reed and colleagues; and a 2011 article published in *Medical Hypotheses* by Daniel Nation, MWB, and colleagues. Dr. Nation was also instrumental in helping to collate and present some of the case presentations in the chapters. We have also drawn on chapters from 2006 by GES with Kejal Kantarci and Mary Machulda in *Perspectives on Mild Cognitive Impairment*, edited by Holly Tuokko and David Hultsch, and by GES with Beth Rush in *Geriatric Neuropsychological Assessment and Intervention*, with Deborah Koltai-Attix and Kathleen Welsh-Bohmer as editors. Finally, in our discussions across chapters on the heuristic value of the cortical/subcortical dementia distinction, we relied heavily on the 2007 *Seminars in Neurology* article by David Salmon and Vince Filoteo.

All of the aforementioned works draw heavily on our good fortune to each work with outstanding teams of collaborators at our respective institutions and Alzheimer's Disease Research Centers. In addition to the colleagues mentioned above we wish to acknowledge collaborators including Jane Cerhan, Dennis Dickson, Neill Graff-Radford, Cliff Jack Jr., Keith Josephs, David Knopman, Joe Parisi, and Ron Petersen, and Angela Lunde at Mayo and from UCSD Jody Corey-Bloom, Dean Delis, Lisa Delano-Wood, Doug Galasko, Lawrence Hansen, Amy Jak, Christina Wierenga, and of course the late Nelson Butters.

It has also been our great professional privilege to work with some of the best clinical neuropsychology postdoctoral residents over our careers. Invariably we have learned more from them than they from us. They have become our colleagues. Their questions and ideas have shaped our thinking and thus influenced this book. Several are listed above but others whose work is reflected in this book include Katherine Bangen, Yu-Ling Chang, Melanie Greenaway, S. Duke Han, Wes Houston, Dona Locke, Matthew Powell, Dawn Schiehser, Nikki Stricker, and Julie Testa Flauta.

We would like to acknowledge Julie Smith's excellent work in managing references and edits to the book. Finally, we would like to thank our American Academy of Clinical Neuropsychology colleagues, who provided the kind offer to have us present our work at its annual meeting and encouraged us to produce this volume on MCI and dementia; and also to Joan Bossert and Oxford University Press for their patience and help in guiding this project from inception to completion.

Overview of the Book

In Chapter 1 we provide a brief history of terminology that has been used to describe the spectrum of cognitive function from normal aging to dementia. We also discuss the current developments noted above that may quickly render this book obsolete. In Chapter 2 we discuss several roles for neuropsychological evaluations in the assessment of cognitive aging, mild cognitive impairment, and dementia. Figure 1.1, though itself an incomplete delineation, includes many conditions we will not review in this book. Chapter 3 provides an abbreviated treatment of the normal aging issues of relevance to clinical neuropsychologists. Then in Chapter 4 we turn to the concept of mild cognitive impairment as a borderland entity between normal aging and dementia and discuss its common assumption as a prodrome for various dementia syndromes. We then attempt to present the remaining chapters in order of presumed prevalencies of the dementias. Thus, we begin in Chapter 5 with a review and discussion of the most common and highly prevalent form of dementia, Alzheimer's disease (AD). Chapter 6 follows with a discussion of vascular dementia, since it too appears to be highly prevalent—though not as prevalent as AD—and is often comorbid with AD (i.e., "mixed" AD plus vascular dementia). Chapter 7 is provided in collaboration with one of our two guest authors, Dr. Tanis Ferman, and focuses on Lewy Body disease. Chapter 8 rounds out our presentation of the most prevalent forms of dementia with a discussion of the frontotemporal lobar dementias. Chapter 9, provided in collaboration with our other guest author, Dr. David Salmon, focuses on some of the rare dementias (e.g., progressive supranuclear palsy, corticobasal degeneration, Creutzfelt-Jacob disease). In the final chapter we close the volume by taking a broader examination of intervention models in the degenerative dementias.

Chapters 3–9 are similarly organized. We begin each chapter with one or two case presentations involving history, relevant medical records and neuropsychological profile. All cases are actual cases from our files. All but one case have autopsy confirmation of the diagnosis, although the case without autopsy confirmation has extensive MRI exams in close proximity to the neuropsychological evaluation. Following the case presentations in each chapter we turn to current diagnostic criteria, epidemiology, neuropathology/neurophysiology, genetics, neuroimaging studies as relevant, associated clinical features, differential neuropsychological features, and possible interventions for each disorder.

As stated at the outset, given the vast array of changes afoot in our field it might not be the ideal time to release this book. Then again, it just might be.

I

Introduction

Terminology for the Continuum from Normal Cognitive Aging to Dementia

In the last 20 years, a plethora of terms and criteria have been proposed to describe the boundary area between normal aging and dementia. In this chapter we will review these terms and criteria. Figure 1.1 is a less-than-complete depiction of the myriad possibilities confronting a clinician when an older adult presents with a cognitive complaint. Although we will venture to some of the other parts of the decision tree in Figure 1.1 and present on atypical forms of dementia (e.g., normal pressure hydrocephalus) in Chapter 9, this book will focus primarily on the right-most nodes of this decision tree (in bold font), namely normal aging, degenerative dementias, and the node between normal aging and dementia. This last node has emerged as a primary focus of dementia research as it has become clear that there may be little utility in intervening with patients after they have dementia.

Benign and Malignant Cognitive Aging

Dating back to the writings of V. A. Kral (1958, 1962), and perhaps before, two forms of cognitive change have been associated with aging. One form is proposed to involve typical, *benign*, and perhaps "developmental" changes in cognition associated with nonspecific histopathological brain changes. The second, *malignant* form includes cognitive and behavioral changes that may

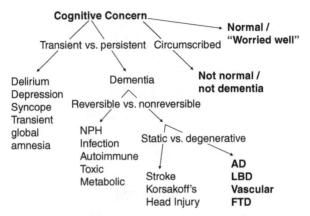

FIGURE 1.1 Schematic diagram of possible differential diagnoses of late life cognitive concerns.

reflect specific underlying brain histopathologies. An extensive nomenclature exists to capture the boundary between normal aging and dementia and can be roughly divided into these two forms of cognitive and behavioral aging. A number of these diagnostic terms are depicted in Figure 1.2.

Benign Cognitive Changes Associated with Normal Aging
Age-Associated Memory Impairment

As originally proposed by a National Institute of Mental Health work group (Crook et al., 1986), the diagnosis of age-associated memory impairment (AAMI) was intended to identify age-related changes in memory performance.

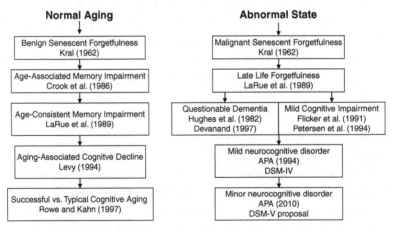

FIGURE 1.2 "Boundary" condition terms proposed over the past five decades.

The method of establishing AAMI diagnoses was predicated on the comparison of older persons to young adult norms on a variety of memory tests (Crook et al., 1986). This method was quickly criticized because it did not recognize that traditional memory measures in clinical neuropsychology have tremendous heterogeneity in terms of their sensitivity to age effects (Smith et al., 1991). Greater specificity in which aspects of memory were to be assessed was called for so that the concept could be reliably applied. Studies using the concept and definition of AAMI continue, many of which originate from Europe and represent clinical trials aimed at mitigating age-related cognitive changes (van Dongen, van Rossum, Kessels, Sielhorst, & Knipschild, 2003). Ultimately, instead of becoming more rigorously defined in DSM-IV, the AAMI concept devolved into a much more loosely defined concept of age-related cognitive decline (ARCD) (American Psychiatric Association [APA], 1994).

Age-Related Cognitive Decline
In recent practice, the term "age-related cognitive decline" (ARCD) has been used interchangeably with "normal aging" (cf., Caccappolo-van Vliet, Miozzo, Marder, & Stern, 2003). The definition of ARCD is not linked to psychometric test performance per se; rather, it is conceptually tied to the focus of interventions on memory that are considered normal for age. Those with ARCD are sometimes described colloquially as the "worried well." The term applies best to the clinical situation where an older person is worried about their memory function—to the degree that they complain to their primary care providers thereby prompting a referral—but there is no objective evidence of memory impairment.

Malignant Cognitive Change
Dementia researchers and clinicians have improved the ability to diagnose and study "at risk" or malignant boundary conditions (see Figure 1.2). Again a variety of terms and criteria have been promoted. Unverzagt et al. (2007) nicely depicted the relationship of these concepts. In Figure 1.3, we have updated his depiction to include newer terms.

Late Life Forgetfulness
Late life forgetfulness (LLF) was suggested by Blackford and LaRue (1989) as a modification to AAMI. It was probably the forebearer of mild cognitive impairment (MCI). LLF was defined by having borderline to impaired

---

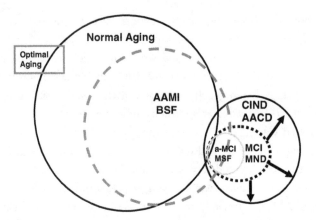

FIGURE 1.3 Overlap of boundary conditions. (Adapted from Unverzagt et al., 2007.) AACD = Age-Associated Cognitive Decline; AAMI = Age-Associated Memory Impairment; BSF = Benign Senescent Forgetfulness; CIND = Cognitive Impairment No Dementia; a-MCI = amnestic Mild Cognitive Impairment; MND = Mild Neurocognitive Disorder; MSF = Malignant Senescent Forgetfulness.

memory function relative to age-matched peers but the absence of dementia. Its usage was quickly usurped by the MCI concept in 1991.

Questionable Dementia/Possible Dementia Prodrome

Prior to the evolution of the MCI concept, it was very difficult to label the growing numbers of elderly patients presenting to outpatient clinics when presenting complaints included cognitive impairment but formal diagnostic criteria for dementia were not met. For this reason, many groups began using a diagnostic category referred to as questionable dementia (QD). Patients were classified with QD if they obtained a Clinical Dementia Rating (CDR) Scale score of 0.5 (Hughes, Berg, Danzinger, Coben, & Martin 1982). Longitudinal follow-ups of these patients yielded mixed outcomes, as some groups found good prognosis in QD groups (Reisberg et al., 1986; Youngjohn & Crook, 1993) whereas other groups showed progressive decline from QD to Alzheimer's dementia (Hughes et al., 1982; Rubin, Kinscherf, & Morris, 1993; Storandt & Hill, 1989). The heterogeneity of diagnostic outcomes emerging from the QD classification established the feasibility of clinical research programs aimed at defining specific clinical and, more specifically, cognitive markers for improving diagnostic accuracy in Alzheimer's disease (AD) and dementia.

Aging-Associated Cognitive Decline

The International Psychogeriatric Association and the World Health Organization criticized AAMI as a concept because it presumed that early malignant cognitive aging surfaces exclusively within the learning and memory domain and not in other cognitive domains (Ritchie, Artero, & Touchon, 2000). As an alternative to AAMI, the term "aging-associated cognitive decline" (AACD) was introduced (Levy, 1994) and defined by (1) performance on a standardized cognitive test that is at least one standard deviation below age-adjusted norms in at least one of any of the following cognitive domains: learning and memory, attention and cognitive speed, language, or visuoconstructional abilities; (2) exclusion of any medical, psychiatric, or neurological disorder that could cause cognitive impairment; and (3) normal activities of daily living and exclusion of dementia according to DSM-IV criteria. AACD differs from AAMI because it is defined by age-adjusted normative data, allows for cognitive impairment in cognitive domains other than memory, and allows for mild cognitive impairment in multiple cognitive domains. Work by Pantel and colleagues (Pantel, Kratz, Essig, & Schroder, 2003) demonstrated that parahippocampal volumes in patients meeting AACD criteria were intermediate between cognitively intact elderly individuals and individuals meeting criteria for AD. As such, AACD criteria appeared to be a feasible approach for establishing diagnostic criteria for preclinical or potentially prodromal Alzheimer's dementia. One glaring omission from the criteria was any assessment of the domain of executive function, which—as we discuss in Chapter 6—would seem particularly relevant for disorders of cerebrovascular origin.

Cognitive Impairment No Dementia

The Canadian Study of Health and Aging (CSHA) utilized multicenter studies to characterize the epidemiology of cognitive impairment among Canadians 65 years of age or older (Graham et al., 1997). A diagnostic concept known as "cognitive impairment no dementia" (CIND) emerged in this population study to describe individuals with demonstrated cognitive impairment (using a modified mini-mental-examination cut-off score) but no clinical evidence of dementia. The CIND classification is a heterogeneous diagnostic category that is nonspecific with regard to the etiology of cognitive impairment. CIND applies to individuals with delirium, chronic alcohol and drug use, depression, psychiatric illness, and mental retardation, although the most prevalent diagnostic subcategory of CIND relates to circumscribed memory impairment. The prevalence of CIND among the Canadian elderly was reported to be about twice that of all dementias combined (Graham et al., 1997). A longitudinal study revealed that, despite the diverse etiologic subcategories of CIND, individuals with CIND had higher rates of progression to dementia, admission to care facilities, and mortality than individuals without cognitive impairment (Tuokko et al., 2003). MCI was recognized as a subcategory of CIND (Fisk, Merry, & Rockwood, 2003), but it remains unclear whether all etiologic subcategories of CIND represent malignant cognitive change (i.e., prodromal stages of dementia).

Mild Cognitive Impairment
The term "mild cognitive impairment" (Flicker, Ferris, & Reisberg, 1991) was initially introduced to describe persons obtaining a score of 3 on the Reisberg Global Deterioration Scale (Reisberg, Ferris, deLeon, & Crook, 1982). The Global Deterioration Scale score is based on clinician assessment/ judgment and ranges from 1 (no impairment) to 7. The score of 7 reflects a vegetative state due to dementia. A score of 3 reflects the "earliest clear cut deficits... obtained only with an intensive interview conducted by a trained geriatric psychiatrist" (Reisberg et al., 1982). Petersen, and colleagues adopted the term "mild cognitive impairment" (MCI) to describe an epoch in the longitudinal course of neurodegenerative disease where cognition is no longer normal relative to age expectations, but also where daily function is not sufficiently disrupted to warrant the diagnosis of dementia (Figure 1.4 broadly

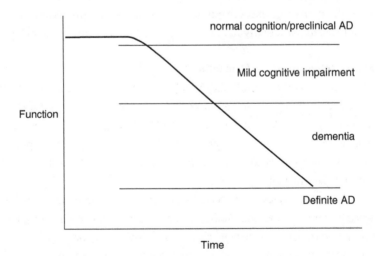

FIGURE 1.4 Mild cognitive impairment as an intermediate stage in the longitudinal course of Alzheimer's disease. (Adapted from Petersen, 2004, with permission.)

Mild Cognitive Impairment and Dementia

depicts this epoch). The initial clinical definition of MCI was proposed to include (1) the presence of a subjective memory concern; (2) normal activities of daily living; (3) normal global cognitive function; and (4) abnormal objective memory function compared to the age and education norms. The development of the Mayo Older American Norms (MOANS; Ivnik et al., 1992) was crucial to the ability to identify MCI. A Clinical Dementia Rating (Morris, 1993) of 0.5 was proposed to corroborate the criteria.

Modifications to the MCI terminology were introduced by Petersen and Morris (2005) to broaden the scope of MCI in order to recognize that non-amnestic forms of MCI are possible, as are deficits in more than one cognitive domain but without appreciable deficits in activities of daily living (Petersen & Morris, 2005). Petersen and Morris (2005) further opined that amnestic and nonamnestic forms of MCI might be associated with different underlying etiologies (e.g., AD vs. vascular dementia, respectively). Today the vast majority of research studies have adopted the use of the concept of MCI and its subtyping terminology (amnestic vs. nonamnestic; single- vs. multidomain) over its many predecessors.

Emerging Terms

Advances in science, technology, and clinical knowledge have created awareness that the neurobiology of most dementias involves long processes with measurable changes occurring perhaps decades before any clinical manifestations of the illness. Jack and colleagues from the Alzheimer Disease Neuroimaging Initiative have captured the temporal dynamics of this process as it pertains to the amyloid cascade hypothesis in AD with a now widely disseminated graphic (see Figure 1.5; Jack et al., 2010).

Similar graphics could be postulated for the tauopathy of frontotemporal dementia (FTD) and the synucleinopathy of dementia with Lewy bodies (DLB) (see Chapter 2).

These new longitudinal perspectives on the dementias are leading to new nosologies for the disorders. As noted in the introduction, both the DSM criteria for cognitive disorders and the joint National Institute of Aging–Alzheimer's Association (NIA-AA) criteria for Alzheimer's disease are undergoing extensive revisions. We will discuss the revisions to the NIA-AA criteria in more detail in Chapters 4–6. Regarding the DSM, the proposed criteria for the DSM-V would do away with the term "dementia" and formal criteria analogous to MCI in lieu of the respective terms "major neurocognitive disorder" and "minor neurocognitive disorder." The draft criteria for each are as follows.

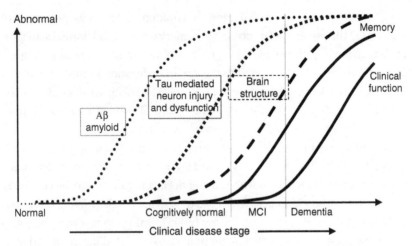

FIGURE 1.5 Dynamic biomarkers of the Alzheimer's disease pathological cascade. (Reproduced from Jack et al., 2010, with permission.)

Proposed DSM-V Criteria for Neurocognitive Disorders

Major Neurocognitive Disorder (APA, 2010b)

A. Evidence of significant cognitive *decline from a previous level of performance* in one or more of the domains outlined above based on:

    1. Reports by the patient or a knowledgeable informant, or observation by the clinician, of clear decline in specific cognitive abilities (attention, language, visual spatial processing, memory, executive functions)

    AND

    2. Clear deficits in objective assessment of the relevant domain (typically >2.0 SD below the mean [or below the 2.5th percentile] of an appropriate reference population [i.e., age, gender, education, premorbid intellect, and culturally adjusted]).

B. The cognitive deficits are sufficient to interfere with independence (e.g., at a minimum requiring assistance with instrumental activities of daily living, i.e., more complex tasks such as finances or managing medications).

C. The cognitive deficits do not occur exclusively in the context of a delirium.

D. The cognitive deficits are not wholly or primarily attributable to another Axis I disorder (e.g., major depressive disorder, schizophrenia).

Minor Neurocognitive Disorder (APA, 2010a)

A. Evidence of minor cognitive decline from a previous level of performance in one or more of the domains outlined above based on:

1. Reports by the patient or a knowledgeable informant, or observation by the clinician, of minor levels of decline in specific
abilities as outlined for the specific domains above. Typically
these will involve greater difficulty performing these tasks, or
the use of compensatory strategies.

AND

2. Mild deficits on objective cognitive assessment (typically 1 to
2.0 SD below the mean [or in the 2.5th to 16th percentile] of
an appropriate reference population; i.e., age, gender, education, premorbid intellect, and culturally adjusted). When serial
measurements are available, a significant (e.g., 0.5 SD) decline
from the patient's own baseline would serve as more definitive
evidence of decline.

B. The cognitive deficits are not sufficient to interfere with independence (instrumental activities of daily living are preserved), but
greater effort and compensatory strategies may be required to maintain independence.

C. The cognitive deficits do not occur exclusively in the context of a
delirium.

D. The cognitive deficits are not wholly or primarily attributable to another Axis I disorder (e.g., major depressive disorder,
schizophrenia).

Whether these proposed changes will be more broadly adopted remains to
be seen. However, at least two concerns to these draft criteria are apparent
and relate to (1) the thresholds of impairment used to separate major from
minor neurocognitive disorder and (2) the use of a one-size-fits-all 0.5 SD
change in performance to denote significant decline. With respect to the
first concern, we have shown that the patterns of Alzheimer-related cognitive impairment and brain atrophy are less salient in the very-old (e.g.,
those over the age of 80) than in the young-old (Bondi et al., 2003; Stricker
et al., 2011). In the study by Stricker et al. (2011), even though the two
groups had similar levels of overall cognitive impairment, the pattern of
changes associated with AD appeared to be less pronounced in people over
the age of 80 (very-old) compared to those between the ages of 69 and 75

(young-old). When compared to their healthy counterparts, executive function, immediate memory, and attention/processing speed were less impaired in the very old compared to the young-old. The very-old also showed less severe thinning of portions of cerebral cortex and the overall cerebrum than the young-old, as compared to their healthy counterparts. This is in part because these brain areas decrease in thickness due to age, so there are fewer differences between the healthy very-old brain and the very-old brain with AD. Therefore, mild cases of AD in the very-old may either go undetected or would be misdiagnosed with "minor" neurocognitive disorder if one expects to see the prototypical pattern *and* severity of cognitive or brain changes that occur in the young-old with AD. The bottom line is that, with the proposed DSM-V criteria, diagnosing major neurocognitive disorder in the very elderly patient may be more difficult.

Regarding the second concern, the use of a one-size-fits-all 0.5 SD change in serial performance ignores critical factors such as measurement error and practice effects on cognitive tests. A growing number of neuropsychological studies of older adults have used reliable change indices (RCI) to account for this systematic variability in cognitive performance over time (Stein, Luppa, Brähler, König, & Riedel-Heller, 2010). Pedraza and colleagues (2007), for example, have used RCI to define reliable declines on the Mattis Dementia Rating Scale (DRS) over two different time periods (7–15 months or 16–24 months), and Clark et al. (2012) have applied these RCI-based DRS declines to examine whether specific measures of executive function predict these RCI-anchored DRS declines in older adults.

This latter application of the direct assessment of within-person change in cognition over time would seem to be a particularly fruitful area for future clinical research efforts for the neuropsychologist and might altogether obviate the need to categorically describe individuals with "major" or "minor" neurocognitive disorders. As Clark et al. (2012) showed, difficulties with complex executive control tasks may herald the onset of more global cognitive declines over time. These findings are consonant with a vast literature demonstrating the utility of neuropsychological performances to predict those who progress to dementia some years later (see Salmon & Bondi, 2009, for review). Identifying those cognitive measures that predict more global declines in cognition would seem to be more helpful for intervention efforts aimed at prevention or maintenance of cognitive function, regardless of the term used to describe that individual's cognitive state.

Conclusion

Diagnostic terminology for the dementias continues to evolve. While great strides have occurred in the shift from belief in pervasive senility to diagnoses like hardening of the arteries to concepts of senile dementia versus AD, and from QD to MCI to minor neurocognitive disorder, it remains likely that additional evolution in concepts and terms will continue. Neuropsychology as a profession has made substantial contributions to our ability to distinguish common cognitive changes associated with aging from cognitive changes that are the harbinger of neurodegenerative disease. Consensus is developing on how to identify prodromes for nearly all neurodegenerative dementias and how to distinguish MCI from typical cognitive aging. Even as we start to use biomarkers, neuroimaging, genetics, and sensitive cognitive measures to identify dementia risk before appreciable cognitive impairment develops, neuropsychological assessment will continue to play an important role in intervention planning, assessment of care needs, and tracking the course of illness for the individual patient with dementia. This philosophy has been articulated in the new American Psychological Association guidelines for the assessment of cognitive aging and dementia (APA, 2011). As strides are made in the early diagnosis of MCI and dementia, continued research is needed to advance the utility of neuropsychological measures in differential diagnosis, prediction of progression, and treatment planning.

References

American Psychiatric Association (APA). (1994). *Diagnostic and statistical manual of mental disorders, fourth edition*. Washington, DC: Author.

American Psychiatric Association. (2010a). *S 12 Mild neurocognitive disorder*. Retrieved 12/1/2011, from http://www.dsm5.org/ProposedRevisions/Pages/proposedrevision.aspx?rid=420

American Psychiatric Association. (2010b). *S 24 Major neurocognitive disorder*. Retrieved 12/1/2011, from http://www.dsm5.org/ProposedRevisions/Pages/proposedrevision.aspx?rid=419

American Psychological Association. (2011). Guidelines for the evaluation of dementia and age-related cognitive change. *American Psychologist*.

Attix, D. K., Story, T. J., Chelune, G. J., Ball, J. D., Stutts, M. L., Hart, R. P., & Barth, J. T. (2009). The prediction of change: Normative neuropsychological trajectories. *Clinical Neuropsychologist*, 23(1), 21–38.

Blackford, R. C., & LaRue, A. (1989). Criteria for diagnosing age associated memory impairment. *Developmental Neuropsychology, 5*, 295–306.

Bondi, M. W., Houston, W. S., Salmon, D. P., Corey-Bloom, J., Katzman, R., Thal, L. J., & Delis, D. C. (2003). Neuropsychological deficits associated with Alzheimer's disease in the very-old: Discrepancies in raw vs. standardized scores. *Journal of the International Neuropsychological Society, 9*(5), 783–795.

Caccappolo-van Vliet, E., Miozzo, M., Marder, K., & Stern, Y. (2003). Where do perseverations come from? *Neurocase, 9*(4), 297–307.

Clark, L. R., Schiehser, D. M., Weissberger, G. H., Salmon, D. P., Delis, D. C., & Bondi, M. W. (2012). Specific measures of executive function predict cognitive decline in older adults. *Journal of the International Neuropsychological Society, 18*, 20–28.

Crook, T., Bartus, R. T., Ferris, S. H., Whitehouse, P., Cohen, G. D., & Gershon, S. (1986). Age-associated memory impairment: Proposed diagnostic criteria and measures of clinical change—Report of a National Institute of Mental Health Work Group. *Developmental Neuropsychology, 2*, 261–276.

Fisk, J. D., Merry, H. R., & Rockwood, K. (2003). Variations in case definition affect prevalence but not outcomes of mild cognitive impairment *Neurology, 61*(9), 1179–1184.

Flicker, C., Ferris, S. H., & Reisberg, B. (1991). Mild cognitive impairment in the elderly: Predictors of dementia. *Neurology, 41*, 1006–1009.

Graham, J. E., Rockwood, K., Beattie, B. L., Eastwood, R., Gauthier, S., Tuokko, H., & McDowell, I. (1997). Prevalence and severity of cognitive impairment with and without dementia in an elderly population. *Lancet, 349*(9068), 1793–1796.

Hughes, C. P., Berg, L., Danzinger, W. L., Coben, L. A., & Martin, R. L. (1982). A new clinical scale for the staging of dementia. *British Journal of Psychiatry, 140*, 566–572.

Ivnik, R. J., Malec, J. F., Smith, G. E., Tangalos, E. G., Petersen, R. C., Kokmen, E., & Kurland, L. T. (1992). Mayo's Older Americans Normative Studies: WAIS-R, WMS-R and AVLT norms for ages 56 through 97. *Clinical Neuropsychologist, 6*(Supplement), 1–104.

Jack, C. R., Jr., Knopman, D. S., Jagust, W. J., Shaw, L. M., Aisen, P. S., Weiner, M. W., . . . Trojanowski, J. Q. (2010). Hypothetical model of dynamic biomarkers of the Alzheimer's pathological cascade. *Lancet Neurology, 9*(1), 119–128.

Kral, V. A. (1958). Senescent memory decline and senile amnestic syndrome. *American Journal of Psychiatry, 115*(4), 361–362.

Kral, V. A. (1962). Senescent forgetfulness: Benign and malignant. *Canadian Medical Association Journal, 86*, 257–260.

Levy, R. (1994). Aging-associated cognitive decline. *International Psychogeriatrics, 6*, 63–68.

Morris, J. C. (1993). The Clinical Dementia Rating (CDR): Current version and scoring rules. *Neurology, 43*(11), 2412–2414.

Pantel, J., Kratz, B., Essig, M., & Schroder, J. (2003). Parahippocampal volume deficits in subjects with aging-associated cognitive decline. *American Journal of Psychiatry, 160*(2), 379–382.

Pedraza, O., Smith, G. E., Ivnik, R. J., Willis, F. B., Ferman, T. J., Petersen, R. C.,...Lucas, J. A. (2007). Reliable change on the Dementia Rating Scale. *Journal of the International Neuropsychological Society, 13*(4), 716–720.

Petersen, R. C. (2004). Mild cognitive impairment as a diagnostic entity. *Journal of Internal Medicine, 256*(3), 183–194.

Petersen, R. C., & Morris, J. C. (2005). Mild cognitive impairment as a clinical entity and treatment target. *Archives of Neurology, 62*, 1160–1163.

Reisberg, B., Ferris, S. H., deLeon, M. J., & Crook, T. (1982). The Global Deterioration Scale for assessment of primary degenerative dementia. *American Journal of Psychiatry, 130*, 1136–1139.

Reisberg, B., Ferris, S. H., Shulman, E., Steinberg, G., Buttinger, C., Sinaiko, E.,...Cohen, J. (1986). Longitudinal course of normal aging and progressive dementia of the Alzheimer's type: A prospective study of 106 subjects over a 3.6 year mean interval. *Progress in Neuro-Psychopharmacology and Biological Psychiatry, 10*(3–5), 571–578.

Ritchie, K., Artero, S., & Touchon, J. (2000). Classification criteria for mild cognitive impairment: A population-based validation study. *Neurology, 56*(1), 37–42.

Rubin, E. H., Kinscherf, B. A., & Morris, J. C. (1993). Psychopathology in younger versus older persons with very mild and mild dementia of Alzheimer type. *American Journal of Psychiatry, 150*, 639–642.

Salmon, D. P., & Bondi, M. W. (2009). Neuropsychological assessment of dementia. *Annual Review of Psychology, 60*, 257–282.

Smith, G. E., Ivnik, R. J., Petersen, R. C., Malec, J. F., Kokmen, E., & Tangalos, E. (1991). Age-associated memory impairment diagnoses: Problems of reliability and concerns for terminology. *Psychology and Aging, 6*, 551–558.

Stein, J., Luppa M., Brähler, E., König, H.-H., & Riedel-Heller, S. G. (2010). The assessment of changes in cognitive functioning: Reliable change indices for neuropsychological instruments in the elderly—A systematic review. *Dementia and Geriatric Cognitive Disorders, 29*, 275–286.

Storandt, M., & Hill, R. D. (1989). Very mild senile dementia of the Alzheimer type: II. Psychometric test performance. *Archives of Neurology, 46*, 383–386.

Stricker, N. H., Chang, Y. L., Fennema-Notestine, C., Delano-Wood, L., Salmon, D. P., Bondi, M. W., & Dale, A. M. (2011). Distinct profiles of brain and cognitive changes in the very old with Alzheimer disease. *Neurology, 77*(8), 713–721.

Tuokko, H., Frerichs, R., Graham, J., Rockwood, K., Kristjansson, B., Fisk, J.,...McDowell, I. (2003). Five-year follow-up of cognitive impairment with no dementia. *Archives of Neurology, 60*(4), 577–582.

Unverzagt, F. W., Gao, S., Lane, K. A., Callahan, C., Ogunniyi, A., Baiyewu, O.,...Hendrie, H. C. (2007). Mild cognitive dysfunction: An epidemiological perspective with an emphasis on African Americans. *Journal of Geriatric Psychiatry and Neurology, 20*, 215–226.

van Dongen, M., van Rossum, E., Kessels, A., Sielhorst, H., & Knipschild, P. (2003). Ginkgo for elderly people with dementia and age-associated memory impairment: A randomized clinical trial. *Journal of Clinical Epidemiology, 56*(4), 367–376.

Youngjohn, J., & Crook, T. (1993). Stability of everyday memory in age-associated memory impairment: A longitudinal study. *Neuropsychology, 7*, 406–416.

2

Role of Neuropsychological Measurement in MCI and Dementia Assessment

As noted in Chapter 1, recent advances in our understanding of the pathophysiology and clinical course of Alzheimer's disease (AD) have culminated in new heuristic models of the dynamic course of dementia development. Models offered by Jack and other leaders of the Alzheimer's Disease Neuroimaging Initiative (Jack, Bernstein, et al., 2010; see Figure 1.5 in Chapter 1) make explicit the idea that brain changes are occurring in patients with Alzheimer's disease decades before the first clinical manifestations become evident, that is, before cognitive changes can be detected. Advances in science allow for the detection of these changes via neuroimaging with techniques like structural magnetic resonance imaging (MRI), positron emission tomography (PET) scanning with radioligands like the Pittsburgh Compound B (PiB), or through assays of cerebrospinal fluid (CSF) or serum measurements of AD markers such as $A\beta_{42}$ or tau_{181} or phosphorylated tau (p-tau) protein concentrations. These models suggest that cognitive changes are a late-arriving phenomenon of the illness. Proposals to revise nosology to permit the diagnosis of neurodegenerative conditions in advance of any (currently) measurable cognitive changes (Jack et al., 2011) have emerged (e.g., see Sperling et al., 2011). This leads to questions about the utility of neuropsychological measurement in neurodegenerative disease.

In addition, with the recent publications of the National Institute of Aging–Alzheimer's Association (NIA-AA) workgroups on revising the criteria for diagnosis of dementia due to Alzheimer's disease (AD; McKhann, 2011), mild cognitive impairment (MCI; Albert et al., 2011), and preclinical AD (Sperling, et al., 2011), it is clear that the neurodegenerative disorders field is entering an era increasingly focused on the role of biomarkers in disease detection, diagnosis, and prognosis. In the nearly three decades since the original publication of McKhann et al.'s criteria on the diagnosis of AD (McKhann et al., 1984), there has been an explosion of research on genetic, neuroimaging, and CSF biomarker correlates of AD. In this era, the concept of MCI was introduced to better characterize the borderland between normal aging and the frank manifestations of mild dementia (Petersen et al., 1995; Petersen et al., 1999).

Yet, despite this volume of work and increasing sophistication in genetics, imaging, and biomarkers in the study of mild forms of cognitive impairment, concomitant sophistication in profiling cognition in MCI has generally been lacking. Part of the problem may stem from a lack of consensus on a uniform set of diagnostic criteria and the widely disparate means by which MCI is diagnosed. Many studies have relied on relatively few measures and clinical judgment. In a commentary on the revised criteria for AD diagnosis published in the *Journal of the American Medical Association*, McKhann (2011) offered that "[t]here are no exact transition points that define when an individual has progressed from the MCI phase to the dementia phase. *It is a question of clinical judgment.*" [italics added] However, research consistently shows actuarial methods to be superior to clinical judgment, given the latter method's susceptibility to a host of errors and biases (see Dawes, Faust, & Meehl, 1989, for discussion). Saxton et al. (2009), for example, have shown how a neuropsychologically based algorithm for MCI diagnosis better predicts progression to dementia than a clinically based interview that stages decline across the spectrum of AD (i.e., Clinical Dementia Rating Scale). The CDR approach produced more "false positive" diagnostic errors (Saxton et al., 2009). In this book, it is our goal to present the neuropsychological methods that are representative examples of empirically supported or best-practice models that rely on actuarial judgment (e.g., operational definitions of impairment, optimal predictive models of progression, etc.).

Neuropsychological measurement continues to play at least five important roles in preclinical and clinical dementia evaluation and care. More specifically, neuropsychological measures (1) serve as biomarkers for illness; (2) serve as potent predictors for development of Alzheimer's disease and other dementias; (3) can dynamically capture countervailing influences on disease trajectory; (4) are proxies for important functional deficits; and (5) can provide insights into interventional targets in early dementia intervention (see Fields et al., 2011). However, in order for neuropsychological measures to serve these important roles in evaluation we must understand and optimize their function. This is the purpose of normative neuropsychological studies (Smith & Ivnik, 2003; Smith et al., 2008).

Understanding and Optimizing Neuropsychological Measures

We and others have sought to clarify (1) what different cognitive measures are measuring exactly, that is, their construct validity; (2) what their normal temporal dynamics are, that is, stability; and (3) what the sources of noise or extraneous variance are that can be mitigated for these measures, that is, appropriate norms.

1. *Construct validity.* A first normative neuropsychology question is what constructs various measures index. Over quite a few years we have completed a series of factor analytic studies (Greenaway et al., 2009; Pedraza et al., 2005; Smith et al., 1994) looking at a common set of neuropsychological measures collected initially with normal older adults. This series of studies suggests that common clinical neuropsychological batteries are likely measuring five to seven broad cognitive domains as depicted in Figure 2.1. These five to seven domains include two typically associated with the concepts of verbal and nonverbal IQ; two reflecting attention and executive function processes; a domain of motor speed; and finally and importantly, two memory domains that separate components of learning (or encoding) and delayed recall (specifically retention). Learning is measured by using immediate recall measures, which is a different memory process than that of delayed recall, which requires the process of retrieval (Squire & Wixted, 2011). It is important to keep these domains and processes distinct. A great deal of discrepancy between amnestic MCI studies arises from treating immediate and delayed recall as interchangeable.

2. *Test stability.* Ivnik et al. (1999) demonstrated for five of the seven broad cognitive domains mentioned above that assessment at roughly annual intervals in cognitively normal older adults, produces an initial rise in scores that likely reflects an exposure effect. In other words, once people have been exposed to these kinds of measures, they perform better the second time around. In subsequent assessments over time, group means tend to stabilize (see Figure 2.2). However, the mean data mask a very important concept that different cognitive constructs have different longitudinal variances. Table 2.1 presents the frequencies of temporal difference scores in a normal sample of

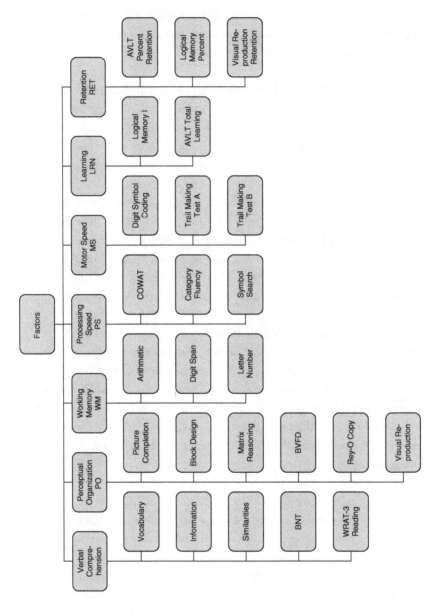

FIGURE 2.1 Factor structure of common neuropsychological tests with normal older adults.

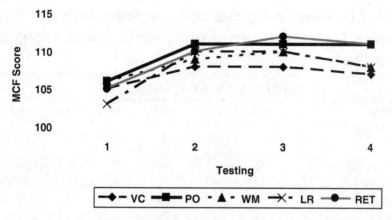

FIGURE 2.2 Mean "practice" effects in approximately annual assessment of nomal older adults.
(From Ivnik et al., 1999)

people tested at least twice over a 3- to 4-year interval. For each assessment, the scale generating the difference scores is an IQ gradient (mean of 100, standard deviation of 15). As reflected in the center column of Table 2.1, only 2% of normal older adults showed change scores as large as one standard deviation on the verbal comprehension index. However, nearly 25% of this sample demonstrated Retention index change scores of a magnitude as large as one standard deviation or greater. In practical terms, this means over 3–4 years, a 15-point change in retention cannot be assumed to be clinically significant, but a 15-point change in verbal comprehension is highly significant. This illustration emphasizes the clinical importance of longitudinal as well as cross-sectional norms, and argues against a single change threshold (e.g., 0.5 SD per the DSM-V draft criteria) for all tests. Moreover, these differences reflect the different temporal stabilities of cognitive measures. Understanding these different temporal stabilities has significant clinical import and is critical to the design of clinical trials.

3. *Demographically corrected norms.* There is debate in the dementia field as to whether it is appropriate to remove the extraneous variance in cognitive measures that is attributable to age (cf. Sliwinski, 2003; G. E. Smith & Ivnik, 2003). Some argue that, since aging is the major risk factor for dementia, it undermines the sensitivity of neuropsychological measures to control for age. *Sensitivity* is the probability that a person with a known condition like Alzheimer's disease will have abnormal test scores, and *specificity* is the probability that a person without AD will have normal test scores. We

Table 2.1 Percent of Cognitively Stable and Normal People with Mayo Cognitive Factor Change Scores of Varying Magnitudes When Retested at 3 to 4 Years

	TEST-RETEST CHANGE SCORES						
MCSF	<5	≥5	≥10	≥15	≥20	≥25	≥30
VC	70	30	7	2	<1	—	—
PO	43	57	27	9	2	<1	—
AC	47	53	28	6	3	1	<1
LRN	36	64	35	13	6	2	1
RET	35	65	43	23	9	5	3

Note: Mayo Cognitive Factor Scores (MCSF) have a Mean of 100 and Standard Deviation of 15
AC = Attention and Concentration; LRN = Learning; PO = Perceptual Organization; VC = Verbal Comprehension; RET = Retention.
(Ivnik et al., 1995). Reprinted with permission

argue that our measures need *positive predictive value* (PPV) rather than sensitivity. PPV is the probability that a person with an abnormal test score will have a condition like Alzheimer's disease. This is statistically more relevant to the diagnostic situation in neuropsychology. We obtain test scores and endeavor to determine the clinical condition. PPV can be expressed as sensitivity/(1-specificity). Enhancements to specificity are more important than enhancements to sensitivity for positive predictive value (Sackett, Haynes, Guyatt, & Tugwell, 1991; Sackett, Straus, Richardson, Rosenberg, & Haynes, 2000). Norms enhance specificity. Several investigators have generated age and education norms for common neuropsychological tests (cf. Ivnik et al., 1992). But cognitive measures have largely been developed and normed in specific majority cultures resulting in cultural biases. Using ethnicity as a proxy for culture, many groups are now trying to improve the performance of neuropsychological measures across cultures through the development of ethnicity specific norms. Lucas et al. (2005a, 2005b) have generated the Mayo Older African American Normative Studies (MOAANS) and in these studies have shown that use of ethnicity-specific norms for African American populations yields vastly improved PPV for the diagnosis of cognitive impairment relative to the application of Caucasian norms to the same population. These studies affirm the notion that the utility of neuropsychological assessment is enhanced with adjustment for demographic sources of extraneous variance.

This need to control for extraneous variance is finally being recognized in guidelines like those being initially proffered by the DSM-V work groups for both major neurocognitive disorder and minor neurocognitive disorder (American Psychiatric Association, 2010).

Five Roles for Neuropsychological Measurement with Preclinical and Clinical Dementia Populations

Neuropsychological Measures as Biomarkers

The National Institutes of Health (NIH) definition of "biomarker" is as follows: "a characteristic that is objectively measured and evaluated as an indicator of normal biologic processes, pathogenic processes, or pharmacologic responses to a therapeutic intervention" (Biomarkers Definitions Working Group, 2001).

Do neuropsychological measures meet this definition of a biomarker? Certainly neuropsychology involves objective measurement. The procedures for collecting neuropsychological data are highly operationalized and show strong reliability (Busch, Chelune, & Suchy, 2006; Lezak, Howieson, & Loring, 2004). However, is it reasonable to suggest that these measures serve as indicators of normal or pathologic processes? As for normal biologic processes, there exists an enormous literature that demonstrates a concordance between cognitive aging and age-related changes in brain structure and function (Hedden & Gabrieli, 2004). Moreover, numerous "validational" studies now show the strong association of objective neuropsychological measures and pathological processes. For example, members of our research group (Powell et al., 2006) demonstrated that an optimized neuropsychological score obtained at enrollment into a Alzheimer's Disease Research Center cohort had adequate sensitivity and specificity for neuropathological findings (both NIA-Reagan diagnosis and Braak neurofibrillary pathology score) obtained on autopsy on average 5.5 years later.

Useful biomarkers for neurodegenerative disease are not just sensitive and specific for any degenerative process, but they are differently sensitive and specific for disorders with different regional and functional pathophysiologies. For example, the utility of CSF tau levels is mitigated if it cannot distinguish AD from frontotemporal dementia. Neuropsychological profiles or patterns can help distinguish the different underlying pathologies because of their different regional affinities. For instance, Whitwell et al. (2009) found a strong association between specific patterns of regional atrophy assessed by voxel-based morphometry and specific patterns of language and memory dysfunction.

They were able to use the combined cognitive and atrophy data to identify subtypes of behavioral variant frontotemporal dementia.

Similarly, Ferman et al. (2006) demonstrated that decreasing scores on visual form discrimination, the Trail Making Test, and memory (AVLT percent retention) measures increase the odds that a person has dementia with Lewy bodies (DLB) *relative* to cognitive normality. However, if we take as a given that the person has cognitive impairment, then differential determination pertains to the likelihood this person has DLB versus the more common AD. In this case the measures perform differently. While lower scores on Trail Making B continue to increase the odds of DLB, scores on Trail Making A and form discrimination no longer contribute to the differential diagnosis. Lower scores on memory (and naming) performance actually reduce the odds of DLB diagnosis relative to Alzheimer's disease.

Neuropsychological changes may be one of the earlier markers of synucleinopathy. In a clinical DLB cohort, we examined informant-reported age of onset for the other cardinal features of DLB, namely, cognitive change, Parkinsonism, hallucinations, and fluctuations. Across the continuum of onset ages, cognitive changes are of course an early marker for DLB, a finding that contrasts with some of the notions of Jack et al. with regard to the purported late appearance of cognitive changes in AD (Jack, Knopman, et al., 2010). This early cognitive change may be more readily detected than any current structural or physiologic neuroimaging marker, leading to a different heuristic model for the emergence of clinically probable DLB (see Figure 2.3).

The final characteristic of a biomarker according to NIH is its ability to detect therapeutic response. It has long been common practice to utilize cognitive measures as a target for therapeutic interventions in dementia clinical trials. In fact, the FDA has institutionalized cognitive measures in this role by requiring that a cognitive measure be a coprimary outcome in studies seeking to show efficacy in dementia (Leber, 1990).

Neuropsychological Measures as Predictors for Development of Alzheimer's Disease and Other Dementias

As noted above, the essence of a biomarker is that it indicates the presence of a pathological process that has *or will* have clinical manifestation. Thus, it is a tautology to say that those measures that serve as biomarkers for dementia would serve as a predictor of the eventual diagnosis of Alzheimer's disease and other dementias. If neuropsychological measures are biomarkers of

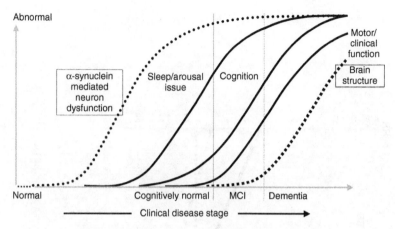

FIGURE 2.3 Dynamic biomarkers of Lewy body pathological cascade.

Alzheimer's disease and other dementias, then they should not only detect the current clinical manifestation of these conditions, but should also predict their future development. And in fact, a meta-analysis of 47 studies involving over 9,000 controls and 1,200 preclinical AD cases (Bäckman, Jones, Berger, Laukka, & Small, 2005) shows large effect sizes for neuropsychological measures (specifically episodic memory) in distinguishing those who progress to AD versus those who do not.

Neuropsychological measures have the potential not only to identify increased risk but also to identify mitigated risk. Locke and colleagues showed how memory scores could be used to positively or negatively modify the risk associated with advancing aging and family history in dementia (Locke et al., 2009). The nomogram shown in Figure 2.4 shows that, relative to a 75-year-old person with no family history of dementia, an 80-year-old with 30% of first-degree relatives affected has a 2.3 times greater relative risk (RR) of dementia within the next five years (see RR column in the middle of the figure). The nomogram further depicts that if the same person obtains an AVLT percent retention standard score one standard deviation below age-adjusted norms that the relative risk increases four-fold. However, if the person scores one standard deviation above the mean, that risk drops to 1, that is, an RR score that represents no increased risk in spite of the increased age and family history. The ability to capture positive deviance (e.g., cognitive reserve) (Stern, 2009), as well as negative deviance, is an underutilized but valuable attribute of neuropsychological measures.

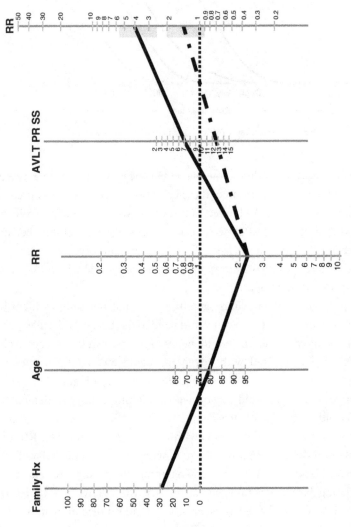

FIGURE 2.4 The interaction of age, family history, and memory performance in predicting 5-year risk for cognitive impairment. Reproduced with permission. (Locke et al., 2009)

Neuropsychological Measures Can Dynamically Capture Countervailing Influences on Disease Trajectory

All degenerative dementias develop over time. They are longitudinal processes, each with their distinct clinical, neuropsychological, and pathophysiological temporal dynamics. It is often assumed in neurodegeneration that these processes run in parallel. In fact, this is implied if not intended in Jack, Knopman et al.'s (2010) diagram of the Alzheimer's pathological cascade (e.g., Figure 1.5 in Chapter 1). That figure shows each marker reaching some critical inflection point and then following a monotonic process to clinical diagnosis. However, at least for cognitive assessments, pooled studies of the preclinical period suggested the possibility that memory functioning does not decline monotonically but has a period of stabilization that could reflect both physiologic and/or neuropsychological compensatory mechanisms (Twamley, Ropacki, & Bondi, 2006). G. Smith et al. (2007) empirically supported a model suggesting a period of stabilization for delayed retention (i.e. memory), but a process of monotonic decline in four other broad cognitive domains (verbal comprehension, perceptual organization, learning, and attention; see Chapter 5, Figure 5.5). Functional MRI studies provide a plausible explanation for this plateau. They show that other brain regions and cognitive processes are recruited in the period after initial memory decline, and that this de facto produces a period of compensated memory performance (Bookheimer et al., 2000; Bondi, Houston, Eyler, & Brown, 2005; Grady et al., 2003; Han et al., 2007). No matter the basis, a period of stabilization has very significant implications for both clinical practice and clinical trials. If people with amnestic mild cognitive impairment (aMCI) have a period of stable memory functioning, then simple stabilization of memory performance in aMCI clinical trials cannot be interpreted as a treatment effect. Instead, it will be necessary to look at other markers, including other cognitive domains. Clinically, we also cannot assume persons with mild but stable memory impairment do not have Alzheimer's disease. While the neuropathological processes may be progressing, memory processes may stabilize due to compensation.

It has become clear that the degree of cognitive dysfunction at any given time is only partially explained by the degree of disease burden. Vemuri and coworkers (Vemuri et al., 2011) demonstrated that at fixed levels of various biomarkers (e.g., cerebrospinal fluid levels of beta amyloid 1–42 and tau, and MRI indices of atrophy and white matter disease), measures of cognitive reserve significantly and independently explained variance in cognitive measures. These authors' depiction of the mediating effects of cognitive reserve

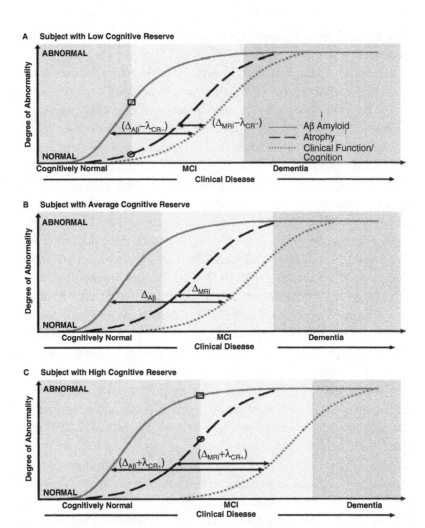

A **Subject with Low Cognitive Reserve**

B **Subject with Average Cognitive Reserve**

C **Subject with High Cognitive Reserve**

FIGURE 2.5 Effect of cognitive reserve on the relationship between biomarkers and cognitive function/clinical disease stage. Subjects with (A) low, (B) average, and (C) high cognitive reserve. At an equivalent level of biomarker abnormalities, people with high cognitive reserve have better cognitive function, and thus better time to clinical diagnostic threshold, than low cognitive reserve persons. (Vemuri et al., 2011, with permission)

on the association of disease burden and cognitive function is depicted in Figure 2.5. The important point is that the cognitive measures capture the impact of not just disease burden but also mediating and moderating factors such as compensation or cognitive reserve.

Neuropsychological Measures Are Proxies for Important Functional Deficits

Neuropsychological measurement may also have two key functions not afforded by physiological or imaging biomarkers. The first, implied by Figure 1.5 in Chapter 1, is that cognitive measures are most proximal to functional outcomes that matter most to patients and families. Patient and families' interest in biomarker levels are generally only in the service of knowing what to expect functionally and prognostically. "Can mother manage her finances, shop, cook, remain safely in her home?" "Will my husband become more confused and agitated?"

In approximately 40% of cases, the older adult patient we are asked to assess is living alone at the time of that initial evaluation for cognitive dysfunction. In these cases, informants may be unreliable reporters of functional status. Yet our cognitive measures can serve as a proxy to estimate functional impairment. Some time ago, Lemsky, Smith, Malec, and Ivnik (1996) demonstrated how iterative partitioning models could be used to deduce classes of instrumental and basic activities of daily living functions based on a brief neurocognitive battery. More recently, Fields et al. (2010) provided a pragmatic analysis of the level of dysfunction across a range of 17 ADLs associated with specific score ranges on the Mattis Dementia Rating Scale (Mattis, 1988; see Table 2.2). This analysis allows clinicians to estimate the likely specific types of functional impairments that a person is having from the Dementia Rating Scale score.

Neuropsychological Measures Can Provide Insights into Interventional Targets

A feature of cognitive measures perhaps least noticed but most important is that they also identify areas of residual cognitive strength. Research is beginning to focus on how to capitalize on residual cognitive strengths, if not to modify the disease course then at least to compensate for deficits in order to compress the morbidity of dementia. For example, if it turns out that procedural memory, that is, the ability to form new habits, is relatively spared in amnestic MCI, then perhaps procedural memory can be used to develop compensatory strategies to mitigate the impact of declarative memory deficits on functional abilities. In fact, as discussed in Chapter 4, Greenaway et al. (2006) adapted procedural-based memory compensation training models long used in traumatic brain injury populations for application with aMCI.

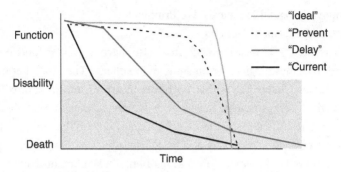

FIGURE 2.6 Heuristic model of prevention versus delay in dementia intervention studies.

Using compensatory interventions to impact functional outcomes is critical. To date, most clinical trials have focused on delaying time to dementia diagnosis without documenting a net reduction in total disability days. Yet without demonstration of decreased net disability, or increased quality of life days, interventions stand to generate only delay rather than prevention of dementia. Figure 2.6 contrasts the theoretical impact of delay versus prevention on total disability burden. If there is merely a shift in the time course of functional decline, then people are older but equally disabled over time. Rather, models of prevention have to focus on inverting the time course of functional impairment to mitigate our degree of disability over time. Using neuropsychological measurement of residual cognitive assets to direct compensation interventions is foundational to dementia prevention.

Summary and Conclusions

Assuming a long lag between the initiation of brain changes and the first appearance of clinical symptoms, the field of neurodegenerative diseases is moving to uncouple neuropathologies from clinical syndromes. It is conceivable to diagnose someone with Alzheimer's disease (preclinical) even if they are cognitively normal. However, just as electrocardiograms provide an important tool linking high cholesterol and poor heart health, neuropsychological measures continue to play an essential role in linking neurodegenerative disease processes to brain function. Neuropsychological measures capture the competing forces of pathologic burden on the one hand and cognitive reserve or compensation on the other. Neuropsychological measures help distinguish clinical syndromes even when pathologies overlap, as in the case of typical Lewy body disease versus Alzheimer's disease. Neuropsychological measures

Mild Cognitive Impairment and Dementia

Table 2.2 Predicted Difficulties and Impairments in Activities of Daily Living Based on ROIL-Part A Score

ROIL-PART A SCORE	0–5	6–10	11–15	16–20	21–25	26–30	31–35	36–40	41–45	46–50
DRS-2 TOTAL SCORE	144–141	140–132	131–126	125–120	119–117	116–105	104–90	89–54	53–45	<45
Basic ADLs										
Eating										D
Toileting									D	D
Dressing							D	D*	D*	I
Washing/Grooming					D	D	D	D*	D*	I
Instrumental ADLs										
Setting the Table						D	D	I	I	I*
Mobility – Home/Neighborhood					D	D	D	D*	I	I†
Using the Telephone					D	D	D*	D*	I	I
Preparing Food				D	D	I	I	I*	I*	I*
Shopping/Handling Cash				D*	D*	I	I*	I*	I*	I*

(continued)

Table 2.2 (Continued)

ROIL-PART A SCORE	0-5	6-10	11-15	16-20	21-25	26-30	31-35	36-40	41-45	46-50
DRS-2 TOTAL SCORE	144-141	140-132	131-126	125-120	119-117	116-105	104-90	89-54	53-45	<45
Responsible for Personal Belongings				D	D	D*	D*	D*	I	I*
Recreation/Organizations				D	D*	D*	D*	I	I	I*
Household Upkeep (Interior/Exterior)			D	D	D*	I	I	I*	I*	I*
Managing Finances			D*	I	I	I*	I*	I*	I*	I*
Function outside Familiar Environment			D	D*	I	I	I*	I*	I*	I*
Driving		D	I	I	I	I*	I*	I*	I*	I*

D = Difficulty; 50% or more patients reported some trouble but required no more than spoken or written assistance

I = Impairment; 50% or more patients reported needing physical assistance or could no longer perform

*75% or more patients with difficulty or impairment;

†100% with difficulty or impairment

ADLs = Activities of Daily Living; CI = Confidence Interval; DRS-2 = Dementia Rating Scale-2; MMSE = Mini-Mental State Examination; ROIL = Record of Independent Living; SD = Standard Deviation. Reprinted with permission (Fields et al., 2010).

help predict not only likely etiology but also current level of functional impairment. Finally, neuropsychological measures help identify residual strengths that can be exploited in interventional models. Even as the science advances, neuropsychological measures remain an essential tool in clinical and research efforts focused on neurodegenerative disease.

Summarizing prior work in mild cognitive impairment, we offer the perspective that the widespread use of cognitive screening measures such as the MMSE across studies diminishes sensitivity to the mildest forms of cognitive impairment, the push for fewer measures populating test batteries reduces reliability and stability of cognitive impairment profiles (Jak et al., 2009; Loewenstein et al., 2009), and the absence of operational definitions of declines in ADL or underutilization of ADL information (Bangen et al., 2010; Chang et al., 2011) limit and diminish the utility of the MCI construct in studying biomarkers and predicting progression to dementia.

We need to do better. Indeed, despite much of this pursuit for imaging and other biomarkers of the dementia prodrome, cognitive variables at baseline remain either comparable or better predictors of progression than other biomarkers (Devanand et al., 2008; Gomar et al., 2011; Heister, Brewer, Magda, Blennow, & McEvoy, 2011; Landau et al., 2010); and these studies have found comparable or superior prediction of progression with *individual* cognitive measures. Outcome studies using more comprehensive neuropsychological assessments – and actuarial examinations of patterns and profiles of neuropsychological dysfunction – have yet to be done. We consider this area of neuropsychological study to be critically needed and to have the potential to help move the field significantly forward.

References

Albert, M., DeKosky, S., Dickson, D., Dubois, B., Feldman, H., Fox, N., et al. (2011). The diagnosis of mild cognitive impairment due to Alzheimer's disease: recommendations from the National Institute on Aging–Alzheimer's Association workgroups on diagnostic guidelines for Alzheimer's disease. *Alzheimer's and Dementia, 7*(3), 270–279.

American Psychiatric Association. (2010). *S 24 Major neurocognitive disorder.* Retrieved 12/1/2011, from http://www.dsm5.org/ProposedRevisions/Pages/proposedrevision.aspx?rid=419

Bäckman, L., Jones, S., Berger, A., Laukka, E., & Small, B. (2005). Cognitive impairment in preclinical Alzheimer's disease: A meta-analysis. *Neuropsychology, 19*(4), 520–531.

Bangen, K. J., Jak, A. J., Schiehser, D. M., Delano-Wood, L., Tuminello, E., Han, S. D., et al. (2010). Complex activities of daily living vary by mild cognitive impairment subtype. *Journal of the International Neuropsychological Society, 16*(4), 630–639.

Biomarkers Definitions Working Group. (2001). Biomarkers and surrogate endpoints: Preferred definitions and conceptual framework. *Clinical Pharmacology and Therapeutics, 69*, 89–95.

Bondi, M. W., Houston, W. S., Eyler, L. T., & Brown, G. G. (2005). FMRI evidence of compensatory mechanisms in older adults at genetic risk for Alzheimer's disease. *Neurology, 64*, 501–508.

Bookheimer, S. Y., Strojwas, M. H., Cohen, M. S., Saunders, A. M., Pericak-Vance, M. A., Mazziotta, J. C., & Small, G. W. (2000). Patterns of brain activation in people at risk for Alzheimer's disease. *New England Journal of Medicine, 343*, 450–456.

Busch, R. M., Chelune, G. J., & Suchy, Y. (2006). Using norms in neuropsychological assessment of the elderly. In D. K. Attix & K. A. Welsh-Bohmer (Eds.), *Geriatric neuropsychology: Assessment and intervention* (pp. 133–157). New York: Guilford Press.

Chang, Y. L., Bondi, M. W., McEvoy, L. K., Fennema-Notestine, C., Salmon, D. P., Galasko, D., et al. (2011). Global clinical dementia rating of 0.5 in MCI masks variability related to level of function. *Neurology, 76*(7), 652–659.

Dawes, R., Faust, D., & Meehl, P. (1989). Clinical versus actuarial judgment. *Science, 243*, 1668–1674.

Devanand, D., Liu, X., Tabert, M., et al. (2008). Combining early markers strongly predicts conversion from mild cognitive impairment to Alzheimer's disease. *Biological Psychiatry, 64*, 871–879.

Ferman, T., Smith, G., Boeve, B., Graff-Radford, N., Lucas, J., Knopman, D., et al. (2006). Neuropsychological differentiation of dementia with Lewy bodies from normal aging and Alzheimer's disease. *The Clinical Neuropsychologist, 20*, 623–636.

Fields, J., Ferman, T., Boeve, B., & Smith, G. (2011). Neuropsychological assessment of patients with dementing illness. *Nature Reviews. Neurology, 7*, 677–687.

Fields, J., Machulda, M., Aakre, J., Ivnik, R., Boeve, B., Knopman, D., et al. (2010). Utility of the DRS for predicting problems in day-to-day functioning. *The Clinical Neuropsychologist, 24*(7), 1167–1180.

Gomar, J., Bobes-Bascaran, M., Conejero-Goldberg, C., Davies, P., & Goldberg, T., for the Alzheimer's Disease Neuroimaging Initiative. (2011). Utility of combinations of biomarkers, cognitive markers, and risk factors to predict conversion from mild cognitive impairment to Alzheimer disease in the Alzheimer's Disease Neuroimaging Initiative. *Archives of General Psychiatry, 68,* 961–969.

Grady, C., McIntosh, A., Beig, S., Keightley, M., Burian, H., & Black, S. (2003). Evidence from functional neuroimaging of a compensatory prefrontal network in Alzheimer's disease. *Journal of Neuroscience, 23*(3), 986–993.

Greenaway, M., Smith, G., Lepore, S., Lunde, A., Hanna, S., & Boeve, B. (2006). Compensating for memory loss in amnestic mild cognitive impairment. *Alzheimer's and Dementia, 2*(Suppl 1), S571.

Greenaway, M., Smith, G., Tangalos, E., Geda, Y., & Ivnik, R. (2009). Mayo Older Americans normative studies: Factor analysis of an expanded neuropsychological battery. *The Clinical Neuropsychologist, 23*(1), 7–20.

Han, Ş. D., Houston, W. S., Eyler, L. T., Brown, G. G., Salmon, D. P., Fleisher, A. S., & Bondi, M. W. (2007). Verbal paired-associate learning by APOE genotype in non-demented older adults: fMRI evidence of a right hemisphere compensatory response. *Neurobiology of Aging, 28,* 238–247.

Hedden, T., & Gabrieli, J. D. (2004). Insights into the ageing mind: A view from cognitive neuroscience. *Nature Reviews. Neuroscience, 5*(2), 87–96.

Heister, D., Brewer, J., Magda, S., Blennow, K., & McEvoy, L., for the Alzheimer's Disease Neuroimaging Initiative. (2011). Predicting MCI outcome with clinically available MRI and CSF biomarkers. *Neurology, 77,* 1619–1628.

Ivnik, R., Malec, J., Smith, G., Tangalos, E., Petersen, R., Kokmen, E., et al. (1992). Mayo's Older Americans Normative Studies: WAIS-R, WMS-R and AVLT norms for ages 56 through 97. *The Clinical Neuropsychologist, 6*(Supplement), 1–104.

Ivnik, R., Smith, G., Lucas, J., Petersen, R., Boeve, B., Kokmen, E., et al. (1999). Testing normal older people three or four times at 1- to 2-year intervals: Defining normal variance. *Neuropsychology, 13*(1), 121–127.

Ivnik, R., Smith, G., Malec, J., Petersen, R., & Tangalos, E. (1995). Long-term stability and inter-correlations of cognitive abilities in older persons. *Psychological Assessment, 7*(155–161).

Jack, C. R., Albert, M. S., Knopman, D. S., McKhann, G. M., Sperling, R. A., Carrillo, M. C., et al. (2011). Introduction to the recommendations from the National Institute on Aging-Alzheimer's Association workgroups on diagnostic guidelines for Alzheimer's disease. [Introductory Research Support, Non-U.S. Gov't]. *Alzheimer's and Dementia, 7*(3), 257–262.

Jack, C R, Bernstein, M., Borowski, B., Gunter, J., Fox, N., Thompson, P., et al. (2010). Update on the magnetic resonance imaging core of the Alzheimer's disease neuroimaging initiative. *Alzheimer's and Dementia 6*(3), 212–220.

Jack, C. R.Knopman, D., Jagust, W., Shaw, L., Aisen, P., Weiner, M., et al. (2010). Hypothetical model of dynamic biomarkers of the Alzheimer's pathological cascade. *Lancet Neurology, 9*(1), 119–128.

Jak, A. J., Bangen, K. J., Wierenga, C. E., Delano-Wood, L., Corey-Bloom, J., & Bondi, MW. (2009). Contributions of neuropsychology and neuroimaging to understanding clinical subtypes of mild cognitive impairment. [Research Support, N.I.H., Extramural Research Support, Non-U.S. Gov't Research Support, U.S. Gov't, Non-P.H.S. Review]. *International Review of Neurobiology, 84,* 81–103.

Landau, S., Harvey, D., Madison, C., Reiman, E., Foster, N., Aisen, P., et al. (2010). Comparing predictors of conversion and decline in mild cognitive impairment. *Neurology, 75*(3), 230–238.

Leber, P. (1990). *Guidelines for the clinical evaluation of antidementia drugs. First draft.* Rockville, MD: US Food and Drug Administration.

Lemsky, C., Smith, G., Malec, J., & Ivnik, R. (1996). Identifying risk for functional impairment using cognitive measures: An application of CART modeling. *Neuropsychology, 10,* 368–375.

Lezak, M., Howieson, D., & Loring, D. (2004). *Neuropsychological assessment* (4th ed.). New York: Oxford University Press.

Locke, D., Ivnik, R., Cha, R., Knopman, D., Tangalos, E., Boeve, B., et al. (2009). Age, family history, and memory and future risk for cognitive impairment. *Journal of Clinical ad Experimental Neuropsychology, 31*(1), 111–116.

Loewenstein, D. A., Acevedo, A., Small, B. J., Agron, J., Crocco, E., & Duara, R. (2009). Stability of different subtypes of mild cognitive impairment among the elderly over a 2- to 3-year follow-up period. *Dementia and Geriatric Cognitive Disorders, 27*(5), 418–423.

Lucas, J., Ivnik, R., Smith, G., Ferman, T., Willis, F., Petersen, R., et al. (2005a). Mayo's Older African Americans Normative Studies: Norms for Boston Naming Test, Controlled Oral Word Association, Category Fluency, Animal Naming, Token Test, Wrat-3 Reading, Trail Making Test, Stroop Test, and Judgment of Line Orientation. *The Clinical Neuropsychologist, 19*(2), 243–269.

Lucas, J., Ivnik, R., Smith, G., Ferman, T., Willis, F., Petersen, R., et al. (2005b). Mayo's Older African Americans Normative Studies: WMS-R norms for African American elders. *The Clinical Neuropsychologist, 19*(2), 189–213.

Mattis, S. (1988). Mattis Dementia Rating Scale (MDRS). Odessa, FL: Psychological Assessment Resources.

McKhann, G. (2011). Changing concepts of Alzheimer disease. *Journal of the American Medical Association, 305,* 2458–2459.

McKhann, G., Drachman, D., Folstein, M., Katzman, R., Price, D., & Stadlan, E. (1984). Clinical diagnosis of Alzheimer's disease: Report of the NINCDS-ADRDA work group under the auspices of Department of Health and Human Services Task Force on Alzheimer's Disease. *Neurology, 34,* 939–944.

Pedraza, O., Lucas, J., Smith, G., Willis, F., Graff-Radford, N., Ferman, T., et al. (2005). Mayo's Older African Americans Normative Studies: Confirmatory factor analysis of a core battery. *Journal of the International Neuropsychological Society, 11,* 184–191.

Petersen, R., Smith, G., Ivnik, R., Tangalos, E., Schaid, D., Thibodeau, S., et al. (1995). Apolipoprotein E status as a predictor of the development of Alzheimer's disease in memory-impaired individuals. *Journal of the American Medical Association, 273,* 1274–1278.

Petersen, R., Smith, G., Waring, S., Ivnik, R., Tangalos, E., & Kokmen, E. (1999). Mild cognitive impairment: Clinical characterization and outcome. *Archives of Neurology, 56(3),* 303–308.

Powell, M., Smith, G., Knopman, D., Parisi, J., Boeve, B., Petersen, R., et al. (2006). Cognitive measures predict Alzheimer's disease pathology. *Archives of Neurology, 63,* 865–868.

Sackett, D. L., Haynes, R. B., Guyatt, G. H., & Tugwell, P. (1991). *Clinical epidemiology: A basic science for clinical medicine* (2nd ed.). New York: Lippincott Williams & Wilkins.

Sackett, D. L., Straus, S. E., Richardson, W. S., Rosenberg, W., & Haynes, R. B. (2000). *Evidence-based medicine: How to practice and teach EBM* (2nd ed.). Edinburgh & New York: Churchill Livingstone.

Saxton, J., Snitz, B., Lopez, O., & et al. (2009). Functional and cognitive criteria produce different rates of mild cognitive impairment and conversion to dementia. *Journal of Neurology, Neurosurgery, and Psychiatry, 80,* 737–743.

Sliwinski, M., Lipton, R., Buschke, H., Wasylyshyn, C. (2003). Optimizing cognitive test norms for detection. In R. Petersen (Ed.), *Mild cognitive impairment* (pp. 89–104). New York: Oxford University Press.

Smith, G., Pankratz, V., Negash, S., Machulda, M., Petersen, R., Boeve, B., et al. (2007). A plateau in pre-clinical Alzheimers disease memory decline: Evidence for compensatory mechanisms? *Neurology, 69,* 133–139.

Smith, G. E., & Ivnik, RJ. (2003). Normative neuropsychology. In R. Petersen (Ed.), *Mild cognitive impairment* (pp. 63–88). New York: Oxford University Press.

Smith, G. E., Ivnik, R. J., & Lucas, J. (2008). Assessment techniques: Tests, test batteries, norms, and methodological approaches. In J. Morgan & J. Ricker

(Eds.), *Textbook of clinical neuropsychology* (pp. 38–57). New York: Taylor & Francis.

Smith, G. E., Ivnik, R. J., Malec, J. F., Petersen, R. C., Kokmen, E., & Tangalos, E. G. (1994). The Mayo Cognitive Factor Scales (MCFS): Derivation of a short battery and norms for factor scores. *Neuropsychology, 9, 194–202.*

Sperling, R., Aisen, P., Beckett, L., Bennett, D., Craft, S., Fagan, A., et al. (2011). Toward defining the preclinical stages of Alzheimer's disease: Recommendations from the National Institute on Aging–Alzheimer's Association workgroups on diagnostic guidelines for Alzheimer's disease. *Alzheimer's and Dementia, 7*(3), 280–292.

Squire, L. R., & Wixted, JT. (2011). The cognitive neuroscience of human memory since H.M. [Historical Article Research Support, N.I.H., Extramural Research Support, U.S. Gov't, Non-P.H.S. Review]. *Annual Review of Neuroscience, 34, 259–288.*

Stern, Y. (2009). Cognitive reserve. *Neuropsychologia, 47*(10), 2015–2028.

Twamley, E., Ropacki, S., & Bondi, M. (2006). Neuropsychological and neuroimaging changes in preclinical Alzheimer's disease. *Journal of the International Neuropsychological Society, 12*(5), 707–735.

Vemuri, P., Weigand, S., Knopman, D., Kantarci, K., Boeve, B., Petersen, R., et al. (2011). Time-to-event voxel-based techniques to assess regional atrophy associated with MCI risk of progression to AD. *Neuroimage, 54*(2), 985–991.

Vemuri, P., Weigand, S. D., Przybelski, S. A., Knopman, D. S., Smith, G. E., Trojanowski, J. Q., et al. (2011). Cognitive reserve and Alzheimer's disease biomarkers are independent determinants of cognition. *Brain, 134*(Pt 5), 1479–1492.

Whitwell, J. L., Przybelski, S. A., Weigand, S. D., Ivnik, R. J., Vemuri, P., Gunter, J. L., et al. (2009). Distinct anatomical subtypes of the behavioural variant of frontotemporal dementia: A cluster analysis study. *Brain, 132*(11), 2932–2946.

3

■ ■ ■

Normal Cognitive Aging

Case Presentation

A 76-year-old retired nurse agreed to serve as a normal control subject in a longitudinal study on aging, cognition, and dementia. The subject and her husband had been married for 50 years. She had been retired for 15 years after being a nurse for over 40 years. She continued to do some private duty nursing after formally retiring and had only completely retired in the last three years. She was a nonsmoker and an occasional drinker. At initial research evaluation, she had hypertension and was on treatment with a calcium channel blocker and diuretic. She denied any current cardiovascular symptoms. Other medical history included osteoporosis, present for over 20 years, mild degenerative joint disease, and a history of compression fractures of the spine with numerous work-ups and evaluations in the Bone Clinic. She was trying to walk as much as she could. Her participation in the research was likely motivated by the fact that her husband had Alzheimer's disease, which was progressing slowly. At her enrollment, her husband was not able to complete normal daytime activities, putting her in a stressful situation on many occasions.

Family History

Her father died in his 40s following complications from surgery. Her mother died at age 88 of a cardiac arrest. One brother died of congestive

(continued)

---

heart failure and respiratory arrest at age 73. One sister had a history of hypertension and died suddenly at age 70. She had two sons.

Medications
She was taking Dyazide, Premarin, calcium carbonate, and Cardizem.

Course of Illness
Her husband died suddenly about four years after her enrollment in the study. She continued to participate in the research undergoing abbreviated annual cognitive evaluations and neuroimaging studies in this context. These evaluations included the Dementia Rating Scale (DRS) and the Rey Auditory Verbal Learning Test (AVLT). Over this interval, her DRS scores were 143,142, 143, and 136. Her AVLT percent retention was never below 100%. Her weakest AVLT total learning score came on the annual evaluation that occurred six months after her husband's death. In subsequent years, this score recorded consistently above average. About 9 years after enrollment, she had a fall and fractured her shoulder. She had a confusional episode following surgery to repair her shoulder. She spent 3 months in nursing home care rehabilitation from this episode.

Ten years after her enrollment, she had a final research MRI as shown below (Figure 3.1). This was read by the radiologist as: "Comparison to

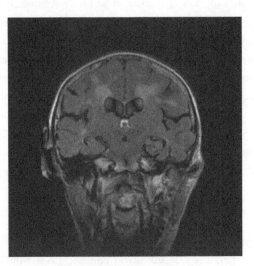

FIGURE 3.1 Normal patient MRI at 10 years after initial evaluation

(continued)

previous scan. There has been further progression of advanced leukoariosis. Stable generalized atrophy. Otherwise unchanged."

She was seen by her primary health care provider in the 12th year after study enrollment. The primary issue for the visit remained her hypertension. Five days after this visit, she died suddenly at age 88 of presumed cardiac causes. She had agreed to brain autopsy as part of the research.

Brain Autopsy

1. Hypoxic encephalopathy, acute (agonal), mild, with (a) Acute ischemic cell change in scattered neocortical and subcortical neurons, rare hippocampal pyramidal cells and cerebellar Purkinje cells. (b) Cerebral edema, mild, generalized, superimposed on mild cerebral atrophy, left hemibrain weight 733 g.
2. Argyrophilic grain (Braak) disease, with medial temporal pretangles, grains, tau-positive astrocytes, and coiled bodies, and ballooned neurons in amygdala and limbic cortices.
3. Nonspecific neurodegenerative changes of the Alzheimer type, mild (CERAD: Normal; Braak & Braak: Stage II; NIA-Reagan: Low likelihood), with (a) Neocortex with moderate diffuse plaques, sparse neuritic plaques and absent neurofibrillary tangles, and absent to sparse pretangles and threads.

Neuropsychological Findings

Figure 3.2 provides age adjusted standard (z-) score data across a variety of cognitive measures from initial evaluation and a 5-year follow-up.

A couple features of this case are instructive. First, note the evidence for a temporary decline in test performance in the aftermath of her husband's death. Also note that the patient was observed on neuroimaging and at autopsy to have noteworthy white matter disease but no evidence of cognitive dysfunction. The frequent occurrence of substantial white matter disease in cognitively normal older adults makes it difficult to interpret the role of white matter disease in many cases of cognitive dysfunction (as we discuss in greater detail in Chapter 6).

(continued)

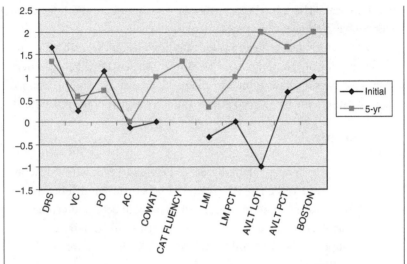

FIGURE 3.2 Neuropsychological profile of normal participant. (All scores are age adjusted z scores). VC = Verbal comprehension, PO = perceptual organization, AC = Attention and Concentration (all from Mayo Cognitive Factor Scores; Smith, Ivnik, Malec, & Tangalos, 1993), COWAT = Controlled Oral Word Association Test (Benton & Hamsher, 1978), Cat Fluency = Category Fluency test, LM1 = Wechsler Memory Scale Revised (WMS-R; Wechsler, 1987), Logical Memory Immediate Recall, LMPCT = WMS-R Logical Memory Delay divided by LM1. AVLTLOT = Rey Auditory Verbal Learning Test (AVLT; Rey, 1964) total of trials 1–5 minus 5*trial 1 (see Ivnik et al., 1992). AVLTPCT = AVLT 30-minute delay divided by AVLT trial 5. Boston = Boston Naming Test (Kaplan, Goodglass, & Weintraub, 1983).

Models of Aging

At least one biological model of development distinguishes two phases of life: growth and aging. This model is based primarily on the observation that for most organisms there is a period of physical growth and differentiation, leading to maturity, then a period of "senescing" (Schroots & Birren, 1996). Senescing refers to a loss of functional capacity and adaptability. Note that disease also tends to produce loss of functional capacity and adaptability. Thus aging and disease are often conflated or at least viewed in parallel in biological aging. A contrasting developmental view is the life-span perspective (Baltes & Reese, 1984). Within this perspective, "the changes (growth, development, aging) shown by people from the time of their conception, throughout their lives, and until the time of their death are usefully conceptualized as development" (Baltes & Reese, 1984, p. 493).

The life-span perspective recognizes changes in functional status as characteristic of the entire life span. It avoids pejorative or abnormality terms for these processes. Within this model "maturation" continues after physical growth, continuing even until the time of death. Throughout maturation, psychological processes change.

Different conceptualizations of age-related cognitive changes can arise from these contrasting views of aging. For example, the senescence model may produce the conclusion that age-related changes require diagnoses and treatment. The condition of presbyopia provides a good example of this model. Accurate identification of common, age-related changes in vision can lead to provision of glasses or surgery that maintain visual function and therefore greater independence. A life-span perspective is likely to view age-related cognitive changes less as a condition and more as a stage of life. Retirement provides a good example. Retirement is typically seen as a developmental phase rather than as "work impairment." The response to this stage may be to change our expectations for the person (i.e., no longer expecting them to work), rather than change the person.

Whether researchers and clinicians embrace a senescence or life-span development model of aging influences their approach to the spectrum from normal aging to disease. Advocates of one or another model of aging will embrace different definitions of normal aging. It should be recognized that choices about models of aging and definitions of normal aging reflect philosophical rather than empirical decisions on the part of researchers and clinicians.

General Considerations in Neuropsychological Assessment with Older Adults

When working with older adults there are a number of general considerations that the neuropsychologist should bear in mind that relate to the choice and administration of appropriate neuropsychological tests. Examples of age-related factors that ought to be considered include sensory changes, physical disabilities, and generalized response slowing (see Bondi, Salmon, & Kaszniak, 1996). For example, hearing loss is quite common, especially in those over 75 years of age, and can easily affect the results of any verbal/auditory tests of cognition. Losses in visual acuity from a number of possible causes (e.g., cataracts, glaucoma, macular degeneration, etc.) also are common and can affect the results of any tests requiring the processing of visual information. Uncorrected visual difficulties, as is the case when individuals forget to bring their reading glasses to testing, can contribute to errors on visual tasks. Thus, if either hearing or visual capabilities are questioned, it may be helpful to administer simple tests of auditory discrimination and visual acuity prior to neuropsychological testing. So too will well-illuminated rooms, clear and direct speech of sufficient volume, and perhaps the use of larger printed materials if available. Finally, the contributions of physical disabilities (e.g., arthritis, fatigue) and generalized response slowing should be borne in mind as well. If severe, the neuropsychologist may wish to rely more heavily on untimed tests that are less likely to be negatively affected by a subject's particular physical difficulties. Neuropsychologists may also wish to "test the limits" by allowing the older individual to continue working on a task after standard cut-off times have passed in order to get a more complete picture of the person's cognitive strengths and weaknesses.

Definitions of Normal Aging: Optimal versus Typical Cognitive Aging

Models of aging influence definitions of normal aging and the methods used to study aging. Experimental neuropsychologists and cognitive-aging researchers often study the effects of aging alone on cognitive function. The definition of aging as the passage of time alone, exclusive of age-related diseases, has been associated with the term "successful aging" (J. W. Rowe & Kahn, 1998). Within this paradigm, older persons with common medical illnesses or taking medications that have the slightest potential to affect cognition (e.g., diabetes, chronic obstructive pulmonary disease) are excluded from study. This strategy enables cognitive aging theorists to isolate the impact of the passage of time alone on the organism's cognition. Cohorts of persons studied in these paradigms are often described as "super normals" because their performances tend to cluster at the upper end of the distribution on measures of mental or physical functioning. Studies of successful aging provide a picture of the impact of uncomplicated but uncommon forms of aging.

An alternate approach in cognitive aging studies is to study *typical* aging. This definition accepts common age-associated diseases as physiologically typical of the aging process, that is, part of development. Within this definition of normal aging, persons with common medical conditions, using common medications, and so forth, are included. Studies of typical aging often provide a different and perhaps less optimistic picture of normal cognitive aging than studies of optimal aging (Smith, Ivnik, & Lucas, 2008).

Cognitive Aging Study Designs

Irrespective of the types of participants included, studies of cognitive aging are typically founded on either cross-sectional (interindividual comparison) or longitudinal (intraindividual comparison) design. Most cross-sectional studies of cognitive aging compare the performance of older adults to the performance of younger adults at a single point in time. This approach is favored for its practicality and its ability to appreciate obvious dimensions of difference between age groups on a given cognitive task. However, a major disadvantage to this approach is that between-group comparisons do not take into account cohort effects (e.g., differential access to quality education). Therefore, cross-sectional studies can provide evidence of cognitive differences between older and younger adult cohorts but may provide misleading information about patterns of functioning over time or rates of decline within individuals.

Longitudinal studies compare levels of performance across serial evaluations within individuals and, therefore, provide information about patterns of performance over time. Longitudinal studies advance our understanding of typical cognitive aging by allowing us to examine individual differences in rates of cognitive change. Longitudinal studies of cognitive aging are expensive and time and labor intensive, and studies that can model intraindividual cognitive change over decades are few. Moreover, longitudinal studies can suffer from selective attrition (the tendency for lower scoring members of a cohort to drop out of studies more rapidly) as well as from cohort effects that limit generalizability. For example, adults currently older than 75 years were exposed to the Great Depression, whereas subsequent cohorts were not.

More complex designs involving shorter longitudinal follow-up of cross-sectional cohorts are tenable. A few key *cross-sequential* studies have used such designs with great success to understand cognitive aging (cf. Schaie, 1994). Cross-sequential designs allow two or more age cohorts to be tested two or more times. Cross-sequential studies of typical aging may be most relevant to clinicians who practice in settings where they must distinguish neuropathology-related impairment (e.g., MCI or dementing disorders) from other age-related processes. Such studies can constitute longitudinal normative studies and generate norms not only for cross-sectional but also for longitudinal assessment. Admittedly, normative studies of aging have a different focus than cognitive aging studies.

Neuropsychology of Cognitive Aging
Successful Cognitive Aging
Successful *cognitive* aging is but one form of successful aging. A few "optimally" aging people may avoid cognitive decline as they age (Powell, 1994). Studies of successful cognitive aging focus on persons whose physical health may or may not be exceptional but whose cognitive function remains exceptional. Nevertheless, and not surprisingly, persons meeting various definitions of successful cognitive aging have better survival and lower risk for functional and cognitive decline (Negash et al., 2011). Negash et al.'s methods are further delineated below.

Typical Cognitive Aging
An exhaustive review of the extensive theorizing, controversies, and research in cognitive aging are well beyond the scope of this chapter. These controversies have been described and discussed elsewhere (see Depp, Harmell, & Vahia, 2012, for discussion). Suffice it to say, most researchers agree that cognitive change is a pervasive part of advancing age (cf. Albert & Killiany, 2001). For most people, cognitive efficiency and flexibility peak in early adulthood. This is followed by a slow loss of cognitive efficiency that may typically accelerate during the fifth decade.

A hallmark of cognitive aging is a reduction in mental processing speed (Salthouse, 2010). Multiple studies have demonstrated that limitations in mental processing speed consequently result in age-related changes in performance across many cognitive domains including attention, language, memory, and executive functions (Finkel & Pederson, 2000; Fisher, Duffy, & Katskiopoulos, 2000; Hertzog & Bleckley, 2001; Meyerson, Adams, Hale, & Jenkins, 2003; Meyerson, Jenkins, Hale, & Sliwinski, 2000; Parkin & Java, 2000; Salthouse, 2010; Zimprich, 2002). Studies of "normal" memory change reveal that, compared to younger adults, healthy older adults are less efficient at encoding to-be-learned information and therefore have greater difficulty recalling information following a delay period (e.g., Brebion, Smith, & Ehrlich, 1997; Frieske & Park, 1999; LaRue, 1992; Light, 1996; Park et al., 1996; Sliwinski & Buschke, 1999).

Implications for Normative Studies

In Chapter 2, we briefly discussed the utility of norms, including age-based norms. The present discussion of successful versus typical cognitive aging is germane to that discussion. The recognition that preclinical dementia-related neuropathology is present in a proportion of normally aging individuals prior to cognitive declines, has given rise to a number of normative neuropsychological studies that propose the use of so-called *robust* norms—a notion first forwarded by Sliwinski and colleagues (Sliwinski, Lipton, Buschke, & Stewart, 1996). Proponents of robust norms argue that normative samples may be "contaminated" with cases of preclinical dementia that can lead to underestimation of the test mean and overestimation of its variance, thus reducing the clinical utility of the norms—particularly for tasks designed for dementia evaluations. Robust norming is an approach that follows a normative cohort for some period of time, identifies those who develop dementia during that follow-up period, and removes those preclinical dementia cases from the normative cohort while retaining only those who remain dementia free. With this method, a handful of studies have shown that longitudinal robust norms are at least as useful as cross-sectional conventional norms in detecting cognitive impairment among older adults and may be more accurate than conventional norms in predicting preclinical dementia cases (De Santi et al., 2008; Marcopulos & McLain, 2003; Pedraza et al., 2010; Sliwinski, et al., 1996). However, the incremental sensitivity of this method may not justify the considerable expense. It may be easier to simply use epidemiological methods to estimate the prevalence of preclinical cases in normative cohorts and adjust cut scores accordingly (Smith et al., 2008).

Genetic Influences on Successful Aging

Most studies to date have focused on the more general question of identifying genetic influences on longevity, or the genetic basis for the human lifespan, although within this broader domain a nascent area of research is growing on the specific genetic influences of successful aging. Glatt, Chayavichitsilp, Depp, Schork, and Jeste (2007) reviewed a number of studies and found several specific genes that hold promise for future studies designed to advance our understanding of the genetic basis of successful aging. They include: apolipoprotein E (APOE), glutathione S-transferase θ1 (GSTT1), interleukins 6 (IL6) and 10 (IL10), paraoxonase 1 (PON1), and sirtuin 3 (SIRT3). While most of these candidate genes are thought to relate to physiologic processes that might jointly influence successful aging (e.g., regulating metabolism, immunity, protein production, cardiovascular output, and the cell cycle), APOE would be representative of a smaller subset of genes that influences cognition given its role in promoting (ε4 allele) or mitigating (ε2 allele) dementia risk generally and Alzheimer's disease in particular.

Impact of Knowledge of Genetic Risks

Aside from the direct genetic influences on successful aging, few have studied whether knowledge of one's own genetic risks would have negative consequences on emotional status or self-efficacy beliefs. These questions are central to some of the current medical ethical debates focused on the risks and benefits of disclosing to individuals knowledge of genetic risks for which there is no effective treatment, and APOE is a gene at the center of this debate. For example, a study by Green et al. (2009) suggests that disclosure has few adverse emotional risks. Groups of healthy nondemented older adults with a living or deceased parent with AD were randomly assigned to a disclosure group informed of their APOE gene status or a nondisclosure group who did not receive this information. They found that the two groups did not differ in levels of depression or anxiety in the year following disclosure. This finding was true regardless of whether disclosure revealed APOE ε4+ or ε4- gene status. Despite the low emotional impact of APOE genotype disclosure shown by Green et al. (2009), Kane and Kane (2009) argue that few benefits are to be gained by informing cognitively normal older adults that they may be at risk for a disease that cannot be prevented and for which available treatments offer only limited help.

The impact of knowledge of one's own APOE genotype on subjective ratings of memory and objective memory test performance of older adults is unknown. Because the devastating impact of AD on the ability to remember is widely known, older adults who know they have a genetic risk for the disease might be more likely to have lower subjective ratings of their memory than those who do not have the risk or do not know their genotype. It is also possible that knowledge of genetic risk for AD could influence objective memory performance. Knowledge that one possesses a characteristic associated with poor cognitive performance can lead to lowered self-efficacy beliefs (i.e., belief in one's capability to produce a given level of performance) that may result in underperformance on objective memory tests due to low confidence, reduced effort, or lack of perseverance (Bandura, 1986). Studies show that negative stereotypes about aging lead to decreased self-efficacy beliefs related to memory ability and decreased memory test performance in older adults (Desrichard & Kopetz, 2005). On the other hand, higher self-efficacy regarding memory ability is associated with better memory test performance (Valentijn et al., 2006). These results suggest that memory test performance might be influenced by the extent to which knowledge of APOE genotype leads them to question or to have confidence in their memory ability.

Salmon and colleagues (Salmon, Lineweaver, Bondi, & Galasko, 2012) administered objective memory tests and self-rating scales of memory function to cognitively normal older adults who either knew or did not know their genotype and genetic risk for AD prior to neuropsychological evaluation. Although APOE genotype did not have an overall main effect on subjective self-ratings, objective memory scores, or depressive affect, a significant interaction effect was observed between genotype and disclosure on several memory rating scales and on tests of immediate and delayed verbal recall. Older adults who knew their APOE ε4+ genotype tended to judge their memory more harshly and performed worse on an objective verbal memory test than did ε4+ adults who did not know. In contrast, older adults who knew theirε4- genotype judged their memory more positively than did ε4- adults who did not know, but these groups did not differ in objective memory test performance (see Figure 3.3). This study provides evidence that informing older adults that they have an APOE genotype associated with increased risk of AD can have adverse consequences not only on their perception of their memory abilities but also on their performances on objective memory tests, despite limited effects on emotional status. Knowledge of genotype and risk of AD should be considered when evaluating cognition in the elderly.

Emerging Issues of Disclosure of Dementia-Associated Risks

Issues related to disclosure are likely to intensify in the coming years as more knowledge of AD risks and biomarkers become more widely available to practitioners and the public. For example, the first amyloid imaging ligand that uses fluorine 18, florbetapir F18 (Amyvid™), has received FDA approval and is likely to be incorporated into clinical practice with increasing regularity. Once this is available, of course people will want to know the results of their specific amyloid burden and what those results may mean. Clinical trials too will likely use amyloid imaging to identify candidates for antiamyloid treatment trials. On the one hand, such information, once disclosed, may help people to cope better when they have this information for future planning purposes. On the other hand, knowledge that one carries a significant amount of Alzheimer's disease plaque pathology in their brain, without access to treatment to eradicate or

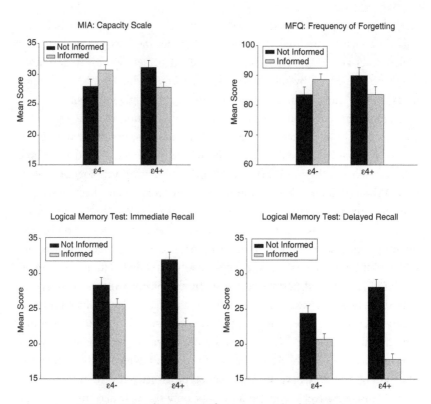

FIGURE 3.3 Mean scores depicting significant genotype by disclosure interaction effects (p < .05) on subscales of the Metamemory in Adulthood (MIA) scale and Memory Functioning Questionnaire (MFQ), and memory test performances for each Genotype (ε4- vs. ε4+) X Disclosure (not informed vs. informed) group. Error bars represent standard error of the mean. From Salmon et al. (2012). From a presentation but not yet published.

lessen that pathology, may have adverse effects—much in the same way that, as Salmon et al. (2012) demonstrated, knowledge of one's own APOE genotypic risk for AD had adverse effects on subjective memory ratings as well as objective memory performances. Similar implications can be drawn for those with knowledge of AD risk based on neuroimaging or CSF biomarkers. The impact of such knowledge could have serious clinical consequences by increasing the likelihood of false-positive diagnosis of dementia or MCI in those who know they carry AD biomarkers or risks, or could distort the results of AD primary prevention clinical trials if those with knowledge of their AD risk is over-represented in an unbalanced way in either the placebo or treatment arm of a trial.

To date, there are no formal guidelines on this issue (see Kane & Kane, 2009; Karlawish, 2011, for discussion). Thus, who should get an amyloid imaging scan and who should be told the results? Most would suggest that only symptomatic individuals should receive such scans at present to aid in diagnosis, although undoubtedly cognitively intact people concerned about their memory will increasingly ask their practitioners for access to such procedures. Given that a "positive scan" finding imparts some probabilistic risk, how should that risk be communicated? Is it acceptable to disclose a "positive scan" result to someone who may then worry over the prospects of a disease they may not express for many years, if at all, and for which there are no effective treatment options? It is reasonable to expect that some people who learn of their "positive scan" results may overinterpret the predictive value of their scan findings, with any number of adverse effects from diminished self-efficacy beliefs, to depression and anxiety, to suicide. Thus, the need for guidelines in this rapidly expanding area of clinical practice and research is acute.

Epidemiology of Cognitive Aging
Successful Cognitive Aging
As noted above, Negash et al. (2011) studied successful cognitive aging in the Mayo Study on Aging cohort. They developed three successful aging models that were not mutually exclusive. The models were based on participants' performance on a basic neuropsychological screening battery that generated four composite scores. These four composites include attention/executive function, language, visual spatial processing and memory. In *Model 1*, a mean global z-score was generated by calculating the mean of the four domain scores. Participants with mean global z-score in the top 10% were then classified as "successful agers," whereas those in the remaining 90% were classified as "typical agers." In *Model 2*, participants' domain scores in each of the cognitive domains were assessed and those with all four domain scores above the 50th percentile were classified as "successful agers." Participants with at least one domain score below the 50th percentile were classified as "typical agers." *Model 3* was conceptualized as the inverse of age-associated memory impairment (AAMI; see Chapter 1 for criteria). AAMI references memory function in older individuals to the performance of younger adults. Specifically, the diagnosis was applied when a person scored 1 SD below the mean established norms for young adults on standardized neuropsychological tests. Thus, in

Model 3 (inverse-age-associated memory impairment i-AAMI), older adults were labeled successful agers if all target raw scores remained above -1 SD compared to norms for young adults (e.g., WMS-R Logical Memory II cutoff score was greater than 12). The three definitions produced successful aging "prevalence" rates of 10% for Model 1 (by definition), 13.5% for Model 2, and 6% for Model 3.

Typical Cognitive Aging

In the same Mayo Study of Aging (MSA) cohort described above, Petersen et al. (2010) noted a prevalence of dementia of approximately 8% and a prevalence of MCI in the *remaining* nondemented cohort of 16.7% (see Chapter 4). Negash et al.'s (2011) numbers from above represent 6%–13% of the *remaining* noncognitively impaired subjects. Thus, in a representative sample of 100 persons over age 70 from Olmsted County, Minnesota, there would be 8 with dementia, 15 with MCI, and between 5 and 10 successful agers. This leaves 67 to 72 typical cognitive agers in the sample. In other words, the "prevalence" of typical cognitive aging is estimated in this sample to be 67%–72%.

Neuroimaging

Structural Change

Morphometry and Diffusion Imaging

There appears to be regional specificity to brain atrophy with aging. This atrophy also appears to accelerate with aging. Association cortices, hippocampus, and cerebellum appear to lose volume more precipitously while entorhinal cortex and primary visual cortex lose little volume over a 5-year span (Raz et al., 2005). Caudate and anterior corpus callosum appear to show more marked shrinkage as well (Raz, et al., 2005; Raz et al., 2003). Loss of white matter integrity, as evidenced both by volume of hyperintensities and on diffusion tensor indices of white matter microstructure, increases with age. Loss of white matter integrity is greater in frontal relative to posterior white matter (Davis et al., 2009). In one of the more comprehensive studies undertaken, Jernigan et al. (2001) studied normal MRI changes from ages 30 to 99 and found the following: (1) Age-related losses in the hippocampus were significantly accelerated relative to gray matter losses elsewhere in the brain. (2) The frontal lobes were disproportionately affected by cortical volume loss and by increased white matter abnormality. (3) Loss of cerebral and cerebellar white matter occurred later than loss of gray matter. Finally, volume losses from age

30 to 90 averaged 14% in the cerebral cortex, 35% in the hippocampus, and 26% in the cerebral white matter.

Amyloid Imaging

A relatively new positron emission tomography (PET) imaging approach to the identification of potential biomarkers for dementia involves the use of the [11]C Pittsburgh Compound B (PIB) (C. C. Rowe et al., 2007; Wolk & Klunk, 2009; Wolk et al., 2009) and other radioligands (e.g., florbetapir F18) capable of binding to brain amyloid and thereby allowing for the visualization of one's *in vivo* amyloid burden. Although the approach of amyloid imaging holds great promise for the study and identification of preclinical dementia, it is costly, few centers nationwide have this imaging capability, and the procedure is more invasive due to exposure to ionizing radiation (see Woodard & Sugarman, 2011, for discussion). In addition, the finding that nearly half of cognitively intact older adults also have significant levels of Aβ plaque burden (Sonnen, Santa Cruz, Hemmy, et al., 2011) suggests that Aβ may be necessary but not a sufficient condition for progression from normal aging to dementia (Zaccai, Brayne, McKeith, et al., 2008). Despite the primacy afforded Aβ positivity by Sperling et al. (2011; Zaccai, et al., 2008) for the research diagnosis of preclinical AD, the lack of sensitivity of Aβ to predict cognitive decline and its weak association with clinical symptoms and disease severity has lessened enthusiasm for cerebral Aβ (e.g., amyloid imaging) to stand alone as a biomarker of AD.

Functional Change
Default Mode Network

In the absence of an explicit task, the brain is clearly not inactive. During this "idling" is observed temporal synchrony of the blood oxygen level dependent (BOLD) signal across distinct brain regions. That is, these brain regions show concurrent oscillations in brain metabolism when the brain is "at rest" versus performing tasks. These linked regions are variably referred to as task free, resting-state, or default mode networks (DMN) (Greicius, Krasnow, Reiss, & Menon, 2003; Raichle et al., 2001) and task positive networks (TPN), respectively (Fox et al., 2005). Taking advantage of this synchrony and its simplicity, resting-state functional MRI has been used to study connectivity in health and disease (Biswal et al., 2010; Buckner, Andrews-Hanna, & Schacter, 2008; Fox & Raichle, 2007; Raichle & Snyder, 2007). The presence of synchronous resting-state BOLD fluctuations was first demonstrated by Biswal, Yetkin, Haughton, and Hyde (1995). Since then, resting-state BOLD connectivity has been evaluated across multiple brain regions. These resting-state networks are consistently identified using voxel-wise correlation (Fox et al., 2005; Fransson, 2005; Greicius et al., 2003; Lowe, Mock, & Sorenson, 1998) and data-driven approaches (Beckmann & Smith, 2004; Damoiseaux et al., 2006; De Luca, Beckmann, De Stefano, Matthews, & Smith, 2006; S. M. Smith et al., 2009). Furthermore, alterations in fMRI default network connectivity have been offered as a putative marker of neuronal injury in preclinical dementia (see Sperling et al., 2011).

Aging appears to change the strength of these concurrent oscillations, both at rest and in transition to stimulus dependent task performance. At rest, the strength of association between anterior and posterior structures (specifically the medial prefrontal cortex and the posterior cingulate) drops to near zero with advanced aging (Andrews-Hanna et al., 2007). With task demands, older adults appear to deactivate DMN less (Sambataro et al., 2010). These changes in default mode network and task positive network activation appear to associate with changes in cognition. Less deactivation, the DMN is correlated with poorer working memory performance across age, and in general older adults deactivate DMN less well (Sambataro, et al., 2010). Debate persists as to whether differences in regionally specific activations and deactivation during TPN networks reflects a compensatory process (Davis, et al., 2009) or a failure of cognitive control (Sambataro, et al., 2010). Suffice it to say, the integrity of both DMN and TPNs diminishes with age.

Cerebral Blood Flow and Metabolism

Studies consistently show reduced resting cerebral blood flow (CBF) and metabolism in normal aging and still further reductions in dementia. Older studies using positron emission tomography (PET) and single photon emission computed tomography (SPECT) have shown age-related reductions in global CBF (Matsuda et al., 2003) as well as regional CBF in the medial temporal lobe (Krausz et al., 1998), hippocampus (Larsson et al., 2001), and parahippocampus (Matsuda et al., 2003). More recent CBF studies using MRI techniques such as arterial spin labeling (ASL) have also shown blood flow reductions, and one early study observed an average decrease in CBF of 0.45% per year from ages 20 to 67 (Parkes, Rashid, Chard, & Tofts, 2004). Several specific regions of reduced CBF via ASL techniques have been implicated in older adults including the frontal cortex, superior temporal cortex, precuneus, hippocampus, and the parahippocampal gyrus (Bangen et al., 2009; Lee et al., 2009; Parkes et al., 2004). Although regional effects of age on CBF appear independent of gray matter atrophy (Chen, Rosas, & Salat, 2011), Asllani et al. (2009) have shown that incorporation of methods to correct for partial volume effects results in lower age-related reductions in gray matter CBF (15%) than previous reports (20%–30%; Parkes et al., 2004; Restom, Bangen, Bondi, Perthen, & Liu, 2007). This methodological control for partial volume effects suggests that increased atrophy may confound CBF measurement if not taken into account. Finally, PET studies using the radio-isotope, fluorodeoxyglucose (FDG), have examined the cerebral metabolic rate of oxygen consumption at rest and demonstrate similar reductions—or hypometabolism—with advancing age (Kantarci et al., 2010) as well as with risk factors for AD (Reiman, 2007).

Contrary to the age reductions in cerebral blood flow at rest, Grady et al. (1994) were the first to show via PET imaging age-related *increases* in regional CBF during performance of a visual processing and matching task. These findings were the first to show this opposing CBF pattern at rest and during task activation. They suggested that aging negatively affects the efficient use of occipital visual areas, which leads to greater reliance by older subjects on other cortical networks, perhaps to compensate for reduced processing efficiency of occipital cortex. Other studies found similar patterns of increased activation in lateralized regions thought to be critical for a given task, as well as bilaterally during cognitive tasks. That is, older adult activity was generally greater unilaterally as well as bilaterally when compared to young adults. This age-related change in hemispheric lateralization during cognitive tasks gave rise to (Cabeza, 2002) model of Hemispheric Asymmetry Reduction in Older Adults (or HAROLD). Explanations for the HAROLD model include compensatory recruitment of brain regions to complete a given task, a reduction in regional specialization with age (dedifferentiation), or connectivity changes across the life span (see Guidotti Breting, Tuminello, & Duke Han, 2011; Woodard & Sugarman, 2011, for reviews).

Functional MRI

A couple years prior to the Grady et al. (1994) initial functional PET imaging study, an MRI technique based on the BOLD signal was discovered (Kwong et al., 1992). Since its inception, BOLD fMRI has enjoyed a rapid development and neuropsychologists were quick to harness its vast potential for examining brain-behavior relationships in both health and disease. Broadly speaking, this technique allows one to observe *in vivo* brain changes that may underlie age-related as well as disease-specific alterations in cognitive processing, and does so with a better time frame than with PET imaging and without the need for injection of a radioactive agent. The BOLD signal is generally interpreted to reflect changes in neural activity, although it is a complex neurovascular signal. The BOLD signal reflects local changes in deoxyhemoglobin content, which in turn exhibits a complex dependence on changes in CBF, cerebral blood volume, and the cerebral metabolic rate of oxygen consumption (Buxton, Uludag, Dubowitz, & Liu, 2004). Thus, factors that affect baseline deoxyhemoglobin content or the coupling between CBF and $CMRO_2$—as occurs in the degenerating AD brain or with cerebrovascular changes, or both—may therefore alter the BOLD response even when neural activity is unchanged, thus complicating its interpretation (D'Esposito, Deouell, & Gazzaley, 2003).

In addition, Woodard and Sugarman (2011) summarize a variety of methodological issues that further complicate BOLD fMRI, including differential atrophy, task performance differences across clinical groups, the nature of the control task, and the choice of an appropriate task to be assessed during fMRI—especially in the absence of foreknowledge of a person's cognitive status.

Neurophysiology of Typical Cognitive Aging

Table 3.1 lists the distribution of diffuse amyloid plaques, cored plaques, neuritic plaques, and Braak neurofibrillary tangle scores (see Chapter 5) in 39 persons coming to autopsy in a longitudinal study on aging. All 39 were deemed cognitively normal within two years of their death in an evaluation that included behavioral neurological examination, neuropsychological assessment, and neuroimaging studies. Note that while diffuse plaques are common, cored plaques are less so, and neuritic plaques are uncommon in normal aging. Note also that 34 out of 39 of these autopsy cases had Braak scores of III or less (Braak score scale ranges from 0 to VI; see Chapter 5). Not shown is the fact that only one of these cases was found to have neocortical Lewy bodies, while four had nigral Lewy bodies. Nine cases had one old infarct and nine more had two old infarcts. Thus, vascular pathology was observed in nearly half (46%) of these cases. Over half of the infarcts were of the subcortical lacunar type. Most were microscopic and would likely have been deemed "silent."

These findings support the idea that cognitive changes that accompany advancing age are a result of several neurophysiological processes including minor deposition of beta-amyloid peptide, rare neurofibrillary tangles, minor vascular insults, occasional Lewy body pathology, as well as a loss of synapses,

Table 3.1 Distribution of AD-Related Changes in Normal Cognitive Aging

CASE NO.	DIFFUSE AMYLOID PLAQUES*	ARGYROPHILIC DENSE CORE PLAQUES*	NEURITIC PLAQUES WITH TAU POSITIVE NEURITIS*	BRAAK AND BRAAK STAGE
17	None	None	None	None
39	None	None	None	I
3	Sparse	None	None	I
4	Sparse	None	None	I
1	Moderate	None	None	I
22	Frequent	Sparse	None	I
24	Frequent	Moderate	None	I
21	Sparse	None	Sparse	I
14	Sparse	Sparse	Sparse	I
20	Moderate	Sparse	Sparse	I
31	Frequent	Moderate	Sparse	I
13	Frequent	Moderate	Sparse	I
9	Frequent	Sparse	None	I-II
26	Moderate	Moderate	None	I-II
18	None	None	None	II
29	None	None	None	II
15	None	None	None	II
16	Sparse	None	None	II
10	Sparse	None	None	II
2	Sparse	None	None	II atypical
19	Sparse	Sparse	Sparse	II
11	Frequent	Sparse	None	II
7	Frequent	None	None	II
34	None	None	None	II-III
12	Frequent	Sparse	Sparse	II-III
23	None	None	None	III
6	Sparse	None	None	III
33	None	None	None	III

(continued)

Table 3.1 (Continued)

CASE NO.	DIFFUSE AMYLOID PLAQUES*	ARGYROPHILIC DENSE CORE PLAQUES*	NEURITIC PLAQUES WITH TAU POSITIVE NEURITIS*	BRAAK AND BRAAK STAGE
5	Sparse	None	None	III
32	Sparse	Sparse	None	III
36	None	Sparse	None	III atypical
28	Moderate	Sparse	Sparse	III atypical
40	Moderate	Sparse	Sparse	III atypical
8	Frequent	Sparse	Sparse	III atypical
35	Frequent	Sparse	Sparse	IV-V atypical
37	Frequent	Moderate	Sparse	IV-V
30	Frequent	Frequent	Moderate	IV-V atypical
38	Frequent	Moderate	Moderate	IV-V atypical
23	Frequent	Sparse	Sparse	V

* The number of each type of plaque was, characterized according to the CERAD rating scheme: none = 1; sparse = 1 to 5 per × 100 field; moderate = 6 to 15 per × 100 field; or frequent = > 15 per × 100 field. The rating of the neocortical area with the highest plaque count was used.
Reprinted with permission (Knopman et al., 2003).

neurons, neurochemical input, and neuronal networks changes perhaps independent of these processes (Fillit, Butler, O'Connell, et al., 2002; West, Coleman, Flood, & Tronosco, 1994). In general, age-related neurophysiological changes appear to reduce the efficiency and net productivity of the neural system, without dramatically altering its structural integrity.

Interventions for Normal Cognitive Aging

Two general approaches for maintaining or improving cognitive function in older adults have emerged. The first approach is focused on direct instruction of putatively useful strategies. Although improvement on cognitive tests is generally seen subsequent to direct strategy instruction, performance gains typically do not generalize beyond tasks corresponding directly to the strategies taught (Fillit et al., 2002). That is, the "far transfer" of these techniques is poor (Zelinski, Dalton, & Smith, 2011). Moreover, it is not clear that older adults continue to use learned strategies over time (Rebok, Carlson, & Langbaum, 2007). As a result, strategy training programs have not been widely adopted.

A second approach is derived from studies in animals (van Praag, Kempermann, & Gage, 2000) and humans (Wilson, Scherr, Schneider, Tang, & Bennett, 2007) that suggest that nonspecific cognitive stimulation reduces the risk of cognitive decline. This approach has led to the practice of encouraging older adults to engage in cognitively stimulating everyday activities (Fillit et al., 2002; Hultsch, Hertzog, Small, & Dixon, 1999). However, the retrospective and/or observational designs of the human studies have led to difficulty in interpreting the direction of causation between cognitive function and cognitively stimulating activities (Hultsch et al., 1999).

Regardless of the design principles, large-scale randomized controlled trials of training programs that are broadly available for patient use are lacking to date, limiting the ability of physicians and other health care professionals to make evidence-based recommendations to older adults experiencing cognitive decline.

As noted above, age-related reductions in the efficiency and quality of information processing, flowing through peripheral and central sensory systems to cognitive systems, contribute to age-related cognitive decline. There is an emerging literature that suggests that the performance improvement of information processing systems via intensive learning and practice is mediated by plastic brain changes across central nervous system networks (Gilbert, Sigman, & Crist, 2001). Consequently, a cognitive training program designed to improve central sensory system function could potentially improve cognitive function in older adults (Mahncke, Bronstone, & Merzenich, 2006). Several investigators (Smith et al., 2009; Zelinski, Spina, et al., 2011) participated in a multisite randomized controlled double-blind treatment trial to investigate the efficacy of computerized cognitive training programs in older adults. The trial examined impact on untrained measures of memory and attention and participant-reported outcomes. Community-dwelling adults age 65 and older (N = 487) without diagnosis of clinically significant cognitive impairment were randomized to receive either a commercially available computerized cognitive training program or an intensity matched general cognitive stimulation program (active control). Duration of training was 1 hour/day, 5 days/ week, for a total of 40 hours. A composite score calculated from six auditory memory and attention subtests of the Repeatable Battery for the Assessment of Neuropsychological Status (Randolph, 1998) was the primary outcome measure for this trial. Secondary measures were derived from performance on the experimental program, standardized neuropsychological assessments of memory and attention, and participant-reported outcomes. Both groups displayed some improvement in the primary outcome score, likely due to practice effects. However, computer training groups showed significantly greater improvement in this score than in the control group for multiple secondary measures (word list total score, word list delayed recall, digits backward, letter-number sequencing; participant-reported outcome measure). At 3-month posttraining follow-up, a significant treatment effect was still present but the effect size had decreased (Zelinski, Spina, et al., 2011). Thus, the computer training paradigm appeared to create benefits that generalized to measures of memory and attention more than an active control program.

Conclusion

Typical cognitive aging occurs in about two-thirds of persons over age 70. It involves modest atrophy of association cortices, hippocampus, caudate, and cerebellum along with decreasing integrity of anterior white matter structures. Diffuse amyloid plaques and rare neurofibrillary tangles may appear, but there is limited gliosis and limited cell loss. These changes are associated with decreased functional connectivity in brain default mode networks but paradoxically less deactivation in these same networks in the presence of task demands. In turn, these findings may associate with the decreased cognitive processing speed and cognitive flexibility that are the hallmarks of cognitive aging. These two cognitive factors impact the efficiency of cognitive functioning across multiple domains, including working memory, learning, and executive function (which themselves are not mutually exclusive cognitive constructs). There is preliminary evidence that cognitive training practices, especially those based on brain plasticity principles, can mitigate normal cognitive aging effects.

References

Albert, M. S., & Killiany, R. J. (2001). Age-related cognitive change and brain-behavior relationships. In J. E. Birren (Ed.), *Handbook of the psychology of aging* (5th ed., pp. 161–185). San Diego, CA: Academic Press.

Andrews-Hanna, J. R., Snyder, A. Z., Vincent, J. L., Lustig, C., Head, D., Raichle, M. E., & Buckner, R. L. (2007). Disruption of large-scale brain systems in advanced aging. *Neuron, 56*(5), 924–935.

Asllani, I., Habeck, C., Borogovac, A., Brown, T. R., Brickman, A. M., & Stern, Y. (2009). Separating function from structure in perfusion imaging of the aging brain. *Human Brain Mapping, 30*(9), 2927–2935.

Baltes, P. B., & Reese, H. W. (1984). The life span perspective in developmental psychology. In M. H. Bornstein & M. E. Lamb (Eds.), *Developmental psychology: An advanced textbook* (pp. 493–532). Hillsdale, NJ: Erlbaum.

Bandura, A. (1986). *Social foundations of thought and action: A social cognitive theory.* Englewood Cliffs, NJ: Prentice-Hall.

Bangen, K. J., Restom, K., Liu, T. T., Jak, A. J., Wierenga, C. E., Salmon, D. P., & Bondi, M. W. (2009). Differential age effects on cerebral blood flow and BOLD response to encoding: associations with cognition and stroke risk. *Neurobiology of Aging, 30*(8), 1276–1287.

Beckmann, C. F., & Smith, S. M. (2004). Probabilistic independent component analysis for functional magnetic resonance imaging. *IEEE Transactions on Medical Imaging, 23*(2), 137–152.

Benton, A. L., & Hamsher, K. (1978). *Multilingual aphasia examination. Manual.* Iowa City: University of Iowa.

Biswal, B. B., Yetkin, F. Z., Haughton, V. M., & Hyde, J. S (1995). Functional connectivity in the motor cortex of resting human brain using echo-planar MRI. *Magnetic Resonance in Medicine, 34,* 537–541.

Biswal, B. B., Mennes, M., Zuo, X.-N., Gohel, S., Kelly, C., Smith, S. M.,...Milham, M. P. (2010). Toward discovery science of human brain function. *Proceedings of the National Academy of Sciences.*

Bondi, M. W., Salmon, D. P., & Kaszniak, A. W. (1996). The neuropsychology of dementia. In I. Grant & K. M. Adams (Eds.), *Neuropsychological assessment of neuropsychiatric disorders* (pp. 164–199). New York: Oxford University Press.

Brebion, G., Smith, M. J., & Ehrlich, M. F. (1997). Working memory and aging: Deficit or strategy differences. *Aging, Neuropsychology, and Cognition, 4,* 58–73.

Buckner, R. L., Andrews-Hanna, J. R., & Schacter, D. L. (2008). The brain's default network: Anatomy, function, and relevance to disease. *Annals of the New York Academy of Sciences, 1124,* 1–38.

Buxton, R. B., Uludag, K., Dubowitz, D. J., & Liu, T. T. (2004). Modeling the hemodynamic response to brain activation. *Neuroimage, 23*(Suppl 1), S220–S233.

Cabeza, R. (2002). Hemispheric asymmetry reduction in older adults: The HAROLD model. [Research Support, Non-U.S. Gov't Review]. *Psychology and Aging, 17*(1), 85–100.

Chen, J. J., Rosas, H. D., & Salat, D. H. (2011). Age-associated reductions in cerebral blood flow are independent from regional atrophy. *Neuroimage, 55*(2), 468–478.

D'Esposito, M., Deouell, L. Y., & Gazzaley, A. (2003). Alterations in the BOLD fMRI signal with ageing and disease: A challenge for neuroimaging. *Nature Reviews. Neuroscience, 4*(11), 863–872.

Damoiseaux, J. S., Rombouts, S. A. R. B, Barkhof, F., Scheltens, P., Stam, C. J., Smith, S. M., & Beckmann, C. F. (2006). Consistent resting-state networks across healthy subjects. *Proceedings of the National Academy of Sciences, 103*(37), 13848–13853.

Davis, S. W., Dennis, N. A., Buchler, N. G., White, L. E., Madden, D. J., & Cabeza, R. (2009). Assessing the effects of age on long white matter tracts using diffusion tensor tractography. *Neuroimage, 46*(2), 530–541.

De Luca, M., Beckmann, C. F., De Stefano, N., Matthews, P. M., & Smith, S. M. (2006). fMRI resting state networks define distinct modes of long-distance interactions in the human brain. *Neuroimage, 29*(4), 1359–1367.

Depp, C. A., Harmell, A., & Vahia, I. V. (2012). Successful cognitive aging. In M.-C. Pardon & M.W. Bondi (Eds.), *Behavioral neurobiology of aging* (pp. 35–50). New York: Springer-Verlag.

De Santi, S., Pirraglia, E., Barr, W., Babb, J., Williams, S., Rogers, K., . . . de Leon, M. J. (2008). Robust and conventional neuropsychological norms: diagnosis and prediction of age-related cognitive decline. *Neuropsychology, 22*(4), 469–484.

Desrichard, O., & Kopetz, C. (2005). A threat in the elder: The impact of task instructions and self-efficacy on memory performance in the elderly. *European Journal of Social Psychology, 35*(4), 537–552.

Fillit, H. M., Butler, R. N., O'Connell, A. W., Albert, M. S., Birren, J. E., Cotman, C. W., . . . Tully, T. (2002). Achieving and maintaining cognitive vitality with aging. *Mayo Clinic Proceedings, 77*(7), 681–696.

Finkel, D., & Pederson, N. L (2000). Contribution of age, genes, and environment to the relationship between perceptual speed and cognitive ability. *Psychology and Aging, 15,* 56–64.

Fisher, D. L., Duffy, S. A., & Katskiopoulos, K. V. (2000). Cognitive slowing among older adults: What kind and how much? In T. J. Perfect & E. A. Maylor (Eds.), *Models of cognitive aging: Debates in psychology* (pp. 87–124). New York: Oxford University Press.

Fox, M. D, & Raichle, M. E. (2007). Spontaneous fluctuations in brain activity observed with functional magnetic resonance imaging. *Nature Reviews. Neuroscience, 8*(9), 700–711.

Fox, M. D., Snyder, A. Z., Vincent, J. L., Corbetta, M., Van Essen, D. C., & Raichle, M. E. (2005). The human brain is intrinsically organized into dynamic, anticorrelated functional networks. *Proceedings of the National Academy of Sciences, 102*(27), 9673–9678.

Fransson, Peter. (2005). Spontaneous low-frequency BOLD signal fluctuations: An fMRI investigation of the resting-state default mode of brain function hypothesis. *Human Brain Mapping, 26*(1), 15–29.

Frieske, D. A., & Park, D. C. (1999). Memory for news in young and old adults. *Psychology and Aging, 14,* 90–98.

Gilbert, C. D., Sigman, M., & Crist, R. E. (2001). The neural basis of perceptual learning. [Review]. *Neuron, 31*(5), 681–697.

Glatt, S. J., Chayavichitsilp, P., Depp, C., Schork, N. J., & Jeste, D. V. (2007). Successful aging: From phenotype to genotype. *Biological Psychiatry, 62*(4), 282–293.

Grady, C. L., Maisog, J. M., Horwitz, B., Ungerleider, L. G., Mentis, M. J., Salerno, J. A.,... Haxby, J. V. (1994). Age-related changes in cortical blood flow activation during visual processing of faces and location. *Journal of Neuroscience, 14*(3 Pt 2), 1450–1462.

Green, R. C., Roberts, J. S., Cupples, L. A., Relkin, N. R., Whitehouse, P. J., Brown, T.,... Farrer, L. A. (2009). Disclosure of APOE genotype for risk of Alzheimer's disease. *New England Journal of Medicine, 361*(3), 245–254.

Greicius, M. D., Krasnow, B., Reiss, A. L., & Menon, V. (2003). Functional connectivity in the resting brain: A network analysis of the default mode hypothesis. *Proceedings of the National Academy of Sciences, 100*(1), 253–258.

Guidotti Breting, L. M., Tuminello, E. R., & Duke Han, S. (2011). Functional neuroimaging studies in normal aging. *Current Topics in Behavioral Neurosciences, 10,* 91–111.

Hertzog, C., & Bleckley, M. K. (2001). Age differences in the structure of intelligence: Influences of information processing speed. *Intelligence, 29,* 191–217.

Hultsch, D. F., Hertzog, C., Small, B. J., & Dixon, R. A. (1999). Use it or lose it: Engaged lifestyle as a buffer of cognitive decline in aging? *Psychology and Aging, 14*(2), 245–263.

Ivnik, R. J., Malec, J. F., Smith, G. E., Tangalos, E. G., Petersen, R. C., Kokmen, E., & Kurland, L. T. (1992). Mayo's Older Americans Normative Studies: Updated AVLT norms for ages 56–97. *The Clinical Neuropsychologist, 6,* 83–104.

Jernigan, T. L., Archibald, S. L., Fennema-Notestine, C., Gamst, A. C., Stout, J. C., Bonner, J., & Hesselink, J. R. (2001). Effects of age on tissues and regions of the cerebrum and cerebellum. *Neurobiology of Aging, 22*(4), 581–594.

Kane, R. A., & Kane, R. L. (2009). Effect of genetic testing for risk of Alzheimer's disease. *New England Journal of Medicine, 361*(3), 298–299.

Karlawish, J. (2011). Addressing the ethical, policy, and social challenges of preclinical Alzheimer disease. *Neurology, 77*, 1487–1493.

Kantarci, K., Avula, R., Senjem, M. L., Samikoglu, A. R., Zhang, B., Weigand, S. D., …Jack, C. R., Jr. (2010). Dementia with Lewy bodies and Alzheimer disease: Neurodegenerative patterns characterized by DTI. *Neurology, 74*(22), 1814–1821.

Kaplan, E. F., Goodglass, H., & Weintraub, S. (1983). *The Boston Naming Test* (2nd ed.). Philadelphia: Lea & Febiger.

Knopman, D. S., Parisi, J. E., Salviati, A., Floriach-Robert, M., Boeve, B. F., Ivnik, R. J., …Petersen, R. C. (2003). Neuropathology of cognitively normal elderly. *Journal of Neuropathology & Experimental Neurology, 62*(11), 1087–1095.

Krausz, Y., Bonne, O., Gorfine, M., Karger, H., Lerer, B., & Chisin, R. (1998). Age-related changes in brain perfusion of normal subjects detected by 99mTc-HMPAO SPECT. *Neuroradiology, 40*(7), 428–434.

Kwong, K. K., Belliveau, J. W., Chesler, D. A., Goldberg, I. E., Weisskoff, R. M., Poncelet, B. P., …et al. (1992). Dynamic magnetic resonance imaging of human brain activity during primary sensory stimulation. *Proceedings of the National Academy of Sciences, 89*(12), 5675–5679.

Larsson, A., Skoog, I., Aevarsson, Arlig, A., Jacobsson, L., Larsson, L., …Wikkelso, C. (2001). Regional cerebral blood flow in normal individuals aged 40, 75 and 88 years studied by 99Tc(m)-d,l-HMPAO SPET. *Nuclear Medicine Communications, 22*(7), 741–746.

LaRue, A. (1992). *Aging and neuropsychological assessment.* New York: Plenum Press.

Lee, C., Lopez, O. L., Becker, J. T., Raji, C., Dai, W., Kuller, L. H., & Gach, H. M. (2009). Imaging cerebral blood flow in the cognitively normal aging brain with arterial spin labeling: Implications for imaging of neurodegenerative disease. *Journal of Neuroimaging, 19*(4), 344–352.

Light, L. L. (1996). Memory and aging. In E. L. Bjork & R. A. Bjork (Eds.), *Memory: Handbook of perception and cognition* (2nd ed., pp. 443–490). New York: Academic Press.

Lowe, M. J., Mock, B. J., & Sorenson, J. A. (1998). Functional connectivity in single and multislice echoplanar imaging using resting-state fluctuations. *Neuroimage, 7*(2), 119–132.

Mahncke, H. W., Bronstone, A., & Merzenich, M. M. (2006). Brain plasticity and functional losses in the aged: Scientific bases for a novel intervention. *Progress in Brain Research, 157,* 81–109.

Marcopulos, B., & McLain, C. (2003). Are our norms "normal"? A 4-year follow-up study of a biracial sample of rural elders with low education. [Comparative Study Research Support, Non-U.S. Gov't Research Support, U.S. Gov't, P.H.S.]. *The Clinical Neuropsychologist, 17*(1), 19–33. doi: 10.1076/clin.17.1.19.15630

Matsuda, H., Ohnishi, T., Asada, T., Li, Z. J., Kanetaka, H., Imabayashi, E.,... Nakano, S. (2003). Correction for partial-volume effects on brain perfusion SPECT in healthy men. [Clinical Trial Comparative Study Validation Studies]. *Journal of Nuclear Medicine, 44*(8), 1243–1252.

Meyerson, J., Adams, D. R., Hale, S., & Jenkins, L. (2003). Analysis of group differences in processing speed: Brinley plots, Q-Q plots, and other conspiracies. *Psychonomic Bulletin and Review, 10,* 224–237.

Meyerson, J., Jenkins, L., Hale, S., & Sliwinski, M. (2000). Individual and developmental differences in working memory across the life span: Reply. *Psychonomic Bulletin and Review, 7,* 734–740.

Negash, S., Smith, G. E., Pankratz, S., Aakre, J., Geda, Y. E., Roberts, R. O.,... Petersen, R. C. (2011). Successful aging: Definitions and prediction of longevity and conversion to mild cognitive impairment. *American Journal of Geriatric Psychiatry, 19*(6), 581–588.

Park, D. C., Smith, A. D., Lautenschlager, G., Earles, J. L., Frieske, D., Zwahr, M., & Gaines, C. L (1996). Mediators of long-term memory performance across the life span. *Psychology and Aging, 11,* 621–637.

Parkes, L. M., Rashid, W., Chard, D. T., & Tofts, P. S. (2004). Normal cerebral perfusion measurements using arterial spin labeling: Reproducibility, stability, and age and gender effects. *Magnetic Resonance in Medicine, 51*(4), 736–743.

Parkin, A. J., & Java, R. I. (2000). Determinants of age-related memory loss. In T. J. Perfect & E. A. Maylor (Eds.), *Models of cognitive aging: Debates in psychology* (pp. 188–203). New York: Oxford University Press.

Pedraza, O., Lucas, J. A., Smith, G. E., Petersen, R. C., Graff-Radford, N. R., & Ivnik, R. J. (2010). Robust and expanded norms for the Dementia Rating Scale. *Archives of Clinical Neuropsychology, 25*(5), 347–358.

Petersen, R. C., Roberts, R. O., Knopman, D. S., Geda, Y. E., Cha, R. H., Pankratz, V. S.,...Rocca, W. A. (2010). Prevalence of mild cognitive impairment is higher in men: The Mayo Clinic Study of Aging. *Neurology, 75*(10), 889–897.

Powell, D. H. (1994). *Profiles in cognitive aging*. Cambridge, MA: Harvard University Press.

Raichle, M. E., & Snyder, A. Z. (2007). A default mode of brain function: A brief history of an evolving idea. *Neuroimage, 37*(4), 1083–1090; discussion 1097–1089.

Raichle, M. E., MacLeod, A. M., Snyder, A. Z., Powers, W. J., Gusnard, D. A., & Shulman, G. L. (2001). A default mode of brain function. *Proceedings of the National Academy of Sciences, 98*(2), 676–682.

Randolph, C. (1998). *Repeatable Battery for the Assessment of Neuropsychological Status (RBANS)*. San Antonio, TX: The Psychological Corporation.

Raz, N., Lindenberger, U., Rodrigue, K. M., Kennedy, K. M., Head, D., Williamson, A.,...Acker, J. D. (2005). Regional brain changes in aging healthy adults: General trends, individual differences and modifiers. *Cerebral Cortex, 15*(11), 1676–1689.

Raz, N., Rodrigue, K. M., Kennedy, K. M., Dahle, C., Head, D., & Acker, J. D. (2003). Differential age-related changes in the regional metencephalic volumes in humans: A 5-year follow-up. *Neuroscience Letters, 349*(3), 163–166.

Rebok, G. W., Carlson, M. C., & Langbaum, J. B. (2007). Training and maintaining memory abilities in healthy older adults: Traditional and novel approaches. *Journals of Gerontology. Series B, Psychological Sciences And Social Sciences, 62* Spec No 1, 53–61.

Reiman, E. M. (2007). Linking brain imaging and genomics in the study of Alzheimer's disease and aging. *Annals of the New York Academy of Sciences, 1097*, 94–113.

Restom, K., Bangen, K. J., Bondi, M. W., Perthen, J. E., & Liu, T. T. (2007). Cerebral blood flow and BOLD responses to a memory encoding task: A comparison between healthy young and elderly adults. *Neuroimage, 37*(2), 430–439.

Rey, A. (1964). *L'examen clinique en psychologie*. Paris: Presses Universitaires de France.

Rowe, C. C., Ng, S., Ackermann, U., Gong, S. J., Pike, K., Savage, G.,... Villemagne, V. L. (2007). Imaging beta-amyloid burden in aging and dementia. *Neurology, 68*(20), 1718–1725.

Rowe, J. W., & Kahn, R. L. (1998). *Successful aging*. New York: Pantheon Books.

Salmon, D. P., Lineweaver, T. T., Bondi, M. W., & Galasko, D. (2012). Knowledge of APOE genotype affects subjective and objective memory performance in healthy older adults. *Alzheimer's & Dementia, 8* (Suppl.), 123–124 (abstract).

Salthouse, T. A. (2010). *Major issues in cognitive aging.* New York: Oxford University Press.

Sambataro, F., Murty, V. P., Callicott, J. H., Tan, H. Y., Das, S., Weinberger, D. R., & Mattay, V. S. (2010). Age-related alterations in default mode network: Impact on working memory performance. *Neurobiology of Aging, 31*(5), 839–852.

Schaie, K. W. (1994). The course of adult intellectual development. *American Psychologist, 49*(4), 304–313.

Schroots, J. J. F., & Birren, J. E. (1996). History, concepts, and theory in the psychology of aging. In J. E. Birren & K. W. Schaie (Eds.), *Handbook of the psychology of aging* (4th ed., pp. 3–23). San Diego, CA: Academic Press.

Sliwinski, M., & Buschke, H. (1999). Cross-sectional and longitudinal relationships among age, cognition, and processing speed. *Psychology and Aging, 14*(1), 18–33.

Sliwinski, M., Lipton, R. B., Buschke, H., & Stewart, W. (1996). The effects of preclinical dementia on estimates of normal cognitive functioning in aging. *Journals of Gerontology. Series B, Psychological Sciences and Social Sciences, 51*(4), P217–P225.

Smith, G. E., Housen, P., Yaffe, K., Ruff, R., Kennison, R. F., Mahncke, H. W., & Zelinski, E. M. (2009). A cognitive training program based on principles of brain plasticity: Results from the Improvement in Memory with Plasticity-based Adaptive Cognitive Training (IMPACT) study. *Journal of the American Geriatrics Society, 57*(4), 594–603.

Smith, G. E., Ivnik, R. J., & Lucas, J. (2008). Assessment techniques: Tests, test batteries, norms, and methodological approaches. In J. Morgan & J. Ricker (Eds.), *Textbook of clinical neuropsychology* (pp. 38–57). New York: Taylor & Francis.

Smith, G. E., Ivnik, R. J., Malec, J. F., & Tangalos, E. G. (1993). Factor structure of the MOANS core battery: Replication in a clinical sample. *Psychological Assessment, 5,* 121–124.

Smith, S. M., Fox, P. T., Miller, K. L., Glahn, D. C., Fox, P. M., Mackay, C. E.,... Beckmann, C. F. (2009). Correspondence of the brain's functional architecture during activation and rest. *Proceedings of the National Academy of Sciences, 106*(31), 13040–13045.

Sonnen, J., Santa Cruz, K., Hemmy, L., et al. (2011). Ecology of the aging human brain. *Archives of Neurology, 68,* 1049–1056.

Sperling, R. A., Aisen, P. S., Beckett, L. A., Bennett, D. A., Craft, S., Fagan, A. M., ... Phelps, C. H. (2011). Toward defining the preclinical stages of Alzheimer's disease: Recommendations from the National Institute on Aging-Alzheimer's Association workgroups on diagnostic guidelines for Alzheimer's disease. *Alzheimer's and Dementia, 7*(3), 280–292.

Valentijn, S. A., Hill, R. D., Van Hooren, S. A., Bosma, H., Van Boxtel, M. P., Jolles, J., & Ponds, R. W. (2006). Memory self-efficacy predicts memory performance: results from a 6-year follow-up study. *Psychology and Aging, 21*(1), 165–172.

van Praag, H., Kempermann, G., & Gage, F. H. (2000). Neural consequences of environmental enrichment. *Nature Reviews. Neuroscience, 1*(3), 191–198.

Wechsler, D. A. (1987). *Wechsler Memory Scale-Revised.* New York: Psychological Corporation.

West, M. J., Coleman, P. D., Flood, D. G., & Tronosco, J. C. (1994). Differences in the pattern of hippocampal neuronal loss in normal ageing and Alzheimer's disease. *Lancet, 344,* 769–772.

Wilson, R. S., Scherr, P. A., Schneider, J. A., Tang, Y., & Bennett, D. A. (2007). Relation of cognitive activity to risk of developing Alzheimer disease. *Neurology, 69*(20), 1911–1920.

Wolk, D. A., & Klunk, W. (2009). Update on amyloid imaging: from healthy aging to Alzheimer's disease. *Current Neurology and Neuroscience Reports, 9*(5), 345–352.

Wolk, D. A., Price, J. C., Saxton, J. A., Snitz, B. E., James, J. A., Lopez, O. L., ... De-Kosky, S. T. (2009). Amyloid imaging in mild cognitive impairment subtypes. *Annals of Neurology, 65*(5), 557–568. doi: 10.1002/ana.21598

Woodard, J. L., & Sugarman, M. A. (2011). Functional magnetic resonance imaging in aging and dementia: Detection of age-related cognitive changes and prediction of cognitive decline. *Current Topics in Behavioral Neurosciences, 10,* 113–36.

Zaccai, J., Brayne, C., McKeith, I., et al. (2008). Patterns and stages of alpha-synucleinopathy: Relevance in a population-based cohort. *Neurology, 70,* 1042–1048.

Zelinski, E. M., Dalton, S. E., Smith, G. E. (2011). *Consumer based brain fitness programs.* New York: Springer.

Zelinski, E. M., Spina, L. M., Yaffe, K., Ruff, R., Kennison, R. F., Mahncke, H. W., & Smith, G. E. (2011). Improvement in memory with plasticity-based adaptive cognitive training: Results of the 3-month follow-up. *Journal of the American Geriatrics Society, 59*(2), 258–265.

Zimprich, D. (2002). Cross-sectionally and longitudinally balanced effects of processing speed on intellectual abilities. *Experimental Aging Research, 28*(3), 231–251.

4

■ ■ ■

Mild Cognitive Impairment

Case Presentation

Background

This patient was an 84-year-old, right-handed, woman with 11 years of education. She was a widow for 21 years at the point of initial evaluation. She had no specific complaint regarding her cognitive function, except for generalized slowing over time. She lived alone independently in an apartment. She wrote checks and was also able to balance her checkbook without difficulty. She did not drive a car as it was inconvenient for her. She did all her own ADLs, but admitted she had help from her children who lived in the area. She was initially recruited as a normal control for a longitudinal research project. However, she was not given that designation following initial clinical evaluation with a short mental status test (Kokmen, Smith, Petersen, Tangalos, & Ivnik, 1991; see exam results below).

Medical/Surgical History.

Of note, she had multiple medical problems, and she had multiple hospital admissions in the year prior due to complications of congestive heart failure and pneumonia. She received one-vessel CABG during an aortic valve replacement. She had hypertension, osteoarthritis with bilateral total

(continued)

hip arthroplasty, cataract surgery, and lower extremity cellulitis. She had a history of right clavicular fracture from a fall.

Family History
Her father died at age 68 due to cancer. Mother died at age 97 due to "old age." She had one living and three deceased brothers. She had one son and four daughters. There was no known family history of Alzheimer's disease or any other neurodegenerative disorder.

Medications
No psychotropic medications.

Neurological Exam
General appearance—she used a walker to aid her balance. On the Kokmen Short Test of Mental Status, she learned all four target items with one trial, but recall was 0 out of 4 at approximately 5-minute delay. Attention/concentration was normal, scoring 6 out of 7 on forward digits. Her total score was 31/38. The rest of the neurologic examination was significant for slight hypomimia; -2 to -3 walk on toes and walk on heels. Romberg sign was positive. Muscle strength was -2 of her thenar and hypothenar muscles. Muscle strength was also -2 to -1 of her iliopsoas and quadriceps. The rest of the examination was unremarkable.

System Review
No history of head injury or loss of consciousness, seizure, meningitis, or encephalitis. She has no history of dry eyes and/or dry mouth. No risk factors for HIV infection.

Course of Illness
The patient continued to live alone in her apartment following her initial evaluation. At about 1.5 years, she entered and completed a project where medication adherence of MCI patients living alone was monitored with in-home video (Smith, Lunde, Hathaway, & Vickers, 2007). As noted below, she continued to have memory problems, but no evidence of cognitive decline or behavioral disturbance. At about 3.5 years following initial evaluation, the patient was diagnosed with acute myelogenous leukemia. She was referred for hospice services and died at home within the month.

(continued)

Mild Cognitive Impairment and Dementia

Autopsy Study

1. Nonspecific neurodegenerative changes, mild (Braak and Braak: stage II-III; NIA-Reagan: low likelihood; CERAD: normal), with:
    a. Neocortex: Sparse to moderate diffuse plaques, absent to focally sparse (parietal) neuritic plaques, and absent to focally rare (temporal) neurofibrillary tangles.
    b. Amygdala, entorhinal cortex, subiculum, and hippocampus: Absent to sparse diffuse and neuritic plaques, rare to frequent neurofibrillary tangles, frequent CA2–3 pretangles, and frequent neuropil grains.
    c. No evidence of cerebral amyloid angiopathy.
    d. Substantia nigra and locus ceruleus: Minimal pigmentary incontinence, sparse neurofibrillary tangles and threads, without Lewy bodies or significant neuronal loss or gliosis; moderate midbrain tegmental neurofibrillary tangles.
    e. Cerebral atrophy, mild, generalized; left hemibrain weight 602 g.
2. Ischemic (lacunar) infarct, old, focal, left putamen at the level of the anterior commissure, 0.5 x 0.2 x 0.2 cm.
3. Cranial arteriolosclerosis, moderate, with prominent cribriform change, white matter pallor, and rarefaction.
4. Mineralization of basal ganglionic blood vessels (Fahr disease), mild.
5. Cranial atherosclerosis: right vertebral, grade 1 (of 4); left vertebral, grade 2; basilar trunk, grade 1; left posterior communicating, grade 1; left internal carotid, grade 1; left middle cerebral (M1 and M2), grade 1; left anterior cerebral, A1 grade 1, A2 focal grade

Neuropsychological Evaluation

As shown in Figure 4.1, this woman displayed "classic" amnestic mild cognitive impairment. Her deficits clustered in the learning and memory domains. Other areas of cognitive function may have been below average but they were not in the impaired range, and she continued to live and function independently without incident despite her circumscribed deficit in learning and memory. Her AVLT percent retention score appeared

(continued)

to be stable but this finding was only because she was already at the floor on the measure (because of her advanced age, a score of 0 still falls at the about the 8th percentile). Her improvement, especially on perceptual organization, reflects that even MCI patients can show some procedural practice effects on longitudinal testing.

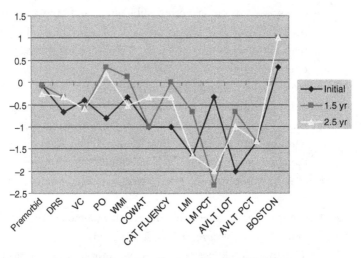

FIGURE 4.1 Neuropsychological profile of woman with mild cognitive impairment. All scores are age adjusted z scores. Premorbid = Wide Range Achievement Test (3rd edition; Wilkinson, 1993), Reading score, DRS = Mattis Dementia Rating Scale (Mattis, 1988) total scores, VC = Verbal comprehension, PO = perceptual organization, WMI = Working Memory Index (all from Wechsler Adult Intelligence Scale-Third edition, 1997), COWAT = Controlled Oral Word Association Test (Benton & Hamsher, 1978), Cat Fluency = Category Fluency test, LM1 = Wechsler Memory Scale Revised (WMS-R; Wechsler, 1987) Logical Memory Immediate Recall, LMPCT = WMS-R Logical Memory Delay divided by LM1. AVLTLOT = Rey Auditory Verbal Learning Test (AVLT; Rey, 1964) total of trials 1–5 minus 5*trial 1 (see R. Ivnik et al., 1992). AVLTPCT = AVLT 30-minute delay divided by AVLT trial 5. Boston = Boston Naming Test (Kaplan, Goodglass, & Weintraub, 1983). DRS, COWAT, Category Fluency, WMS-R, AVLT and Boston scores are based on Mayo Older American's Normative Studies (MOANS) norms.

MCI as a Diagnostic Concept

As noted in Chapter 1, a variety of terms have been proposed in the last 50 years to capture the concept of a not-normal but not-demented clinical state. From these terms *mild cognitive impairment* has emerged as the most widely used. A current PUBMED search on isolated memory impairment, questionable dementia, cognitive impairment not demented, AAMI, and separately for MCI, will generate about 10 times more hits on MCI than all other terms combined. Clearly the concept of MCI has gained widest acceptance.

As originally conceived, Petersen (Petersen et al., 1995; Petersen et al., 1999) defined MCI by the following criteria: (1) a subjective complaint of a memory disturbance (preferably supported by an informant); (2) objective evidence of a memory deficit; (3) generally preserved cognitive functions; (4) intact activities of daily living; and (5) the absence of dementia. Representative examples of this diagnostic scheme include the large donepezil/vitamin E study of MCI (Petersen et al., 2005) or multisite initiatives like the Alzheimer's Disease Neuroimaging Initiative (ADNI) that operationally defined the above criteria in the following way: (1) presence of a subjective memory complaint (corroborated by an informant); (2) -1.5 SD or more impairment on 20-minute delayed recall of Story A of the Wechsler Memory Scale's Logical Memory subtest; (3) normal general cognition as indexed by a score of 24–30 on the MMSE; (4) generally intact ADLs as indexed by a global CDR score of 0.5 (Morris, 1993); and (5) consensus diagnosis of the absence of dementia. This "historical" diagnostic scheme was the norm for some time prior to—and during—the period when MCI subtyping methods were proposed (see "Evolution of MCI Concept" below).

With respect to groups of people, MCI constitutes that level of cognitive function wherein low-functioning normal older persons and high functioning dementia patients cannot be reliably distinguished (Figure 4.2 depicts this overlap). If all persons labeled as MCI are conceived of as belonging in either a normal population, not destined to develop dementia, or from a population that is developing dementia, then MCI can be thought of not as a "condition" present in the patient, but rather as a state of uncertainty in the clinician. Since the group from which that individual arose is uncertain, the clinician turns to the MCI label. As it turns out, that state of uncertainty can be thought of as constituting a risk factor for the patient with respect to subsequent development of dementia. This finding is due to the finite trajectories for someone with MCI (see Figure 4.3); the most common is likely to be the one involving ongoing deterioration leading to dementia, although other trajectories include stable but mild cognitive impairment or reversion back to normal levels.

On average, persons with MCI as originally defined by Petersen et al. have intermediate degrees of hippocampal atrophy impairment compared to

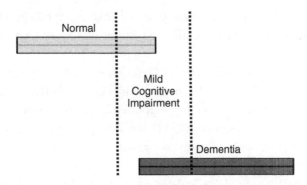

FIGURE 4.2 Mild cognitive impairment as a concept. The region of cognitive over-lap between low functioning normal and the earliest signs of a dementia process.

healthy control subjects and AD patients (Jack et al., 1999), and intermediate changes in regional cerebral metabolic patterns (Kantarci et al., 2000). Note however that these previously reported data represent mean values and could reflect averaging measurements taken from patients developing dementia along with those of normal (or nonprogressing) individuals. MCI patients show similar apolipoprotein E allelic frequencies to AD patients (Petersen, et al., 1995). These same neuroimaging and genetic variables help predict progression to dementia (see Figure 4.4b and 4.4c).

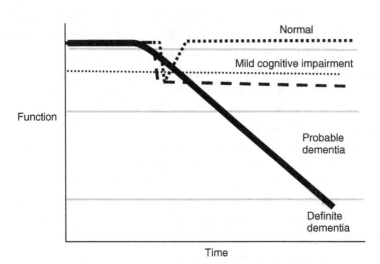

FIGURE 4.3 Finite trajectories for an individual with MCI.

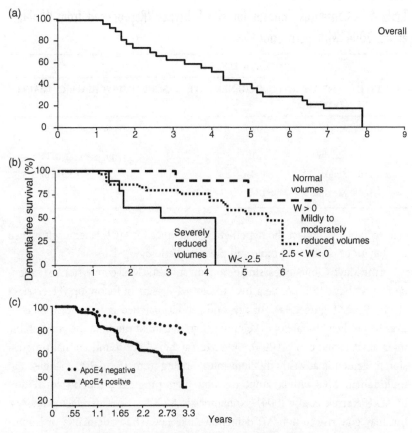

FIGURE 4.4 Risk for progression from MCI to dementia, (a) overall, (b) by hippocampal volume (reproduced from Jack et al., 1999 with permission) and (c) by apolipoprotein E status (reproduced from Petersen et al., 1995 with permission).

Evolution of the MCI Diagnostic Concept

Of course not all dementia is due to Alzheimer's disease, so the idea that mild cognitive impairment could only include memory problems was quickly recognized to be a limitation of the concept (Petersen et al., 2001a). For example, we know that early in subcortical dementias such as Parkinson's disease, memory may be relatively spared but basic attention and processing speed is compromised. Such notions led to a broadening of the concept of MCI to include presentations that are not amnestic or not exclusively amnestic in nature. A 2004 consensus conference (Winblad et al., 2004) produced the scheme listed in Table 4.1. The profile is established by clinical and neuropsychological evaluation. Presumed etiology is assessed by clinical history, clinical evaluation, and appropriate studies. The

Table 4.1 Consensus Concept for MCI Subtypes (Reproduced from Winblad et al., 2004 with permission)

MCI TYPE	# OF AFFECTED DOMAINS	ETIOLOGY			
		DEGENERATIVE	VASCULAR	PSYCHIATRIC	TRAUMA
Amnestic	Single	AD		Depression	TBI
	Multiple	AD	VaD	Depression	TBI
Nonamnestic	Single	FTD			TBI
	Multiple	DLB	VaD		TBI

cells in Table 4.1 reflect the hypothetical outcomes for MCI patients with given combinations of clinical profile and presumed etiology.

In the Mayo Clinic series, single-domain amnestic MCI conversion to dementia rate is about 12% per year over the initial 7 years of follow-up (Petersen et al., 1999; see Figure 4.4a). An age- and gender-matched group of normal controls had only a 5% rate of developing cognitive impairment in the comparable interval (Petersen et al., 1995). Other researchers have found annual progression to dementia at vastly different rates ranging from 1% to 20%. Single- and multidomain MCI with an amnestic component progress at roughly equal rates to AD (Petersen et al., 2004). Nonamnestic MCI is also a risk factor for AD, but may give rise to non-AD dementias, like Lewy body dementia or frontotemporal dementia, more commonly than does amnestic MCI (Boeve et al., 2004; Ferman et al., 2006; Petersen et al., 2001b). Yet the reported rates of amnestic to nonamnestic MCI have varied greatly. Petersen et al. (2009) have asserted that there is roughly a 2:1 ratio between amnestic and nonamnestic MCI subtypes, suggesting that amnestic MCI makes up the majority of MCI cases. However, other studies have suggested the converse: that multidomain MCI or single nonmemory domain MCI may be more common than amnestic MCI (Lopez et al., 2002). A summary of 41 studies compiled for meta-analysis by Mitchell and Shiri-Feshki (2009) is provided in Table 4.2.

Methodology Matters

Table 4.2 obviously reveals great variability in rates of progression from MCI to dementia (e.g., from a low of 3% to a high of 63%). As far back as 2002, Lopez et al. (2002) similarly noted that differences in the methods and criteria used for MCI diagnosis resulted in widely disparate prevalence rates (3%–54%).

Table 4.2 Statistical summary of rates of progression from Mild Cognitive Impairment (MCI) to dementia, Alzheimer's disease (AD), or vascular dementia (VaD), and the annual conversion rate (ACR) for each of those three groups (Reproduced from Mitchell and Shiri-Feshki (2009) with permission)

STUDY	DURATION (YEARS, MEAN)	SETTING	MCI SAMPLE SIZE	PROPORTION DEVELOPING DEMENTIA	PROPORTION DEVELOPING AD	PROPORTION DEVELOPING VAD	ACR DEMENTIA	ACR AD	ACR VAD
Mayo Clinic Definition of MCI									
Visser, Kester, Jolles, & Verhey, (2006)	10	Specialist center	64	0.438	0.438		0.044	0.044	0.044
Annerbo, Wahlund, & Lökk, (2006)	6	Specialist center	93	0.344	0.344		0.057		
Hansson, Buchhave, Zetterberg, et al. (2009)	5.2	Specialist center	167	0.563	0.413	0.108	0.108	0.079	
Visser & Verhey (2008)	5	Specialist center	119		0.378			0.076	
Gabryelewicz, Styczynska, Barczak, et al. (2008)	5	Specialist center	105	0.295	0.248	0.038	0.059	0.050	
R. Petersen et al. (1999)	4	Specialist center	76	0.474	0.474			0.118	

(continued)

Table 4.2 (Continued)

STUDY	DURATION (YEARS, MEAN)	SETTING	MCI SAMPLE SIZE	PROPORTION DEVELOPING DEMENTIA	PROPORTION DEVELOPING AD	PROPORTION DEVELOPING VAD	ACR DEMENTIA	ACR AD	ACR VAD
Tabert et al. (2006a)	3.88	Specialist center	148		0.264			0.068	
Bombois et al. (2008)	3.8	Specialist center	170	0.394	0.171	0.041	0.104	0.045	
Jack et al. (2004)	3.6	Specialist center	41		0.634			0.176	
Gabryelewicz et al. (2007)	3.02	Specialist center	105	0.210	0.181	0.029	0.069	0.060	0.009
Yaffe, Petersen, Lindquist, Kramer, & Miller (2006)	3.1	Specialist center	327	0.609			0.196		
Herukka, Hallikainen, Soininen, & Pirttila (2005)	3	Specialist center	78		0.295			0.098	
Marcos, Gil, & Barabash (2006)	3	Specialist center	82		0.463			0.154	
Ravaglia et al. (2006)	3	Specialist center	165	0.291	0.206	0.085	0.097	0.069	0.028

Study		Setting	N						
Ganguli, Dodge, Shen, & Dekosky (2004)	10	Community	40	0.275	0.225		0.028	0.023	
Busse, Hensel, Guhne, Angermeyer, & Riedel-Heller (2006)	6	Community	91	0.385			0.064		
Dickerson, Sperling, Hyman, Albert, & Blacker (2007)	5	Community	42		0.405			0.081	
Artero et al. (2008)	4	Community	2882	0.066	0.042	0.007	0.016	0.011	
K. Palmer et al. (2007)	3	Community	47		0.574			0.191	
Zanetti et al. (2006)	3	Community	65	0.308	0.169	0.138	0.103	0.056	0.046
Larrieu et al. (2002)	5	Community	58		0.448			0.090	
Ritchie, Artero, & Touchon (2001)	3	Community	27	0.111			0.037		
Non–Mayo Clinic Definition of MCI									
Devanand et al. (2008)	5	Specialist center	139		0.266			0.053	
Bozoki, Giordani, Heidebrink, Berent, & Foster (2001)	5	Specialist center	48		0.438			0.088	
Storandt, Grant, Miller, & Morris (2002)	4.4	Specialist center	59		0.322			0.073	

(continued)

Table 4.2 (Continued)

STUDY	DURATION (YEARS, MEAN)	SETTING	MCI SAMPLE SIZE	PROPORTION DEVELOPING DEMENTIA	PROPORTION DEVELOPING AD	PROPORTION DEVELOPING VAD	ACR DEMENTIA	ACR AD	ACR VAD
Alexopoulos, Grimmer, Perneczky, Domes, & Kurz (2006)	3.49	Specialist center	81	0.407			0.117		
Tyas et al. (2007)	8	Community	949	0.075			0.009		
Aggarwal, Wilson, Beck, Bienias, & Bennett (2005)	5.1	Community	218	0.385	0.376		0.076	0.074	
Grober, Lipton, Hall, & Crystal (2000)	5	Community	68	0.294			0.059		
Hogan & Ebly (2000)	5	Community	210	0.162	0.105		0.032	0.021	
Ishikawa & Ikeda (2007)	5	Community	98	0.224	0.112	0.051	0.045	0.022	0.010
Heun, Kölsch, & Jessen (2006)	4.7	Community	633	0.088	0.028	0.014	0.019	0.006	0.003
Bennett et al. (2002)	4.5	Community	188		0.340			0.076	
Lopez, Kuller, & Becker (2007)	4.3	Community	136	0.515			0.120		
Di Carlo et al. (2007)	3.9	Community	445	0.052					

Jak, Urban, et al. (2009) have also shown that, in the *same* sample of subjects, MCI prevalence rates vary from 11% to 74% depending on the diagnostic criteria used. How can such wide variations exist? It is instructive to dissect how MCI has been diagnosed across studies in order to gain a better appreciation of its variability in the research literature. A review of this literature reveals several important dimensions along which studies of predementia conditions must be compared in order to understand their discrepant findings, including the (1) population sampled; (2) nature of cognitive complaint; (3) number of cognitive domains assessed; (4) number of tests/measures per cognitive domain; (5) sensitivity of tests in each domain; and (6) quandary of establishing functional status to rule out dementia. We turn to each methodological issue.

Population Sampled
It is important to distinguish MCI studies using clinical samples from studies for which MCI "patients" are culled from a population sample or a normal volunteer sample of older adults. Mayo studies, and those of several others (e.g., Bowen et al., 1997; Tierney et al., 1996), have used clinical samples. The fact that a clinical concern exists for these patients increases the likelihood that they are drawn from a predementia group.

A variety of studies of MCI-like conditions have identified their cohorts by recruiting normal older adults (e.g., Albert & Killiany, 2001; Ritchie & Touchon, 2000). These samples are composed of individuals who either served as control participants in clinical trials or longitudinal aging studies, or were selected as a community sample of older adults in order to describe cognitive function in a group conceived to be representative of elderly from a general population. MCI "patients" are often culled from these normal samples by using a psychometric cutoff based on their memory performance. Thus, by definition, normal patients scoring at the lowest end of the memory score distributions receive a diagnosis of MCI. Selection in this fashion necessarily increases the likelihood that these MCI patients arise from the normal population, rather than from a cognitively impaired population depicted in Figure 4.2.

Nature of Cognitive Complaint
The original Mayo criteria (Petersen, et al., 1999) for MCI propose that a memory complaint must be present. Differences in the nature of memory complaints across studies are a corollary of differences in recruitment methods. In clinical samples, memory complaints are generally "spontaneous." Complaints arise as a concern from some member of the health care process

(e.g., patient, family, provider). Such memory concerns, especially from family or physicians, may have a better correspondence with objectively established cognitive dysfunction (c.f., Carr, Gray, Baty, & Morris, 2000). In studies that recruit general or normal samples, a memory complaint is typically established by administration of standardized subjective ratings of memory function. Numerous studies have demonstrated that scores on such instruments are more likely to associate with mood or self-efficacy than with actual cognitive dysfunction (Smith, Petersen, Ivnik, Malec, & Tangalos, 1996; Taylor, Miller, & Tinklenberg, 1992).

Number and Type of Cognitive Domains Assessed
The number and type of cognitive domains assessed in studies of MCI is important since MCI criteria typically stipulate no dementia. Commonly accepted dementia criteria require impairment in at least two cognitive domains. Since MCI patients must have at least one domain of cognitive impairment, statistical applications of dementia criteria will exclude from MCI samples any person with scores falling below some cutoff in any additional domain. Many, if not most, early MCI studies used the MMSE as the measure that sampled all other cognitive domains, and the original cutoff score recommended by Folstein, Folstein, and McHugh, (1975) of 24 and above was typically used to demonstrate the absence of dementia. However, this suggested MMSE cutoff for the presence of dementia is more than three decades old and most neuropsychologists would consider it to be far too conservative, although it continues to be routinely used. For example, a study by Salmon et al. (2002) showed that individuals—all of whom had MMSE scores of 24 and greater— were accurately diagnosed with AD based on other sensitive measures such as delayed recall and verbal fluency (Salmon et al., 2002). These findings demonstrate the ineffectiveness of the MMSE's suggested cutoff of 23 and below for the presence of dementia and attest to the clinical utility of targeted neuropsychological measures for early diagnosis.

Although the use of the MMSE in MCI studies has had its limitations, a different concern is borne from the use of additional neuropsychological tests. That is, as the number of cognitive domains and the number of measures per domain assessed increases (see below), there is an increasing probability in any given individual that at least one cognitive measure in more than one domain will fall below a given cutoff by chance alone (Schretlen, Testa, Winicki, Pearlson, & Gordon, 2008). An amnestic MCI study by Ritchie et al. (2001) provides an example of this problem. In this study, seven nonmemory domains were assessed. Seventy-five percent of persons with a loosely defined memory impairment (scores worse than 1 SD below age norms) also had at least one nonmemory score fall below this cutoff. Only 7% of the remaining 25% of their "MCI" patients continued to have memory scores below their cutoff at follow-up. By excluding persons with modestly low nonmemory scores from their sample, these investigators appeared to exclude persons with true memory impairments from their MCI sample.

With respect to multidomain MCI, an astute observer will ask, "how can a person have scores in the impaired range in two cognitive domains and not have dementia?" Two fundamentals of neuropsychology are relevant in this regard. First, a low score is not necessarily the same thing as impairment. A certain percentage of the normal population will score below clinical cutoffs on any measure (see, Heaton, Miller, Taylor, & Grant, 2004), and this is certainly the case for older adults as well (Palmer, Boone, Lesser, & Wohl, 1998). If the cutoff is liberally set at –1 SD, 16% of the general population will fall below the cutoff, although this cut point also has shown the advantage of maximally separating the normal from neurologic samples of the Heaton et al. normative studies (Heaton, et al., 2004). In persons with commiserate histories (e.g., low academic attainment, low IQ), it is entirely possible for a score below this cutoff to be deemed clinically normal for that person. Dementia criteria require a decline from a higher level of cognitive function. The second fundamental issue is that low scores on tests do not necessarily imply "significant impairment in social or occupational functioning" (American Psychiatric Association, 1994). There are plenty of people who live normal day-to-day lives that would "fail" the Wisconsin Card Sorting Test. Of course, it is also entirely possible that a proportion of MCI studies have not routinely or adequately assessed ADL function beyond rudimentary screenings, if at all, and thus may have missed very mild dementia in proportions of multi-domain MCI cases (see Chang et al., 2011, for discussion).

Number of Tests per Cognitive Domain

When studies began subcategorizing MCI by subtypes, the criteria were generally modified to include specific neuropsychological tests of other cognitive functions in lieu of the MMSE (e.g., verbal fluency, Trailmaking test, etc.). Thus, the "typical" MCI diagnostic scheme included specific tests of attention, executive function, language, and visuospatial skills, and usually retained its cutoff criterion of -1.5 SDs for each of these measures. While this approach included a broader assessment of cognition than its "historical" predecessor, diagnostic challenges to the MCI concept also increased. For example, when multiple tests are given, a certain percentage of healthy persons will score below cutoffs (Brooks & Iverson, 2010). Heaton et al. (2004), for example, have shown in their comprehensive norms that the modal number of test performances of their neurologically normal group that fall below their recommended 1 SD cutpoint (demographically corrected T-scores < 40) is about 10%. Schretlen et al. (2008) have also carefully demonstrated that rates of abnormal test scores increase as the number of tests in a battery increases and decrease as the cutoff used to define abnormality is lowered (from 1 to 2 SDs).

 That said, many studies using neuropsychological tests to more broadly sample cognitive domains have typically used only one test in a particular domain (Tabert et al., 2006b; Lopez et al., 2007). For example, memory is often solely represented by a single measure of delayed free recall (usually of a story paragraph), language might be solely represented by the total score on the Boston Naming Test, executive function by Trails B, visuospatial function by Block Design, and so on. However, investigators taking a broader view of, say, memory have shown that a sizable minority of amnestic MCI cases are likely missed if visual memory (Alladi, Arnold, Mitchell, Nestor, & Hodges, 2006) or learning (Chang et al., 2010) is not examined. Other studies have shown that verbal list learning tests are among the most sensitive in MCI (de Jager, Hogervorst, Combrinck, & Budge, 2003; Rabin, Pare, Saykin, & et al., 2009) and to the earliest stages of an evolving dementia (Bondi, Salmon, Galasko, Thomas, & Thal, 1999; Lange et al., 2002; Tierney, Yao, Kiss, & McDowell, 2005). Inaccurate identification of MCI subtypes due to insufficient evaluation is of significant concern, given findings that subtypes differ in diagnostic outcomes and likelihood of progression to dementia. Busse et al., (2006) have shown, for example, that multidomain nonamnestic MCI is more likely to result in a non-AD dementia, and that the single-domain nonamnestic subtype appears to be most apt to revert to normalcy (see also Ganguli, Snitz, Saxton, et al., 2011; Jak, Bangen, et al., 2009).

Relying on more than one test to sample a cognitive domain has clearly not been the norm in MCI studies. Nevertheless, some MCI studies have begun to explore the use of different numbers of tests (Jak, Bondi, et al., 2009; Loewenstein et al., 2009) and different cutoffs (e.g., 1 SD: Busse, et al., 2006; 1.96 SD: Bickel, Mosch, Seigerschmidt, Siemen, & Forstl, 2006), and still others have avoided the use of cutoff scores altogether in favor of clinical judgments based on evidence of memory impairment out of proportion to an individual's other cognitive scores or domains (e.g., Jicha et al., 2006). This latter diagnostic strategy unfortunately rests on a rather faulty assumption of rough equivalency of ability levels across cognitive domains. For example, individuals with high IQs would be expected to demonstrate equally high memory abilities, although conormed instruments like the WAIS and WMS have shown relatively modest proportions of variance in memory accounted for by IQ (roughly on the order of 20%–30%).

Given these different operational criteria across studies, investigators began examining diagnostic algorithms (Bondi et al., 2008; Jak, Bangen, et al., 2009) and sought to characterize how the different diagnostic approaches would impact the classification of individuals as normal or MCI. Thus, to the same sample of subjects the "historical" criteria and its more modern variant, the "typical" criteria, were applied to that of a third neuropsychologically defined scheme. In this latter comprehensive neuropsychological method, as shown in Table 4.3 a battery of five broad domains was constructed (memory, attention, language, visuospatial skills and executive functions) with at least three measures in each domain and in light of multiple pieces of evidence that reflect the difficulty of interpreting an isolated test score. These notions included the statistical maxim that multiple measures tend to provide a more reliable estimate of a cognitive construct than a single measure (Anastasi & Urbina, 1997); a cutoff score of 1 SD provides the best balance of sensitivity and specificity (Busse et al., 2006; Heaton et al., 2004); and a sizable minority of healthy older adults will obtain an impaired score in two different cognitive domains but fewer, less than 5%, earn two or more impaired scores in the same domain (Palmer et al., 1998). To strike a balance between reliability and sensitivity to detect mild impairment, we adopted a lower cutoff for impairment of 1 SD below normative data, alongside the requirement that two or more tests within a cognitive domain be impaired for that domain to contribute to the MCI classification. Individuals were classified as normal if, at most, performance on one measure within one or two cognitive domains fell more than 1 SD below demographically corrected norms.

Examining the different diagnostic schemes resulted in prevalence rates of 11% for the historical criteria, 49% for the typical criteria, and an intermediate rate of 34% for the more comprehensive neuropsychological criteria (see Figure 4.5); the latter criteria were also shown to be a relatively stable diagnostic strategy over time. These findings indicate that varying

Table 4.3 Neuropsychological Test Battery Used by Jak et al. (2009) to Diagnose Mild Cognitive Impairment

MEMORY	ATTENTION	LANGUAGE	VISUOSPATIAL FUNCTIONING	EXECUTIVE FUNCTIONS
WMS-R Logical Memory (immediate, delayed free recall)	DRS attention	BNT	WISC-R Block Design	WCST-48-card version (categories achieved and perseverative errors)
WMS-R Visual Reproduction (immediate, delayed free recall)	WAIS-R Digit Span	Letter fluency	D-KEFS Visual Scanning	TMT, Part B
CVLT Trials 1–5 total, long delay free recall	TMT Part A	Category fluency	D-KEFS Design Fluency (empty and filled dot conditions)	D-KEFS Color-Word Interference Test (inhibition and inhibition/switching)
			DRS construction	D-KEFS fluency switching (visual and verbal)
			Clock drawing	

Wechsler Memory Scale—Revised (D. Wechsler, 1987) (WMS-R), California Verbal Learning Test (Delis, Kramer, Kaplan, & Ober, 1987) (CVLT), Wechsler Adult Intelligence Scale-Revised (Wechsler, 1981) (WAIS-R), Trail Making Test (Reitan & Wolfson, 1985) (TMT), Part A, Boston Naming Test (Kaplan, Goodglass, & Weintraub, 1983) (BNT), Wechsler Intelligence Scale for Children-Revised (Wechsler, 1974) (WISC-R), Delis-Kaplan Executive Function System (Delis, Kaplan, & Kramer, 2001) (D-KEFS), modified Wisconsin Card Sorting Test (Lineweaver; Bondi, Thomas, & Salmon, 1999) (WCST-48-card version), Trail Making Test (Reitan & Wolfson, 1985) (TMT), Part B, Normative data was drawn from Mayo's Older Americans Normative Studies (MOANS) (R. J. Ivnik et al., 1992) or from other published norms (Delis et al., 2001; Delis et al., 1987; Gladsjo et al., 1999; Kaplan et al., 1983; Lineweaver et al., 1999; Norman, Evan, Miller, & Heaton, 2000; Reitan & Wolfson, 1985; Wechsler, 1974, 1981, 1987) except for block design, which used age and education adjusted norms drawn from local unpublished data derived from the UCSD Alzheimer Disease Research Center.

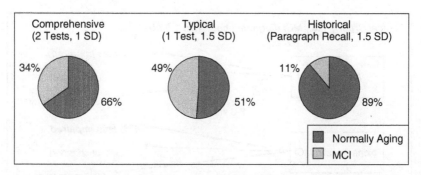

FIGURE 4.5 Prevalence of Mild Cognitive Impairment (MCI) According to Different Definitional Criteria.
Adapted from Jak et al. (2009) with permission.

the number of tests used to determine objective impairment, or the cutoffs used to define mildly impaired cognition in older adults, can alter MCI classification rates substantially. The historical criteria's prevalence rate of 11%, based on its circumscribed focus on amnestic MCI, is very close to the 12% rate shown repeatedly by Petersen and colleagues; the 49% prevalence for the typical criteria is consonant with the upper range of prevalence rates in other studies, as well as consistent with Schretlen et al.'s notion that rates of abnormal test scores increase with the number of tests administered; and our diagnostic algorithm, given its intermediate prevalence between these other two approaches, does appear to strike a balance between increased sensitivity coupled with reliability.

Loewenstein et al. (2009) have also presented compelling data that diagnostic algorithms, based on the requirement of two or more tests for an MCI diagnosis, are superior to those based on a single test's positive finding (see Figure 4.6). Impressively, none of the subjects diagnosed with amnestic MCI on the basis of two or more memory tests reverted to normal over a 2–3 year follow-up; half remained stably impaired, while the other half worsened over time. Similar patterns of low reversion to normal levels and high rates of stability or worsening were also seen for the nonamnestic MCI group (with the two or more test requirement). On the other hand, the typical criteria for MCI based on a single abnormal test score showed far more instability over time, where about half of aMCI or naMCI groups reverted to normal during the follow-up period.

Researchers have sought to further validate the more comprehensive neuropsychological approach via the study of brain-behavior relationships.

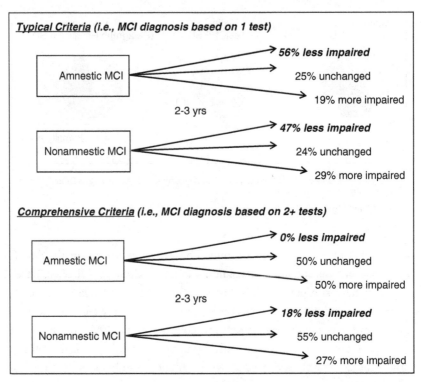

FIGURE 4.6 Stability of different subtypes of MCI, over a 2- to 3-year follow-up period based on whether the diagnosis of MCI is made on a single test or multiple tests.
Adapted from Loewenstein et al. (2009).

In an initial study in this area, Jak et al. examined whether hippocampal volumes and cerebrovascular risk factors in individuals, characterized by a comprehensive neuropsychological definition of MCI subtypes, would differ from more typical definitional schemes (Jak, Urban, et al., 2009). The investigators found this to be the case, such that the comprehensive neuropsychological definition of MCI resulted in expected anatomical results: hippocampal volumes were significantly smaller in the amnestic MCI group as compared to cognitively normal or nonamnestic MCI groups. However, the typical criteria for classifying MCI based only on the presence of one impaired score within a cognitive domain did not result in hippocampal differences between groups. Furthermore, relationships between stroke risk and cognitive performance varied by diagnostic scheme. The comprehensive approach demonstrated associations between stroke risk and cognition (both in healthy control and MCI groups), whereas the typical criteria did not.

Thus, research is beginning to show that the use of more sophisticated clinical decision-making and diagnostic approaches that incorporate comprehensive neuropsychological assessment techniques is supported by a convergence of cognitive, MRI, and stroke risk findings. The studies reviewed also suggest that MCI diagnostic stability improves when based on the requirement of two or more impaired test performances. Therefore, more comprehensive approaches may be the better choice for researchers and clinicians looking for a more stable diagnostic strategy. It is likely that this latter approach better approximates clinical decision-making processes. Clinicians typically will inspect multiple scores within a cognitive domain and base decisions on consistency of findings and patterns of impairment rather than isolated deficit scores. The findings reviewed here provide empirical support for an operational definition of clinical subtypes of MCI using comprehensive neuropsychological assessments based on multiple measures, as opposed to the typical screening approaches found in many MCI studies (e.g., one delayed recall measure, MMSE, and CDR) or reliance on isolated impaired test scores.

Statistically Determined MCI Classifications
Researchers have begun to explore statistically determined MCI classifications, and the initial findings are intriguing since they suggest optimal clusterings of neuropsychological dysfunction along three dimensions, or subtypes, and not necessarily the four MCI subtypes proposed by Winblad et al. (2004). In an initial study, Delano-Wood and investigators (Delano-Wood et al., 2010) found evidence for an amnestic group, a mixed amnestic and language group, and a third group demonstrating impairment on tests measuring executive control and information processing speed. In a separate study, Libon et al. (2010) also found evidence for two distinct amnestic and dysexecutive groups, and similar to Delano-Wood et al. (2010), a third multiple-domain group was also identified with reduced scores on fluency, naming, and delayed free recall (but importantly with intact recognition memory).

In a detailed follow-up study of the memory characteristics of the three statistically determined MCI subtypes, Libon et al. (2011) showed that their amnestic MCI group presented with low scores on delayed free recall and recognition (along with a proclivity for intrusions and false positive errors); the mixed or multidomain MCI group had higher scores on recognition relative to free recall; and the dysexecutive MCI group had relatively intact scores on both recall and recognition (Libon et al., 2011). Such memory performance dissociations are often associated with those typified in cortical versus subcortical dementia syndromes (i.e., equally impaired recall and recognition indicative of rapid forgetting in the case of cortical dementias such as Alzheimer's disease versus impaired recall but improved recognition indicative of retrieval-based difficulties in the case of subcortical dementias such as Huntington's disease), and they are suggestive of differing underlying neuropathologies (see Salmon & Bondi, 2009). What remains to be determined is whether these optimal cognitive clusterings indeed correspond to dissociable neuropathologic substrates and whether they reliably predict progression to dementia. Nevertheless, when combined with other research findings (e.g., Lopez et al., 2003; Salmon et al., 2002), neuropsychological tests selected on the basis of known brain-behavior relationships may make a substantial contribution to understanding cognitive manifestations underlying MCI.

These findings based on cluster analyses also appear at odds with some of the conventional thinking on MCI and its subtypes. For example, Petersen et al. (2009) suggest that amnestic MCI is twice as prevalent as nonamnestic MCI, although the findings of Delano-Wood et al. and Libon et al. suggest that early cognitive declines in nonamnestic MCI may be more prevalent than an isolated deficit in delayed free recall. It is likely that the higher amnestic MCI prevalence noted by Petersen et al. may also relate to the prior decade's focus on amnestic MCI coupled with fewer studies using broader neuropsychological characterizations of subtypes. Prior work has shown that MCI presents with more heterogeneous cognitive profiles more often than a circumscribed amnesia (Delano-Wood, et al., 2010) and that, instead, supports that difficulties with complex executive control tasks (Clark et al., 2012) or semantic memory (Mickes et al., 2007; Woodard, Seidenberg, Nielson, & et al., 2010), in addition to episodic memory (Bondi et al., 1999), may herald the onset of more global cognitive declines. Whether different MCI subtypes reflect different underlying etiologies and represent reliable prodromes of dementia will require additional follow-up. To date, the data are not compelling that different MCI subtypes relate to distinct neuropathologic substrates (e.g., Busse et al., 2006; Schneider, Arvanitakis, Leurgans, & Bennett, 2009), although it remains to be determined if more sophisticated neuropsychological approaches to MCI and its subtypes will yield improvements in this area. Statistically defined MCI subtypes, based on carefully chosen neuropsychological tests and perhaps via optimal clusterings of test performance patterns, may improve on MCI diagnosis and cognitive characterizations, and ultimately may engender improvements in the use of biomarkers in disease detection.

Sensitivity of Cognitive Measures

Another key difference across studies of predementia conditions has to do with the manner in which memory is assessed. The term "memory impairment" has been used to describe a wide variety of cognitive impairments, which may have different neural substrates. Most studies have focused on episodic memory, and most assessments of episodic memory have been based on delayed recall of a story paragraph. However, even within the realm of episodic memory, differences may exist in the particular test(s) used and the extent to which impairments are associated with risk for subsequent decline to dementia. It is important to distinguish between encoding and retrieval phases of memory tasks. Encoding is typically assessed by measures of immediate recall, whereas retrieval is assessed by delayed recall. The encoding phase of memory is sensitive to aging effects alone, but may be insensitive relative to indices of delayed recall for detecting incipient dementia (Petersen, Smith, Ivnik, Kokmen, & Tangalos, 1994; Petersen, Smith, Kokmen, Ivnik, & Tangalos, 1992). For example, a recent study of nine people who died and were observed to have healthy brains, compared to five people who were nondemented at death but observed to have Alzheimer's disease changes in the brain, revealed no difference in the cognitive profiles between groups. However, all memory test scores in this very small study focused on immediate recall (Goldman et al., 2001). Numerous studies suggest delayed recall measures appear to be most sensitive for early discrimination of dementia (Bondi et al., 1994; Ivnik et al., 2000; Tierney et al., 1996). Studies that focus on immediate recall (encoding) versus delayed recall (retrieval) in establishing the memory impairment criteria for MCI may engender very different samples and different rates of progression to MCI.

That said, a number of investigators have argued that prodromal AD is characterized predominantly by an acquisition deficit (Greene, Baddeley, & Hodges, 1996) rather than one of accelerated forgetting, and a consistent but less well-known literature exists on the utility of learning measures in preclinical dementia detection. For example, Masur et al. (Masur, Fuld, Blau, Crystal, & Aronson, 1990) were among the first to show about equal sensitivity in either learning or delayed recall measures in predicting the development of dementia 1 to 2 years later. Grober and Kawas (1997) further showed—with the same free and cued selective reminding (FCSR) procedure used by Masur and colleagues—that a retention deficit is not present in preclinical AD when hallmark learning deficits can be documented, suggesting that detection of preclinical and very early AD may be best accomplished by using robust learning measures. They go on to suggest that the particular conditions of the FCSR test maximize recall by circumventing certain age-associated decrements in attention and processing capacity and by inducing deep semantic processing, thereby promoting retention rates. Indeed, retention rates for the preclinical AD group was nearly the same as control participants at baseline (both were around 100% retention), whereas it was poorer at follow-up 3 years later in the AD participants (i.e., it dropped to 87%). Although retention was impaired in AD participants at follow-up, 87% of the initially learned material was still retained in comparison with much lower levels observed for patients with mild AD on, for example, the CERAD list learning test (e.g., 37% in Welsh, Butters, Hughes, Mohs, & Heyman, 1991) which is an uncontrolled learning test. Grober and Kawas (1997) concluded that measurement of learning deficits with sensitive tests such as the FCSR procedure is likely to be more valuable for the early diagnosis of AD than measures of delayed recall.

Bondi and colleagues (Bondi et al., 1999) showed that, in a survival analysis to identify those baseline variables that best predicted progression to AD, the APOE ε4 allele and CVLT Trials 1–5 Total Learning were retained as predictors of progression in the model, whereas MMSE, CVLT delayed free recall and cued recall intrusion errors were not retained in the final model. Given the high correlation between CVLT measures, it is not surprising that the remaining CVLT measures did not improve prediction once the other variable was in the list of predictors. Thus, when the summary learning measure was withheld from a second survival analysis, the remaining two CVLT measures (long delay free recall and cued recall intrusions) both provided significant predictive utility. Both of the survival analyses underscore the notion that measures of either learning or retention appear to be among the most salient markers of preclinical AD. These findings were reinforced by Rabin et al. (2009), who showed that the CVLT-II Trials 1–5 Total Learning score was the most sensitive and specific individual measure for distinguishing MCI from normal aging (90% sensitivity; 84% specificity), and that the addition of delayed recall measures both further enhanced classification accuracies and improved prediction of progression to AD dementia.

The Quandary of Functional Assessment to Rule Out Dementia

Once deficits in two or more areas of cognition are identified, the clinician is faced with the challenging task of determining whether the cognitive disturbances are also associated with decline in ADL. This determination is eased when reliable and, ideally, multiple collateral sources such as a spouse and son, daughter, or other relative are available, although a separate decision is periodically required to ascertain the veracity and reliability of an informant's opinion (American Psychological Association, 2011).

Unfortunately, the research literature is generally not very helpful in guiding this critical determination, and in many ways it may boil down to an issue of semantics and the choice of which diagnostic scheme one uses. For example, some schemes such as that proposed by Winblad et al. (2004) allow for the diagnosis of MCI in those individuals with mild declines in complex instrumental activities of daily living (IADL; e.g., medications, finances, driving, etc.), whereas others do not. Complicating matters further, Jefferson and colleagues (Jefferson et al., 2008) have shown dissociations between various ADL measures in the same sample of patients diagnosed with MCI (diagnosed as such under the Winblad et al. scheme). This observation suggests that some of the more traditional measures assessing global ADLs may not be sensitive to early functional changes related to MCI, whereas others may be more useful in capturing subtle evolving functional declines. These findings help to underscore the variability between measures but do not necessarily resolve which instrument(s) or sources of information to use and how to gauge mild versus more substantive declines in complex IADLs.

Bangen et al. (2010) have shown that performance-based IADL assessments from the Independent Living Scales (Loeb, 1996) were significantly lower in MCI individuals than in normally aging individuals. However, MCI individuals were still within normal limits (i.e., T-scores ≥ 40) on this scale. They also showed that IADL scores varied by MCI subtype. Specifically, individuals with amnestic MCI demonstrated significant decrements in financial management, whereas those with nonamnestic MCI showed poorer performance in abilities related to health and safety. These results support the need for better delineation of functional decline in MCI, perhaps even by subtype. Given the important ramifications of determining one's functional status for diagnosis and possible treatment of MCI or dementia, better operational definitions of functional status are clearly needed. One recommendation might be the direct assessment of functional abilities, thereby circumventing the need for informant reports and their susceptibility to errors and biases in reporting. However, direct lab based IADL assessments have their own limitations because they are necessarily conducted outside of a person's familiar environment and routine and could thereby overestimate degree of impairment. These assessments require their own form of independent validation. This is an area for further exploration, especially if specific IADL decrements are associated with specific cognitive deficit profiles and thus permit targeted compensatory treatment strategies.

In another study, Chang and colleagues (2011) evaluated whether ratings on the Clinical Dementia Rating (CDR) scale are associated with cognitive or brain morphometric characteristics of participants diagnosed with MCI. The CDR is perhaps the most widely used instrument for gathering IADL information. On the CDR, a global score of 0.5 implies the MCI state (i.e., intermediate between no decline [CDR = 0] and mild but evident decline [CDR = 1]). The most heavily weighted component of the CDR score is memory function. CDR nonmemory components, including the three IADL categories, receive less weighting in the assignment of the global score. Consequently, two MCI individuals with the same global CDR score of 0.5 can noticeably differ in IADL ratings. This lack of specificity in characterizing IADL changes might prevent identification of meaningful clinical differences within the global CDR level associated with MCI. Chang et al. examined baseline cognitive and morphometric data, as well as clinical outcome 2 years later, in 283 individuals from the Alzheimer's Disease Neuroimaging Initiative diagnosed with MCI (all of whom had a global CDR of 0.5). MCI subjects were divided into two groups (impaired and intact) based on their scores on the three CDR categories assessing IADL. As shown in Figure 4.7, the impaired IADL MCI group showed a more widespread pattern of gray matter loss involving frontal and parietal regions. Cognitively, the impaired IADL MCI group showed worse episodic memory and executive functions, and a significantly higher percentage of individuals progressed to AD than the "intact" IADL MCI group. These results demonstrate the importance of considering functional information captured by the CDR when evaluating individuals with MCI, even though it is not afforded equal weight in the assignment of the global CDR score of 0.5.

Since the MCI group with impaired IADL were more likely than those with intact IADL to progress to a clinical diagnosis of probable AD, this difference suggests that the two MCI subgroups may be at different points along an MCI-to-AD continuum, with the impaired IADL group having progressed farther toward AD than the intact IADL group. This possibility was also supported by

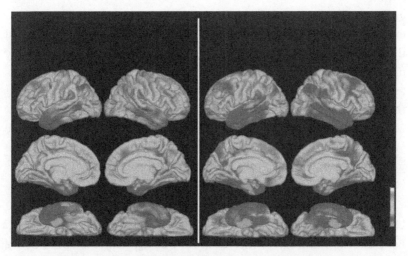

FIGURE 4.7 Reconstructed cortical surface maps representing the average mean difference in cortical thickness for the intact (high) or impaired (low) IADL groups, relative to the healthy control group. Darkened brain areas indicate greater cortical thinning. IADL = Instrumental Activities of Daily Living. From Chang et al. (2011) with permission.

the fact that the impaired IADL group showed higher scores on the Functional Assessment Questionnaire than the intact IADL group. We could also argue that the findings might be more supportive of a mild dementia diagnosis rather than MCI—at least in a subset of the individuals with impaired IADL. In other words, the presence of deficits in two or more areas of cognition (i.e., episodic memory and executive function), coupled with documented difficulties in IADL, would be supportive of a diagnosis of mild dementia rather than MCI. At a minimum, the conventional practice of relying on the global CDR score as currently computed underutilizes valuable IADL information available in the scale, and may delay identification of an important subset of MCI individuals who are at higher risk of clinical decline and in whom some may already show sufficient evidence for a diagnosis of mild dementia.

Critiques of the MCI Concept

Dubois et al. (2007) were among the first to offer a critique of the MCI concept—particularly as a transitional state of Alzheimer's disease—suggesting that distinctive and reliable biomarkers of AD are now available through structural MRI, amyloid imaging, and CSF assays, and that the prevailing MCI diagnostic methods have fallen behind. Instead, they advanced new criteria that focused on a central core criterion of episodic memory impairment that is gradual and progressive and either isolated or not. There must also be at least one or more abnormal biomarkers as supportive evidence. They concluded that these criteria would eliminate the MCI construct and its arbitrary binary outcome (e.g., conversion vs. no conversion to AD) in the clinical characterization process. While not eliminating the MCI construct, it is clear that the subsequent NIA-Alzheimer's Association workgroups (Albert et al., 2011; McKhann, 2011; Sperling et al., 2011) have embraced this focus and reliance on the role of biomarkers in diagnosis, although the sole reliance on episodic memory impairment has generally not been supported by autopsy studies (see discussion below on the neuropathology of MCI).

Current Diagnostic Criteria for MCI

Both the American Psychiatric Association and a joint committee of the National Institute of Aging and Alzheimer's Association have proposed new criteria for MCI-like conditions. The criteria for minor neurocognitive disorder proposed by the APA were presented in Chapter 1. The NIA-Alzheimer's Association task force criteria for MCI (Albert et al., 2011) are as follows:

A.MCI—Criteria for the Clinical and Cognitive Syndrome

1. **Concern regarding a change in cognition.** There should be evidence of concern about a change in cognition, in comparison to the person's prior level. This concern can be obtained from the patient, from an informant who knows the patient well, or from a skilled clinician observing the patient.

2. **Impairment in one or more cognitive domains.** There should be evidence of lower performance in one or more cognitive domains that is greater than would be expected for the patient's age and educational background. If repeated assessments are available, then a decline in performance should be evident over time. This change can occur in a variety of cognitive domains, including: memory, executive function, attention, language, and visuospatial skills. An impairment in episodic memory (i.e., the ability to learn and retain new information) is seen most commonly in MCI patients who subsequently progress to a diagnosis of AD (see the section on the cognitive characteristics below, for further details).

3. **Preservation of independence in functional abilities.** Persons with MCI commonly have mild problems performing complex functional tasks they used to be able to perform, such as paying bills, preparing a meal, or shopping at the store. They may take more time, be less efficient, and make more errors at performing such activities than in the past. Nevertheless, they

generally maintain their independence of function in daily life, with minimal aids or assistance.

4. Not demented. These cognitive changes should be sufficiently mild that there is no evidence of a significant impairment in social or occupational functioning. It should be emphasized that the diagnosis of MCI requires evidence of intraindividual change. If an individual has only been evaluated once, change will need to be inferred from the history and/or evidence that cognitive performance is impaired beyond what would have been expected for that individual. Serial evaluations are of course optimal, but may not be feasible in a particular circumstance.

As noted above and in the NIA-Alzheimer Association statement, after criteria of MCI are met, the clinician endeavors to determine the cause of the MCI. The criteria for MCI due to AD versus other causes are discussed in Chapters 5 and 6.

Epidemiology of MCI

As noted above, the reported incidence and prevalence (number of cases at a given point in time) of MCI has varied widely based on diagnostic methods. The incidence (number of new cases in a given period such as one year) of MCI is reported to range between 5.1 and 7.7 per 100 person/years. In contrast, the annual incidence of dementia in the over 65 population is well established at 1%–2% (Edland, Rocca, Petersen, Cha, & Kokmen, 2002). This incidence rate is strongly associated with age. Work from the Mayo Clinic suggests that about 12% of MCI patients will progress to dementia per year (Figure 4.3a) and that 7%–10% of MCI patients will not ultimately have a progressive neuropathology at autopsy. These data provide the basis for establishing what the prevalence of MCI "should" be. If we assume that all dementia patients will pass through the MCI state before displaying dementia, then we can use the percentages above to estimate MCI prevalence. Since the 1%–2% annual incidence of dementia represents the outcome of 12% of all prevalent MCI progressing to dementia that year, the estimated prevalence of MCI (that will progress to dementia) would be 1%–2% divided by 12% or 8.3%–16.6%. The 8.3%–16.6% progressive MCI prevalence would then be roughly 90% of all MCI, so the total theoretical estimated prevalence would be 9%–18%.

We note above that reported prevalence varies widely from 3% to 54% mainly because of the different methods and criteria used (Bennett et al., 2002; Larrieu et al., 2002; Lopez et al., 2002). The Cardiovascular Health Study

(CHS) evaluated several definitions of MCI in their nondemented cohort 65 years of age or older and provided useful prevalence figures (Lopez, et al., 2002). The CHS included amnestic MCI and multidomain MCI defined in a very similar fashion to that above. They concluded that the prevalence of MCI among nondemented individuals was 19%, and it increased with increasing age. These results are strikingly similar to the estimate of MCI prevalence calculated above. They found a ratio of 2.5:1 for the prevalence of multiple domain type MCI (which included memory impairment) to single-domain amnestic MCI (Lopez, et al., 2002). The Mayo Clinic Study of Aging (MCSA) reported an overall MCI prevalence of exactly 16%, partitioned into an 11.1% rate for amnestic MCI and 4.9% for nonamnestic MCI. Single-domain amnestic MCI was the most common form observed. The MCSA study suggests a higher prevalence of MCI in men, a finding that is relatively unique and as yet unreplicated (see Figure4.8).

The CHS and MCSA prevalence findings fall within the expected range that can be derived from dementia incidence and prevalence rates. Ultimately, these theoretic rates provide a check on MCI criteria and diagnostic methods. If population studies use criteria and methods that generate prevalence rates outside of the 9%–20% range, those criteria and methods should be carefully scrutinized.

Neuropathology of MCI

Petersen et al. (2006) studied 15 Mayo Alzheimer's Disease Patient Registry cases who died while their clinical classification was still amnestic MCI (one of which was the case presented at the beginning of this chapter). The brains were processed using standard neuropathological techniques and classified according to Katchaturian (1985), CERAD (Mirra, Heyman, McKeil, Sumi, & Crain, 1991), and National Institute on Aging–Reagan (Hyman & Trojanowski, 1997) neuropathological criteria. Eight of these cases did not meet any of the three neuropathological criteria for Alzheimer's disease (AD), though their pathology suggested a transitional state of evolving AD. In these cases, there was also a great deal of concomitant pathology including argyrophilic grain disease, hippocampal sclerosis and vascular lesions. One of the 15 cases had no identifiable neuropathology.

These findings concur with a larger autopsy study by Schneider et al. (2009) that found, of 134 persons who died with final antemortem diagnoses of MCI, little more than half met pathological criteria for AD. Interestingly, in those who met pathologic criteria for "definite" AD, they

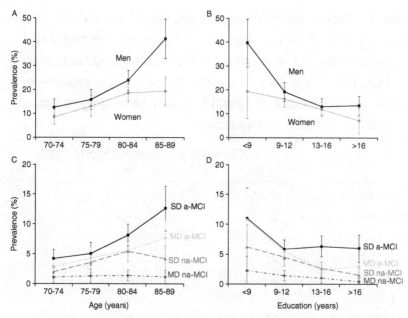

FIGURE 4.8 Patterns of Mild Cognitive Impairment (MCI) prevalence by age, sex, education, and type of MCI. (A) Age- and sex-specific prevalence of MCI in Olmsted County, MN. Men had consistently higher prevalence than women at all ages. (B) Education- and sex-specific prevalence of MCI. The prevalence decreased with increasing education in both men and women. (C) Age- and type-specific prevalence of MCI. The increase of prevalence with age was consistent for single-domain amnestic MCI (SD a-MCI), multiple-domain amnestic MCI (MD a-MCI), single-domain nonamnestic MCI (SD na-MCI), and multiple-domain nonamnestic MCI (MD na-MCI). (D) Education- and type-specific prevalence of MCI. The decline in prevalence with increasing education was consistent across the four types of MCI. (Petersen et al., 2010). Reproduced with permission.

were roughly divided equally between amnestic and nonamnestic MCI subtypes, and another 20% had mixed pathologies—again with similar proportions of amnestic (22.7%) and nonamnestic (15.3%) antemortem diagnoses (see Table 4.4).

Collectively, these findings would argue that it is not appropriate to simply conclude that all MCI, including amnestic MCI, is simply early AD (cf. Morris et al., 2001). Rather, MCI looks to be a pathologically heterogeneous disorder, whether diagnosed in its amnestic or nonamnestic form, with many persons exhibiting mixed pathologies. In addition, these neuropathological findings suggest that MCI is not just a state of uncertainty in the clinician, but

Table 4.4 Number and percentage of autopsied subjects with no pathology, one type of pathology, or mixed pathology with final clinical diagnoses of amnestic or nonamnestic Mild Cognitive Impairment prior to death. AD = Alzheimer's disease; MCI = mild cognitive impairment; NIA = National Institute on Aging; LB = Lewy bodies. Adapted from Schneider et al. (2009) with permission

	AMNESTIC MCI, n = 75	NONAMNESTIC MCI, n = 59
One pathology	41 (54.7%)	32 (54.2%)
AD path diagnosis	27 (36%)	20 (33.9%)
NIA high	6 (8.0%)	4 (6.8%)
NIA intermediate	21 (28.0%)	16 (27.1%)
Infarcts	10 (13.3%)	11 (18.6%)
LB	4 (5.3%)	1 (1.7%)
Mixed pathology	17 (22.7%)	9 (15.3%)
AD + infarcts	15 (20.0%)	8 (13.6%)
AD + LB	2 (2.7%)	1 (1.7%)
AD + infarcts + LB	0	0
Infarcts + LB	0	0
No AD, infarcts, or LB	17 (22.7%)	18 (30.5%)

that the clinical syndrome of MCI may (in many but not all patients) reflect a transitional neuropathological state—in whom some meet the underlying pathological criteria for AD and some who do not. If it is ultimately possible to arrest the development of neuropathology at this point, it would be tantamount to preventing dementia.

Neuroimaging Studies in MCI
Structural Magnetic Resonance Imaging (MRI)
Early MRI studies in MCI examined hippocampal volume (Jack et al., 1999) and found that degree of hippocampal atrophy at baseline was associated with the development of Alzheimer's disease. Follow-up studies addressed whether MRI-based measurements of the transentorhinal/entorhinal cortex

are more sensitive than hippocampal volume in discriminating normal controls, MCIs, and ADs, given that the earliest pathology of AD has been identified in this brain region (Xu et al., 2000). Contrary to expectations, measurements of the hippocampus and entorhinal cortex were approximately equivalent at discriminating between the two patient groups, although other studies have found increased sensitivity of the entorhinal cortex relative to hippocampal volumes (Tapiola et al., 2008) as well as associations between entorhinal cortex and CSF biomarkers of AD pathology (Aβ/p-tau concentrations; Desikan, McEvoy, Thompson, et al., 2011) among MCI patients.

Serial MRI scans were subsequently found to serve as a biomarker of disease progression along the continuum from normal aging to MCI to AD. The first of these studies focused on rate of hippocampal atrophy (Jack et al., 2000). The annualized rate of hippocampal volume loss was greatest in the AD patients, followed by MCI, and then the normal control groups. Control participants and those with MCI who experienced a greater loss of hippocampal volume over time also showed more decline in their cognitive status. Jack et al. also examined whole brain and ventricular volume in addition to medial temporal lobe structures (i.e., hippocampus, entorhinal cortex) in individuals with MCI and found that atrophy rates in all four brain regions were greater in subjects who evidenced clinical decline than in those who remained stable (Jack et al., 2004). A more recent serial MRI study examined atrophy rates in these same brain regions in normal elderly and subjects with MCI over a relatively short period of time (i.e., 1–2 year interval) (C. Jack et al., 2004). Interestingly, whole brain and ventricular volume atrophy rates were helpful in predicting progression in the MCI subjects, while the hippocampal and entorhinal cortex measures were not. There was, however, overlap in the atrophy rates in the medial temporal lobe structures between the subjects who converted versus those who did not.

Examining the possibility that regional atrophy rates derived from serial structural MRI also contribute to domain-specific cognitive changes in MCI, McDonald et al. (2012) demonstrated that left temporal lobe atrophy rates over a 24-month period were associated with naming decline, whereas bilateral temporal, left frontal, and left anterior cingulate atrophy rates were associated with semantic fluency decline (McDonald et al., 2012). Left entorhinal cortex atrophy rate was associated with memory decline and bilateral frontal atrophy rates were associated with executive function decline (see Figure 4.9). These important data using high-throughput image analyses and examination

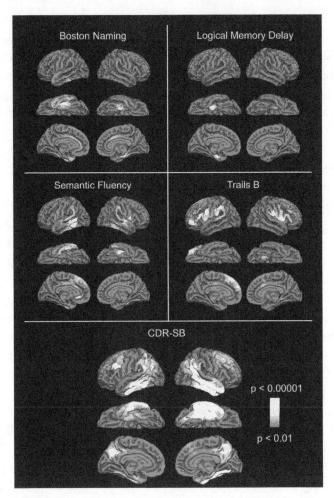

FIGURE 4.9 Significance maps of correlations between 2-year atrophy rates and 2-year decline on the cognitive scores and Clinical Dementia Rating Scale Sum of Boxes (CDR-SB) (bottom panel) in MCI (*n* = 103). Statistical maps show areas of significant correlation after regressing out age, gender, baseline performance, and CDR-SB decline for the four cognitive measures. Age, gender, and baseline performance are regressed out of the CDR-SB statistical maps. McDonald et al 2012. Reproduced with permission.

of specific brain-behavior relationships provide evidence that regional atrophy rates in MCI contribute to domain-specific cognitive declines, which appear to be partially independent of disease progression. MRI measures of regional atrophy can provide valuable information for understanding the neural basis of cognitive impairment in MCI.

A recent structural MRI study further highlights some of the importance of the above discussion in profiling cognition in MCI and AD with sophisticated neuropsychological and neuroimaging methods to better determine the specific features of those cognitive losses in the transitional period to AD. Chang et al. (2010) examined the utility of both learning (L) and retention (R) measures in (1) the diagnosis of MCI, (2) predicting progression to AD, and (3) their underlying brain morphometric correlates via cortical thickness maps derived from FreeSurfer (Fischl & Dale, 2000). A total of 607 participants were assigned to three MCI groups (high L-low R; low L-high R; low L-low R) and one control group (high L-high R) based on the *Rey Auditory Verbal Learning Test*. Results showed that MCI individuals with predominantly a learning deficit showed a widespread pattern of gray matter losses at baseline, whereas individuals with retention deficit showed more focal MTL loss (see Figure 4.10). Either learning or retention measures provided good predictive value for longitudinal clinical outcome over two years, although impaired learning had modestly better predictive power than impaired retention. As expected, impairments in both learning and retention provided the best predictive power. These findings have important implications for the diagnosis of MCI, given the conventional practice of relying solely on the use of delayed recall in studies of MCI. Specifically, these results suggest that this sole reliance on delayed recall misses an important subset of older adults at risk of developing AD. These results highlight the importance of including learning measures in addition to retention measures when making a diagnosis of MCI and predicting outcome.

¹H Magnetic Resonance Spectroscopy

Proton MR spectroscopy (¹H MRS) is a diagnostic imaging technique that is sensitive to the changes in the brain at the cellular level. With ¹H MRS, major proton-containing metabolites in the brain include N-acetyl aspartate (NAA), myo-inositol (MI), choline, and creatine, and are measured during a common data acquisition period. The NAA metabolite is a marker for neuronal integrity, and decreases in a variety of neurological disorders including AD (Kantarci et al., 2000; Klunk et al., 2004). The MI spectrographic peak consists of glial metabolites that are responsible for osmoregulation (Urenjak, Williams, Gadian, & Noble, 1993). Elevated MI levels correlate with glial proliferation in inflammatory CNS demyelination (Bitsch et al., 1999). The largest amount of choline in the brain is bound in

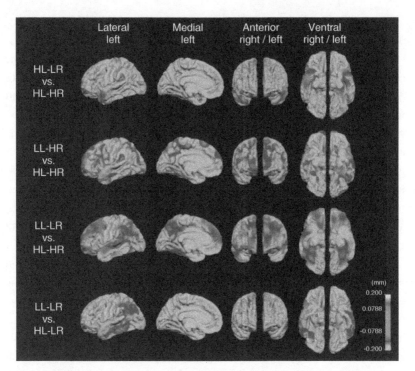

FIGURE 4.10 Cortical surface maps representing the average difference in thickness (mm, $p < .002$) for the three groups with low learning (LL) or low retention (LR) relative to an intact group with high learning and high retention (HL-HR) on the *Rey Auditory Verbal Learning Test* (top three rows), and the combined low learning and low retention (LL-LR) group relative to the group with isolated poor retention (HL-LR) (bottom row). The two groups with impaired learning ability showed a more widespread pattern of cortical thinning involving temporal, frontal and posterior cingulate cortex regions, whereas the impaired participants with isolated low retention (HL-LR) showed significant thinning of medial temporal and posterior cingulate cortical regions relative to the intact group (HL-HR). From Chang et al. (2010), with permission.

membrane phospholipids that are precursors of choline and acetylcholine synthesis. It has been postulated that the elevation of the choline peak is the consequence of membrane phosphatidylcholine catabolism in order to provide free choline for the chronically deficient acetylcholine production in AD. The observed result is that NAA is decreased and MI and choline are increased in MCI relative to normal values (Kantarci et al., 2000). The metabolite changes in MCI are generally intermediate between normal elderly and patients with AD. MI levels also correlate with performance on the Auditory Verbal Learning Test and Dementia Rating Scale in patients with MCI (Kantarci et al., 2000). We speculate that the elevation of the MI peak is related to glial proliferation and astrocytic activation during the evolution of AD pathology.

Diffusion Weighted MR Imaging (DWI)

DWI is sensitive to the random motion of water molecules in brain tissue. When molecules are free to move in any direction, as would be more likely in a sphere, such unrestricted movement would be termed "isotropic." However, if movement were restricted along one axis, as would be more likely in a tube or the principle axis of a neuron, such restricted movement would be more "anisotropic." Measures of fractional anisotropy (FA) or apparent diffusion coefficient (ADC) from DWI can quantify the alterations in water diffusivity resulting from microscopic structural changes. The apparent diffusion coefficient measurements of DWI indicate that the diffusivity of water is higher in the hippocampus of patients with MCI and AD than cognitively normal elderly (Fellgiebel et al., 2004; Kantarci et al., 2001). We attribute the elevation of the apparent diffusion coefficients in the hippocampi of people with MCI and AD to the expansion of the extracellular space owing to the loss of neuron cell bodies and dendrites. In a comparative study of different MR techniques in MCI, Kantarci et al. found that hippocampal diffusivity was not superior to hippocampal volumetry in distinguishing patients with MCI from normal (Kantarci et al., 2002). However, when patients with MCI were followed, elevated hippocampal diffusivity predicted progression to AD as well or better than hippocampal volumetry (Kantarci et al., 2005)

In another pair of studies, Delano-Wood and colleagues examined cognitively normal and MCI groups in whom diffusion tensor imaging FA values were obtained for the genu and splenium of the corpus callosum, as well as for the posterior cingulum (Delano-Wood, et al., 2010; Delano-Wood et al., 2012). Examining anterior (genu) and posterior (splenium) regions of the corpus callosum capitalizes on the large white matter fiber bundles contained within it. In addition, the posterior cingulate cortex has been implicated in preclinical AD, as Reiman et al. (1996) found hypometabolism in this region in cognitively normal middle-aged APOE ε4/ε4 homozygotes. In their first study, Delano-Wood et al. (2010) found that splenium FA was significantly lower in MCI than in NC participants, despite no differences in

A

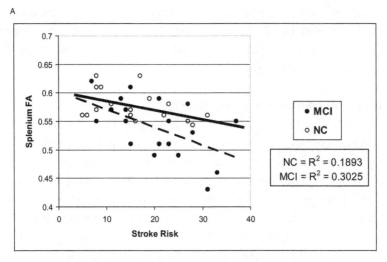

FIGURE 4.11 Group by stroke risk interaction of mean splenial fractional anisotropy (FA) values for normal control (NC) and mild cognitive impairment (MCI) groups. Stroke risk was based on the mean Framingham Stroke Risk Profile. From Delano-Wood et al. (2010), with permission.

gross morphometry or hippocampal volumes. In the overall sample, higher stroke risk was associated with lower white matter integrity, particularly in the genu.

However, as shown in Figure 4.11, increased stroke risk was more strongly associated with poorer splenium FA in those with MCI than in normal elderly. Finally, splenium FA significantly predicted performance on verbal memory, adjusting for the effects of age, education, and whole brain volume. In a follow-up study, Delano-Wood et al. (2012) found that MCI also demonstrated considerably diminished white matter integrity in the posterior cingulum (PC; Delano-Wood et al., 2012). Additionally, results showed that, above and beyond the effects of age, stroke risk, hippocampal volume, and whole brain volume, diminished white matter integrity of the PC was strongly predictive of MCI status, as well as neuropsychological performance on recall and recognition memory tasks. Finally, exploratory analyses showed that those with amnestic MCI showed decreased white matter integrity of the PC. Taken together, findings demonstrate a relationship between increased vascular burden and white matter changes, and they support the possibility that posterior white matter pathology may contribute to the development of MCI-related cognitive changes.

Mild Cognitive Impairment and Dementia

Functional Magnetic Resonance Imaging
Task Activated fMRI Studies

Functional MRI is a noninvasive technology that offers the ability to examine changes in blood oxygenation (i.e., an indirect measure of neuronal activity) as subjects engage in cognitive tasks while being scanned. The vast majority of studies in this area have focused on interrogating memory functions, given the early occurrence of known AD pathologic change in the medial temporal lobes and the reliance on these structures for learning and memory. Machulda and coworkers studied fMRI activation during a complex scene-encoding task in a group of normal elderly individuals, a group with MCI, and individuals with early AD. Using ROC curve analysis, it was found that activation in the medial temporal lobe was greater in normal subjects than in patients with MCI and AD, while the MCI patients were not significantly different from AD patients (Machulda et al., 2003). Decreased hippocampal activation has also been reported in a subgroup of subjects with "isolated memory decline" during a face-encoding task (Small, Perera, DeLaPaz, Mayeux, & Stern, 1999). Another study found that the medial temporal lobe response during repeated presentations of faces is compromised in individuals with MCI (Johnson et al., 2004). In contrast, Dickerson et al. showed that a subgroup of MCI subjects who demonstrated greater clinical impairment over time activated a greater extent of the right parahippocampal gyrus during a scene-encoding task compared to subjects who remained clinically stable (Dickerson et al., 2004). However, they did not require that their MCI subjects demonstrate objective memory impairment, which is one of the criteria for MCI required by most research groups.

One of the more interesting facets of BOLD fMRI findings in MCI groups is the apparent dynamic change that may take place in activation patterns across the range of cognitive severity of MCI patients. For example, studies appear to indicate that, within the medial temporal lobes (MTL), less impaired MCI subjects show increased BOLD response compared to control groups, whereas more impaired MCI subjects demonstrate decreased BOLD response similar to the diminished levels seen in mild AD patients (De Santi et al., 2008; Dickerson et al., 2004; Dickerson et al., 2005; Johnson et al., 2006; Machulda et al., 2003). Dickerson et al. (2004) reported a positive association between the extent of MTL activation with memory performance in MCI but, in a paradoxical fashion, found that greater clinical impairment, as determined by the Dementia Rating Scale, was associated with recruitment of a larger region of the right parahippocampal gyrus during encoding. Johnson et al. (2004)

provided further evidence for hippocampal dysfunction in MCI, whereby a reduction in hippocampal adaptation during repetition of a picture encoding task was found in an amnestic MCI group with poor learning, suggesting that adults with MCI do not habituate to increasingly familiar items in the same manner as healthy older adults who show expected reductions in BOLD response to repeated items over time (Johnson et al., 2004).

Despite the overwhelming focus on memory and medial temporal lobe function in most task activated BOLD fMRI studies, a number of other studies have examined language function and semantic network changes in MCI. In general, these studies, though diverse in terms of the semantic tasks employed, have generally shown upsurges in BOLD response in MCI groups. Woodard and others (Woodard et al., 2009) have found that MCI patients show functional compensation in brain regions subserving semantic memory systems that generally equals or exceeds that observed in cognitively intact individuals at risk for AD. In another pair of studies, Wierenga et al. examined word retrieval in AD as well as in nondemented APOE ε4 carriers with fMRI. In one study (Wierenga et al., 2011) the underlying neural correlates of word retrieval deficits in AD were examined and widespread differences were found in the categorical representation of semantic knowledge in several language-related brain areas in AD. Findings support the notion of a disrupted semantic network in AD that does not appear to clearly respect the living/nonliving categorical dimension or the global/local featural distinctions seen in normal aging. Interestingly, the AD group showed increased brain response for word retrieval in inferior frontal and rostral cingulate zones, suggestive of frontally mediated compensation in the face of semantic network decline. In another study, Weirenga et al. (2010) further examined whether nondemented APOE ε4 carriers exhibited BOLD changes in this same task and found that, despite equivalent naming accuracy, APOE ε4 adults showed more widespread BOLD response with greater signal change in the left fusiform gyrus and bilateral medial prefrontal cortex, but no significant group differences in inferior frontal gyrus. Taken together, this pair of studies suggests a continuum of semantic impairment across the spectrum of dementia risk that culminates in widespread changes in AD, and they provide further support for frontal lobe–mediated compensatory mechanisms in early AD. That is, executive functions mediated by the frontal lobes may be better preserved than temporal lobe-mediated episodic or semantic memory functions during the period of decline from MCI to AD (Mickes et al., 2007).

Task Free fMRI Studies

Consistent with the findings of BOLD fMRI activation studies, examination of changes in the resting state reveals alterations in MCI as well. For example, studies have shown greater memory-related *de*activation (e.g., reduction in brain activity) in medial and lateral parietal regions in less impaired MCI adults, and a loss of deactivation in more impaired MCI and mild AD adults (De Santi et al., 2008). In fact, the proposed "default mode network" is thought to be comprised of regions with a high resting state metabolism, including the posterior cingulate, medial frontal and parietal cortices, to explain decreases in brain activity that occur during task performance (Greicius, Krasnow, Reiss, & Menon, 2003; Raichle et al., 2001; Rombouts, Barkhof, Goekoop, Stam, & Scheltens, 2005). Thus, regions in the default mode network in healthy adults are thought to be more involved during resting states due to a number of factors, including engagement in attending to environmental stimuli, reviewing past knowledge and planning future behavior, spontaneous semantic processing, and the allocation of resources to perform a task. Alterations in the default mode network have been reported in both MCI and AD patients, and a study by Rombouts, Goekoop, Stam, Barkhof, & Scheltens (2005) showed that MCI patients showed less deactivation than healthy control subjects, but more than AD (see also Lustig et al., 2003; Sliwinski, Lipton, Buschke, & Stewart, 1996; Wang et al., 2006). Their findings were thought to be consistent with the notion of proposed early changes in MCI in the posterior cingulate cortex and precuneus, and suggest that altered activity in the default mode network may act as an early marker for AD pathology. This possibility was reinforced by the recent NIA-Alzheimer's Association workgroup definition of preclinical AD by Sperling et al., (2011), who offered the possibility that fMRI measurement of default network connectivity holds promise as a possible preclinical AD marker.

Postitron Emission Tomography (PET)
Fluorodeoxyglucose (FDG) PET

As with other imaging modalities, FDG PET findings in MCI suggest that MCI is an intermediate stage between normality and AD. The spatial distribution of the decrease in glucose metabolism in patients with MCI is similar to but less pronounced than patients with AD (Kantarci et al., 2004). In keeping with the distribution of the early neurofibrillary pathology of AD, the decrease in glucose metabolism involves the limbic and paralimbic cortex, as well as the temporal and parietal association cortices in MCI. Longitudinal studies indicate that FDG PET may predict progression to AD in people with MCI (Drzezga et al., 2003).

Amyloid Imaging

Amyloid imaging represents a major advance in the study of dementia, and it has rapidly become one of the central biomarkers of interest in the study of AD progression. As stated in the previous chapter, the (11)carbon-labeled Pittsburgh Compound-B (^{11}C-PIB) is the most commonly studied and utilized tracer to date and appears to bind to brain fibrillar Aβ deposits. As Rabinovici and Jagust (2009) have highlighted, PIB-PET has quickly become a powerful tool to examine in vivo the relationship between amyloid deposition, clinical symptoms, and structural and functional brain changes in the continuum between normal aging and AD. They further note that amyloid imaging studies generally support a model in which amyloid deposition is an early event in the pathogenesis of dementia, beginning insidiously in cognitively normal individuals, and accompanied by subtle cognitive decline and functional and structural brain changes suggestive of incipient AD. As individuals progress to MCI and dementia, clinical decline and neurodegeneration accelerate and appear to proceed independently of amyloid accumulation.

This supposition largely concurs with the model of dynamic changes, proposed by Jack et al. (2010), wherein AD biomarkers will be most informative in the preclinical period. Although Aβ pathology is thought to be causative, clinical symptoms nevertheless appear to be more closely related to neurofibrillary tangles than amyloid deposition. The finding that a substantial proportion of cognitively intact older adults also have significant levels of Aβ plaque burden (Sonnen, Santa Cruz, Hemmy, et al., 2011) further suggests that Aβ may be necessary but not sufficient for progression (Zaccai, Brayne, McKeith, et al., 2008). The lack of sensitivity of Aβ to predict cognitive decline and its weak association with clinical symptoms and disease severity has lessened enthusiasm for cerebral Aβ (e.g., amyloid imaging) to stand alone as a biomarker of AD. Nonetheless, as discussed in Chapter 3, FDA approval of the first amyloid imaging ligand, florbetapir F18 (Amyvid□), all but assures that amyloid imaging will be increasingly utilized in diagnosis and treatment—despite its prohibitive cost and limited access.

Rabinovici & Jagust (2009) suggest that, in the future, amyloid imaging is likely to supplement clinical evaluation in selecting patients for antiamyloid therapies, while MRI and FDG-PET may be more appropriate markers of clinical progression. Laforce and Rabinovici (2011) further note that amyloid imaging may be increasingly helpful in individuals with mild cognitive impairments or atypical presentations, and in those who are younger (e.g., middle aged to young-old age ranges). For example, amyloid imaging may help to differentiate early-onset AD from frontotemporal dementias (see Chapter 8), although the positive predictive value of amyloid imaging in older patients will likely be lower. What these and other authors often fail to include in that cadre of markers of clinical progression is the role of cognition. In the few studies that have directly compared biomarkers to cognitive markers, it is clear that cognitive variables at baseline remain either comparable or better (Devanand, Liu, Tabert, et al., 2008; Gomar et al., 2011; Heister et al., 2011; Jedynak et al., 2012; Landau et al., 2010) predictors of progression than biomarkers; and these studies have found comparable or superior prediction with *individual* cognitive measures.

Setting aside the issue of the importance of cognition and its utility as a predictor of decline, as well as an essential marker of clinical progression, Quigley et al. (2011) summarize that most amyloid imaging studies have shown that PIB uptake is intermediate between AD and nondemented normal control groups, although we would point out that there is great variability in this finding (Quigley, Colloby, & O'Brien, 2011). As Figure 4.12, from a representative PIB study of MCI by Mormino et al. (2009) demonstrates, the variability of PIB uptake values appears to range from the lowest levels of the NC group to the highest levels of the AD group. Furthermore, there does not appear to be much year-to-year change in PIB uptake levels, and Jack et al. (2009) have shown that a simple measure of annual change in ventricular volume on MRI nicely separates cognitively normal from MCI from AD groups, whereas PIB does not (Jack et al., 2009). Thus, the clinical symptoms would appear to be more highly coupled with a marker of neurodegeneration and not with amyloid deposition, echoing the conclusions drawn by Rabinovici and Jagust (2009) that clinical decline and neurodegeneration proceed independently of amyloid accumulation (Rabinovici & Jagust, 2009).

Despite such circumspection of the proximal role of brain amyloid levels to the prediction of clinical progression, PIB levels of amyloid binding have shown significant associations with episodic memory and hippocampal volumes. Mormino et al. (2009) discussed that their results were consistent with a model in which PIB index, hippocampal volume, and episodic memory are sequentially related, with hippocampal volume mediating the relationship

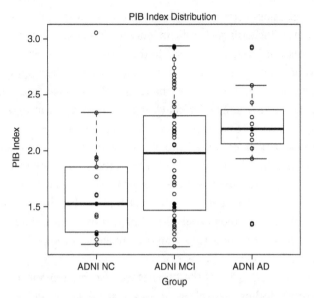

FIGURE 4.12 Box and whiskers plot showing the distribution of PIB uptake values in clinical groups from the Alzheimer's Disease Neuroimaging Initiative (ADNI). NC = control group; MCI = mild cognitive impairment; AD = Alzheimer's disease. Taken from Mormino et al. (2009). With permission.

between PIB index and episodic memory. In other words, the relationship between PIB and memory is no longer present after controlling for hippocampal volume. Thus, these latter findings concur with the notion of the relative insensitivity of amyloid imaging to the prediction of progression from normal aging to MCI to AD. Rather, it appears that the likely role of amyloid imaging will be in its straightforward assay of underlying amyloid burden and thus serve as a putative marker of the relative risk of developing dementia— analogous to the role of the APOE gene or the presence of mild cognitive impairment.

Given this early occurrence of amyloid deposition many years prior to the emergence of clinical symptoms, Sperling et al. (2011) propose a staging framework wherein amyloidosis represents the initial stage of necessary but not sufficient change in the cascade of events leading to Alzheimer's disease. The second stage would then include, in addition to the abnormal levels of β-amyloid, markers of brain neurodegeneration. The third and final stage would include the features of stage 2 plus reveal the presence of subtle cognitive changes leading to MCI and Alzheimer's dementia (see Figure 4.13).

Mild Cognitive Impairment and Dementia

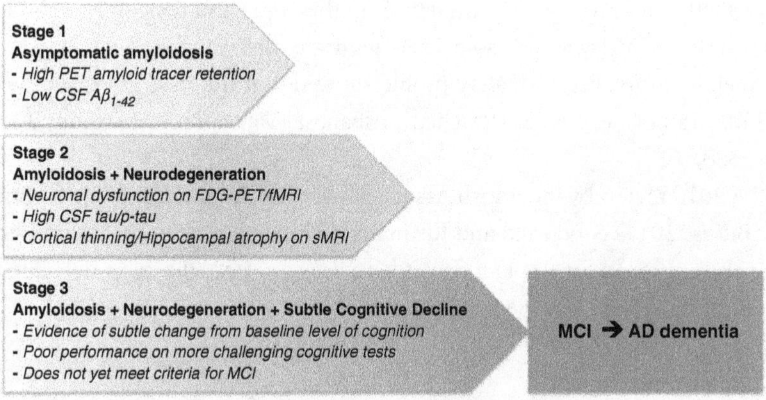

Stage 1
Asymptomatic amyloidosis
- *High PET amyloid tracer retention*
- *Low CSF Aβ₁₋₄₂*

Stage 2
Amyloidosis + Neurodegeneration
- *Neuronal dysfunction on FDG-PET/fMRI*
- *High CSF tau/p-tau*
- *Cortical thinning/Hippocampal atrophy on sMRI*

Stage 3
Amyloidosis + Neurodegeneration + Subtle Cognitive Decline
- *Evidence of subtle change from baseline level of cognition*
- *Poor performance on more challenging cognitive tests*
- *Does not yet meet criteria for MCI*

MCI → AD dementia

FIGURE 4.13 Model of a proposed staging for preclinical AD brain changes. Adapted from Sperling et al 2011 with permission.

Knopman et al. (2012) recently examined the ability of these recommended staging criteria for preclinical AD to predict progression to cognitive impairment. They found that the proportion of subjects who progressed to MCI or dementia increased with each advancing stage of the Sperling et al. criteria. Specifically, 5% of those in Stage 0 progressed over the 1–4 years of follow-up, 11% in Stage 1, 21% in Stage 2, and 43% in Stage 3. Despite the short follow-up period (median = 1.3 years for all four groups), the preclinical AD staging criteria proposed by Sperling et al. (2011) confirmed that advancing preclinical stage led to higher proportions of subjects who progressed to MCI or dementia. These findings by Knopman et al. (2012) represent a preliminary view of the possible utility of the preclinical AD staging criteria for assessing prognosis. Again, however, these findings were borne of expensive PIB-PET imaging and it remains to be seen whether such efforts are worth the costs involved and whether more cost-effective and less-invasive methods (e.g., cognitive variables) can accomplish many of the same results regarding prognosis.

Interventions

Pharmacological

As might well be expected, investigators have sought to determine if current Alzheimer's medications, namely the cholinesterase inhibitors (see Chapter 5), could impact outcomes for MCI, especially amnestic forms of MCI. In 2007,

Raschetti et al. reviewed the literature on this topic and concluded, "the use of ChEIs in MCI was not associated with any delay in the onset of AD or dementia. Moreover, the safety profile showed that the risks associated with ChEIs are not negligible" (Raschetti, Albanese, Vanacore, & Maggini, 2007, p. e388).

A 2010 review by the British Association for Psychopharmacology (O'Brien & Burns, 2011) concurred and further added memantine to the list of medications approved for AD *that do not have demonstrated efficacy* in delaying or preventing dementia in persons with MCI.

Nonpharmacological

Cognitive rehabilitation approaches that enhance functional independence in traumatic brain injury (TBI) may be applicable to MCI. Clinical practice guidelines in TBI include evidence-based memory rehabilitation techniques that improve cognition and functional ability (Cicerone et al., 2000). Memory rehabilitation can take two forms: (1) "memory building" or restorative techniques in which the goal is to regain memory function through repetitive training paradigms; or (2) "memory compensation" or techniques focused on using external aids to help compensate for memory loss. Memory notebooks are a form of memory compensation with validated efficacy in TBI patients (Sohlberg & Mateer, 1989).

There has been relatively little research regarding cognitive rehabilitation techniques in patients with MCI. Recent trials of a computer training program have suggested modest benefit on cognition and mood in patients with MCI (Talassi et al., 2007). Belleville et al. (2006) also reported positive outcomes for their program mixing education, computer-based attention training, and internal memory compensatory training (Belleville et al., 2006). These authors reported improved list recall memory and face name association performance, as well as improvements in subjective memory report and sense of subject well-being. Barnes et al. also reported no significant benefit from brain fitness training in MCI (Barnes et al., 2009). Note however that the effect size they observed was nearly the same as that reported as significant by Smith et al. (2009) in normal older adults. This suggests that the Barnes (and other studies) may be underpowered to see the modest beneficial effect of computer training. A randomized, case-control trial of a computer training program demonstrated improvements in short story recall, abstract reasoning, and behavioral problems in participants with MCI (Rozzini et al., 2007). Hampsted et al. examined fMRI patterns in MCI subjects taught mnemonic strategies (face-name and object-location associations) (Hampstead, Sathian, Moore, Nalisnick, & Stringer, 2008). These authors found that training on a specific set of faces or object locations resulted in significantly better memory for that information that persisted at a 1-month follow-up session, and resulted in increased medial and lateral frontoparietal activation (i.e., working memory and executive control areas) and connectivity between these regions.

In contrast to the above studies, a subgroup of participants from the ACTIVE trial who showed memory impairment on a neuropsychological measure but normal functional status, there was no benefit of memory training focused on improving ability to learn new information using internal memory strategies (Unverzagt et al., 2007). None of the above trials, however, include an external memory compensatory strategy for MCI patients and none used a functional outcome measure designed for MCI patients. We have produced preliminary evidence that a memory compensatory strategy using external aides can benefit persons with amnestic MCI (Greenaway et al., 2006). An important distinction yet to be explored relates to the nature of the memory disorder in MCI. Recall the above discussion on statistically determined MCI subtypes, some of which may demonstrate equally impaired delayed recall and recognition abilities and some that demonstrate improvements on delayed recognition relative to recall (Libon et al., 2010, 2011). Such distinctions between MCI subtypes may relate to differences in treatment response to memory training interventions.

Physical activity interventions are also being explored as a means to minimize cognitive decline in MCI. One study (Lautenschlager et al., 2008) observed significant improvement in memory in participants that engaged in a 24-week physical regimen exercise. However these participants did not necessarily meet contemporary criteria for MCI.

The emerging trend is to consider multicomponent interventions for persons with MCI. Rapp and colleagues investigated a multifaceted intervention that included education on memory, relaxation skills, mnemonic strategies, and cognitive restructuring to change beliefs about memory control (Rapp, Brenes, & Marsh, 2002). In this small sample study, the treatment group showed improvement in their perception of their memory abilities, as well as their belief in their ability to control their memory. Investigators at Mayo Clinic have launched a multicomponent MCI intervention program called Healthy Action to Benefit Independence and Thinking (HABIT). In its current form, this program is a 10-day, 50-hour program. It includes five components:

(1) memory compensation training with a calendar/journaling tool; (2) "brain fitness" with the computerized tool studied by Barnes et al. (2009) and Smith et al. (2009); (3) physical fitness; (4) caregiver and patient support groups; and (5) educational programming. While this program has not been subjected to randomized clinical trials, preliminary program evaluation data suggest positive impact on self-efficacy outcomes for patients and caregivers, as well as positive impact on patient functional outcomes. Additional information about this program is available at http://mayoresearch.mayo.edu/mayo/research/alzheimers_center/habit.cfm.

Conclusion

Early detection has become a watch word in dementia research and clinical practice. Mild cognitive impairment has emerged as the leading predementia concept, although the name could ultimately be replaced by "minor neurocognitive disorder." The proposed DSM-V criteria for minor neurocognitive disorder are similar but not identical to MCI. Regardless of whether the MCI or MND or other labels and criteria ultimately gain widest acceptance, there is likely to be substantial research and clinical benefit to including a predementia condition in DSM-V as a "legitimate" diagnosis.

MCI patients are clearly at elevated risk for progressing to dementia. MCI samples are probably comprised of patients with incipient dementia, persons with static neuropathology *and* normal older persons with stably poor cognitive function. The relative proportion of each group in an MCI sample will be influenced by the sampling frame (clinical vs. general or normal), the nature of the memory complaint (spontaneous vs. elicited), the type of memory assessment used in selecting patients (e.g., single vs. multiple measures; story vs. list learning), and the number, type, and interpretation of measures of nonmemory domains. These factors need to be considered when comparing outcomes from studies of predementia conditions.

Using a predementia diagnosis avoids the problem of knowing for sure whether a person with mildly compromised performance has a disease entity or not. It enables an alternative to attempts to predict which individual normal people will develop dementia. Instead, predementia conditions themselves can be diagnosed. These diagnoses acknowledge the overlapping distributions yet identify risk status. Identifying persons in this way permits their involvement in intervention research and practice. In fact, being able to identify such persons provides impetus to early intervention research.

References

Aggarwal, N., Wilson, R., Beck, T., Bienias, J., & Bennett, D. (2005). Mild cognitive impairment in different functional domains and incident Alzheimer's disease. *Journal of Neurology, Neurosurgery, and Psychiatry, 76,* 1479–1484.

Albert, M., DeKosky, S., Dickson, D., Dubois, B., Feldman, H., Fox, N.,...Phelps, C. (2011). The diagnosis of mild cognitive impairment due to Alzheimer's disease: Recommendations from the National Institute on Aging–Alzheimer's Association workgroups on diagnostic guidelines for Alzheimer's disease. *Alzheimer's and Dementia, 7*(3), 270–279.

Albert, M., & Killiany, R. (2001). Age-related cognitive change and brain-behavior relationships. In J. Birren (Ed.), *Handbook of the psychology of aging* (5th ed., pp. 161–185). San Diego, CA: Academic Press.

Alexopoulos, P., Grimmer, T., Perneczky, R., Domes, G., & Kurz, A. (2006). Progression to dementia in clinical subtypes of mild cognitive impairment. *Dementia and Geriatric Cognitive Disorders, 22,* 27–34.

Alladi, S., Arnold, R., Mitchell, J., Nestor, P. J., & Hodges, J. R. (2006). Mild cognitive impairment: Applicability of research criteria in a memory clinic and characterization of cognitive profile. *Psychological Medicine, 36*(4), 507–515.

American Psychiatric Association. (1994). *Diagnostic and statistical manual of mental disorders, fourth edition.* Washington, DC: Author.

American Psychological Association. (2011). Guidelines for the evaluation of dementia and age-related cognitive change. *The American Psychologist.*

Anastasi, A., & Urbina, S. (1997). *Psychological testing* (7th ed.): Upper Saddle River: Prentice Hall.

Annerbo, S., Wahlund, L.-O., & Lökk, J. (2006). The significance of thyroid-stimulating hormone and homocysteine in the development of Alzheimer's disease in mild cognitive impairment: A 6-year follow-up study. *American Journal of Alzheimers Disease and Other Dementias, 21,* 182.

Artero, S., Ancelin, M.-L., Portet, F., Dupuy, A., Berr, C., Dartigues, J.,...Ritchie, K. (2008). Risk profiles for mild cognitive impairment and progression to dementia are gender specific. *Journal of Neurology, Neurosurgery, and Psychiatry, 79,* 979–984.

Attix, D. K., Story, T. J., Chelune, G. J., Ball, J. D., Stutts, M. L., Hart, R. P., & Barth, J. T. (2009). The prediction of change: Normative neuropsychological trajectories. *The Clinical Neuropsychologist, 23*(1), 21–38.

Bangen, K. J., Jak, A. J., Schiehser, D. M., Delano-Wood, L., Tuminello, E., Han, S. D.,...Bondi, M. W. (2010). Complex activities of daily living vary by mild cognitive impairment subtype. *Journal of the International Neuropsychological Society, 16*(4), 630–639.

Barnes, D. E., Yaffe, K., Belfor, N., Jagust, W. J., DeCarli, C., Reed, B. R., & Kramer, J. H. (2009). Computer-based cognitive training for mild cognitive impairment: results from a pilot randomized, controlled trial. *Alzheimer Disease and Associated Disorders, 23*(3), 205–210.

Belleville, S., Gilbert, B., Fontaine, F., Gagnon, L., Menard, E., & Gauthier, S. (2006). Improvement of episodic memory in persons with mild cognitive impairment and healthy older adults: Evidence from a cognitive intervention program. *Dementia and Geriatric Cognitive Disorders, 22*(5–6), 486–499.

Bennett, D., Wilson, R., Schneider, J., Evans, D., Beckett, L., Aggarwal, N., ... Bach, J. (2002). Natural history of mild cognitive impairment in older persons. *Neurology, 59*, 198–205.

Benton, A., & Hamsher, K. (1978). *Multilingual aphasia examination: Manual.* Iowa City: University of Iowa.

Bickel, H., Mosch, E., Seigerschmidt, E., Siemen, M., & Forstl, H. (2006). Prevalence and persistence of mild cognitive impairment among elderly patients in general hospitals. *Dementia and Geriatric Cognitive Disorders, 21*(4), 242–250.

Bitsch, A., Bruhn, H., Vougioukas, V., Stringaris, A., Lassmann, H., Frahm, J., & Bruck, W. (1999). Inflammatory CNS demyelination: Histopathologic correlation with in vivo quantitative proton MR spectroscopy. *American Journal of Neuroradiology, 20*(9), 1619–1627.

Boeve, B., Ferman, T., Smith, G., Knopman, D., Jicha, G., Geda, Y., ... Petersen, R. (2004). Mild cognitive impairment preceding dementia with Lewy bodies (abstract). *Neurology, 62*(Suppl 5), A86–A87.

Bombois, S., Debette, S., Bruandet, A., Delbeuck, X., Delmaire, C., Leys, D., & Pasquier, F. (2008). Vascular subcortical hyperintensities predict conversion to vascular and mixed dementia in MCI patients. *Stroke, 39*, 2046–2051.

Bondi, M., Monsch, A., Galasko, D., Butters, N., Salmon, D., & Delis, D. (1994). Preclinical cognitive markers of dementia of the Alzheimer type. *Neuropsychology, 8*, 374–384.

Bondi, M. W., Jak, A. J., Delano-Wood, L., Jacobson, M. W., Delis, D. C., & Salmon, D. P. (2008). Neuropsychological contributions to the early identification of Alzheimer's disease. *Neuropsychology Review, 18*(1), 73–90.

Bondi, M. W., Salmon, D. P., Galasko, D., Thomas, R. G., & Thal, L. J. (1999). Neuropsychological function and apolipoprotein E genotype in the preclinical detection of Alzheimer's disease. *Psychology and Aging, 14*(2), 295–303.

Bowen, J., Teri, L., Kukall, W., McCormick, W., McCurry, S., & Larson, E. (1997). Progression to dementia in patients with isolated memory loss. *Lancet, 349*, 763–765.

Bozoki, A., Giordani, B., Heidebrink, J., Berent, S., & Foster, N. (2001). Mild cognitive impairments predict dementia in nondemented elderly patients with memory loss. *Archives of Neurology, 58*(3), 411–416.

Brooks, B. L., & Iverson, G. L. (2010). Comparing actual to estimated base rates of "abnormal" scores on neuropsychological test batteries: Implications for interpretation. *Archives of Clinical Neuropsychology, 25*(1), 14–21.

Busse, A., Hensel, A., Guhne, U., Angermeyer, M., & Riedel-Heller, S. (2006). Mild cognitive impairment: Long-term course of four clinical subtypes. *Neurology, 67*, 2176–2185.

Carr, D., Gray, S., Baty, J., & Morris, J. (2000). The value of informant versus individual's complaints of memory impairment in early dementia. *Neurology, 55*, 1724–1727.

Chang, Y. L., Bondi, M. W., Fennema-Notestine, C., McEvoy, L. K., Hagler, D. J., Jr., Jacobson, M. W., & Dale, A. M. (2010). Brain substrates of learning and retention in mild cognitive impairment diagnosis and progression to Alzheimer's disease. *Neuropsychologia, 48*(5), 1237–1247.

Chang, Y. L., Bondi, M. W., McEvoy, L. K., Fennema-Notestine, C., Salmon, D. P., Galasko, D.,... Dale, A. M. (2011). Global clinical dementia rating of 0.5 in MCI masks variability related to level of function. *Neurology, 76*(7), 652–659.

Cicerone, K. D., Dahlberg, C., Kalmar, K., Langenbahn, D. M., Malec, J. F., Bergquist, T. F.,... Morse, P. A. (2000). Evidence-based cognitive rehabilitation: Recommendations for clinical practice. *Archives of Physical Medicine and Rehabilitation, 81*(12), 1596–1615.

Clark, L., Schiehser, D., Weissberger, G., Salmon, D., Delis, D., & Bondi, M. (2012). Specific measures of executive function predict cognitive decline in older adults. *Journal of the International Neuropsychological Society, 18*, 118–127.

de Jager, C., Hogervorst, E., Combrinck, M., & Budge, M. (2003). Sensitivity and specificity of neuropsychological tests for mild cognitive impairment, vascular cognitive impairment and Alzheimer's disease. *Psychological Medicine, 33*, 1039–1050.

De Santi, S., Pirraglia, E., Barr, W., Babb, J., Williams, S., Rogers, K.,... de Leon, M. J. (2008). Robust and conventional neuropsychological norms: Diagnosis and prediction of age-related cognitive decline. *Neuropsychology, 22*(4), 469–484.

Delano-Wood, L., Bondi, M. W., Jak, A. J., Horne, N. R., Schweinsburg, B. C., Frank, L. R., . . . Salmon, D. P. (2010). Stroke risk modifies regional white matter differences in mild cognitive impairment. *Neurobiology of Aging, 31*(10), 1721–1731.

Delano-Wood, L., Stricker, N., Sorg, S., Nation, D., Jak, A., Woods, S., . . . Bondi, M. (2012). Posterior cingulum white matter disruption and its associations with verbal memory and stroke risk in mild cognitive impairment. *Journal of Alzheimer's Disease, 29*, 589–603.

Delis, D. C., Kaplan, E., & Kramer, J. H. (2001). *Delis-Kaplan Executive Function System (D-KEFS)*. San Antonio, TX: The Psychological Corporation.

Delis, D. C., Kramer, J. H., Kaplan, E., & Ober, B. A. (1987). *The California Verbal Learning Test*. New York: Psychological Corporation.

Desikan, R., McEvoy, L., Thompson, W., et al. (2011). Amyloid-beta associated volume loss occurs only in the presence of phospho-tau. *Annals of Neurology, 70*, 657–661.

Devanand, D., Liu, X., Tabert, M., et al. (2008). Combining early markers strongly predicts conversion from mild cognitive impairment to Alzheimer's disease. *Biological Psychiatry, 64*, 871–879.

Di Carlo, A., Lamassa, M., Baldereschi, M., Inzitari, M., Scafato, E., Farchi, G., & Inzitari, D. (2007). CIND and MCI in the Italian elderly, frequency, vascular risk factors, progression to dementia. *Neurology, 68*, 1909–1916.

Dickerson, B., Salat, D., Bates, J., Atiya, M., Killiany, R., Greve, D., . . . Sperling, R. (2004). Medial temporal lobe function and structure in mild cognitive impairment. *Annals of Neurology, 56*(1), 27–35.

Dickerson, B., Salat, D., Greve, D., Chua, E., Rand-Giovanetti, E., Rentz, D., . . . Sperling, R. A. (2005). Increased hippocampal activation in mild cognitive impairment compared to normal aging and AD. *Neurology, 65*(3), 404–411.

Dickerson, B., Sperling, R., Hyman, B., Albert, M., & Blacker, D. (2007). Clinical prediction of Alzheimer disease dementia across the spectrum of mild cognitive impairment. *Archives of General Psychiatry, 64*, 1443–1450.

Drzezga, A., Lautenschlager, N., Siebner, H., Riemenschneider, M., Willoch, F., Minoshima, S., . . . Kurz, A. (2003). Cerebral metabolic changes accompanying conversion of mild cognitive impairment into Alzheimer's disease: A PET follow-up study. *European Journal of Nuclear Medicine and Molecular Imaging, 30*(8), 1104–1113.

Dubois, B., Feldman, H., Jacova, C., DeKosky, S., Barberger-Gateau, P., Cummings, J., . . . Scheltens, P. (2007). Research criteria for the diagnosis of Alzheimer's disease: Revising the NINCDS-ADRDA criteria. *Lancet, 6,* 734–746.

Edland, S., Rocca, W., Petersen, R., Cha, R., & Kokmen, E. (2002). Dementia and Alzheimer's disease incident rates do not vary by sex in Rochester, Minnesota. *Archives of Neurology, 59,* 1589–1593.

Fellgiebel, A., Wille, P., Muller, M. J., Winterer, G., Scheurich, A., Vucurevic, G.,...Stoeter, P. (2004). Ultrastructural hippocampal and white matter alterations in mild cognitive impairment: A diffusion tensor imaging study. *Dementia and Geriatric Cognitive Disorders, 18*(1), 101–108.

Ferman, T. J., Smith, G. E., Boeve, B. F., Graff-Radford, N. R., Lucas, J. A., Knopman, D. S.,...Dickson, D. W. (2006). Neuropsychological differentiation of dementia with Lewy bodies from normal aging and Alzheimer's disease. *The Clinical Neuropsychologist, 20*(4), 623–636.

Fischl, B., & Dale, A. M. (2000). Measuring the thickness of the human cerebral cortex from magnetic resonance images. *Proceedings of the National Academy of Sciences, 97*(20), 11050–11055.

Folstein, M., Folstein, S., & McHugh, P. (1975). "Mini-mental state." A practical method for grading the cognitive state of patients for the clinician. *Journal of Psychiatry Research, 12*(3), 189–198.

Gabryelewicz, T., Styczynska, M., Barczak, A., et al. (2008). Conversion to dementia over a five-year period among patients with mild cognitive impairment in a Polish follow-up study. *Alzheimer's and Dementia, 4,* P1–P189.

Gabryelewicz, T., Styczynska, M., Luczywek, E., Barczak, A., Pfeffer, A., Androsiuk, W.,...Barcikowska, M. (2007). The rate of conversion of mild cognitive impairment to dementia: Predictive role of depression. *International Journal of Geriatric Psychiatry, 22,* 563–567.

Ganguli, M., Dodge, H., Shen, V., & Dekosky, S. (2004). Mild cognitive impairment, amnestic type an epidemiologic study. *Neurology, 63,* 115–121.

Ganguli, M., Snitz, B., Saxton, J., et al. (2011). Outcomes of mild cognitive impairment by definition: A population study. *Archives of Neurology, 68,* 761–767.

Gladsjo, J. A., Schuman, C. C., Evans, J. D., Peavy, G. M., Miller, S. W., & Heaton, R. K. (1999). Norms for letter and category fluency: Demographic corrections for age, education, and ethnicity. *Assessment, 6*(2), 147–178.

Goldman, W., Price, J., Storandt, M., Grant, E., McKeel, D., Jr., Rubin, E., & Morris, J. (2001). Absence of cognitive impairment or decline in preclinical Alzheimer's disease. *Neurology, 56,* 361–367.

Gomar, J., Bobes-Bascaran, M., Conejero-Goldberg, C., Davies, P., Goldberg, T., & for the Alzheimer's Disease Neuroimaging Initiative. (2011). Utility of combinations of biomarkers, cognitive markers, and risk factors to predict conversion from mild cognitive impairment to Alzheimer disease in the Alzheimer's Disease Neuroimaging Initiative. *Archives of General Psychiatry, 68*, 961–969.

Greenaway, M., Smith, G., Lepore, S., Lunde, A., Hanna, S., & Boeve, B. (2006). Compensating for memory loss in amnestic mild cognitive impairment. *Alzheimer's and Dementia, 2*(Suppl 1), S571.

Greene, J. D., Baddeley, A. D., & Hodges, J. R. (1996). Analysis of the episodic memory deficit in early Alzheimer's disease: Evidence from the doors and people test. *Neuropsychologia, 34*(6), 537–551.

Greicius, M., Krasnow, B., Reiss, A., & Menon, V. (2003). Functional connectivity in the resting brain: A network analysis of the default mode hypothesis. *Proceedings of the National Academy of Sciences, 100*(1), 253–258.

Grober, E., & Kawas, C. (1997). Learning and retention in preclinical and early Alzheimer's disease. *Psychology and Aging, 12*(1), 183–188.

Grober, E., Lipton, R., Hall, C., & Crystal, H. (2000). Memory impairment on free and cued selective reminding predicts dementia. *Neurology, 54*, 827–832.

Hampstead, B., Sathian, K., Moore, A., Nalisnick, C., & Stringer, A. (2008). Explicit memory training leads to improved memory for face-name pairs in patients with mild cognitive impairment: Results of a pilot investigation. *Journal of the International Neuropsychological Society, 14*(5), 883–889.

Hansson, O., Buchhave, P., Zetterberg, H., et al. (2009). Combined rCBF and CSF biomarkers predict progression from mild cognitive impairment to Alzheimer's disease. *Neurobiology of Aging, 30*(2), 165–173.

Heaton, R. K., Miller, S. W., Taylor, M. J., & Grant, I. (Eds.). (2004). *Revised comprehensive norms for an expanded Halstead-Reitan battery: Demographically adjusted neuropsychological norms for African American and Caucasian adults—Professional manual* (3rd ed.). Lutz, FL: Psychological Assessment Resources.

Heister, D., Brewer, J., Magda, S., Blennow, K., & McEvoy, L., for the Alzheimer's Disease Neuroimaging Initiative. (2011). Predicting MCI outcome with clinically available MRI and CSF biomarkers. *Neurology, 77*, 1619–1628.

Herukka, S.-K., Hallikainen, M., Soininen, H., & Pirttila, T. (2005). CSF A 42 and tau or phosphorylated tau and prediction of progressive mild cognitive impairment. *Neurology, 64*, 1294–1297.

Heun, R., Kölsch, H., & Jessen, F. (2006). Risk factors and early signs of Alzheimer's disease in a family study sample: Risk of AD. *European Archives of Psychiatry and Clinical Neuroscience, 256*, 28–36.

Hogan, D., & Ebly, E. (2000). Predicting who will develop dementia in a cohort of Canadian seniors. *Canadian Journal of Neurological Sciences, 27,* 18–24.

Hyman, B., & Trojanowski, J. (1997). Consensus recommendations for the postmortem diagnosis of Alzheimer's disease from the National Institute on Aging and the Reagan Institute Working Group on diagnostic criteria for the neuropathological assessment of Alzheimer's disease. *Journal of Neuropathology and Experimental Neurology, 56,* 1095–1097.

Ishikawa, T., & Ikeda, M. (2007). Mild cognitive impairment in a population-based epidemiological study. *Psychogeriatrics, 7,* 104–108.

Ivnik, R., Malec, J., Smith, G., Tangalos, E., Petersen, R., Kokmen, E., & Kurland, L. (1992). Mayo's Older Americans Normative Studies: Updated AVLT norms for ages 56–97. *The Clinical Neuropsychologist, 6,* 83–104.

Ivnik, R., Smith, G., Petersen, R., Boeve, B., Kokmen, E., & Tangalos, E. (2000). Diagnostic accuracy of four approaches to interpreting neuropsychological test data. *Neuropsychology, 14,* 163–177.

Ivnik, R. J., Malec, J. F., Smith, G. E., Tangalos, E. G., Petersen, R. C., Kokmen, E., & Kurland, L. T. (1992). Mayo's Older Americans Normative Studies: WMS-R norms for ages 56–94. *The Clinical Neuropsychologist, 6,* 49–82.

Jack, C., Jr., Knopman, D., Jagust, W., Shaw, L., Aisen, P., Weiner, M.,...Trojanowski, J. (2010). Hypothetical model of dynamic biomarkers of the Alzheimer's pathological cascade. *Lancet Neurology, 9*(1), 119–128. 6

Jack, C., Jr., Lowe, V., Weigand, S., Wiste, H., Senjem, M., Knopman, D.,...Alzheimer's Disease Neuroimaging Initiative. (2009). Serial PIB and MRI in normal, mild cognitive impairment and Alzheimer's disease: Implications for sequence of pathological events in Alzheimer's disease. *Brain, 132*(Pt 5), 1355–1365.

Jack, C., Jr., Shiung, M., Gunter, J., O'Brien, P., Weigand, S., Knopman, D.,...Petersen, R. (2004). Comparison of different MRI brain trophy rate measures with clinical disease progression in AD. *Neurology, 62,* 591–600.

Jack, C. R., Jr., Petersen, R. C., Xu, Y. C., O'Brien, P. C., Smith, G. E., Ivnik, R. J.,...Kokmen, E. (1999). Prediction of AD with MRI-based hippocampal volume in mild cognitive impairment. *Neurology, 52*(7), 1397–1403.

Jack, C. R., Jr., Petersen, R., Xu, Y., O'Brien, P., Smith, G., Ivnik, R.,...Kokmen, E. (2000). Rates of hippocampal atrophy correlate with change in clinical status in aging and AD. *Neurology, 55*(4), 484–489.

Jak, A. J., Bangen, K. J., Wierenga, C. E., Delano-Wood, L., Corey-Bloom, J., & Bondi, M. W. (2009). Contributions of neuropsychology and neuroimaging to understanding clinical subtypes of mild cognitive impairment. *International Review of Neurobiology, 84*, 81–103.

Jak, A. J., Bondi, M. W., Delano-Wood, L., Wierenga, C., Corey-Bloom, J., Salmon, D. P., & Delis, D. C. (2009). Quantification of five neuropsychological approaches to defining mild cognitive impairment. *American Journal of Geriatric Psychiatry, 17*(5), 368–375.

Jak, A. J., Urban, S., McCauley, A., Bangen, K. J., Delano-Wood, L., Corey-Bloom, J., & Bondi, M. W. (2009). Profile of hippocampal volumes and stroke risk varies by neuropsychological definition of mild cognitive impairment. *Journal of the International Neuropsychological Society, 15*(6), 890–897.

Jedynak, B. M., Lang, A., Liu, B., Katz, E., Zhang, Y., Wyman, B. T., Raunig, D., Jedynak, C. P., Caffo, B., Prince, J. L. for the Alzheimer's Disease Neuroimaging Initiative. (2012). A computational neurodegenerative disease progression score: Method and results with the Alzheimer's disease neuroimaging initiative cohort. *Neuroimage, 63*(3), 1478–1486.

Jefferson, A. L., Byerly, L. K., Vanderhill, S., Lambe, S., Wong, S., Ozonoff, A., & Karlawish, J. H. (2008). Characterization of activities of daily living in individuals with mild cognitive impairment. *American Journal of Geriatric Psychiatry, 16*(5), 375–383.

Jicha, G. A., Parisi, J. E., Dickson, D. W., Johnson, K., Cha, R., Ivnik, R. J.,...Petersen, R. C. (2006). Neuropathologic outcome of mild cognitive impairment following progression to clinical dementia. *Archives of Neurology, 63*(5), 674–681.

Johnson, S., Baxter, L., Susskind-Wilder, L., Connor, D., Sabbagh, M., & Caselli, R. (2004). Hippocampal adaptation to face repetition in healthy elderly and mild cognitive impairment. *Neuropsychologia, 42*(7), 980–989.

Johnson, S., Schmitz, T., Trivedi, M., Ries, M., Torgerson, B., Carlsson, C.,...Sager, M. (2006). The influence of Alzheimer disease family history and APOE e4 on mesial temporal lobe activation. *Journal of Neuroscience, 26*, 6069–6076.

Kantarci, K., Jack, C., Jr., Xu, Y., Campeau, N., O'Brien, P., Smith, G.,...Petersen, R. (2000). Regional metabolic patterns in mild cognitive impairment and Alzheimer's disease: A 1 H MRS study. *Neurology, 55*, 210–217.

Kantarci, K., Jack, C., Jr., Xu, Y., Campeau, N., O'Brien, P., Smith, G.,...Petersen, R. (2001). Mild cognitive impairment and Alzheimer disease: Regional diffusivity of water. *Radiology, 219*(1), 101–107.

Kantarci, K., Petersen, R. C., Boeve, B. F., Knopman, D. S., Tang-Wai, D. F., O'Brien, P. C.,...Jack, C. R., Jr. (2004). 1H MR spectroscopy in common dementias. *Neurology, 63*(8), 1393–1398.

Kantarci, K., Petersen, R. C., Boeve, B. F., Knopman, D. S., Weigand, S. D., O'Brien, P. C., ... Jack, C. R., Jr. (2005). DWI predicts future progression to Alzheimer disease in amnestic mild cognitive impairment. *Neurology, 64*(5), 902–904.

Kantarci, K., Xu, Y., Shiung, M., O'Brien, P., Cha, R., Smith, G., ... Jack, C., Jr., (2002). Comparative diagnostic utility of different MR modalities in mild cognitive impairment and Alzheimer's disease. *Dementia and Geriatric Cognitive Disorders, 14*(4), 198–207.

Kaplan, E., Goodglass, H., & Weintraub, S. (1983). *The Boston Naming Test* (2nd ed.). Philadelphia: Lea & Febiger.

Katchaturian, Z. (1985). Diagnosis of Alzheimer's disease. *Archives of Neurology, 42*, 1097–1105.

Klunk, W. E., Engler, H., Nordberg, A., Wang, Y., Blomqvist, G., Holt, D. P., ... Langstrom, B. (2004). Imaging brain amyloid in Alzheimer's disease with Pittsburgh Compound-B. *Annals of Neurology, 55*(3), 306–319.

Knopman, D. S., Jack, C. R., Jr., Wiste, H. J., Weigand, S. D., Vemuri, P., Lowe, V., ... Petersen, R. C.. (2012). Short-term clinical outcomes for stages of NIA-AA preclinical Alzheimer disease. *Neurology, 78*(20):1576–1582.

Kokmen, E., Smith, G. E., Petersen, R. C., Tangalos, E., & Ivnik, R. C. (1991). The short test of mental status: Correlations with standardized psychometric testing. *Archives of Neurology, 48*(7), 725–728.

Laforce, R., Jr., Rabinovici, G. D. (2011). Amyloid imaging in the differential diagnosis of dementia: Review and potential clinical applications. *Alzheimers Research and Therapy, 3*(6):31

Landau, S., Harvey, D., Madison, C., Reiman, E., Foster, N., Aisen, P., ... Jagust, W. (2010). Comparing predictors of conversion and decline in mild cognitive impairment. *Neurology, 75*(3), 230–238.

Lange, K., Bondi, M., Salmon, D., Galasko, D., Delis, D., Thomas, R., & Thal, L. (2002). Decline in verbal memory during preclinical Alzheimer's disease: Examination of the effect of APOE genotype. *Journal of the International Neuropsychological Society, 8*(7), 943–955.

Larrieu, S., Letenneur, L., Orgogozo, J., Fabrigoule, C., Amieva, H., Le Carret, N., ... Dartigues, J. (2002). Incidence and outcome of mild cognitive impairment in a population-based prospective cohort. *Neurology, 59*, 1594–1599.

Lautenschlager, N. T., Cox, K. L., Flicker, L., Foster, J. K., van Bockxmeer, F. M., Xiao, J., ... Almeida, O. P. (2008). Effect of physical activity on cognitive function in older adults at risk for Alzheimer disease: A randomized trial. *Journal of the American Medical Association, 300*(9), 1027–1037.

Libon, D., Eppig, J., Xie, S., Wicas, G., Lippa, C., Bettcher, B., & Wambach, D. (2010). The heterogeneity of mild cognitive impairment: A neuropsychological analysis. *Journal of the International Neuropsychological Society, 16*, 84–93.

Libon, D. J., Bondi, M. W., Price, C. C., Lamar, M., Eppig, J., Wambach, D. M.,...Penney, D. L. (2011). Verbal serial list learning in mild cognitive impairment: A profile analysis of interference, forgetting, and errors. *Journal of the International Neuropsychological Society, 17*(5), 905–914.

Lineweaver, T. T., Bondi, M. W., Thomas, R. G., & Salmon, D. P. (1999). A normative study of Nelson's (1976) modified version of the Wisconsin Card Sorting Test in healthy older adults. *The Clinical Neuropsychologist, 13*(3), 328–347.

Loeb, P. (1996). *Independent living scales.* San Antonio: The Psychological Corporation.

Loewenstein, D. A., Acevedo, A., Small, B. J., Agron, J., Crocco, E., & Duara, R. (2009). Stability of different subtypes of mild cognitive impairment among the elderly over a 2- to 3-year follow-up period. *Dementia and Geriatric Cognitive Disorders, 27*(5), 418–423.

Lopez, O., Kuller, L., & Becker, J. (2007). Incidence of dementia in mild cognitive impairment in the Cardiovascular Health Study Cognition Study. *Archives of Neurology, 64*, 416–420.

Lopez, O., Kuller, L., DeKosky, S., Becker, J., Jagust, W., Dulberg, C., & Fitzpatrick, A. (2002). Prevalence and classification of mild cognitive impairment in a population study. *Neurobiology of Aging, 23*, S138.

Lopez, O. L., Jagust, W. J., DeKosky, S. T., Becker, J. T., Fitzpatrick, A., Dulberg, C.,...Kuller, L. H. (2003). Prevalence and classification of mild cognitive impairment in the Cardiovascular Health Study Cognition Study: Part 1. *Archives of Neurology, 60*(10), 1385–1389.

Lustig, C., Snyder, A., Ghakta, M., O'Brien, K., McAvoy, M., Raichle, M.,...Buckner, R. (2003). Functional deactivations: Change with age and dementia of the Alzheimer type. *Proceedings of the National Academy of Sciences, 100*, 14505–14509.

Machulda, M., Ward, H., Borowski, B., Gunter, J., Cha, R., O'Brien, P.,...Jack, C., Jr. (2003). Comparison of memory fMRI response among normal, MCI, and Alzheimer's patients. *Neurology, 61*(4), 500–506.

Marcos, A., Gil, P., & Barabash, A. (2006). Neuropsychological markers of progression from mild cognitive impairment to Alzheimer's disease. *American Journal of Alzheimers Disease and Other Dementia, 21*, 189–196.

Masur, D. M., Fuld, P. A., Blau, A. D., Crystal, H., & Aronson, M. K. (1990). Predicting development of dementia in the elderly with the Selective Reminding Test. *Journal of Clinical and Experimental Neuropsychology, 12*(4), 529–538.

Mattis, S. (1988). *Mattis Dementia Rating Scale (MDRS)*. Odessa, FL: Psychological Assessment Resources.

McDonald, C., Gharapetian, L., McEvoy, L., Fennema-Notestine, C., Hagler, D., Jr, Holland, D.,...Alzheimer's Disease Neuroimaging Initiative. (2012). Relationship between regional atrophy rates and cognitive decline in mild cognitive impairment. *Neurobiology of Aging, 33*(2), 242–253.

McKhann, G. (2011). Changing concepts of Alzheimer disease. *Journal of the American Medical Association, 305*, 2458–2459.

Mickes, L., Wixted, J. T., Fennema-Notestine, C., Galasko, D., Bondi, M. W., Thal, L. J., & Salmon, D. P. (2007). Progressive impairment on neuropsychological tasks in a longitudinal study of preclinical Alzheimer's disease. *Neuropsychology, 21*(6), 696–705.

Mirra, S., Heyman, M., McKeil, D., Sumi, S., & Crain, B. (1991). The Consortium to Establish a Registry for Alzheimer's Disease (CERAD). Part II. Standardization of the neuropathologic assessment of Alzheimer's disease. *Neurology, 41*(4), 479–486.

Mitchell, A., & Shiri-Feshki, M. (2009). Rate of progression of mild cognitive impairment to dementia—Meta-analysis of 41 robust inception cohort studies. *Acta Psychiatrica Scandinavica, 119*(4), 252–265.

Mormino, E., Kluth, J., Madison, C., Rabinovici, G., Baker, S., Miller, B.,...Alzheimer's Disease Neuroimaging Initiative. (2009). Episodic memory loss is related to hippocampal-mediated beta-amyloid deposition in elderly subjects. *Brain, 132*, 1310–1323.

Morris, J. C. (1993). The Clinical Dementia Rating (CDR): Current version and scoring rules. *Neurology, 43*(11), 2412–2414.

Morris, J. C., Storandt, M., Miller, J. P., McKeel, D. W., Price, J. L., Rubin, E. H., & Berg, L. (2001). Mild cognitive impairment represents early-stage Alzheimer disease. *Archives of Neurology, 58*(3), 397–405.

Norman, M. A., Evan, J. D., Miller, W. S., & Heaton, R. K. (2000). Demographically corrected norms for the California Verbal Learning Test. *Journal of Clinical and Experimental Neuropsychology, 22*(1), 80–95.

O'Brien, J. T., & Burns, A. (2011). Clinical practice with anti-dementia drugs: A revised (second) consensus statement from the British

Association for Psychopharmacology. *Journal of Psychopharmacology, 25*(8), 997–1019.

Palmer, B. W., Boone, K. B., Lesser, I. M., & Wohl, M. A. (1998). Base rates of "impaired" neuropsychological test performance among healthy older adults. *Archives of Clinical Neuropsychology, 13*(6), 503–511.

Palmer, K., Berger, A., Monastero, Winblad, B., Backman, L., & Fratiglioni, L. (2007). Predictors of progression from mild cognitive impairment to Alzheimer disease. *Neurology, 68,* 1596–1602.

Petersen, R., Doody, R., Kurz, A., Mohs, R., Morris, J., Rabins, P., . . . Winblad, B. (2001). Current concepts in mild cognitive impairment. *Archives of Neurology, 58,* 1985–1992.

Petersen, R., Ivnik, R., Boeve, B., Knopman, D., Smith, G., & Tangalos, E. (2004). Outcome of clinical subtypes of MCI (abstract). *Neurology, 62,* A29S.

Petersen, R., Roberts, R., Knopman, D., Boeve, B., Geda, Y., Ivnik, R., . . . Jack, C., Jr. (2009). Mild cognitive impairment: Ten years later. *Archives of Neurology, 66*(12), 1447–1455.

Petersen, R., Roberts, R., Knopman, D., Geda, Y., Cha, R., Pankratz, V., . . . Rocca, W. (2010). Prevalence of mild cognitive impairment is higher in men. The Mayo Clinic Study of Aging. *Neurology, 75*(10), 889–897.

Petersen, R., Smith, G., Ivnik, R., Kokmen, E., & Tangalos, E. (1994). Memory function in very early Alzheimer's disease. *Neurology, 44,* 867–872.

Petersen, R., Smith, G., Ivnik, R., Tangalos, E., Schaid, D., Thibodeau, S., . . . Kurland, L. (1995). Apolipoprotein E status as a predictor of the development of Alzheimer's disease in memory-impaired individuals. *Journal of the American Medical Association, 273,* 1274–1278.

Petersen, R., Smith, G., Kokmen, E., Ivnik, R., & Tangalos, E. (1992). Memory function in normal aging. *Neurology, 42,* 396–401.

Petersen, R., Smith, G., Waring, S., Ivnik, R., Tangalos, E., & Kokmen, E. (1999). Mild cognitive impairment: Clinical characterization and outcome. *Archives of Neurology, 56*(3), 303–308.

Petersen, R. C., Parisi, J. E., Dickson, D. W., Johnson, K. A., Knopman, D. S., Boeve, B. F., . . . Kokmen, E. (2006). Neuropathologic features of amnestic mild cognitive impairment. *Archives of Neurology, 63*(5), 665–672.

Petersen, R. C., Thomas, R. G., Grundman, M., Bennett, D., Doody, R., Ferris, S., . . . Thal, L. J. (2005). Vitamin E and donepezil for the treatment of mild cognitive impairment. *New England Journal of Medicine, 352*(23), 2379–2388.

Quigley, H., Colloby, S., & O'Brien, J. (2011). PET imaging of brain amyloid in dementia: a review. *International Journal of Geriatric Psychiatry, 10*, 991–999.

Rabin, L., Pare, N., Saykin, A., et al. (2009). Differential memory test sensitivity for diagnosing amnestic mild cognitive impairment and predicting conversion to Alzheimer's disease. *Aging, Neuropsychology, and Cognition, 16*, 357–376.

Rabinovici, G., & Jagust, W. (2009). Amyloid imaging in aging and dementia: testing the amyloid hypothesis in vivo. *Behavioural Neurology, 21*(1), 117–128.

Raichle, M., MacLeod, A., Snyder, A., Powers, W., Gusnard, D., & Shulman, G. (2001). A default mode of brain function. *Proceedings of the National Academy of Sciences, 98*(2), 676–682.

Rapp, S., Brenes, G., & Marsh, A. (2002). Memory enhancement training for older adults with mild cognitive impairment: A preliminary study. *Aging and Mental Health, 6*(1), 5–11.

Raschetti, R., Albanese, E., Vanacore, N., & Maggini, M. (2007). Cholinesterase inhibitors in mild cognitive impairment: A systematic review of randomised trials. *PLoS Medicine, 4*(11), e338.

Ravaglia, G., Forti, P., Maioli, F., Martelli, M., Servadei, L., Brunetti, N., ... Mariani, E. (2006). Conversion of mild cognitive impairment to dementia: Predictive role of mild cognitive impairment subtypes and vascular risk factors. *Dementia and Geriatric Cognitive Disorders, 21*, 51–58.

Reiman, E., Caselli, R., Yun, L., Chen, K., Bandy, D., Minoshima, S., ... Osborne, D. (1996). Preclinical evidence of Alzheimer's disease in persons homozygous for the epsilon 4 allele for apolipoprotein E. *New England Journal of Medicine, 21*, 752–758.

Reitan, R. M., & Wolfson, D. (1985). *The Halstead-Reitan Neuropsychological Test Battery*. Tucson, AZ: Neuropsychology Press.

Rey, A. (1964). *L'examen clinique en psychologie*. Paris: Presses Universitaires de France.

Ritchie, K., Artero, S., & Touchon, J. (2001). Classification criteria for mild cognitive impairment: A population-based validation study. *Neurology, 56*(1), 37–42.

Ritchie, K., & Touchon, J. (2000). Mild cognitive impairment: Conceptual basis and current nosological status. *Lancet, 15*, 225–228.

Rombouts, S., Barkhof, F., Goekoop, R., Stam, C., & Scheltens, P. (2005). Altered resting state networks in mild cognitive impairment and mild Alzheimer's disease: An FMRI study. *Human Brain Mapping, 26*, 231–239.

Rombouts, S., Goekoop, R., Stam, C., Barkhof, F., & Scheltens, P. (2005). Delayed rather than decreased BOLD response as a marker for early Alzheimer's disease. *Neuroimage, 26*(4), 1078–1085.

Rozzini, L., Costardi, D., Chilovi, B., Franzoni, S., Trabucchi, M., & Padovani, A. (2007). Efficacy of cognitive rehabilitation in patients with mild cognitive impairment treated with cholinesterase inhibitors. *International Journal of Geriatric Psychiatry, 22*(4), 356–360.

Salmon, D., & Bondi, M. (2009). Neuropsychological assessment of dementia. *Annual Review of Psychology, 60,* 257–282.

Salmon, D., Thomas, R., Pay, M., Booth, A., Hofstetter, C., Thal, L., & Katzman, R. (2002). Alzheimer's disease can be accurately diagnosed in very mildly impaired individuals. *Neurology, 59*(7), 1022–1028.

Schneider, J., Arvanitakis, Z., Leurgans, S., & Bennett, D. (2009). The neuropathology of probable Alzheimer disease and mild cognitive impairment. *Annals of Neurology, 66,* 200–208.

Schretlen, D., Testa, S., Winicki, J., Pearlson, G., & Gordon, B. (2008). Frequency and bases of abnormal performance by healthy adults on neuropsychological testing. *Journal of the International Neuropsychological Society, 14*(3), 436–445.

Sliwinski, M., Lipton, R. B., Buschke, H., & Stewart, W. (1996). The effects of preclinical dementia on estimates of normal cognitive functioning in aging. *Journals of Gerontology. Series B, Psychological Sciences and Social Sciences, 51*(4), P217–P225.

Small, S., Perera, G., DeLaPaz, R., Mayeux, R., & Stern, Y. (1999). Differential regional dysfunction of the hippocampal formation among elderly with memory decline and Alzheimer's disease. *Annals of Neurology, 45*(4), 466–472.

Smith, G., Lunde, A., Hathaway, J., & Vickers, K. (2007). Telehealth home monitoring of solitary persons with mild dementia. *American Journal of Alzheimer's Disease and Related Disorders, 22*(1), 20–26.

Smith, G., Petersen, R., Ivnik, R., Malec, J., & Tangalos, E. (1996). Subjective memory complaints, psychological distress, and longitudinal change in objective memory performance. *Psychology and Aging, 11,* 272–279.

Smith, G. E., Housen, P., Yaffe, K., Ruff, R., Kennison, R. F., Mahncke, H. W., & Zelinski, E. M. (2009). A cognitive training program based on principles of brain plasticity: Results from the Improvement in Memory with Plasticity-based Adaptive Cognitive Training (IMPACT) study. *Journal of the American Geriatrics Society, 57*(4), 594–603.

Sohlberg, M. M., & Mateer, C. A. (1989). Training use of compensatory memory books: A three stage behavioral approach. *Journal of Clinical and Experimental Neuropsychology, 11*(6), 871–891.

Sonnen, J., Santa Cruz, K., Hemmy, L., et al. (2011). Ecology of the aging human brain. *Archives of Neurology, 68*, 1049–1056.

Sperling, R., Aisen, P., Beckett, L., Bennett, D., Craft, S., Fagan, A., ... Phelps, C. (2011). Toward defining the preclinical stages of Alzheimer's disease: Recommendations from the National Institute on Aging-Alzheimer's Association workgroups on diagnostic guidelines for Alzheimer's disease. *Alzheimer's and Dementia, 7*(3), 280–292.

Sperling, R. A., Jack, C. R., Jr., Black, S. E., Frosch, M. P., Greenberg, S. M., Hyman, B. T., ... Schindler, R. J. (2011). Amyloid-related imaging abnormalities in amyloid-modifying therapeutic trials: Recommendations from the Alzheimer's Association Research Roundtable Workgroup. *Alzheimer's and Dementia, 7*(4), 367–385.

Storandt, M., Grant, E., Miller, J., & Morris, J. (2002). Rates of progression in mild cognitive impairment and early Alzheimer's disease. *Neurology, 59*, 1034–1041.

Tabert, M., Manly, J., Liu, X., Pelton, G., Rosenblum, S., Jacobs, M., ... Devanand, D. (2006a). Neuropsychological prediction of conversion to Alzheimer's disease in patients with mild cognitive impairment. *Archives of General Psychiatry, 63*, 916–924.

Tabert, M., Manly, J., Liu, X., Pelton, G., Rosenblum, S., Jacobs, M., ... Devanand, D. (2006b). Neuropsychological prediction of conversion to Alzheimer disease in patients with mild cognitive impairment. *Archives of General Psychiatry, 63*(8), 916–924.

Talassi, E., Guerreschi, M., Feriani, M., Fedi, V., Bianchetti, A., & Trabucchi, M. (2007). Effectiveness of a cognitive rehabilitation program in mild dementia (MD) and mild cognitive impairment (MCI): A case control study. *Archives of Gerontologic Geriatrics, 44*(Suppl 1), 391–399.

Tapiola, T., Pennanen, C., Tapiola, M., Tervo, S., Kivipelto, M., Hänninen, T., ... Soininen, H. (2008). MRI of hippocampus and entorhinal cortex in mild cognitive impairment: A follow-up study. *Neurobiology of Aging, 29*(1), 31–38.

Taylor, J., Miller, T., & Tinklenberg, J. (1992). Correlates of memory decline: A four-year longitudinal study of older adults with memory complaints. *Psychology and Aging, 7*, 185–193.

Tierney, M., Szalai, J., Snow, W., Fisher, R., Nores, A., Nadon, G., ... St. George-Hyslop, P. (1996). Prediction of probable Alzheimer's disease in memory-impaired patients: A prospective longitudinal study. *Neurology, 46*, 661–665.

Tierney, M., Yao, C., Kiss, A., & McDowell, I. (2005). Neuropsychological tests accurately predict incident Alzheimer disease after 5 and 10 years. *Neurology, 64*, 1853–1859.

Tyas, S., Salazar, J., Snowdon, D., Desrosiers, M., Riley, K., Mendiondo, M., & Kryscio, R. (2007). Transitions to mild cognitive impairments, dementia, and death: Findings from the nun study. *American Journal of Epidemiology, 165*, 1231–1238.

Unverzagt, F., Kasten, L., Johnson, K., Rebok, G., Marsiske, M., Koepke, K.,…Tennstedt, S. (2007). Effect of memory impairment on training outcomes in ACTIVE. *Journal of the International Neuropsychological Society, 13*, 953–960.

Urenjak, J., Williams, S. R., Gadian, D. G., & Noble, M. (1993). Proton nuclear magnetic resonance spectroscopy unambiguously identifies different neural cell types. *Journal of Neuroscience, 13*(3), 981–989.

Visser, P., Kester, A., Jolles, J., & Verhey, F. (2006). Ten-year risk of dementia in subjects with mild cognitive impairment. *Neurology, 67*, 1201–1207.

Visser, P., & Verhey, F. (2008). Mild cognitive impairment as predictor for Alzheimer's disease in clinical practice: Effect of age and diagnostic criteria. *Psychological Medicine, 38*, 113–122.

Wang, P., Saykin, A., Flashman, L., Wishart, H., Rabin, L., Santulli, R.,…Mamouriuan, A. (2006). Regionally specific atrophy of the corpus callosum in AD, MCI and cognitive complaints. *Neurobiology of Aging, 27*, 1613–1617.

Wechsler, D. (1974). *Wechsler Intelligence Scale for Children-Revised*. New York: Psychological Corporation.

Wechsler, D. (1981). *Wechsler Adult Intelligence Scale-Revised Manual*. San Antonio, TX: The Psychological Corporation.

Wechsler, D. (1987). *Wechsler Memory Scale—Revised*. New York: Psychological Corporation.

Wechsler, D. (1997). *Wechsler Adult Intelligence Scale–Third Edition*. San Antonio, TX: Psychological Corporation.

Welsh, K., Butters, N., Hughes, J., Mohs, R., & Heyman, A. (1991). Detection of abnormal memory decline in mild cases of Alzheimer's disease using CERAD neuropsychological measures. *Archives of Neurology, 48*, 278–281.

Wierenga, C. E., Stricker, N. H., McCauley, A., Simmons, A., Jak, A. J., Chang, Y. L.,…Bondi, M. W. (2010). Increased functional brain response during word retrieval in cognitively intact older adults at genetic risk for Alzheimer's disease. *Neuroimage, 51*(3), 1222–1233.

Wierenga, C. E., Stricker, N. H., McCauley, A., Simmons, A., Jak, A. J., Chang, Y. L.,... Bondi, M. W. (2011). Altered brain response for semantic knowledge in Alzheimer's disease. *Neuropsychologia, 49*(3), 392–404.

Wilkinson, G. S. (1993). *Wide Range Achievement Test-Third Edition Administration Manual* Wilmington, DE: Wide Range.

Winblad, B., Palmer, K., Kivipelto, M., Jelic, V., Fratiglioni, L., Wahlund, L.,... Petersen, R. (2004). Mild cognitive impairment—beyond controversies, towards a consensus: Report of the International Working Group on Mild Cognitive Impairment. *Journal of Internal Medicine, 256*, 240–246.

Woodard, J., Seidenberg, M., Nielson, K., et al. (2010). Prediction of cognitive decline in healthy older adults using fMRI. *Journal of Alzheimer's Disease, 21*, 871–885.

Woodard, J. L., Seidenberg, M., Nielson, K. A., Antuono, P., Guidotti, L., Durgerian, S.,... Rao, S. M. (2009). Semantic memory activation in amnestic mild cognitive impairment. *Brain, 132*(Pt 8), 2068–2078.

Xu, Y., Jack, C. R., Jr., O'Brien, P. C., Kokmen, E., Smith, G. E., Ivnik, R. J.,... Petersen, R. C. (2000). Usefulness of MRI measures of entorhinal cortex versus hippocampus in AD. *Neurology, 54*(9), 1760–1767.

Yaffe, K., Petersen, R., Lindquist, K., Kramer, J., & Miller, B. (2006). Subtype of mild cognitive impairment and progression to dementia and death. *Dementia and Geriatric Cognitive Disorders, 22*, 312–319.

Zaccai, J., Brayne, C., McKeith, I., et al. (2008). Patterns and stages of alpha-synucleinopathy: Relevance in a population-based cohort. *Neurology, 70*, 1042–1048.

Zanetti, M., Ballabio, C., Abbate, C., Cutaia, C., Vergani, C., & Bergamaschini, L. (2006). Mild cognitive impairment subtypes and vascular dementia in community-dwelling elderly people: A 3-year follow-up study. *Journal of the American Geriatrics Society, 54*, 580–586.

5

■ ■ ■

Alzheimer's Disease

Case Presentation

A 72-year-old married, right-handed man with 16 years of education presented for initial evaluation. He was a retired computer company manager. He and his wife estimated that approximately three years prior to presentation he had an insidious and spontaneous onset of forgetfulness for events. In the last year, they noticed some emotional volatility. At presentation, he was forgetting events and conversations. The prior summer, he had to give up his job as a cashier in a shop because, under pressure, he was having difficulty calculating or using the cash register. He had also noticed that he was more irritable than before. In activities of daily living, he was independent in everything, but he did not like to drive in unfamiliar places. Separately the wife mentioned personality changes, including more irritability, especially at hockey games, which the patient had decided to no longer attend.

History

Past Medical/Surgical: Hypertension. Elevated cholesterol and hyperuricemia.
Social History: He lived with his wife in their home. He drank one to two ounces of alcohol a day. He did not use tobacco.

(continued)

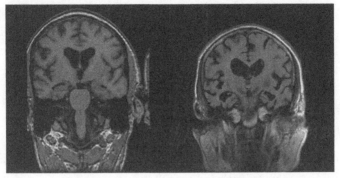

YEAR 2   YEAR 10

FIGURE 5.1 Coronal slices of MRI scans taken at year 2 (T1 SPGR) and again at year 10 (Flair). Note: scans are depicted in radiologic orientation (i.e., left is right).

Family History: Before his death, his father was forgetful but was not clearly demented. His mother was 93 and well. There was no other history of dementia or Alzheimer's disease in the family.

Medications: metoprolol, allopurinol, Lescol, Lotensin, Ascriptin, Niacin

Neuroimaging Studies of AD Case

The radiologist reported the following at the year 2 evaluation of our AD patient (see Figure 5.1):

> Examination demonstrates a few tiny foci of T2 signal increase in the white matter of both cerebral hemispheres consistent with chronic small vessel ischemic change, mild in extent allowing for the patient's age. Minimal diffuse cerebral atrophy. Relative enlargement of the temporal horn of the right lateral ventricle without clear asymmetry of the hippocampal formations.

The patient underwent a number of interim scans within the context of the longitudinal research protocol. His last scan was conducted at year 10, 11 months before his death (see again Figure 5.1). The radiologist noted,

> Minimal T2 hyperintensities in the periventricular white matter and both cerebral hemispheres, with disproportional ventricular dilatation, asymmetric, worse on the right and most prominent in the perisylvian locations.

Single voxel MR spectroscopy (TE of 30), with region of interest placed at the posterior cingulate gyrus. The NAA to creatine ratio measures 1.79, choline to creatine ratio measures 0.73, and myo-inositol to creatine ratio measures 0.58.

These values were all within normal limits.

Disease Course

The patient remained at home for 8 years and eventually came to be cared for by his wife. She became a regular attendee of a caregiver support group, cosponsored by the Alzheimer's Association and medical center. He was thrice seen in the emergency room, twice with chest pains and once for a fall. Eight years after initial presentation, the patient was relocated to a local assisted living facility. This was a locked facility designed primarily for dementia care. Three years later, he was twice admitted to a geriatric psychiatry unit due to aggressive behavior during personal cares. Specifically, he had become incontinent, but when staff went to change him he would resist their efforts via striking out. Antipsychotic medications were tried, and his behavior improved slightly. However, the patient stopped eating and the family elected to move to a palliative care approach. He was eventually discharged to a hospice facility and died there one day later.

Autopsy Brain Findings

1. Alzheimer disease (NIA-Reagan criteria high likelihood) with:
   a. Neuritic plaques, frequent, mesial temporal structures (amygdala, hippocampus, entorhinal cortex, and subiculum) and neocortex (frontal, temporal, parietal, occipital lobes, and insula).
   b. Neurofibrillary tangles, frequent, mesial temporal structures (amygdala, hippocampus, entorhinal cortex, and subiculum) and neocortex (frontal, temporal, parietal, occipital lobes, and insula), Braak and Braak stage 6 of 6.
   c. Amyloid angiopathy, moderate to severe, predominantly leptomeningeal (frontal greater than occipital lobe).
   d. No Lewy body/alpha-synuclein pathology.
   e. Cerebral atrophy, predominantly hippocampal (posterior); left hemi brain weight 661 g (fixed).

(continued)

Neuropsychological Case Findings

The patient was seen for initial cognitive evaluation, and then enrolled in an Alzheimer's Disease Patient Registry, where he was seen for annual neuropsychological evaluations for almost ten years, until he was no longer testable. The battery used was limited per the research protocol. Figure 5.2 lists performances across several key measures over time. For purposes of clarity, only initial, year 4, year 6, and year 9 evaluations are listed. The patient died 2 years after the year 9 evaluation. Several aspects of the presentation are noteworthy. First, the only measures falling below -1 SD z-score at initial evaluation are memory measures. Over

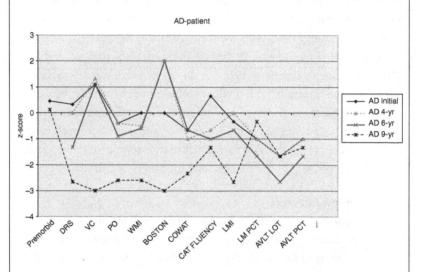

FIGURE 5.2 All scores are age-adjusted z scores. Premorbid = Wide Range Achievement Test 3rd edition (Wilkinson, 1993); Reading score, DRS = Mattis Dementia Rating Scale (Mattis, 1988); total scores, VC = Verbal comprehension, PO = perceptual organization, WMI = Working Memory Index (all from Wechsler, 1997); COWAT = Controlled Oral Word Association Test (Benton & Hamsher, 1978); Cat Fluency = Category Fluency test; LM1 = Wechsler Memory Scale Revised (WMS-R; Wechsler, 1987). Logical Memory Immediate Recall, LMPCT = WMS-R Logical Memory Delay divided by LM1. AVLTLOT = Rey Auditory Verbal Learning Test (AVLT; Rey, 1964) total of trials1–5 minus 5*trial 1 (see Ivnik et al., 1992). AVLTPCT = AVLT 30-minute delay divided by AVLT trial 5. Boston = Boston Naming Test (Kaplan, Goodglass, & Weintraub, 1983). DRS, COWAT, Category Fluency, WMS-R, AVLT and Boston scores are based on Mayo Older American's Normative Studies (MOANS) norms.

time, he shows a pattern that reflects the problem of floor effects on percent retention measures. With increasing age, a 0-point recall score becomes normatively less rare, so z-scores improve as raw scores on learning decline and age increases. Second, this is a bright man with above average verbal comprehension skills, and these skills remain strong 6 years into the illness. Third, a "premorbid estimator," namely reading level, does appear to "hold" even at year 9, when all other measures have floored. Fourth, in this case, naming is stable until quite late. In fact, in the early phases of the illness, he appears to show a practice effect on the *Boston Naming Test*. Fifth, while letter fluency remains relatively stable over the initial years of assessment, category fluency shows a steady deterioration.

Diagnostic Criteria

As noted in Chapter 1, consensus criteria for AD diagnosis have recently been updated by various task forces empaneled by the National Institute on Aging and the Alzheimer's Association (McKhann et al., 2011). The current proposals for AD related diagnoses follow.

Operational Research Criteria for Defining Preclinical AD (Sperling et al., 2011)

1. Biomarker evidence of amyloid-β accumulation (Stage 1 = asymptomatic cerebral amyloidosis)
    a. Elevated tracer retention on PET amyloid imaging and/or low Aβ42 on CSF assay
2. Biomarker evidence of synaptic dysfunction and/or early neurodegeneration (Stage 2 = evidence of amyloid positivity + presence of one or more additional AD markers)
    a. Elevated CSF tau or phospho-tau
    b. Hypometabolism in an AD-like pattern (i.e., posterior cingulate, precuneus, and/or temporoparietal cortices) on FDG-PET
    c. Cortical thinning/grey matter loss in AD-like anatomic distribution (i.e., lateral and medial parietal, posterior cingulate and lateral temporal cortices) and/or hippocampal atrophy on volumetric MRI

3. Evidence of subtle cognitive decline, but does not meet criteria for MCI or dementia (Stage 3 = amyloid positivity + markers of neuro-degeneration + very early cognitive symptoms)
   a. Demonstrated cognitive decline over time on standard cognitive tests, but not meeting criteria for MCI
   b. Subtle impairment on challenging cognitive tests, particularly accounting for level of innate ability or cognitive reserve but not meeting criteria for MCI.

Clinical Criteria for the Diagnosis of MCI due to AD (Albert et al., 2011)

Generic MCI Criteria

The work group in this area has proposed a two-step process in which, first, a clinical diagnosis of "generic" MCI is rendered then biomarker information is used to assign AD as the etiology with increasing levels of confidence. Low confidence is reflected in the term "MCI with neurodegenerative etiology." Intermediate confidence is described as "MCI with presumed AD," and highest confidence is termed "prodromal AD." The "generic" criteria for MCI are presented in Chapter 4. If those criteria are met, then the clinician considers AD as the etiology.

Proposed Terminology for Classifying Individuals with "MCI due to AD" with Varying Levels of Certainty

1. MCI of a Neurodegenerative Etiology. The criteria outlined above for MCI with a presumed degenerative etiology represents the typical presentation of individuals who are at an increased risk of progressing to AD dementia. As noted above, these individuals typically have a prominent impairment in episodic memory, but other patterns of cognitive impairment can also progress to AD dementia over time (e.g., executive dysfunction). Note that negative or ambiguous biomarker evidence (from either topographic or molecular biomarkers) is still consistent with the possibility that the patient with MCI has underlying AD pathology. However, if the biomarkers are negative for AD neuropathology, the likelihood that the diagnosis is due to AD, as opposed to an alternate cause, is low.

2. MCI of the Alzheimer Type. If the subject meets the MCI criteria above but, in addition, has one or more topographic biomarkers associated with the "downstream" effects of AD pathology (e.g., MRI evidence of medial temporal atrophy, or FDG PET evidence of decreased temporoparietal metabolism, adjusting for age), then there is increased likelihood that the outcome will be AD dementia. It should be noted that the absence of molecular biomarker information (or equivocal findings from molecular biomarkers) is still consistent with an intermediate level of certainty that the individual will progress to AD dementia over time.

3. Prodromal Alzheimer's Dementia. If the subject meets the MCI criteria above, and in addition has a positive biomarker for the molecular neuropathology of the Alzheimer's disease, this provides the highest level of certainly that over time the individual will progress to AD dementia. This level of certainty would be increased even further if the individual has positive topographic biomarker evidence of AD. However, the absence of such topographic biomarker evidence (or equivocal or normal findings) is still consistent with the highest level of certainty that the individual will progress to AD dementia over time.

Criteria for the Diagnosis of AD Dementia (McKhann et al., 2011)
The third and final article in this series of publications was charged with revising the criteria for the diagnosis of dementia due to Alzheimer's disease developed in 1984 and was again chaired by Dr. Guy McKhann, who chaired the original workgroup proceedings nearly three decades earlier. The revised criteria include the following:

- Insidious onset. Symptoms have a gradual onset over months to years, and the onset was not sudden over hours or days; and,
- Clear-cut history of worsening of cognition by report or observation; and,
- Cognitive deficits are evident on history and examination in one of the two categories:
- (1) Amnestic presentation: The most common syndromic presentation of AD dementia. The deficits should include impairment in learning and recall of recently learned information. There should also be evidence of cognitive dysfunction in other cognitive domains as defined above.
- (2) Nonamnestic presentations:
  o Language presentation: The most prominent deficits are in word-finding, but dysfunction in other cognitive domains should be present.

o Visual presentation: The most prominent deficits are in spatial cognition, including object agnosia, impaired face recognition, simultanagnosia and alexia. Deficits in other cognitive domains should be present.

o Executive dysfunction: The most prominent deficits are in impaired reasoning, judgment, and problem solving. Deficits in other cognitive domains should be present.

They proposed the following characterization for AD Dementia:

1. Pathologically Proven AD Dementia
  a. Meets clinical and cognitive criteria for probable AD dementia during life
  b. Proven AD by pathological examination (see "Neuropathology" section below)

2. Clinical AD Dementia—Degrees of Certainty. They propose to maintain the "Probable" and "Possible" qualifiers of the 1984 criteria (G. McKhann et al., 1984):

A. *Probable AD Dementia*. Meets clinical and cognitive criteria for AD dementia given above, AND without evidence of any alternative diagnoses, in particular, no significant cerebrovascular disease. In persons who meet the basic criteria for probable AD dementia, the diagnosis of probable AD dementia can be enhanced by one of these three features that increase certainty:

  1. *Documented Decline*: Has evidence of progressive cognitive decline on subsequent evaluations based on information from informants and cognitive testing in the context of either brief mental status examinations or formal neuropsychological evaluation;
  OR

  2. *Biomarker Positive*: Has one or more of the following supporting biomarkers.
     a. low CSF Abeta42, elevated CSF tau or phospho tau
     b. positive amyloid PET imaging
     c. decreased FDG uptake on PET in temporoparietal cortex
     d. disproportionate atrophy on structural MR in medial temporal lobe (esp. hippocampus), basal and lateral temporal lobe, and medial parietal isocortex;

OR

3. *Mutation Carrier*: Meets clinical and cognitive criteria for AD Dementia
   and has a proven AD autosomal dominant genetic mutation (PSEN1,
   PSEN2, APP).

B. **Possible AD Dementia**.

1. *Atypical Course*: Evidence for progressive decline is lacking or
   uncertain but meets other clinical and cognitive criteria for AD
   dementia;

OR,

2. *Biomarkers Obtained and Negative*: Meets clinical and cognitive criteria for AD dementia but biomarkers (CSF, structural or functional
   brain imaging) do not support the diagnosis;

OR,

3. Mixed Presentation: Meets clinical and cognitive criteria for AD
   dementia but there is evidence of concomitant cerebrovascular disease; this would mean that there is more than one lacunar infarct;
   or a single large infarct; or extensive and severe white matter
   hyperintensity changes; or evidence for some features of dementia with Lewy bodies that do not achieve a level of a diagnosis of
   probable DLB.

C. **Not AD Dementia**. Does not meet clinical criteria for AD dementia;
OR

Has sufficient evidence for an alternative diagnosis such as HIV,
Huntington's disease, or others that rarely, if ever, overlap with AD.

Table 5.1 provides an encapsulation of the role of biomarkers in the new
Alzheimer's disease diagnosis scheme.

Epidemiology

The prevalence of AD in the United States in 2011 was estimated at 5.4
million (Alzheimer's Association, 2011). This includes 3.4 million women
over the age of 65. The nearly 2:1 ratio in numbers of women to men
ensues almost entirely from the association of AD with aging combined
with women's greater longevity. Roughly 17% of women versus 9% of
men living to age 65 will receive a diagnosis of AD before death. In 2010,
454,000 people received a new diagnosis of AD (Alzheimer's Association,
2011). Left unchanged, by 2050 it is estimated that there will 13.2 million

Table 5.1 Summary of Alzheimer's Disease Diagnostic Criteria Incorporating Biomarkers

STAGE OF PRECLINICAL AD	EVIDENCE OF SUBTLE COGNITIVE CHANGE	AB (PET OR CSF)	NEURONAL INJURY (TAU, FDG, SMRI)	DESCRIPTION
Stage 1	-	+	-	Asymptomatic cerebral amyloidosis
Stage 2	-	+	+	Asymptomatic cerebral amyloidosis + downstream neurodegeneration
Stage 3	+	+	+	Asymptomatic cerebral amyloidosis + neuronal injury + subtle cognitive/behavioral change

MCI CRITERIA WITH BIOMARKER DATA	AB (PET OR CSF)	NEURONAL INJURY	BIOMARKER PROBABILITY OF AD ETIOLOGY
MCI -Core clinical criteria	?	?	Uninformative
MCI-unlikely due to AD	-	-	Lowest
Due to AD- intermediate likelihood	+	?	Intermediate
Due to AD- intermediate likelihood	?	+	Intermediate
Due to AD- high likelihood	+	+	Highest

AD CRITERIA WITH BIOMARKER DATA	AB (PET OR CSF	NEURONAL INJURY	BIOMARKER PROBABILITY OF AD ETIOLOGY
Probable AD Clinical criteria	?	?	Uninformative
Dementia-unlikely due to AD	-	-	Lowest
Probable AD- intermediate likelihood	+	?	Intermediate
Probable AD- intermediate likelihood	?	+	Intermediate
Probable AD- high likelihood	+	+	Highest
Possible AD (atypical presentation) Clinical criteria	?	?	Uninformative
Possible AD (atypical presentation)	+	+	High but does not exclude second etiology

Abbreviations: AD = Alzheimer's disease, AB = amyloid beta, PET = positron emission tomography, CSF-cerebrospinal fluid, FD G-fluorodeoxyglucose, sMRI = structural magnetic resonance imaging, MCI = mild cognitive impairment, ? = untested/indeterminate/conflicting, + = positive, – = negative.

Americans with AD (Alzheimer's Association, 2011). Worldwide projections are for the number of people with AD to move from 26.6 million in 2006 to 107 million in 2050 (Brookmeyer, Johnson, Ziegler-Graham, & Arrighi, 2007). More than 7 out of 10 people with Alzheimer's disease in the United States live at home (Alzheimer's Association, 2003). Almost 4 out of 10 are living alone at the time of diagnosis (Smith, Kokmen, & O'Brien, 2000; Smith, O'Brien, Ivnik, Kokmen, & Tangalos, 2001). Almost 80% of home care is provided by family and friends. Combined health care and long-term care payments for an individual with AD cost an average of $42,000 per year (Alzheimer's Association, 2011). Survival time from diagnosis of Alzheimer's disease varies with age of diagnosis and ranges from about seven years in those with diagnosis in their 60s to three years for those with diagnosis in their 90s (Brookmeyer, Corrada, Curriero, & Kawas, 2002). Across ages, men's survival is about 88% of women's survival time. Persons with AD will commonly succumb to pneumonia or cardiovascular failure (Beard et al., 1996). Approximately 90% of patients with dementia will require custodial care at some point during their illness (Smith et al., 2000) with median time to placement from diagnosis at 5.3 years (Smith et al., 2001). Cognitive function and functional status at diagnosis are important predictors of time to institutionalization (Smith et al., 2000; Smith et al., 2001).

Neurophysiology and Neuropathology

The Choline Hypothesis

Three of four currently approved medications for the treatment of Alzheimer's disease target the neurotransmitter acetylcholine. This is due to the fact that, before the emergence of the amyloid hypothesis, the choline hypothesis pervaded the field. This hypothesis emanated from neuropathological studies that found massive loss of cholinergic cells in the basal forebrain of persons with AD (Whitehouse et al., 1983). Specifically, the nucleus basalis of Meynert was found to be atrophied in AD autopsies. The nucleus basalis is known to be a key producer of acetylcholine in the brain. Acetylcholine is processed to generate choline, which had been found to be important to learning and memory in a variety of animal and human studies (Furey, 2011). Thus, there appeared to be a consistency between the neuropathology, the neurotransmitter, and the clinical syndrome. Since choline is degraded for reuptake by cholinesterase, research began to pursue the notion that maintaining bioavailability of choline could be neuroprotective. Several acetylcholine compounds were subsequently developed, tested, approved, and marketed (see "Pharmacologic Interventions" section). However, it has become increasingly clear that nucleus basalis degeneration and choline depletion is a late-stage issue in AD (Gilmor et al., 1999). This fact may explain why cholinesterase inhibition has not produced compelling results in the treatment of AD.

The Vascular Hypothesis

Of the lesions first recognized by Alois Alzheimer in his original 1907 publication, clearly the neuritic plaque and the neurofibrillary tangle are the best known. Within a few decades of his original observations, it was also recognized that amyloid accumulated in the vessels in AD and that infiltration of small blood vessel walls by Aβ is present in all but a few cases of AD. More recent studies have also noted that cerebrovascular disease (CVD) pathology observed by MRI (e.g., white matter hyperintensities, lacunes) occurs more often in patients with Alzheimer's disease than in normal aging (DeCarli, 2006). Thus, the presence of cerebral amyloid angiopathy (CAA), as well as overrepresentation of CVD pathology in AD, has led to the vascular hypothesis, which posits that CVD plays an important role in the pathogenesis of AD (de la Torre, 2004). Critics of the vascular hypothesis point to the modest associations between CVD pathology, particularly small vessel ischemic disease, and cognition. In contrast, Cordonnier and van der Flier (2011) offer that brain microbleeds represent a plausible intersection between the amyloid cascade hypothesis (discussed below) and the vascular hypothesis, given that they are an expression of vascular damage and at the same time are closely related to amyloid deposition. Thus, cerebral microbleeds may serve as an additional argument for the notion that amyloid and CVD pathology act in synergy to cause AD.

In a study supportive of this notion, Arvanitakis et al. (2011) found that CAA pathology is associated with AD pathology, and that moderate-to-severe levels of CAA are also associated with cognitive deficits in perceptual speed and episodic memory—independent of the effects of AD pathology (Arvanitakis, Leurgans, Wang, et al., 2011). These data support a separate role for CAA in lowering specific cognitive functions in older persons with and without AD pathology. In another study, Bell et al. (2012) found in an animal model of AD that the epsilon-4 variant of apolipoprotein E (APOE4; discussed further below) triggers a cascade of events that damages the brain's vascular system at the level of the blood-brain barrier (BBB). This relationship between APOE4 and BBB breakdown leads to neuronal uptake of multiple blood-derived neurotoxic proteins, and microvascular and cerebral blood flow reductions. This study provides an important direct link in the complex interplay between beta-amyloid and APOE4, and it furthers our understanding that damage to the brain's vascular system may also play a central role in AD.

The Amyloid Cascade Hypothesis

The amyloid hypothesis (Selkoe, 2001) is currently the most widely accepted model for explaining the development of Alzheimer's neuropathology (see Figure 5.3). The model posits that misprocessing of the amyloid precursor protein leads to amyloid fragments that are insoluble in the brain. These fragments begin to aggregate to form plaques in the extracellular space in the brain, producing a mild inflammatory response. The plaques and inflammation prove neurotoxic, especially to certain neuron populations. As these neurons die, their processes tangle (i.e., neurofibrillary tangles develop). Some neural fibrils also get incorporated in the plaques. Thus, on autopsy, the hallmark features of Alzheimer's disease are filamentous amyloid plaques and

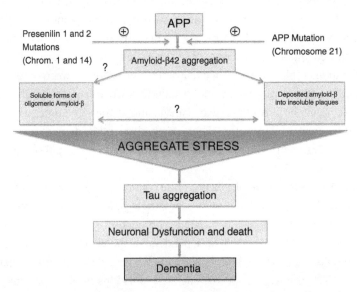

FIGURE 5.3 Schematic diagram of the amyloid cascade hypothesis. Ab42 = the 42-amino acid form of the amyloid-b protein. Tau = the protein associated with tangle formations. Karran, Mercken & De Strooper (2011). Reproduced with permission.

neurofibrillary tangles. The dynamic time course for these developments has been outlined by Jack et al. (2010) and is depicted in Figure 1.5 in Chapter 1 (Jack et al., 2010).

The development of this histopathology is variable. Amyloid plaques can be seen in persons with normal cognitive aging. Tangles can occur in other supposedly unrelated conditions, like frontotemporal dementia or head trauma. As a consequence, the pathological diagnosis of AD is made on a semiquantitative basis.

Braak and Braak Neuropathological Staging System

The movement toward the concept of preclinical Alzheimer's disease was launched in part by the seminal work of Braak and Braak (1991). These neuropathologists demonstrated the presence of neurofibrillary tangles (NFTs) in entorhinal cortex in people as young as 30 years of age. Their work led to a neuropathological staging system that depicts a progression of pathology from its initial presence in hippocampal pathways through the pervasive neocortical NFT dispersal (see Figure 5.4). This progression of pathology has obvious implications for the presentation and progression of cognitive deficits in preclinical and clinical AD. The Braak staging system for Alzheimer's disease is prominently reflected in contemporary criteria for the neuropathological diagnosis of AD (see below).

Insulin and Other Causes

Of course there are numerous other hypothesized mechanisms for the development of AD pathology. Recent research posits a "type-III" diabetes, wherein central nervous system insulin resistance impairs amyloid beta regulation, leading to amyloid plaques (Baker et al., 2011). Preliminary studies of direct delivery of insulin to CNS via inhalation have provided mixed supported for this hypotheses (Craft et al., 2011). Additional recent research raises hypoxia as an instigating event in the development of amyloid pathology (Oresic et al., 2011). Note that these hypotheses are subsidiaries of the amyloid hypothesis as they merely seek to explain how amyloid plaques develop, assuming that the rest of the amyloid cascade hypothesis is correct.

Critiques of the Amyloid Cascade Hypothesis

The success of the amyloid hypothesis has primarily centered on its explicit prediction that AD relates to amyloid production and clearance, and the known deterministic gene mutations for the disease directly relate

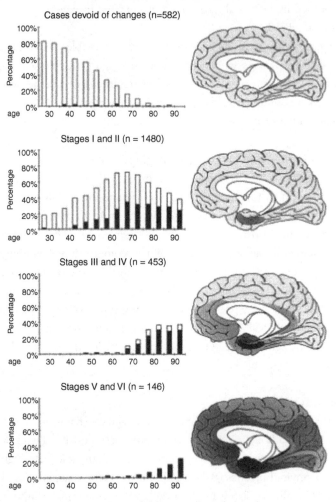

FIGURE 5.4 Distribution of neurofibrillary tangle pathology by age at autopsy. (Braak & Braak, 1991). Reproduced with permission.

to amyloid production. Despite this prevailing evidence in support of the amyloid hypothesis on the genetics front, there remain a number of unanswered questions. And, there have been increasing criticisms that the amyloid hypothesis is not delivering effective therapies for the disease in the wake of a multitude of unsuccessful clinical trials. Hardy (2009) reviews a number of the difficulties of the amyloid hypothesis. First, that amyloid/Aβ should be toxic, although Aβ toxicity has rarely been convincingly demonstrated.

While newer species of smaller soluble Aβ oligomers have shown some toxicity, "none of this amounts to convincing toxicity: these subtle alterations ... are a far cry from the massive cell loss seen in Alzheimer's disease." Second, the amyloid hypothesis sequences the cascade of events such that amyloid/Aβ should initiate tau-related alterations and tangle dysfunction, although little data are available on the pathway linking these two molecules as of yet. Third, the most important prediction of the amyloid hypothesis is that reducing Aβ and plaques should lead to improvements in the symptoms associated with Alzheimer's disease. The amyloid immunization trials, though unsuccessful and stopped because of their vascular and other neurologic complications, seemed to show that amyloid could be cleared from the brain. On this point, Hardy (2009) notes the "clearance of visible plaques is remarkable and runs completely counter to the previous wisdom that amyloid plaques were forever." Unfortunately, it had little to no effect on ameliorating the dementia in those few individuals who showed amyloid clearance. It remains to be seen whether amyloid clearance at more mild stages of dementia, or in MCI individuals, will have greater effects on cognition, if clinical trials eventually and safely get to that phase.

As discussed in the previous chapter, amyloid deposition does not correlate with dementia severity or extent of neurodegeneration, and it does not account for the role of tau in the pathophysiology of AD (Cordonnier & van der Flier, 2011). Amyloid is regarded as one of the initiating events, and other processes such as tangle formation leading to neuronal dysfunction and neurodegeneration then become key pathologic processes later in the course of decline (Jack et al., 2010; R. A. Sperling et al., 2011). The link between these two essential lesions is unknown.

Proposed Neuropathological Criteria for AD

In concert with the update to the clinical criteria for AD, new NIA-Alzheimer's Association neuropathological criteria were proposed in 2011.

Classification

AD neuropathologic change should be ranked along three parameters (Table 5.2) to obtain an "ABC score":

Genetics

The pursuit of early detection and prevention efforts has also been spurred by the identification of genes associated with dementia. Increasingly, more genes

Table 5.2 Level of AD Neuropathologic Change

| A | C | B NFT STAGE (BRAAK)[1] | | | |
AβDEPOSITS (THAL PHASES)[2]	NEURITIC PLAQUE SCORE (CERAD)[3]	0 (NONE)	1 (I/II)	2 (III/IV)	3 (V/VI)
0	0 (none)	Not AD	Not AD[4]	Not AD[4]	Not AD[4]
1, 2, or 3	0 (none)	Low	Low	Low	Low to Intermediate[5]
1, 2, or 3	1 (sparse)	Low	Low	Low	Intermediate[5]
1, 2, or 3	2 or 3 (moderate or frequent)	Low[6]	Low[6]	Intermediate	High

1. NFT stage should be determined by the method of Braak and Braak (Braak & Braak, 1991). Note that Braak staging should be attempted in all cases regardless of the presence of coexisting diseases.
2. Aβ deposits should be determined by the method of Thal et al. (Thal, Rub, Orantes, & Braak, 2002).
3. Neuritic plaque score should be determined by the method of CERAD (Mirra, Heyman, McKeil, Sumi, & Crain, 1991).
4. Medial temporal lobe NFT in the absence of significant Aβ or neuritic plaque accumulation. This occurs in older people and may be seen in individuals without cognitive impairment, mild impairment, or those with cognitive impairment from causes other than AD. Consider other diseases when clinically indicated (Nelson et al., 2009).
5. Widespread NFT with some Aβ accumulation but limited to neuritic plaques. These two categories are relatively infrequent, and other diseases, particularly a tauopathy, should be considered. Such cases may not fit easily into a specific Braak stage, which is intended for categorization of AD-type NFT. AD neuropathologic change should be categorized as "low" for Thal phases 1 and 2 and "intermediate" for Thal phase 3.
6. Moderate or frequent NPs with low Braak stage. Consider contribution of comorbidities like vascular brain injury, Lewy body disease, or hippocampal sclerosis. Also, consider additional sections as well as repeat or additional protocols to demonstrate other non-AD lesions. Adapted from (Alzheimer's Association, 2011b)

will be found and more ways in which genes associate with Alzheimer's disease will be discovered. At this time, it is reasonable to discuss the four known genes as either causative or susceptibility genes. Knowledge of causative and susceptibility genes offers great promise for our early detection and prevention efforts in Alzheimer's disease. The early diagnosis in a person with some equivocal evidence of cognitive decline can be facilitated by knowledge of his/her genes (Roses, 1997). Whole populations without evidence of cognitive decline, but with genetic risk, can be studied (e.g., Reiman et al., 1996) and even entered into prevention trials. It remains unclear the extent to which these polymorphisms directly impact cognitive function or simply serve as markers for the underlying pathology impacting cognition. In other words, do the genes directly influence cognition in the absence of AD-related neuropathology (Bennett et al., 2003; Bondi, Salmon, Galasko, Thomas, & Thal, 1999; Brainerd, Reyna, Petersen, Smith, & Taub, 2011)?

Causative Genes

At the time of this writing, there are three genetic mutations that appear to have a causative link to Alzheimer's disease. These gene mutations are called causative because whenever a person with the genetic mutation lives to the age of risk, he or she invariably develops dementia. Moreover, members of the family who live through the age of risk without developing dementia are not carriers. These gene mutations include the Amyloid Precursor Protein (APP) gene on chromosome 21, the Presenilin 1 gene on chromosome 14, and the Presenilin 2 gene on chromosome 1. All of these genes have a role in amyloid processing (Selkoe, 2001). Yet, these genetic mutations account for less than 5% of all Alzheimer's disease cases (Campion et al., 1999). All of the Alzheimer's disease causative gene mutations are associated with an early age of onset (i.e., AD occurring before the age of 65). The identification of these deterministic genes is significant because it demonstrates that Alzheimer's disease can have a genetic cause, and it has multiple genetic causes with a common final clinical expression. It is possible that a portion of the common late onset form of Alzheimer's disease will have a genetic cause as well, although no causative gene mutations have been identified.

Susceptibility Genes

In addition to genetic mutations that apparently cause Alzheimer's disease, several genetic variations have been identified that increase Alzheimer's disease susceptibility. Recently identified or confirmed by a large-scale genome-wide association study are common genetic variants at *MS4A4/MS4A6E*, *CD2AP*, *CD33*, *EPHA1*, *CR1*, *CLU*, *BIN1*, and *PICALM* (Naj et al., 2011). Even in combination, however, these newly identified genes do not approach the strength of association seen between the apolipoprotein E (APOE) gene and late-onset AD.

The APOE gene is located on chromosome 19 (Strittmatter et al., 1993). This gene has three common isoforms labeled epsilon-2 (E2), epsilon-3 (E3), and epsilon-4 (E4), and a person receives one from each parent to combine to one of six possible genotypic combinations (e.g., E2/E2, E2/E3, E2/E4, E3/E3, E3/E4, and E4/E4). People who possess the E4 genotype are at increased risk for developing late-onset AD, whereas people who possess the E2 genotype may be at decreased risk (Corder et al., 1993; Saunders et al., 1993). A variety of brain changes are associated with the APOE ε4 allele in AD, including increased counts of neuritic plaques and neurofibrillary tangle pathology, as well as greater depletions of cholinergic markers in a variety of regions. In nondemented older adults, the APOE ε4 allele has been associated with structural (e.g., Plassman et al., 1997; Soininen et al., 1995) and functional brain changes (e.g., Bondi et al., 2005; Bookheimer et al., 2000; Reiman, et al., 1996), as well as with subtle neuropsychological deficits (e.g., Bondi et al., 1999; Bondi et al., 1995; Smith et al., 1998). In a study that examined for the presence of neurofibrillary tangle pathology in autopsied young adults (ages 22–46), Ghebremedhin, Schultz, Braak, & Braak (1998) found at least some evidence of neurofibrillary tangle accumulation in the entorhinal cortex (i.e., Stage I) in twice the number of E4 carriers compared with non-E4 carriers. This finding again suggests that AD pathology begins decades—and not years—prior to clinical diagnosis, although it is interesting to note that the Braak and Braak neuropathological staging primarily depicts the neurofibrillary tangle severity. The findings of Ghebremedhin et al. (1998) therefore run counter to the prevailing emphasis on the early preclinical appearance of amyloid and later appearance of tau pathology. It appears that early tau pathology can and does occur, and its early appearance is associated with the major susceptibility gene for AD.

Unlike causative genes, some people with the susceptibility gene do live through the age of risk without developing AD. It is likely that some people with late-onset AD do not carry any of the known susceptibility genes. As such, these genes remain neither necessary nor sufficient for the development of AD. Still, these genes are overrepresented in Alzheimer's disease, and inheriting one increases one's risk for developing the disease. For example, being a carrier of one of the APOE ε4 alleles (e.g., ε2/ε4, ε3/ε4 heterozygotes) increases risk approximately four-fold and inheriting both ε4 alleles (e.g., ε4/ε4 heterozygote) increases risk on the order of 16 times. Identifying such a significant increased risk for AD may justify intervention with ε4 carriers before they show signs of dementia.

Whether APOE genotype directly influences cognitive function remains a source of debate. Studies have shown that by the time of AD diagnosis, ε4 carriers' memory performance is more impaired than ε4 noncarriers (Smith et al., 1998). Other studies fail to demonstrate this effect in clinically evident AD patients (Lange et al., 2002b). Several reports have also suggested that, in asymptomatic persons, in the 50–70 year age range (i.e., less than two decades from age of risk), ε4 carriers perform more poorly on cognitive tasks than noncarriers (Greenwood, Sunderland, Friz, & Parasuraman, 2000) and have noted subtle weaknesses in visual attention and working memory among ε4 carriers. Caselli et al. (1999) reported steeper decline on immediate and delayed recall in ε4 homozygotes relative to ε4 heterozygotes and non-ε4 carriers (Caselli et al., 1999), although they failed to replicate these findings in a second sample (Caselli et al., 2001). Cognitive differences across APOE groups may disappear when persons that subsequently develop dementia are removed from the sample (Bondi et al., 1999). Whether or not cognitive differences exist in ε4 carriers younger than 50 years of age is equivocal.

It may be that complex interactions between APOE genotype and nongenetic factors exist, such as a prior head injury (Jordan, 2000; R. Mayeux et al., 1995; R. Mayeux et al., 1993), nutritional status (Bunce, Kivipelto, & Wahlin, 2004), and diabetes (Dore, Elias, Robbins, Elias, & Nagy, 2009; Irie, Fitzpatrick, Lopez, et al., 2008), to modify the vulnerability to developing Alzheimer's disease. A study by Bunce et al. (2004) highlights the importance of examining for gene-environment interactions in AD. They found that low vitamin B_{12} among ε4 carriers resulted in poor free recall performance, and these results remained after removing incident dementia cases that occurred up to six years later. Although it is clear that gene variations such as APOE appear to predispose one to developing Alzheimer's disease, a significant proportion that carry the risk factor do not go on to develop AD. Identifying other factors that may interact with the APOE gene to influence further one's vulnerability to developing AD are clearly needed, and Bunce et al. (2004) demonstrate that nutritional factors may be one important influence.

Clearly, a combination of risk factors (e.g., both MCI and APOE ε4 genotype) may impart a relatively greater risk of conversion to AD than that conferred by either risk factor alone, although consensus workgroups warn against utilizing APOE genotype information for diagnostic considerations (Knopman et al., 2001; G. Small et al., 1997). Nevertheless, others have argued that APOE genotype is useful for predicting the development of AD in individuals with mild cognitive impairment (MCI) (Petersen et al., 1995; Petersen, Waring, Smith, Tangalos, & Thibodeau, 1996; Smith et al., 1998), and helps identify those that may benefit from treatment (Petersen et al., 2005). Some have argued that, in those with established familial risk, knowing APOE status may be useful (Green et al., 2009).

Associated Clinical Features

Behavioral disturbances are common in AD and often represent a greater burden to the caregiver than do the cognitive symptoms of the disease. Across studies, prevalence rates of psychosis in AD have ranged from 22% to 56% (see Rabins, 1999, for review). Wragg and Jeste (1989) conservatively reported a median prevalence of hallucinations and delusions in 28% and 34% of patients, respectively (Wragg & Jeste, 1989), and a study by Paulsen and colleagues (2000) found that the incidence (e.g., onset of new cases) of psychosis increased over time (Paulsen et al., 2000). Specifically, the cumulative incidence of hallucinations and delusions was 20% at one year, 36% at two, 50% at three, and 51% at four years. Ferman has shown that late onset is one feature distinguishing hallucinations in AD from those of Lewy body dementia (Ferman et al., 2003). Significant behavioral disturbances often accompany the cognitive symptoms of AD, at various stages, and a growing literature suggests that these noncognitive symptoms are not intransigent to treatment but are responsive to specific therapies (Rodda, Morgan, & Walker, 2009; Rovner, Steele, Shmuely, & Folstein, 1996; Schneider, Pollock, & Lyness, 1990; Small et al., 1997; Sultzer et al., 2008; Teri et al., 1992).

Neuropsychology of AD

Earliest Neuropsychological Changes of AD

It is now well accepted that the pathophysiologic changes of AD begin years prior to the clinically evident manifestations of the disease. As depicted in Figure 5.4, these neurodegenerative changes, and particularly the neurofibrillary tangles (NFTs) associated with AD, begin primarily in the medial temporal lobe limbic structures (e.g., entorhinal/transentorhinal cortex, hippocampus) and then spread to the association cortices of the frontal, temporal, and parietal lobes over time (Braak & Braak, 1991). As the NFTs continue to accumulate and spread, a threshold is gradually reached wherein the clinical symptoms of the disease, and particularly the cognitive deficits, appear. As we discuss below, the pattern and progression of these neuropsychological changes fit well with the proposed distribution and spread of AD pathologic accumulations.

The pattern of these cognitive deficits in AD has often been heuristically characterized as a "cortical" dementia, and distinct from the "subcortical" or frontal-subcortical dementias of Huntington's disease (HD) or vascular dementia (described in the next chapter). Although it is well understood that pathologic changes in various cortical and subcortical dementias are not restricted to either cortical or subcortical brain regions, the cortical-subcortical dementia distinction serves as a useful model for describing the profile and pattern of neuropsychological changes that are observed in these patient groups. The reliance on pattern analysis (e.g., recall vs. recognition, letter vs. category fluency), demonstrable experimental neuropsychological dissociations (e.g., implicit vs. explicit memory, cortical disconnectivity), qualitative or process approach distinctions (e.g., intrusion errors, naming errors, cognitive asymmetries and discrepancies), and well-established brain-based distinctions (e.g., AD vs. HD) all provide evidence for the utility of this model in understanding brain-behavior relationships in neurodegenerative disorders.

Distinctions drawn on tests of episodic and semantic memory, visuospatial skills, and specific aspects of attention, working memory, and executive functions, are important considerations in the differential diagnosis of AD versus other predominantly subcortical dementias. The general profile of impairment in the cortical dementia of AD is characterized by a prominent anterograde amnesia with additional deficits in language and semantic memory, abstract reasoning, "executive" functions, attention, and constructional and visuospatial abilities. Subcortical dementias, such as HD, in addition to their motor disorder, usually demonstrate slowness of thought and deficits in executive functions and visuoperceptual and constructional abilities, although they often show only mild or moderate memory and language impairments that are both quantitatively and qualitatively different from those of cortical dementia patients.

Much of our clinical research has centered on the demonstration of detectable cognitive declines in patients with incipient AD well before the clinical diagnosis is made. Most studies examining this early period of decline have focused on the episodic memory impairment, which is primarily characterized by deficits in delayed recall due to rapid forgetting in the case of AD, although a growing body of evidence points to cognitive declines in AD that may be more global in nature (Twamley, Ropacki, & Bondi, 2006). Deterioration of semantic knowledge is evident on demanding naming and category fluency measures (Mickes et al., 2007; Powell et al., 2006b), and executive function deficits are also apparent (Brandt et al., 2009; Clark et al., 2012; Eppig et al., 2011). Asymmetric cognitive test performance distinctions may also be apparent prior to significant decline in global cognition (Jacobson, Delis, Bondi, & Salmon, 2002). Salmon (2011) also notes that cognitive neuropsychological measurement strategies of episodic memory are beginning to show increasing utility in early identification studies, and they include the recollective aspect of recognition memory, associative memory necessary for "binding" representations of two or more stimuli, pattern separation necessary to distinguish between two similar memory representations, prospective memory required to remember a delayed intention to act at a certain time in the future, and autobiographical memory for specific episodes that occurred in one's past. Collectively, many of the above findings related to the pattern of changes fit well with the known pathologic encroachments of AD and represent important cognitive markers of early disease. We review these cognitive domains in turn.

Episodic Memory

Given the early appearance and prominence of pathologic changes in the medial temporal lobe, coupled with the fact that these structures are critical for learning and recall of new material, a wealth of neuropsychological evidence supports that episodic memory impairment is usually the first and most salient cognitive manifestation of AD. Salmon and Bondi (2009) review a number of characteristics of the episodic memory changes that are quite effective in differentiating between mild AD patients and normal older adults. First, very mild AD patients are particularly impaired on delayed recall measures. Second, to-be-remembered information is not accessible after a delay even if retrieval demands are reduced through recognition testing. The combination of poor recall and poor recognition connotes that AD patients have abnormally rapid forgetting of material over time. Third, AD patients exhibit an abnormal serial position effect characterized by an attenuation of the recall of words from the beginning of a list (i.e., reduced primacy effect). Fourth, semantic or "deep" encoding of material is less effective in improving performance in AD. Finally,

AD patients have a proclivity for producing intrusion errors, presumably due to increased sensitivity to interference effects or disinhibition.

The saliency of the episodic memory deficit in AD is further demonstrated in its appearance *prior* to the diagnosis of either dementia or MCI. Most studies of nondemented adults who later develop AD are done more proximally to the typical onset-age in older adulthood. These studies have shown that a subtle decline in episodic memory often occurs prior to the emergence of the obvious cognitive and behavioral changes required for a clinical diagnosis of the disease (Albert & Killiany, 2001; Bäckman, Small, & Fratiglioni, 2001; Bondi et al., 1994; Chen et al., 2001; Fuld, Masur, Blau, Crystal, & Aronson, 1990; Grober & Kawas, 1997; Howieson et al., 1997; Jacobs et al., 1995; Lange et al., 2002b). Often this decline in episodic memory is evident some years prior to the development of dementia (Albert, Moss, Tanzi, & Jones, 2001; Bäckman et al., 2001; M. Bondi et al., 1999; Chen et al., 2001; Lange et al., 2002b; Masur, Sliwinski, Lipton, Blau, & Crystal, 1994) and has been shown to predict the subsequent development of AD (Albert et al., 2001; Bondi et al., 1994; Lange et al., 2002b; Smith & Ivnik, 1998). In an early study Bondi et al. (1999) compared the neuropsychological test performances and clinical outcomes of nondemented older adults who were carriers or noncarriers of the APOE ε4 allele and found that cognitively normal APOE ε4 carriers performed significantly worse than comparable noncarriers on measures of delayed recall from the California Verbal Learning Test but not on a host of other cognitive measures. Results also revealed that APOE ε4 allele status and measures of overall learning and delayed recall were significant independent predictors of subsequent progression to AD (Table 5.3). Furthermore, when individuals who developed AD were removed from analyses of baseline performance, there was no longer any difference between the two APOE genotype groups on memory or other cognitive measures, supporting the idea that poor recall is an early sensitive neuropsychological marker of preclinical AD and not simply a cognitive phenotype of the ε4 genotype.

The importance of mild preclinical memory changes for the early detection of AD has led the intense focus on, and original criteria for, what is now termed single-domain amnestic MCI (Petersen et al., 1999) and more recently MCI due to Alzheimer's disease (Albert, et al., 2011), as well as the development of practice parameters that recommend systematically monitoring patients with these early-identified memory changes for subsequent progression to AD (Petersen, 2001).

Table 5.3 Cox proportional hazards analyses of the presence of the apolipoprotein E (APOE) ε4 genotype, learning (CVLT Trials 1–5 Total Recall), and delayed recall (CVLT Long Delay Free Recall; Cued Recall Intusions) measures in the prediction of progression to Alzheimer's disease among initially nondemented older adults

BASELINE VARIABLE	RISK RATIO (95% CI)	OVERALL MODEL χ^2	P-VALUE
1st Model–Learning		24.1	p < .001
APOE ε4 Carrier	7.65 (0.87–67.4)		
CVLT List A Trials 1–5 Total Recall	5.18 (1.55–17.3) [a]		
2nd Model–Memory		26.2	p < .001
APOE ε4 Carrier	6.19 (0.60–63.9)		
CVLT Long Delay Free Recall	3.37 (1.15–9.88)		
CVLT Cued Recall Intrusions	2.90 (1.10–7.64)		

[a] Odds ratio represents relative risk of progression to disease over the follow-up period per SD decline independent of other variables in the model. CVLT = California Verbal Learning Test (Delis, Kramer, Kaplan & Ober, 1987). CI = confidence interval.

We would also note that the early appearance of known declines in episodic memory in preclinical AD is not well reflected in the much-publicized hypothetical curve of preclinical AD changes presented by Jack et al. (2010) (see Figure 1.5, Chapter 1); rather, the figure suggests a late appearance of cognitive changes in AD, well after neuroimaging changes and just prior to demonstrable functional declines. This proposed late staging of the cognitive declines of AD would appear to ignore this large body of literature on preclinical episodic memory changes and its predictive power for the development of AD some years later. Despite the hot pursuit for imaging and biomarkers of the dementia prodrome, cognitive variables at baseline—and especially episodic memory measures of delayed free recall—remain among the best predictors of progression and often outperform other biomarkers in the preclinical period (See Table 5.4, for summary of recent studies).

Table 5.4 Summary of three studies from the Alzheimer's Disease Neuroimaging Initiative that compared the utility of similar biomarkers and neuropsychological measures, and their combinations, to predict progression from mild cognitive impairment to Alzheimer's disease. Average follow-up periods for examination of progression to AD ranged from 2 to 3 years

STUDY	VARIABLES	HAZARD RATIOS	ROC ANALYSES (OVERALL ACCURACY, %; AUC = AREA UNDER CURVE)	SIGNIFICANCE
		Odds Ratio/ΔR^2	AUC	
(Gomar et al., 2011)	Logical Memory delay	1.01/.06	0.80	<.001
	Rey AVLT delay	0.80/.04	0.80	<.001
	Middle temporal lobe volume	0.02/.18	0.77	<.001
	CSF: t-tau/$A\beta_{1-42}$ ratio	0.03/.11	0.64	<.001
	Best combination	− /.34	0.80	<.001
	(LM + MTL + AVLT)	(.18 + .10 + .06)		
(Heister et al., 2011)	Rey AVLT total learning	4.1	0.97	<.001
	CSF: p-tau/$A\beta_{1-42}$ ratio	3.8	0.85	<.001
	CSF: t-tau/$A\beta_{1-42}$ ratio	4.1	0.85	<.001
	Hippocampal occupancy (HOC)	3.9	0.91	<.001
	Hippocampal volume	2.3	0.90	<.001
	Best Combination	29.0		
	(Rey AVLT + HOC atrophy)			

Table 5.4 (Continued)

STUDY	VARIABLES	HAZARD RATIOS	ROC ANALYSES (OVERALL ACCURACY, %; AUC = AREA UNDER CURVE)	SIGNIFICANCE
(Landau et al., 2010)	Rey AVLT total learning	4.68	90%	.01/.01
	CSF: p-tau/Aβ_{1-42} ratio	3.99	78%	.03/.01
	CSF: t-tau/Aβ_{1-42} ratio	ns	81%	ns/ns
	FDG-PET	2.94	76%	.02/.04
	Hippocampal volume	2.49	81%	.04/.06
	Best Combination (Rey AVLT + FDG-PET)	11.7		

AVLT = Auditory Verbal Learning Test; CSF = cerebrospinal fluid; t-tau = total tau; p-tau = hyperphosphorylated tau; Aβ = amyloid beta 1–42 fragments; HOC = hippocampal occupancy score, ratio of hippocampal volume to hippocampal volume plus volume of the inferior lateral ventricle; hippocampal volume = hippocampal volume as a percent of intracranial volume; FDG-PET = [^{18}F]fluorodeoxyglucose position emission tomography (measure of glucose metabolism)

The importance of episodic memory in predicting the development of dementia was also highlighted in a recent study by Jedynak et al. (2012). This ADNI-based study examined healthy older adults, MCI, and AD patients and computed an *Alzheimer's disease progression score* that standardized individual subject timelines of expected disease onset and progression onto a common temporal scale. The points at which various CSF biomarkers, imaging indices and cognitive measures changed during the course of progression were compared. The order of biomarker dynamic changes proposed by Jack et al. (2010) was reproduced, with the important exception that change in the 30-minute delayed free recall measure of the *Rey Auditory Verbal Learning Test* significantly preceded all other biomarkers, including hippocampal volumes, CSF markers of Aβ and tau, and other cognitive measures (see Figure 5.5). In fact, the MMSE, CDR Sum of Boxes, and ADAS cognitive subscale were the least sensitive markers, confirming that they are poor choices for the diagnostician interested in detecting the earliest cognitive manifestations of Alzheimer's disease.

Few studies systematically examined the course of episodic memory changes during the preclinical phase of the disease, despite strong evidence of subtle memory decline prior to the development of the dementia of AD (Bondi et al. 1999; Bäckman et al., 2001; Chen et al., 2001; Lange et al., 2002b; Rubin et al., 1998; Small, Nava, Perera, Delapaz, & Stern, 2000). In two representative studies that have addressed this issue, Small et al. (2000) and Bäckman et al. (2001) examined longitudinal changes in episodic memory in older

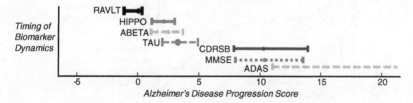

FIGURE 5.5 Timing of a number of biomarkers at the threshold point from 'normal' to 'abnormal' dynamic change as a function of disease progression. Note that the RAVLT measure significantly precedes all other biomarkers, connoting its value in the preclinical detection of Alzheimer's disease. Bars represent the 90% confidence intervals for the inflection point of each biomarker. RAVLT = 30-minute delayed free recall from the Rey Auditory Verbal Learning Test; ABETA = cerebrospinal fluid (CSF) Aβ$_{42}$ concentration; TAU = CSF tau concentration; HIPPO = hippocampal volume; CDRSB = Clinical Dementia Rating Sum of Boxes score; MMSE = Mini-Mental State Exam; ADAS = Alzheimer's Disease Assessment Scale – Cognitive subscale. Adapted from Jedynak et al. (2012) with permission.

adults who eventually developed AD and found they had mild impairment of episodic memory at an evaluation 6 years prior to diagnosis but little change in memory performance over the next 3 years. Their studies suggested that this long period of lowered but stable memory capacity in individuals with preclinical AD is followed by a relatively precipitous decline in the period immediately preceding the development of overt dementia. Consistent with this notion, Chen et al. (2001) found a significant decline in episodic memory and executive functions in individuals with preclinical AD during the period from 3.5 years to 1.5 years prior to diagnosis and, Lange et al. (2002b) demonstrated a precipitous decline in episodic memory 1 to 2 years prior to the onset of the dementia syndrome. Cerhan et al. (2007) found that at 4 years prior to onset of symptoms, persons that progressed to AD had lower learning and retention scores. In contrast to matched control participants, these incipient AD cases showed further decline in learning at follow-up 1.5 years prior to symptom onset, but they did not show a further significant decline in retention. Interestingly, whereas the incipient AD cases did not show poor verbal comprehension (VC) performance at 4 years prior to onset, they did show a decline in subsequent VC score in contrast to the matched normal group who showed, on average, an improvement (practice effect) at follow-up testing. Figure 5.6 depicts a hypothetical model of episodic memory function and decline in the preclinical phase of AD.

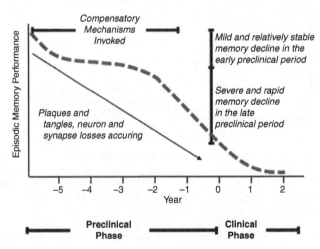

FIGURE 5.6 Proposed model of episodic memory decline (Twamley, Ropacki, & Bondi, 2006). Reprinted with permission.

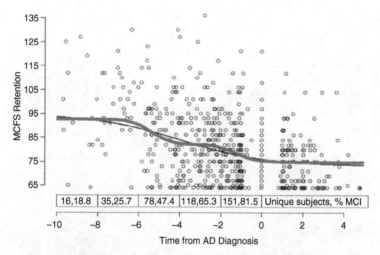

FIGURE 5.7 Mixed effects model of memory (RET) Decline in the 10 Years Prior to
Alzheimer's Disease diagnosis.
(Smith et al., 2007). Reproduced with permission.

Smith et al. (2007) sought to test whether a plateau model (depicted in
Figure 5.6 above) or a monotonic model of decline (depicted in Figure 4.3,
Chapter 4) better fit the longitudinal course of decline in episodic memory
in a cohort of 199 persons followed from normal or MCI status to clinically
probable AD. Modeling revealed that the plateau model did in fact better
fit the data for delayed percent retention (see Figure 5.7) but not for other
cognitive domains, including verbal comprehension, perceptual organization,
attention/concentration, and learning (see Figure 5.8 a–d).

Language and Semantic Knowledge

As the neuropathology of AD spreads beyond the medial temporal lobes to
adjacent lateral temporal cortex, patients with AD often develop a semantic memory deficit that is characterized by a loss of general knowledge and
impairment of language abilities. The meta-analytic work by Henry, Crawford,
and Phillips (2004) confirmed that AD patients exhibit a more pronounced
impairment on category fluency than letter fluency, again suggesting a breakdown in semantic knowledge or at least in its successful access to semantic information in AD (Henry, Crawford, & Phillips, 2004). This conclusion
is supported by the observation that AD patients also exhibit a differential
impairment on another common test of semantic knowledge, the Boston

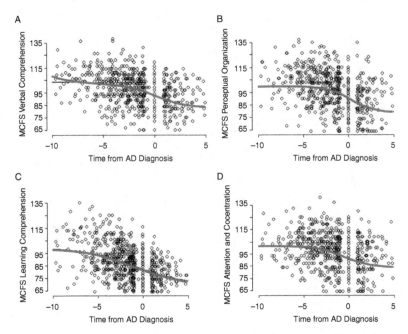

FIGURE 5.8 Mixed effect models: Other mayo cognitive factor Scores. (A) Verbal comprehension. (B) Perceptual Organization. (C) Learning. (D) Attention and Concentration.
(Smith et al., 2007). Reprinted with Permission.

Naming Test (BNT; Kaplan, et al., 1983), and dissociations in the language abilities of patients with cortical and subcortical dementia syndromes are apparent on tests of object naming. Numerous studies show that AD patients have a significant naming impairment that is not equaled by patients with Huntington's disease (Hodges, Salmon, & Butters, 1991) and examination of the naming errors on the BNT has shown that AD patients make more semantic errors such as a superordinate naming error (e.g., naming a pelican a "bird" or an "animal") and HD patients make more perceptually based (e.g., naming a stalk of asparagus a "pencil") or coordinate (e.g., naming an acorn a "peanut") errors. The tendency of AD patients to make semantically based errors is consistent with a disruption of the structure and organization of semantic knowledge that may arise from damage to the lateral temporal lobes, as well as to cortical association areas in the temporal, parietal, and frontal lobes (Salmon & Filoteo, 2007). Such losses in semantic knowledge, or in its organization, do not occur in the subcortical dementia syndrome exhibited by patients with HD. In addition, subcortical dementia patients appear to benefit more from phonemic cues because the cues help to obviate some of their word retrieval difficulties.

That said, Testa, Ivnik, and Smith, (2003) have noted that, although early AD patients may have confrontation naming deficits, they are neither necessary nor sufficient findings for the diagnosis of early AD. Nonetheless, naming impairments are common in moderate to severe AD and impart important functional limitations at these stages. Verbal comprehension skills are typically thought to be spared early in the course of the disease. Powell et al. (2006) showed that, after memory retention scores, initial evaluation verbal comprehension scores were most useful in predicting findings of AD at autopsy. This observation occurred in spite of the fact that most autopsy-confirmed AD cases in the cohort had initial scores within the normal range. It appears that low normal VC scores add to retention values in identifying early AD. The VC scores are more powerful than initial perceptual organization, attention, or learning index scores in making this prediction.

Verbal Fluency

As noted, there appear to be early changes in category fluency that may represent a breakdown of semantic networks (Monsch et al., 1994). In a meta-analysis of 153 studies involving nearly 16,000 participants, Henry, Crawford, and Phillips (2004) observe:

> DAT patients were significantly more impaired on tests of semantic relative to phonemic fluency ($r = 0.73$ and 0.57, respectively) ... confrontation naming, a measure of semantic memory that imposes only minimal demands upon effortful retrieval was significantly more impaired than phonemic fluency ($r = 0.60$ versus 0.55, respectively). However, since semantic fluency was also significantly more impaired than confrontation naming ($r = 0.73$ versus 0.61), deficits in semantic memory and effortful retrieval may be additive. Semantic, but not phonemic, fluency was significantly more impaired than measures of verbal intelligence and psychomotor speed. Thus, the semantic memory deficit in DAT qualifies as a differential deficit, but executive dysfunction as indexed by phonemic fluency does not constitute an additional isolated feature of the disorder. (p. 1212)

The differential sensitivity of various language tasks noted by Henry et al. (e.g., category fluency < naming < letter fluency) was also demonstrated in a study by Mickes and colleagues (2007), who examined the

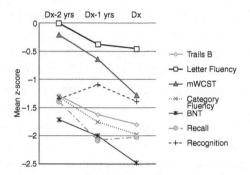

FIGURE 5.9 Mean z-scores (relative to normal control subjects) on measures of episodic memory, semantic memory, and executive functions in initially normal older adults who cognitively declined from 2 years prior to a change in diagnosis (Dx–2 yrs), to 1 year prior to diagnosis (Dx–1 r), to the year of change in diagnosis (Dx). All progressed to probable Alzheimer's disease diagnoses at this latter year or thereafter.
Adapted from Mickes et al. (2007).

degree to which various cognitive functions are impaired and the speed with which they decline during the preclinical period (Henry et al., 2004; Mickes et al., 2007). The results of detailed neuropsychological evaluations of initially normal older adults who went on to develop AD dementia were retrospectively examined. Tasks were divided into three cognitive domains: (1) episodic memory (recall and recognition tasks), (2) semantic memory (BNT and category fluency), and (3) executive functions (perseverative errors on Wisconsin Card Sorting Test, Trails A and B, and letter fluency). Evaluations over the course of 3 years were examined up to and including the first year of a nonnormal diagnosis (e.g., MCI or probable AD, although all developed probable AD). As shown in Figure 5.9, performance falls off rapidly in all three areas of cognition prior to the time a diagnosis of MCI or dementia can be made, but abilities thought to be mediated by the medial and lateral temporal lobes (episodic and semantic memory, respectively) appear to be substantially more impaired than those thought to be dependent on the frontal lobes (executive function). Therefore, the findings concur with the possibility that category fluency and naming decline prior to letter fluency. It is also of note that the work of Henry et al. (2004) and that of Mickes et al. (2007) both conceptualized category fluency as a measure of semantic memory whereas letter fluency was conceptualized as one of executive function. Many other studies, however, will place both fluency measures within a single domain and not separate them into different cognitive domains, so it is important to be aware of these differences when comparing studies.

Executive Functions

While the Henry et al. (2004) meta-analysis argues that executive function as indexed by letter fluency is not an early feature of AD, other measures of (other aspects of) executive function do appear to be impacted early. Salmon and Bondi (2009) note early impairments in cognitive processes involved in "concurrent mental manipulation of information, concept formation, problem solving, and cue-directed behavior" (pp. 259–260). These deficits are expected from the relatively early encroachment of tangle pathology on to frontal association areas. Executive dysfunction has been consistently noted in early AD (Albert et al., 2001; Bäckman, Jones, Berger, Laukka, & Small, 2005; Chen et al., 2001; Dickerson, Sperling, Hyman, Albert, & Blacker, 2007; Bisiacchi, Borella, Bergamaschi, Carretti, & Mondini, 2008) and may even be evident in prodromal stages. Consistent with this possibility, many studies have shown that poor performance on episodic memory and executive function measures in nondemented elderly predicts cognitive decline and progression to AD over as many as 6 years (Albert et al., 2001; Bäckman, et al., 2005; M. W. Bondi, Salmon, Galasko, Thomas, & Thal, 1999; Chen et al., 2001; Fine et al., 2008; Lange et al., 2002a). As such, decrements in executive function, particularly on complex tasks, may be evident in prodromal AD and signal future global cognitive decline.

Deficits in executive functions are evident in MCI as well, particularly since the advent of the subtyping diagnostic schemes and among studies that formally assessed other cognitive functions, and such deficits have also been shown to be predictive of progression to AD in individuals with MCI. Due to the heterogeneous nature of MCI, it is difficult to predict which individuals with MCI will eventually progress to AD. Studies comparing the development of dementia across subtypes of MCI suggest that consideration of executive functions, or the relationship between episodic memory and executive function, may increase the accuracy of these predictions. Consistent with that notion are studies showing progression rates to AD to be higher for MCI patients with deficits in multiple cognitive domains than for those with isolated memory impairments (Ganguli, Snitz, Saxton, et al., 2011; Mitchell & Shiri-Feshki, 2009; Tabert et al., 2006). For example, one study by Tabert et al. (2006) found that the combined predictive accuracy of deficits in verbal memory and executive function, for progression from MCI to AD over three years, was 86%, a level higher than any other potential cognitive predictors. A similar study by Chapman et al. (2010) found that the combination of memory and speeded executive function measures was the strongest predictor of progression to AD.

In another study, Clark et al. (2012) found that performance on select executive function measures was useful in discriminating nondemented older adults with subsequent global cognitive decline (as measured by Reliable Change Indices from the Dementia Rating Scale; Pedraza et al., 2007) from those who remained cognitively stable. The decline and no-decline groups did not differ on demographic characteristics or on allele frequencies for the AD susceptibility gene (i.e., APOE), nor on total DRS scores in the year prior to decline. However, when controlling for important covariates including age and education, the decline group demonstrated poorer executive function performance in the year prior to global cognitive decline, particularly on measures with inhibitory or semantic processing demands such as D-KEFS Color-Word Interference Test (CWIT), Inhibition/Switching and Verbal Fluency/Switching subtests. Furthermore, the CWIT measure significantly improved the prediction of decline, independently of learning and memory measures. These results are similar to previous findings that switching or shifting between sets of items or different tasks is impaired in older adults with MCI (Brandt et al., 2009; Schmitter-Edgecombe, Woo, & Greeley, 2009; Traykov et al., 2007) or early AD (Logie, Cocchini, Delia Sala, & Baddeley, 2004) and extend these findings to the prediction of global cognitive decline in a sample of *either* cognitively normal older adults or individuals with MCI.

Another pair of studies by Brandt and colleagues (Brandt et al., 2009; Aretouli, Okonkwo, Samek, & Brandt, 2011) examined no less than 18 different executive function measures across six broad categories (e.g., flexibility, inhibition, planning/sequencing, concept formation/set shifting, decision-making, and working memory) and found three that explained the lion's share of variance in principal components analysis (e.g., planning/problem-solving, working memory, and judgment). They found planning/problem-solving and working memory, but not judgment, to be selectively impaired in MCI, and even patients with "pure" amnestic MCI (the least impaired subgroup overall) displayed major impairments in these two executive domains. Finally, their multiple-domain MCI patients (i.e., those with deficits in at least two domains [of episodic memory, language, and spatial cognition]) had more significant planning/problem-solving and working memory deficits than single-domain patients. In a longitudinal follow-up study, Aretouli et al. (2011) found that three of the individual executive function measures (e.g., the Alternate Uses Test; the Hayling Test, and the Verbal Concept Attainment Test) predicted progression in the MCI sample, but that none of them added to the predictive ability of a model that first considered demographic, other cognitive (delayed recall, category fluency, clock drawing), and ADL variables. The lack of predictive value of executive function over other measures contrasts with a number of other studies (Albert et al., 2001; Clark et al., 2012; Elias et al., 2000), although most of these other studies did not examine the prognostic value of executive functions after first controlling for other factors, with the exception of the Clark et al. (2012) study. In one recent study from our group that examined the morphometric characteristics associated with executive dysfunction in amnestic MCI (Chang et al., 2010), the MCI group with poor executive functioning showed significant cortical thinning in dorsolateral prefrontal and bilateral posterior cingulate cortices compared with MCI patients with intact executive function performances (see Figure 5.10). Clinical outcome

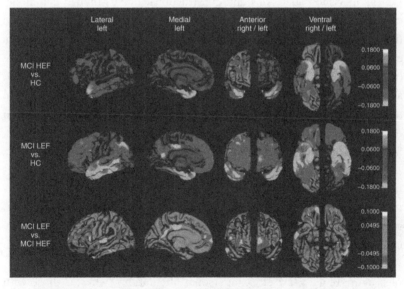

FIGURE 5.10 Average mean differences in cortical thickness (mm) for the 2 MCI groups relative to Healthy Control (top 2 rows) and the MCI LEF group relative to the MCI HEF group (bottom row) are shown on the reconstructed cortical surface, after controlling for the effects of age and gender. Blue and cyan indicate thinning. The MCI LEF group shows more widespread thinning of posterior cingulate as well as frontal and temporal regions. LEF = Low Executive Function; HEF = High Executive Function. Chang et al, 2010. Reproduced with permission.

of the MCI groups one year later was significantly different also, with more than twice the number of low executive functioning MCI patients progressing to AD relative to the high executive functioning MCI patients (26% vs. 11%, respectively).

Collectively, the above findings demonstrate some discrepancies in results across studies regarding the predictive utility of executive function measures, which is not surprising given the vast array of abilities and cognitive processes subsumed under the rubric of executive functions. Nonetheless, the studies are consistent with the notion that impairment of executive function in MCI is not global; only certain higher-order domains appear to be affected. The findings at least suggest that, in addition to episodic and semantic memory performance, executive dysfunction is associated with greater cortical involvement and may add to the prediction of declines in cognitive functioning in subsets of individuals at risk for progression to dementia.

Visuospatial Skills

Deficits in visuospatial skills and constructional praxis, though commonly observed in Alzheimer's disease, tend to emerge later in the course of the disease (e.g., Locascio, Growdon, & Corkin, 1995) and do not appear to be evident in the preclinical stages or among MCI patients. A few studies have begun to show evidence for relatively subtle visual processing difficulties in amnestic MCI. Some of these studies have found increased latencies on visual tasks (Bonney et al., 2006; Bublak et al., 2011), and another has shown an impaired ability of amnestic MCI patients to detect visual motion (Mapstone, Steffenella, & Duffy, 2003)

Although visuospatial deficits are observed in both cortical and subcortical dementias, few studies have directly contrasted the types of dementing disorders on tests of visuospatial functions. Among the few that have, some interesting distinctions have been demonstrated. An early study by (Brouwers, Cox, Martin, Chase, & Fedio, 1984) found that patients with AD, but not those with HD, were impaired in their ability to copy a complex figure (e.g., a test of extrapersonal orientation), whereas those with HD, but not AD, were impaired on the Money Road Map Test (e.g., a test of personal orientation). In another study, Lineweaver, Salmon, Bondi, & Corey-Bloom, (2005) examined the ability of AD and HD patients to mentally rotate representations of objects. They found that HD patients were significantly slower, but just as accurate as normal control subjects in making the necessary rotations to get the items correct, whereas the AD patients were just as quick as normal control subjects, but were not accurate in the rotation task. The impaired ability of AD patients to perform mental rotation may reflect a deficit in extrapersonal visual orientation due to damage or dysfunction in brain regions involved in processing visual motion (e.g., middle temporal gyrus; see Salmon & Filoteo, 2007, for discussion). Another study by Festa et al. (2005) demonstrated dissociations between AD and HD on a visual sensory integration task, such that AD patients had a unique difficulty binding motion and color information. Motion and color information is thought to rely on distinct cortical visual processing pathways (i.e., the dorsal visual stream for motion and the ventral visual stream for color), and the difficulty of AD patients to bind these two features is interpreted to reflect a loss of effective interaction between these distinct neocortical regions.

Distinctions between cortical and subcortical dementia syndromes have been observed on tests of clock drawing. Rouleau, Salmon, Butters, Kennedy, and McGuire (1992) showed that qualitative distinctions were evident in the clock drawings of AD and HD patients. HD patients tended to produce graphic, visuospatial, or planning errors in the command and copy conditions, whereas patients with AD tended to make conceptual errors. Examples of conceptually based errors included misrepresenting the clock by drawing a face without numbers or with an incorrect use of numbers, misrepresenting the time by failing to include the hands, incorrectly setting the time when using the hands (often with a stimulus bound component such that the hands are drawn to the 10 and 11 to represent "10 after 11"), or writing the time in the clock face. These errors also were shown to occur in the command condition but not the copy condition. What these performance distinctions call attention to is the disparate processing deficits in the cortical and subcortical dementia syndromes. That is, HD appears to manifest planning and motor deficits that accompany disruptions of frontal-subcortical circuits, whereas AD reflects a deficit in accessing knowledge of the attributes, features, and meaning of a clock.

Finally, there also exists so-called visual variant-AD, also known as posterior cortical atrophy (PCA). While a variety of pathologies are seen in PCA, the predominant pathology is plaque and tangle disease, that is, AD (Tang-Wai et al., 2004), but may also occur in the context of the neuropathologic changes of Lewy body dementia or Creutzfeld-Jacob disease (Renner et al., 2004). Autopsy studies show greater atrophy and lesion pathology in posterior parietal and occipital cortices (Renner et al., 2004) and imaging has shown PET hypometabolism in these same posterior cortical regions, with particular involvement of the dorsal visual processing stream (Nestor, Caine, Fryer, Clarke, & Hodges, 2003) as well as a disproportional posterior cortical distribution of amyloid binding (Tenovuo, Kemppainen, Aalto, Nagren, & Rinne, 2008). Neuropsychologically, PCA patients have prominent deficits in tasks requiring visual processing including reading, writing, and object naming (McMonagle, Deering, Berliner, & Kertesz, 2006).

Salmon (2011) discusses the interesting possibility that PCA could be conceptualized as a form of single domain MCI because memory, language, and judgment and insight are relatively preserved until the late stages of disease. Patients with PCA usually have prominent visual agnosia (sometimes including prosopagnosia) and constructional apraxia, and exhibit many or all of the features of Balint's syndrome including optic ataxia, gaze apraxia, and simultanagnosia (i.e., they can detect visual details of an object but cannot organize them into a meaningful whole). They may also exhibit components of Gerstmann's syndrome including acalculia, right-left disorientation, finger agnosia, and agraphia (Renner et al., 2004; Tang-Wai et al., 2004). A visual field defect, decreased visual attention, impaired color perception, or decreased contrast sensitivity may also occur (Della Sala, Kinnear, Spinnler, & Stangalino, 1996)

Visual and Verbal Asymmetries

Although the episodic memory decline described above appears to be one of the most salient markers of preclinical AD, a study by Jacobson and colleagues (2002) suggests that mild asymmetric cognitive decline may also detect preclinical AD. In this case-control study, Jacobson et al. (2002) demonstrated that the initial presentation of cognitive deficits in AD may have asymmetrical involvement as a common feature (i.e., language decrements significantly greater than visuospatial decrements, or vice versa). Despite both groups showing similar mean scores on tests of memory, language, and visuospatial ability, the absolute difference between verbal (Boston Naming Test) and visuospatial (Block Design) scores was significantly greater in the preclinical AD group. The preclinical AD group showed significantly larger discrepancies in performance between naming and visuoconstructive skills relative to matched control participants, and a higher frequency of asymmetric cognitive profiles compared to a larger normative group. These results suggest that there is a subgroup of patients with preclinical AD who have asymmetric cognitive decline that may be obscured when cognitive scores are averaged over the entire group.

Although the neuropsychologic mechanism underlying cognitive asymmetry in preclinical AD remains unknown, the findings are consistent with a number of reports of lateralized onset with asymmetric neuroanatomic changes (Franceschi et al., 1995; Giannakopoulos, Hof, & Bouras, 1994; Thompson et al., 1998) or metabolic asymmetry in the early presentation of AD in a subset of patients (Grady et al., 1990; Reiman et al., 1996; Soininen et al., 1995; Soininen et al., 1994). Others studies have also shown that these cognitive asymmetries may be associated in part with APOE genotype in AD (Finton et al., 1998), as well as in nondemented groups (Houston et al., 2005; Jacobson, Delis, Bondi, & Salmon, 2005).

Neuropsychological Changes at Later Stages of AD

As AD progresses deficits accumulate to extend beyond those in episodic learning and memory, loss of semantic knowledge, and executive dysfunction. Deterioration in language skills (e.g., anomia, paraphasias), visuospatial impairments (e.g., clock drawing, visuoconstructional skills), apraxia, and more basic attention deficits appear. AD patients can exhibit agnosia and often demonstrate a general under awareness of their cognitive problems, termed anosognosia.

Interventions

Nonpharmacological Interventions for Cognitive and Functional Symptoms

An early review of research into memory rehabilitation in AD primarily focused on *memory building* techniques with mixed results of effectiveness (Clare et al., 2003). A meta-analysis of cognitive training, broadly defined, in AD showed an overall moderate effect size (d = 0.47) (Sitzer, Twamley, & Jeste, 2006). Mean effect size for restorative techniques (d = 0.54) was not statistically different from the mean effect size for compensatory techniques (d = 0.36). There was also no statistical difference between studies comparing cognitive training to a wait-list control group or to an attention-control placebo group. Two of the largest effect sizes were for informant-based ratings of cognitive problems in restorative (d = 0.95) or compensatory (d = 0.68) cognitive training (Sitzer et al., 2006). It is noted that most of the exploration of *memory compensation* aids in AD have focused on using notebooks and calendars as a way of orienting significantly impaired individuals to date, basic schedules, and personal information with some success (Loewenstein, Acevedo, Czaja, & Duara, 2004). A recent, mixed rehabilitation approach demonstrated that individuals with MCI, but not early AD, showed improvements in mood, memory, and functional abilities (Kurz, Pohl, Ramsenthaler, & Sorg, 2009). This speaks to the importance of early, or indeed preclinical, diagnosis as discussed in Chapter 4.

Pharmacological Interventions for Cognitive and Functional Symptoms

Two classes of drugs are currently approved by the FDA for treatment of cognitive symptoms of AD. The first of these are the cholinesterase inhibitors. These drugs were developed based on the now out-of-fashion choline hypothesis describe previously. The three cholinesterase inhibitors commonly prescribed in the United States are donepezil (Aricept), galantamine (Razadyne), and rivastigmine (Exelon). Cochrane Reviews (Birks, 2006) note that

> The results of 10 randomized, double blind, placebo controlled trials demonstrate that treatment for 6 months, with donepezil, galantamine or rivastigmine, at the recommended dose for people with mild, moderate, or severe dementia due to Alzheimer's disease, produced improvements in cognitive function, on average, -2.7 points (95% CI -3.0 to -2.3, p < 0.00001), in the mid-range of the 70-point ADAS-Cog Scale. Study clinicians rated global clinical state more positively in treated patients. Benefits of treatment were also seen on measures of activities of daily living and behavior. None of these treatment effects are large. The main side effects noted for these drugs include diarrhea, nausea and vomiting.

Of note, Cochrane Reviews does not support the use of cholinesterase inhibitors with MCI.

The second class is the glutamate antagonist medications with only memantine (Namenda) FDA-approved for AD. FDA approval is currently for memantine use in combination with a cholinesterase inhibitor. Pooled data suggests that relative to placebo, memantine contributes to retention of less than 1 point the ADAS-Cog over six months of dosing. Memantine's most common side effect is dizziness (McShane, Areosa Sastre, & Minakaran, 2006).

Nonpharmacologic Approaches for Behavioral Symptoms

As noted above, behavioral disturbance is common in Alzheimer's disease. A pervasive problem with the literature on the management of behavioral symptoms is the poor nomenclature and assessment of the root causes of disruptive behavioral symptoms. Nonpharmacologic approaches to disruptive behaviors are often cited as the first-line treatment choice. Descriptions regarding how to proceed with these approaches are limited. In Chapter 10, we will discuss behavioral approaches to managing disruptive behavior within a framework that is not etiologically specific. For now, we will simply acknowledge that major clusters of disruptive behavioral symptoms include classic mood disorders of depression, mania, anxiety, and "agitated" behavior.

Medication Approaches for Behavioral Symptoms
Depression/Mania/Anxiety

Clinically significant depression is present in 20%–30% of Alzheimer's patients cross-sectionally. Mood disorders in AD appear to respond to standard treatments including antidepressant, mood stabilizing, and anxiolytic medications. Use of benzodiazepine anxiolytics, however, are associated with further impairments in cognition and falls (Hartikainen & Lonnroos, 2010).

Agitated Behavior

The large scale Clinical Antipsychotic Trials of Intervention Effectiveness—Alzheimer's Disease (CATIE-AD) study demonstrated modest and selective efficacy for the atypical antipsychotics in treating agitated behavior in AD. However, meta-analyses have suggested that treatment with these agents is associated with increased risk for cerebrovascular events and death. This led Cochrane Reviews to state:

> Evidence suggests that risperidone and olanzapine are useful in reducing aggression and risperidone reduces psychosis, but both are associated with serious adverse cerebrovascular events and extrapyramidal symptoms. Despite the modest efficacy, the significant increase in adverse events confirms that neither risperidone nor olanzapine should be used routinely to treat dementia patients with aggression or psychosis unless there is severe distress or risk of physical harm to those living and working with the patient. (Ballard, Waite, & Birks, 2006)

Although insufficient data were available from the considered trials, a meta-analysis of seventeen placebo controlled trials of atypical neuroleptics for the treatment of behavioral symptoms in people with dementia, conducted by the Food and Drug Administration, suggested a significant increase in mortality (OR 1.7). A peer-reviewed meta-analysis (Schneider, Dagerman, & Insel, 2005) of 15 placebo controlled studies (nine unpublished) found similarly increased risk in mortality (OR = 1.54, 95% CI 0.004 to 0.02, p = 0.01) for the atypical neuroleptics. The FDA has now placed a "black box" warning on atypical neuroleptics regarding their use in dementia.

Conclusion

Alzheimer's disease is the most common form of dementia, with a prevalence ranging from about 0.5% for those 60–64 years of age to about 25% of those over age 90. Current theories suggest it arises from the misprocessing of beta-amyloid that generates plaque formation, which is neurotoxic. Mesial temporal and frontal brain regions are especially sensitive, producing the earliest neurofibrillary tangle accumulations. This anatomical specificity helps explain the early episodic and semantic memory and executive function deficits observed in AD. Alzheimer's disease is also associated with a variety of behavioral disturbances that are as variable as the people affected. Current FDA approved therapies based on the cholinergic deficit hypothesis are not particularly effective. "Treatment" at this time continues to involve primarily symptom management and caregiver education and support. Prevention models are more likely to impact AD morbidity than are treatment models once dementia is present.

References

Albert, M., DeKosky, S., Dickson, D., Dubois, B., Feldman, H., Fox, N., & Phelps, C. (2011). The diagnosis of mild cognitive impairment due to Alzheimer's disease: Recommendations from the National Institute on Aging-Alzheimer's Association workgroups on diagnostic guidelines for Alzheimer's disease. *Alzheimer's and Dementia, 7*(3),

Albert, M., & Killiany, R. (2001). Age-related cognitive change and brain-behavior relationships. In J. Birren (Ed.), *Handbook of the psychology of aging* (5th ed., pp. 161–185). San Diego, CA: Academic Press.

Albert, M., Moss, M., Tanzi, R., & Jones, K. (2001). Preclinical prediction of AD using neuropsychological tests. *Journal of the International Neuropsychological Society, 7*, 631–639.

Alzheimer's Association. (2003). Statistics: About Alzheimer's disease, 2003. http://www.alz.org/AboutAD/overview.htm

Alzheimer's Association. (2011a). 2011 Alzheimer's disease facts and figures. Retrieved December 30, 2011, from http://www.alz.org/alzheimers_disease_facts_figures.asp

Alzheimer's Association. (2011b). Guidelines for the Neuropathologic Assessment of Alzheimer's Disease: Proposed Recommendations from the National Institute on Aging and the Alzheimer's Association Workgroup. Retrieved December 31, 2011.

Aretouli, E., Okonkwo, O. C., Samek, J., & Brandt, J. (2011). The fate of the 0.5s: Predictors of 2-year outcome in mild cognitive impairment. *Journal of the International Neuropsychological Society, 17*(2), 277–288.

Arvanitakis, Z., Leurgans, S., Wang, Z., et al. (2011). Cerebral amyloid angiopathy pathology and cognitive domains in older persons. *Annals of Neurology, 69*, 320–327.

Bäckman, L., Jones, S., Berger, A., Laukka, E., & Small, B. (2005). Cognitive impairment in preclinical Alzheimer's disease: A meta-analysis. *Neuropsychology, 19*(4), 520–531.

Bäckman, L., Small, B., & Fratiglioni, L. (2001). Stability of the preclinical episodic memory deficit in Alzheimer's disease. *Brain, 124*, 96–102.

Baker, L. D., Cross, D. J., Minoshima, S., Belongia, D., Watson, G. S., & Craft, S. (2011). Insulin resistance and Alzheimer-like reductions in regional cerebral glucose metabolism for cognitively normal adults with prediabetes or early type 2 diabetes. *Archives of Neurology, 68*(1), 51–57.

Ballard, C., Waite, J., & Birks, J. (2006). Atypical antipsychotics for aggression and psychosis in Alzheimer's disease. *Cochrane Database of Systematic Reviews.*

Beard, C., Kokmen, E., Sigler, C., Smith, G., Petterson, T., & O'Brien, P. (1996). Cause of death in Alzheimer's disease. *Annals of Epidemiology, 6*(3), 195–200.

Bell, R. D., Winkler, E. A., Singh, I., Sagare, A. P., Deane, R., Wu, Z., … Zlokovic, B. V . (2012). Apolipoprotein E controls cerebrovascular integrity via cyclophilin A. *Nature,*

Bennett, D., Wilson, R., Schneider, J., Evans, D., Aggarwal, N., Arnold, S., & Bienias, J. (2003). Apolipoprotein E epsilon4 allele, AD pathology, and the clinical expression of Alzheimer's disease. *Neurology, 60*(2), 246–252.

Benton, A., & Hamsher, K. (1978). *Multilingual aphasia examination: Manual.* Iowa City: University of Iowa.

Birks, J. (2006). Cholinesterase inhibitors for Alzheimer's disease. *Cochrane Database of Systematic Reviews* (1), CD005593.

Bisiacchi, P. S., Borella, E., Bergamaschi, S., Carretti, B., & Mondini, S. (2008). Interplay between memory and executive functions in normal and pathological aging. *Journal of Clinical and Experimental Neuropsychology, 30*(6), 723–733.

Bondi, M., Goldin, P., Eyler Zorrilla, L., Lange, K. L., & Brown, G. (2002). Novel picture learning in nondemented older adult at genetic risk for Alzheimer's disease: A functional MRI study (abstract). *Neurobiology of Aging, 23,* S359.

Bondi, M., Monsch, A., Galasko, D., Butters, N., Salmon, D., & Delis, D. (1994). Preclinical cognitive markers of dementia of the Alzheimer type. *Neuropsychology, 8,* 374–384.

Bondi, M., Salmon, D., Galasko, D., Thomas, R., & Thal, L. (1999). Neuropsychological function and apolipoprotein E genotype in the preclinical detection of Alzheimer's disease. *Psychology and Aging, 14,* 295–303.

Bondi, M., Salmon, D., Monsch, A., Galasko, D., Butters, N., Klauber, M., Saitoh, T. (1995). Episodic memory changes are associated with the APOE-e4 allele in nondemented older adults. *Neurology, 45,* 2203–2206.

Bondi, M. W., Salmon, D. P., Galasko, D., Thomas, R. G., & Thal, L. J. (1999). Neuropsychological function and apolipoprotein E genotype in the preclinical detection of Alzheimer's disease. *Psychology and Aging, 14*(2), 295–303.

Bondi, M.W., Houston, W.S., Eyler, L.T., & Brown, G.G. (2005). FMRI evidence of compensatory mechanisms in older adults at genetic risk for Alzheimer's disease. *Neurology, 64,* 501–508

Bonney, K. R., Almeida, O. P., Flicker, L., Davies, S., Clarnette, R., Anderson, M., & Lautenschlager, N. T. (2006). Inspection time in non-demented older adults with mild cognitive impairment.. *Neuropsychologia, 44*(8), 1452–1456.

Bookheimer, S., Strojwas, M., Cohen, M., Saunders, A., Pericak-Vance, M., Mazziotta, J., & Small, G. (2000). Patterns of brain activation in people at risk for Alzheimer's disease. *New England Journal of Medicine, 343,* 450–456.

Braak, H., & Braak, E. (1991). Neuropathological staging of Alzheimer-related changes. *Acta Neuropathologica, 82,* 239–259.

Brainerd, C. J., Reyna, V. F., Petersen, R. C., Smith, G. E., & Taub, E. S. (2011). Is the apolipoprotein e genotype a biomarker for mild cognitive impairment? Findings from a nationally representative study. *Neuropsychology, 25*(6), 679–689.

Brandt, J., Aretouli, E., Neijstrom, E., Samek, J., Manning, K., Albert, M. S., & Bandeen-Roche, K. (2009). Selectivity of executive function deficits in mild cognitive impairment. *Neuropsychology*, *23*(5), 607–618. d

Brookmeyer, R., Corrada, M., Curriero, F., & Kawas, C. (2002). Survival following a diagnosis of Alzheimer disease. *Archives of Neurology*, *59*(11), 1764–1767.

Brookmeyer, R., Gray, S., & Kawas, C. (1998). Projections of Alzheimer's disease in the United States and the public health impact of delaying disease onset. *American Journal of Public Health*, *88*(9), 1337–11342.

Brookmeyer, R., Johnson, E., Ziegler-Graham, K., & Arrighi, H. M. (2007). Forecasting the global burden of Alzheimer's disease. *Alzheimer's and dementia*, *3*(3), 186–191.

Brouwers, P., Cox, C., Martin, A., Chase, T., & Fedio, P. (1984). Differential perceptual-spatial impairment in Huntington's and Alzheimer's dementias. *Archives of Neurology*, *41*(10), 1073–1076.

Bublak, P., Redel, P., Sorg, C., Kurz, A., Forstl, H., Muller, H. J., & Finke, K. (2011). Staged decline of visual processing capacity in mild cognitive impairment and Alzheimer's disease.. *Neurobiology of Aging*, *32*(7), 1219–1230.

Bunce, D., Kivipelto, M., & Wahlin, A. (2004). Utilization of cognitive support and episodic free recall as a function of Apolipoprotein E and vitamin B12 or folate among adults aged 75 years and older. *Neuropsychology*.

Campion, D., Dumanchin, C., Hannequin, D., Dubois, B., Belliard, S., Puel, M., & Frebourg, T. (1999). Early-onset autosomal dominant Alzheimer disease: Prevalence, genetic heterogeneity, and mutation spectrum.. *American Journal of Human Genetics*, *65*(3), 664–670.

Caselli, R., Graff-Radford, N., Reiman, E., Weaver, A., Osborne, D., Lucas, J., & Thibodeau, S. (1999). Preclinical memory decline in cognitively normal apolipoprotein E-epsilon4 homozygotes. *Neurology*, *53*(1), 201–207.

Caselli, R., Osborne, D., Reiman, E., Hentz, J., Barbieri, C., Saunders, A., & Alexander, G. (2001). Preclinical cognitive decline in late middle-aged asymptomatic apolipoprotein E-e4/4 homozygotes: A replication study. *Journal of the Neurological Sciences*, *189*(1–2), 93–98.

Cerhan, J. H., Ivnik, R. J., Smith, G. E., Machulda, M. M., Boeve, B. F., Knopman, D. S., & Tangalos, E. G. (2007). Alzheimer's disease patients' cognitive status and course years prior to symptom recognition. *Neuropsychology, Development, and Cognition. Section B, Aging, Neuropsychology and Cognition*, *14*(3), 227–235.

Chang, Y. L., Jacobson, M. W., Fennema-Notestine, C., Hagler, D. J., Jr., Jennings, R. G., Dale, A. M., & McEvoy, L. K. (2010). Level of executive function influences verbal memory in amnestic mild cognitive impairment and predicts prefrontal and posterior cingulate thickness. *Cerebral Cortex, 20*(6), 1305–1313.

Chapman, R. M., Mapstone, M., Porsteinsson, A. P., Gardner, M. N., McCrary, J. W., DeGrush, E., Guillily, M. D. (2010). Diagnosis of Alzheimer's disease using neuropsychological testing improved by multivariate analyses. *Journal of Clinical and Experimental Neuropsychology, 32*(8), 793–808.

Chen, P., Ratcliff, G., Belle, S., Cauley, J., DeKosky, S., & Ganguli, M. (2001). Patterns of cognitive decline in presymptomatic Alzheimer disease: A prospective community study. *Archives of General Psychiatry, 58*(9), 853–858.

Clare, L., Woods, R. T., Moniz Cook, E. D., Orrell, M., & Spector, A. (2003). Cognitive rehabilitation and cognitive training for early-stage Alzheimer's disease and vascular dementia. *Cochrane Database of Systematic Reviews* (4), CD003260.

Clark, L., Schiehser, D., Weissberger, G., Salmon, D., Delis, D., & Bondi, M. (2012). Specific measures of executive function predict cognitive decline in older adults. *Journal of the International Neuropsychological Society, 18,* 118–127.

Corder, E., Saunders, A., Strittmatter, W., Schmechel, D., Gaskell, P., Small, W., & Pericak-Vance, M. (1993). Gene dose of apolipoprotein E type 4 allele and the risk of Alzheimer's disease in late onset families. *Science, 261,* 921–923.

Cordonnier, C., & van der Flier, W. M. (2011). Brain microbleeds and Alzheimer's disease: Innocent observation or key player? *Brain, 134*(Pt 2), 335–344.

Craft, S., Baker, L. D., Montine, T. J., Minoshima, S., Watson, G. S., Claxton, A., & Gerton, B. (2011). Intranasal insulin therapy for Alzheimer disease and amnestic mild cognitive impairment: A pilot clinical trial. *Archives of Neurology.*

de la Torre, J. C . (2004). Is Alzheimer's disease a neurodegenerative or a vascular disorder? Data, dogma, and dialectics. *Lancet neurology, 3*(3), 184–190.

DeCarli, C. S. (2006). When two are worse than one: Stroke and Alzheimer disease. *Neurology, 67*(8), 1326–1327.

Delis, D. C., Kramer, J. H., Kaplan, E., & Ober, B. A. (1987). The California Verbal Learning Test. New York: The Psychological Corporation.

Della Sala, S., Kinnear, P., Spinnler, H., & Stangalino, C. (1996). Color-to-Figure Matching in Alzheimer's Disease. *Archives of Clinical Neuropsychology, 15*(7), 571–585.

Dickerson, B., Sperling, R., Hyman, B., Albert, M., & Blacker, D. (2007). Clinical prediction of Alzheimer disease dementia across the spectrum of mild cognitive impairment. *Archives of General Psychiatry, 64*, 1443–1450.

Dore, G., Elias, M., Robbins, M., Elias, P., & Nagy, Z. (2009). Presence of APOE e4 allele modifies the relationship between type 2 diabetes and cognitive performance: The Maine-Syracuse study. *Diabetologia, 52*, 255`–2560.

Elias, M. F., Beiser, A., Wolf, P. A., Au, R., White, R. F., & D'Agostino, R. B. (2000). The preclinical phase of Alzheimer disease: A 22-year prospective study of the Framingham Cohort. *Archives of Neurology, 57*(6), 808–813.

Eppig, J., Wambach, D., Nieves, C., Price, C. C., Lamar, M., Delano-Wood, L., & Libon, D. J. (2011). Dysexecutive functioning in mild cognitive impairment: Derailment in temporal gradients. *Journal of the International Neuropsychological Society*, 1–9.

Ferman, T., Dickson, D., Graff-Radford, N., Arvanitakis, Z., DeLucia, M., Boeve, B., & Brassler, S. (2003). Early onset of visual hallucinations in dementia distinguishes pathologically-confirmed Lewy body disease from AD. *Neurology, 60*(5), A264.

Festa, E. K., Insler, R. Z., Salmon, D. P., Paxton, J., Hamilton, J. M., & Heindel, W. C. (2005). Neocortical disconnectivity disrupts sensory integration in Alzheimer's disease. *Neuropsychology, 19*(6), 728–738.

Fine, E. M., Delis, D. C., Wetter, S. R., Jacobson, M. W., Hamilton, J. M., Peavy, G., & Salmon, D. P. (2008). Identifying the "source" of recognition memory deficits in patients with Huntington's disease or Alzheimer's disease: Evidence from the CVLT-II. *Journal of Clinical and Experimental Neuropsychology, 30*(4), 463–470.

Finton, M., Lucas, J., Smith, G., Ivnik, R., Bohac, D., Waring, S., Graf-Radford, N. (1998). Differences in cognitive phenotypes associated with Apolipoprotein-E genotypes in probable Alzheimer's disease. *Journal of the International Neuropsychological Society*, 4, 35.

Franceschi, M., Alberoni, M., Bressi, S., Canal, N., Comi, G., Fazio, F., & Volonte, M. (1995). Correlations between cognitive impairment, middle cerebral artery flow velocity and cortical glucose metabolism in the early phase of Alzheimer's disease. *Dementia, 6*(1), 32–38.

Fuld, P., Masur, D., Blau, A., Crystal, H., & Aronson, M. (1990). Object-memory evaluation for prospective detection of dementia in normal functioning elderly: Predictive and normative data. *Journal of Clinical and Experimental Neuropsychology, 12*(4), 520–528.

Furey, M. L. (2011). The prominent role of stimulus processing: Cholinergic function and dysfunction in cognition. *Current Opinion in Neurology, 24*, 364–370.

Ganguli, M., Snitz, B., Saxton, J., et al. (2011). Outcomes of mild cognitive impairment by definition: A population study. *Archives of Neurology, 68*, 761–767.

Ghebremedhin, E., Schultz, C., Braak, E., & Braak, H. (1998). High frequency of apolipoprotein E epsilon4 allele in young individuals with very mild Alzheimer's disease-related neurofibrillary changes. *Experimental Neurology, 153*(1), 152–155.

Giannakopoulos, P., Hof, P., & Bouras, C. (1994). Alzheimer's disease with asymmetric atrophy of the cerebral hemispheres: Morphometric analysis of four cases. *Acta Neuropathologica, 88*(5), 440–447.

Gilmor, M., Erickson, J., Varoqui, H., Hersh, L., Bennett, D., Cochran, E., & Levey, A. (1999). Preservation of nucleus basalis neurons containing choline acetyltransferase and the vesicular acetylcholine transporter in the elderly with mild cognitive impairment and early Alzheimer's disease. *Journal of Comparative Neurology, 411*(4), 693–704.

Gomar, J., Bobes-Bascaran, M., Conejero-Goldberg, C., Davies, P., & Goldberg, T., for the Alzheimer's Disease Neuroimaging Initiative. (2011). Utility of combinations of biomarkers, cognitive markers, and risk factors to predict conversion from mild cognitive impairment to Alzheimer disease in the Alzheimer's Disease Neuroimaging Initiative. *Archives of General Psychiatry, 68*, 961–969.

Grady, C., Haxby, J., Schapiro, M., Gonzalez-Aviles, A., Kumar, A., Ball, M., & Rapoport, S. (1990). Subgroups in dementia of the Alzheimer type identified using positron emission tomography. *Journal of Neuropsychiatry and Clinical Neurosciences, 2*(4), 373–384.

Green, R. C., Roberts, J. S., Cupples, L. A., Relkin, N. R., Whitehouse, P. J., Brown, T., & Farrer, L. A. (2009). Disclosure of APOE genotype for risk of Alzheimer's disease. *New England Journal of Medicine, 361*(3), 245–254.

Greenwood, P., Sunderland, T., Friz, J., & Parasuraman, R. (2000). Genetics and visual attention: Selective deficits in healthy adult carriers of the epsilon 4 allele of the apolipoprotein E gene. *Proceedings of the National Academy of Sciences, 97*(21), 11661–11666.

Grober, E., & Kawas, C. (1997). Learning and retention in preclinical and early Alzheimer's disease. *Psychology and Aging, 12*(1), 183–188.

Hardy, J. (2009). The amyloid hypothesis for Alzheimer's disease: A critical reappraisal. *Journal of Neurochemistry, 110*(4), 1129–1134.

Hartikainen, S., & Lonnroos, E. (2010). Systematic review: Use of sedatives and hypnotics, antidepressants and benzodiazepines in older people significantly increases their risk of falls. *Evidence-Based Medicine, 15*(2), 59.

Heister, D., Brewer, J., Magda, S., Blennow, K., & McEvoy, L., for the Alzheimer's Disease Neuroimaging Initiative. (2011). Predicting MCI outcome with clinically available MRI and CSF biomarkers. *Neurology, 77,* 1619–1628.

Henry, J., Crawford, J., & Phillips, L. (2004). Verbal fluency performance in dementia of the Alzheimer's type: a meta-analysis. [Meta-Analysis Review]. *Neuropsychologia, 42*(9), 1212–1222.

Hodges, J. R., Salmon, D. P., & Butters, N. (1991). The nature of the naming deficit in Alzheimer's and Huntington's disease. *Brain, 114* (Pt 4), 1547–1558.

Houston, W. S., Delis, D. C., Lansing, A., Jacobson, M. W., Cobell, K. R., Salmon, D. P., & Bondi, M. W. (2005). Executive function asymmetry in older adults genetically at-risk for Alzheimer's disease: Verbal versus design fluency. *Journal of the International Neuropsychological Society, 11*(7), 863–870.

Howieson, D., Dame, A., Camicioli, R., Sexton, G., Payami, H., & Kaye, J. (1997). Cognitive markers preceding Alzheimer's dementia in the healthy oldest old. *Journal of the American Geriatrics Society, 45*(5), 584–589.

Irie, F., Fitzpatrick, A., Lopez, O., et al. (2008). Enhanced risk for Alzheimer disease in persons with type 2 diabetes and APOE E4. *Archives of Neurology, 65,* 89–93.

Ivnik, R., Malec, J., Smith, G., Tangalos, E., Petersen, R., Kokmen, E., & Kurland, L. (1992). Mayo's Older Americans Normative Studies: WAIS-R, WMS-R and AVLT norms for ages 56 through 97. *The Clinical Neuropsychologist, 6*(Suppl), 1–104.

Jack, C., Jr, Knopman, D., Jagust, W., Shaw, L., Aisen, P., Weiner, M., & Trojanowski, J. (2010). Hypothetical model of dynamic biomarkers of the Alzheimer's pathological cascade. *Lancet Neurology, 9*(1), 119–128.

Jacobs, D., Sano, M., Dooneief, G., Marder, K., Bell, K., & Stern, Y. (1995). Neuropsychological detection and characterization of preclinical Alzheimer's disease. *Neurology, 45,* 957–962.

Jacobson, M., Delis, D., Bondi, M., & Salmon, D. (2002a). Do neuropsychological tests detect preclinical Alzheimer's disease: Individual-test versus cognitive-discrepancy score analyses. *Neuropsychology, 16*(2), 132–139.

Jacobson, M. W., Delis, D. C., Bondi, M. W., & Salmon, D. P. (2005). Asymmetry in auditory and spatial attention span in normal elderly genetically at risk for Alzheimer's disease. *Journal of clinical and experimental neuropsychology*, 27(2), 240–253.

Jedynak, B. M., Lang, A., Liu, B., Katz, E., Zhang, Y., Wyman, B. T., Raunig, D., Jedynak, C. P., Caffo, B., Prince, J. L. for the Alzheimer's Disease Neuroimaging Initiative. (2012). A computational neurodegenerative disease progression score: Method and results with the Alzheimer's disease neuroimaging initiative cohort. *Neuroimage*, 63(3), 1478–1486.

Jordan, B. D. (2000). Chronic traumatic brain injury associated with boxing. *Seminars in Neurology*, 20(2), 179–185.

Kaplan, E., Goodglass, H., & Weintraub, S. (1983). *The Boston Naming Test* (2nd ed.). Philadelphia: Lea & Febiger.

Karran, E., Mercken, M., & De Strooper, B. (2011). The amyloid cascade hypothesis for Alzheimer's disease: an appraisal for the development of therapeutics. *Nature Reviews*, 10, 698–712.

Knopman, D., DeKosky, S., Cummings, J., Chui, H., Corey-Bloom, J., Relkin, N., & Stevens, J. (2001). Practice parameter: Diagnosis of dementia (an evidence-based review): Report of the Quality Standards Subcommittee of the American Academy of Neurology. *Neurology*, 56, 1143–1153.

Kurz, A., Pohl, C., Ramsenthaler, M., & Sorg, C. (2009). Cognitive rehabilitation in patients with mild cognitive impairment. *International Journal of Geriatric Psychiatry*, 24(2), 163–168.

Landau, S., Harvey, D., Madison, C., Reiman, E., Foster, N., Aisen, P., & Jagust, W. (2010). Comparing predictors of conversion and decline in mild cognitive impairment. *Neurology*, 75(3), 230–238.

Lange, K., Bondi, M., Salmon, D., Galasko, D., Delis, D., Thomas, R., & Thal, L. (2002a). Decline in verbal memory during preclinical Alzheimer's disease: Examination of the effect of APOE genotype. *Journal of the International Neuropsychological Society*, 8(7), 943–955.

Lange, K., Bondi, M., Salmon, D., Galasko, D., Delis, D., Thomas, R., & Thal, L. (2002b). Decline in verbal memory during preclinical Alzheimer's disease: Examination of the effect of APOE genotype. *Journal of the International Neuropsychological Society*, 8(7), 943–955.

Lineweaver, T. T., Salmon, D. P., Bondi, M. W., & Corey-Bloom, J. (2005). Differential effects of Alzheimer's disease and Huntington's disease on the performance of mental rotation. *Journal of the International Neuropsychological Society*, 11(1), 30–39.

Locascio, J. J., Growdon, J. H., & Corkin, S. (1995). Cognitive test performance in detecting, staging, and tracking Alzheimer's disease. *Archives of Neurology, 52*(11), 1087–1099.

Loewenstein, D. A., Acevedo, A., Czaja, S. J., & Duara, R. (2004). Cognitive rehabilitation of mildly impaired Alzheimer disease patients on cholinesterase inhibitors. *American Journal of Geriatric Psychiatry, 12*(4), 395–402.

Logie, R. H., Cocchini, G., Delia Sala, S., & Baddeley, A. D. (2004). Is there a specific executive capacity for dual task coordination? Evidence from Alzheimer's disease. *Neuropsychology, 18*(3), 504–513.

Mapstone, M., Steffenella, T. M., & Duffy, C. J. (2003). A visuospatial variant of mild cognitive impairment: getting lost between aging and AD. *Neurology, 60*(5), 802–808.

Masur, D., Sliwinski, M., Lipton, R., Blau, A., & Crystal, H. (1994). Neuropsychological prediction of dementia and the absence of dementia in healthy elderly persons. *Neurology, 44,* 1427–1432.

Mattis, S. (1988). *Mattis Dementia Rating Scale (MDRS)*. Odessa, FL: Psychological Assessment Resources.

Mayeux, R., Ottman, R., Maestre, G., Ngai, C., Tang, M., Ginsberg, H., & Shelanski, M. (1995). Synergistic effects of traumatic head injury and apolipoprotein-epsilon 4 in patients with Alzheimer's disease. *Neurology, 45,* 555–557.

Mayeux, R., Ottman, R., Tang, M. X., Noboa-Bauza, L., Marder, K., Gurland, B., & Stern, Y. (1993). Genetic susceptibility and head injury as risk factors for Alzheimer's disease among community-dwelling elderly persons and their first-degree relatives. *Annals of Neurology, 33*(5), 494–501.

McKhann, G., Drachman, D., Folstein, M., Katzman, R., Price, D., & Stadlan, E. (1984). Clinical diagnosis of Alzheimer's disease: Report of the NINCDS-ADRDA work group under the auspices of Department of Health and Human Services Task Force on Alzheimer's Disease. *Neurology, 34,* 939–944.

McKhann, G. M., Knopman, D. S., Chertkow, H., Hyman, B. T., Jack, C. R., Jr., Kawas, C. H., & Phelps, C. H. (2011). The diagnosis of dementia due to Alzheimer's disease: Recommendations from the National Institute on Aging-Alzheimer's Association workgroups on diagnostic guidelines for Alzheimer's disease. *Alzheimer's and Dementia, 7*(3), 263–269.

McMonagle, P., Deering, F., Berliner, Y., & Kertesz, A. (2006). The cognitive profile of posterior cortical atrophy. *Neurology, 66*(3), 331–338.

McShane, R., Areosa Sastre, A., & Minakaran, N. (2006). Memantine for dementia. *Cochrane Database of Systematic Reviews* (2), CD003154.

Mickes, L., Wixted, J. T., Fennema-Notestine, C., Galasko, D., Bondi, M. W., Thal, L. J., & Salmon, D. P. (2007). Progressive impairment on neuropsychological tasks in a longitudinal study of preclinical Alzheimer's disease. *Neuropsychology, 21*(6), 696–705.

Mirra, S., Heyman, M., McKeil, D., Sumi, S., & Crain, B. (1991). The Consortium to Establish a Registry for Alzheimer's Disease (CERAD). Part II. Standardization of the neuropathologic assessment of Alzheimer's disease. *Neurology, 41*(4), 479–486.

Mitchell, A., & Shiri-Feshki, M. (2009). Rate of progression of mild cognitive impairment to dementia—meta-analysis of 41 robust inception cohort studies. *Acta Psychiatrica Scandinavica, 119*(4), 252–265.

Monsch, A., Bondi, M., Butters, N., Paulsen, J., Salmon, D., Brugger, P., & Swenson, M. (1994). A comparison of category and letter fluency in Alzheimer's disease and Huntington's disease. *Neuropsychology, 8,* 25–30.

Naj, A. C., Jun, G., Beecham, G. W., Wang, L. S., Vardarajan, B. N., Buros, J., & Schellenberg, G. D. (2011). Common variants at MS4A4/MS4A6E, CD2AP, CD33 and EPHA1 are associated with late-onset Alzheimer's disease. *Nature Genetics, 43*(5), 436–441.

Nelson, P., Abner, E., Schmitt, F., Kryscio, R., Jicha, G., Santacruz, K., & Markesbery, W. (2009). Brains with medial temporal lobe neurofibrillary tangles but no neuritic amyloid plaques are a diagnostic dilemma but may have pathogenetic aspects distinct from Alzheimer disease. *Journal of Neuropathology and Experimental Neurology, 68*(7), 774–784.

Nestor, P. J., Caine, D., Fryer, T. D., Clarke, J., & Hodges, J. R. (2003). The topography of metabolic deficits in posterior cortical atrophy (the visual variant of Alzheimer's disease) with FDG-PET. *Journal of Neurology, Neurosurgery, and Psychiatry, 74*(11), 1521–1529.

Oresic, M., Hyötyläinen, T., Herukka, S., Sysi-Aho, M., Mattila, I., Seppänan-Laakso, T., Soininen, H. (2011). Metabolome in progression to Alzheimer's disease. *Translational Psychiatry, Epub.*

Paulsen, J., Salmon, D., Thal, L., Romero, R., Weisstein-Jenkins, C., Galasko, D., & Jeste, D. (2000). Incidence of and risk factors for hallucinations and delusions in patients with probable AD. *Neurology, 54*(10), 1965–1971.

Pedraza, O., Smith, G., Ivnik, R., Willis, F., Ferman, T., Petersen, R., Lucas, J. (2007). Reliable change on the Dementia Rating Scale. *Journal of the International Neuropsychological Society,13*(4), 716–720.

Petersen, R. (2001). Mild cognitive impairment: transition from aging to Alzheimer's disease. In K. Iqbal, S. Sisodia & B. Winblad (Eds.), *Alzheimer's disease: advances in etiology, pathogenesis and therapeutics* (pp. 141–151). West Sussex, England: Wiley.

Petersen, R., Smith, G., Ivnik, R., Tangalos, E., Schaid, D., Thibodeau, S., & Kurland, L. (1995). Apolipoprotein E status as a predictor of the development of Alzheimer's disease in memory-impaired individuals. *Journal of the American Medical Association, 273,* 1274–1278.

Petersen, R., Smith, G., Waring, S., Ivnik, R., Tangalos, E., & Kokmen, E. (1999). Mild cognitive impairment: Clinical characterization and outcome. *Archives of Neurology, 56*(3), 303–308.

Petersen, R., Waring, S., Smith, G., Tangalos, E., & Thibodeau, S. (1996). Predictive value of APOE genotyping in incipient Alzheimer's disease. *Annals of the New York Academy of Sciences, 802,* 58–69.

Petersen, R. C., Thomas, R. G., Grundman, M., Bennett, D., Doody, R., Ferris, S., & Thal, L. J. (2005). Vitamin E and donepezil for the treatment of mild cognitive impairment. *New England Journal of Medicine, 352*(23), 2379–2388.

Plassman, B., Welsh-Bohmer, K., Bigler, E., Johnson, S., Anderson, C., Helms, M., & Breitner, J. (1997). Apolipoprotein E e4 allele and hippocampal volume in twins with normal cognition. *Neurology, 48,* 985–989.

Powell, M., Smith, G., Knopman, D., Parisi, J., Boeve, B., Petersen, R., & Ivnik, R. (2006). Cognitive measures predict Alzheimer's disease pathology. *Archives of Neurology, 63,* 865–868.

Rabins, P. (1999). The history of psychogeriatrics in the United States. *International Psychogeriatrics, 11*(4), 371–373.

Reiman, E., Caselli, R., Yun, L., Chen, K., Bandy, D., Minoshima, S., & Osborne, D. (1996). Preclinical evidence of Alzheimer's disease in persons homozygous for the epsilon 4 allele for apolipoprotein E. *New England Journal of Medicine, 21,* 752–758.

Renner, J. A., Burns, J. M., Hou, C. E., McKeel, D. W., Jr., Storandt, M., & Morris, J. C. (2004). Progressive posterior cortical dysfunction: a clinico-pathologic series. *Neurology, 63*(7), 1175–1180.

Rey, A. (1964). *L'examen clinique en psychologie.* Paris: Presses Universitaires de France.

Rodda, J., Morgan, S., & Walker, Z. (2009). Are cholinesterase inhibitors effective in the management of the behavioral and psychological symptoms of dementia in Alzheimer's disease? A systematic review of randomized, placebo-controlled trials of donepezil, rivastigmine and galantamine. *International Psychogeriatrics, 21*(5), 813–824.

Roses, A. (1997). The predictive value of APOE genotyping in the early diagnosis of dementia of the Alzheimer type: Data from three independent series. In K. Iqbal, B. Winblad, T. Nishimura, M. Takeda & H. Wisniewski (Eds.), *Alzheimer's disease: Biology, diagnosis and therapeutics* (pp. 85–91). West Sussex, England: Wiley.

Rouleau, I., Salmon, D. P., Butters, N., Kennedy, C., & McGuire, K. (1992). Quantitative and qualitative analyses of clock drawings in Alzheimer's and Huntington's disease. *Brain and Cognition, 18*(1), 70–87.

Rovner, B., Steele, C., Shmuely, Y., & Folstein, M. (1996). A randomized trial of dementia care in nursing homes. *Journal of the American Geriatrics Society, 44*(1), 7–13.

Rubin, D., Storandt, M., Miller, J., Kinscherf, D., Grant, E., Morris, J., & Berg, L. (1998). A prospective study of cognitive function and onset of dementia in cognitively healthy elders. *Archives of Neurology, 55*, 395–401.

Salmon, D., & Bondi, M. (2009). Neuropsychological assessment of dementia. *Annual Review of Psychology, 60*, 257–282.

Salmon, D., & Filoteo, J. (2007). Neuropsychology of cortical vs subcortical dementia. *Seminars in Neurology, 27*, 7–21.

Salmon, D. P. (2011). Neuropsychological Features of Mild Cognitive Impairment and Preclinical Alzheimer's Disease. *Current Topics in Behavioral Neurosciences.*

Saunders, A., Strittmatter, W., Schmechel, D., St. George-Hyslop, P., Pericak-Vance, M., Joo, S., & Rose, A. (1993). Association of apolipoprotein E allele E4 with late-onset Alzheimer's disease. *Neurology, 43*, 1467–1472.

Schmitter-Edgecombe, M., Woo, E., & Greeley, D. R. (2009). Characterizing multiple memory deficits and their relation to everyday functioning in individuals with mild cognitive impairment. *Neuropsychology, 23*(2), 168–177.

Schneider, L., Pollock, V., & Lyness, S. (1990). A meta-analysis of controlled trials of neuroleptic treatment in dementia. *Journal of the American Geriatrics Society, 38*, 553–563.

Schneider, L. S., Dagerman, K. S., & Insel, P. (2005). Risk of death with atypical antipsychotic drug treatment for dementia: meta-analysis of randomized placebo-controlled trials. *Journal of the American Medical Association, 294*(15), 1934–1943.

Selkoe, D. J. (2001). Alzheimer's disease: Genes, proteins, and therapy. *Physiological Reviews, 81*(2), 741–766.,

Sitzer, D., Twamley, E., & Jeste, D. (2006). Cognitive training in Alzheimer's disease: A meta-analysis of the literature. *Acta Psychiatrica Scandinavica, 114*, 75–90.

Small, G., Rabins, P., Barry, P., Buckholtz, N., DeKosky, S., Ferris, S., Tune, L. (1997). Diagnosis and treatment of Alzheimer disease and related disorders. Consensus statement of the American Association for Geriatric Psychiatry, the Alzheimer's Association, and the American Geriatrics Society. *Journal of the American Medical Association, 278*(16), 1363–1371.

Small, S., Nava, A., Perera, G., Delapaz, R., & Stern, Y. (2000). Evaluating the function of hippocampal subregions with high-resolution MRI in Alzheimer's disease and aging. *Microscopy Research and Technique, 51*(1), 101–108.

Smith, G., Bohac, D., Waring, S., Kokmen, E., Tangalos, E., Ivnik, R., & Petersen, R. (1998). Apolipoprotein E genotype influences cognitive "phenotype" in patients with Alzheimer's disease but not in healthy control subjects. *Neurology, 50,* 355–362.

Smith, G., & Ivnik, R. (1998). Normative neuropsychology in aging and disease. In R. Petersen (Ed.), *Mild cognitive impairment: Normal aging to Alzheimer's disease.* New York: Oxford University Press.

Smith, G., Kokmen, E., & O' Brien, P. (2000). Risk factors for nursing home placement in a population-based dementia cohort. *Journal of the American Geriatrics Society, 48,* 519–525.

Smith, G., O' Brien, P., Ivnik, R., Kokmen, E., & Tangalos, E. (2001). Prospective analysis of risk factors for nursing home placement of dementia patients. *Neurology, 57,* 1467–1473.

Smith, G., Pankratz, V., Negash, S., Machulda, M., Petersen, R., Boeve, B., & Ivnik, R. (2007). A plateau in pre-clinical Alzheimers disease memory decline: Evidence for compensatory mechanisms? *Neurology, 69,* 133–139.

Soininen, H., Partanen, K., Pitkanen, A., Hallikainen, M., Hanninen, T., Helisalmi, S., & Riekkinen, P. S. (1995). Decreased hippocampal volume asymmetry on MRIs in nondemented elderly subjects carrying the apolipoprotein E epsilon 4 allele. *Neurology, 45,* 391–392.

Soininen, H., Partanen, K., Pitkanen, A., Vainio, P., Hanninen, T., Hallikainen, M., & Rukkinen, P. (1994). Volumetric MRI analysis of the amygdala and the hippocampus in subjects with age-associated memory impairment: Correlation to visual and verbal memory. *Neurology, 44,* 1660–1668.

Sperling, R., Aisen, P., Beckett, L., Bennett, D., Craft, S., Fagan, A., & Phelps, C. (2011). Toward defining the preclinical stages of Alzheimer's disease: Recommendations from the National Institute on Aging-Alzheimer's Association workgroups on diagnostic guidelines for Alzheimer's disease. *Alzheimer's and Dementia, 7*(3), 280–292.

Sperling, R. A., Jack, C. R., Jr., Black, S. E., Frosch, M. P., Greenberg, S. M., Hyman, B. T., & Schindler, R. J. (2011). Amyloid-related imaging abnormalities in amyloid-modifying therapeutic trials: recommendations from the Alzheimer's Association Research Roundtable Workgroup. *Alzheimer's and Dementia, 7*(4), 367–385.

Strittmatter, W., Saunders, A., Schmechel, D., Pericak-Vance, M., Enghild, J., Salvesen, G., & Roses, A. (1993). Apolipoprotein E: High avidity binding to beta-amyloid and increased frequency of type 4 allele in late-onset familial Alzheimer disease. *Proceedings of the National Academy of Sciences, 90*, 1977–1981.

Sultzer, D. L., Davis, S. M., Tariot, P. N., Dagerman, K. S., Lebowitz, B. D., Lyketsos, C. G., & Schneider, L. S. (2008). Clinical symptom responses to atypical antipsychotic medications in Alzheimer's disease: Phase 1 outcomes from the CATIE-AD effectiveness trial. [Randomized Controlled Trial]. *American Journal of Psychiatry, 165*(7), 844–854.

Tabert, M., Manly, J., Liu, X., Pelton, G., Rosenblum, S., Jacobs, M., & Devanand, D. (2006). Neuropsychological prediction of conversion to Alzheimer disease in patients with mild cognitive impairment. *Archives of General Psychiatry, 63*(8), 916–924.

Tang-Wai, D. F., Graff-Radford, N. R., Boeve, B. F., Dickson, D. W., Parisi, J. E., Crook, R., & Petersen, R. C. (2004). Clinical, genetic, and neuropathologic characteristics of posterior cortical atrophy. *Neurology, 63*(7), 1168–1174.

Tenovuo, O., Kemppainen, N., Aalto, S., Nagren, K., & Rinne, J. O. (2008). Posterior cortical atrophy: A rare form of dementia with in vivo evidence of amyloid-beta accumulation. *Journal of Alzheimer's Disease, 15*(3), 351–355.

Teri, L., Truax, P., Logsdon, R., Zarit, S., Uomoto, J., & Vitaliano, P. (1992). Assessment of behavioral problems in dementia: The Revised Memory and Behavior Problems Checklist. *Psychology and Aging, 7*, 622–631.

Testa, J., Ivnik, R., & Smith, G. (2003). Diagnostic Utility of the Boston Naming Test in MCI and Alzheimer's disease. *Journal of the International Neuropsychological Society, 9*, 306.

Thal, D., Rub, U., Orantes, M., & Braak, H. (2002). Phases of A beta-deposition in the human brain and its relevance for the development of AD. *Neurology, 58*, 1791–1800.

Thompson, P., Moussai, J., Zohoori, S., Goldkorn, A., Khan, A., Mega, M., & Toga, A. (1998). Cortical variability and asymmetry in normal aging and Alzheimer's disease. *Cerebral Cortex, 8*(6), 492–509.

Traykov, L., Raoux, N., Latour, F., Gallo, L., Hanon, O., Baudic, S., & Rigaud, A. S. (2007). Executive functions deficit in mild cognitive impairment. *Cognitive and Behavioral Neurology, 20*(4), 219–224.

Twamley, E., Ropacki, S., & Bondi, M. (2006). Neuropsychological and neuroimaging changes in preclinical Alzheimer's disease. *Journal of the International Neuropsychological Society, 12*(5), 707–735.

Twamley, E., Ropacki, S., & Bondi, M. (2006). Neuropsychological and neuroimaging changes in preclinical Alzheimer's disease. *Journal of the International Neuropsychological Society, 12*(5), 707–735.

Wechsler, D. (1987). *Wechsler Memory Scale-Revised*. New York: Psychological Corporation.

Wechsler, D. (1997). *Wechsler Adult Intelligence Scale-III*. New York: Psychological Corporation.

Whitehouse, P. J., Struble, R. G., Hedreen, J. C., Clark, A. W., White, C. L., Parhad, I. M., & Price, D. L. (1983). Neuroanatomical evidence for a cholinergic deficit in Alzheimer's disease. *Psychopharmacology Bulletin, 19*(3), 437–440.

Wilkinson, G. S. (1993). *Wide Range Achievement Test-Third Edition Administration Manual* Wilmington, DE: Wide Range.

Wragg, R., & Jeste, D. (1989). Overview of depression and psychosis in Alzheimer's disease. *American Journal of Psychiatry, 146*(5), 577–587.

6
■ ■ ■

Vascular Dementia

Case Presentation No. 1

A 60-year-old, married, right-handed, Caucasian man with 18 years of education presented for evaluation. He was a recently retired accountant who volunteered to participate in our local Alzheimer's Disease Research Center, secondary to self-reported (and spouse corroborated) forgetfulness, memory problems, and word-finding difficulty of about 2 year's duration. He reported independence in basic and complex instrumental activities of daily living, but recounted some increased difficulty at work related to cognitive problems prior to his retirement.

History
Past Medical. Gastrectomy (decades ago), hypertension (blood pressure: 170/100), hyperlipidemia, diabetes mellitus, peripheral neuropathy of the left plantar nerve (left leg decreased sensation to pain, vibration, touch), remote Bell's palsy episode, smoking.

Social. He lived with his wife in their home. He had a longstanding history of alcohol abuse and reported current use of approximately two drinks per day.

Family. Extensive family history of coronary heart disease, although there is no family history of dementia. He has one son with Down's syndrome.

(continued)

Medications

Xanax, hydrochlorothiazide, Diabinese, clofibrate, potassium chloride, niacin

Neuroimaging

In the year prior to evaluation, the patient experienced an episode diagnosed as Bell's palsy that prompted neuroimaging. A brain MRI scan at that time found no evidence of focal atrophy but did reveal an area of infarction in the right posterior internal capsule extending into the right thalamus. MRI also demonstrated substantial subcortical white matter disease with both anterior and posterior periventricular regional involvement, as well as involvement within the corona radiata and centra semiovale.

Course of Decline

The patient was seen over the course of 4 years. He was diagnosed as cognitively normal in the first year but steadily declined thereafter. Two years following initial evaluation he was hospitalized after falling into a diabetic coma. By the third year of testing he was diagnosed with vascular dementia, diagnosed again as such on the fourth year, and he died the following year.

Neuropsychological Case Findings

Figure 6.1 shows performances across several key measures over each of the 4 years of evaluation. Several aspects of the presentation are noteworthy. First, the only measures falling below -1 SD z-score at initial evaluation are visuoconstructive and category fluency tests. By the second evaluation, however, the initial two deficit performances remain present, and clear declines are now also noted on executive function tests (WCST, Trails B, letter fluency). By contrast, global cognitive status (DRS total score) as well as learning and memory were within normal limits, and learning and memory remained within normal limits on all subsequent evaluations. Only by the fourth and final evaluation was this individual below normal limits on the DRS. This case profile illustrates early and progressive visuospatial and executive dysfunction in the face of intact learning and memory abilities.

Autopsy Brain Findings

Neuropathology revealed an old infarct in the right posterior internal capsule and diffuse microcortical infarcts. There was also evidence of mild

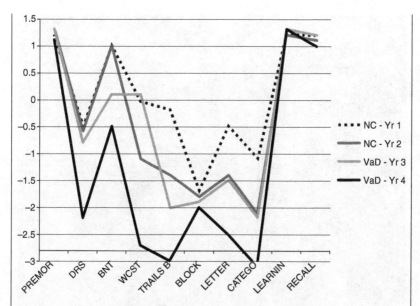

FIGURE 6.1 Neuropsychological test results over four consecutive years in an individual with autopsy-confirmed vascular dementia (and without AD neuropathology). The neuropsychological test battery used by the UCSD Alzheimer's Disease Research Center at the time of this individual's participation is described in detail in Salmon and Butters (1992). Updated variants of these same or similar measures can be found in the Alzheimer's Disease Centers' Uniform Data Set (Weintraub et al., 2009).

atherosclerosis within the circle of Willis. Braak and Braak neuropathological tangle severity was listed as Stage I, although the readings indicated zero counts of neuritic plaques, neurofibrillary tangles, or other amyloid. His APOE genotype was ε3/ε3.

Case Presentation No. 2

A 78-year-old, right-handed, Caucasian man initially presented with a 1–2 year history of word-finding difficulties, prompting a neuropsychological evaluation that demonstrated normal cognition at that time. Then the following year he suffered a left-hemisphere cerebrovascular accident (CVA), with subsequent nonfluent aphasia. However, his language deficits appear to be worsening over the past 2 years since his CVA (i.e., he now exhibits comprehension difficulties), and he has additional memory complaints. He reported being able to read despite some difficulty but has more trouble

(continued)

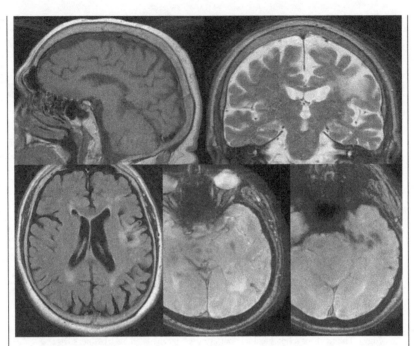

FIGURE 6.2 Brain MRI scans of Case Presentation No. 2 taken two years following left hemisphere stroke that resulted in nonfluent aphasia.

with spelling. Short-term memory problems have been noted by clinicians and acknowledged by the patient. Although he denies difficulty with independent functioning (e.g., driving, managing finances, managing medications), he acknowledges that he stays home more because of his language difficulties.

Neuroimaging

As shown in Figure 6.2, brain MRI scanning around the time of his second neuropsychological evaluation showed an old infarction in the lateral left middle frontal gyrus extending inferiorly to the left inferior frontal gyrus, including the left frontal operculum (Broca's area). Patchy posterior periventricular and bilateral deep subcortical white matter chronic hypertensive changes. Small sulcal hemosiderin-staining in the lateral posterior left temporal lobe, and a smaller punctate focus of old hemosiderin in the mid lateral left temporal lobe, which could represent sequelae of old

(continued)

trauma versus old hypertensive microbleeds. Moderate parenchymal volume loss for age, manifested by prominent CSF around the cerebral convexities, and prominent sylvian fissures. Ventricles are normal in size and temporal horns are not dilated.

Behavioral Observations and Mental Status

Speech was fluent (e.g., normal rate, length of utterance, prosody) but marred by mild word-finding difficulty, circumlocutions, word substitution, grammatical errors, and paraphasias. For example, when discussing hearing difficulties, he stated, "I didn't know it but I was liping." When asked to describe his mood he stated, "I don't like the stroke." In describing recent news events, he stated, "I had 'sock.' Now I don't have any stock." He stated his son's age as "sixty-zero." Repetition was relatively intact for most simple words and phrases, but was impaired on longer phrases. Language comprehension problems were evident during the interview and testing and, when asked questions, he would frequently respond with unrelated information. He was able to provide responses to most interview questions, but some responses were incomprehensible. For example, when asked to describe events recently reported in the news, he said, "there were some stars over there…a lady died, I don't remember her name." He was oriented to person, place, date, and time, though he initially stated the year as "2009" before correcting himself and stating that it was "two-hundred, one, one." When asked about current events he said, "my house is under the water," "there are no jobs," and "we have a depression."

Neuropsychological Case Findings

This patient's neuropsychological profile was consistent with the diagnosis of vascular dementia, with deficits in executive functions, language (naming, language comprehension, and repetition), as well as a mild retrieval-based memory deficit. He also exhibited some disinhibition and perseverative responses during interview and testing, and he was impaired on both verbal and nonverbal executive function tests. Although his speech was somewhat fluent in terms of rate, prosody, and length of utterance, he exhibited significant word-finding problems indicating residual mild nonfluent aphasia from his left frontal stroke. He also showed some comprehension difficulties on interview. Formal language testing revealed

(continued)

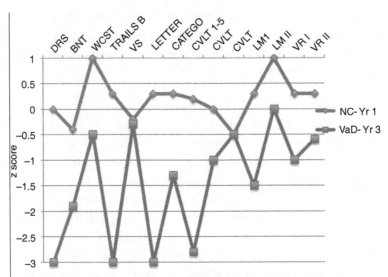

FIGURE 6.3 Neuropsychological test results over two test sessions separated by two years in an individual who suffered a left hemisphere stroke in the interval between the two test sessions. California Verbal Learning Test – Second Edition (CVLT); Block Design (VS) subtest of the Wechsler Abbreviated Scale of Intelligence (WASI); Boston Naming Test (BNT); Mattis Dementia Rating Scale (DRS); Visual Reproduction and Logical Memory subtests of the Wechsler Memory Scale – Fourth Edition (LM; VR); Trailmaking and Verbal Fluency tests from the Delis-Kaplan Executive Function Scale (D-KEFS); Wisconsin Card Sorting Test-64 (WCST) perseverative errors. Figure presents z-scores recalculated from the T-scores of the Heaton et al. (Heaton, Miller, Taylor, & Grant, 2004) normative dataset and are corrected for age, gender, ethnicity, and completion of 18 years of education. Standard scores reported for the Wechsler tests (WAIS-4, WMS-4, and WASI) were obtained from the most recent standardization samples associated with each test and are corrected for age. The z-score reported for the WCST-64 is corrected for age and education (Kongs et al., 2000). The standard scores reported for the D-KEFS are corrected for age (Delis et al., 2001). The standard scores reported for the CVLT-2 are corrected for age and gender (Delis et al., 2000).

severe deficits in language comprehension (e.g., he was able to understand only simple sentences on the MAE Token Test). He also failed to accurately repeat most complex phrases and even some simple phrases and single words. Consistent with his subjective complaints, memory abilities declined when compared to his original neuropsychological testing 4 years ago. These deficits were mild, retrieval-based (e.g., no rapid forgetting), and his performance was normal when provided a structured format, even on tests with high verbal demand (e.g., WMS-IV Logical Memory).

Additional Testing:			
BOSTON DIAGNOSTIC APHASIA EXAM			
Complex Ideational Material	__10_/12 T= __30__	___2__ %ile	
Word Repetition	____8_/10		
High probability phrase	____5_/8		
Low probability phrase	____3_/8		
MAE TOKEN TEST	__10_/44	<1 %ile	
WAIS-IV MATRIX REASONING T= ___62___		89 %ile	

The patient demonstrated a relative strength in nonverbal abstract reasoning, which is consistent with his presentation on interview and high level of premorbid functioning. It is likely that these abilities, together with his relatively preserved insight, allowed him to compensate for his deficits to some degree, which may have masked his substantial decline in language comprehension and other cognitive abilities.

The patient's cognitive deficits are consistent with his history of extensive cerebrovascular disease, including ischemic and hemorrhagic lesions within his left frontal and temporal cortices, as well as subcortical white matter disease. His cognitive profile was not characteristic of Alzheimer's disease (e.g., no evidence of rapid forgetting). Although it is difficult to completely rule out the less likely possibility of an overlying semantic dementia, the extent and distribution of his cerebrovascular lesions appear to be sufficient to account for the deficits he exhibited on testing. Additionally, his deficits are not limited to the language domain, which suggests that his cognitive decline is due to vascular disease throughout a variety of brain areas, rather than circumscribed neurodegeneration within his left temporal lobe. His mild mood dysfunction may have had limited impact on some test scores but cannot account for his overall cognitive profile.

Introduction

Disorders of the cerebrovascular system account for significant morbidity and represent important underlying pathologies in the development of dementia, despite their sometimes "silent" or elusive impact on cognition. Reed and colleagues (Reed et al., 2007) underscore that cerebrovascular or Alzheimer pathology, or both, underlie the great majority of cases of dementia and mild forms of cognitive impairment among older adults; and, their accurate clinical detection and differential diagnosis are important challenges for neuropsychology. Therefore, a better understanding of the risks of cerebrovascular pathologies, their effects, and their cognitive and functional consequences, will become increasingly important in the decades ahead.

Furthermore, the growing recognition of pathologic overlap or "mixed" causes of dementia, such as co-occurring Alzheimer's and vascular dementia, provides additional impetus to better understand the contributions of cerebrovascular disorders on cognition and daily function. For example, Schneider et al. (Schneider, Arvanitakis, Leurgans, & Bennett, 2009) found that in a consecutive series of initially cognitively normal subjects who later received final clinical diagnoses of MCI or probable AD prior to autopsy, mixed cerebrovascular disease (CVD) and AD pathology were nearly as common as "pure" AD. And among MCI diagnoses, amnestic versus nonamnestic subtypes made little difference in the underlying pathologies. This result may not be surprising if one relies on the use of a single delayed recall variable (without inspection of learning, recognition memory, presence of intrusion errors, etc.) or composites to separate amnestic from nonamnestic forms. Knopman et al. (Knopman et al., 2001), in their important practice parameter article on the diagnosis of dementia, recommended more than a decade ago that more "[e]xplicit recognition of the pathologic overlap of AD . . . [and] VaD . . . in the diagnostic criteria might lead to a more realistic approach to clinical diagnosis." Unfortunately, only one paragraph is devoted to etiologically mixed presentations in the revised McKhann et al. (2011) criteria on AD diagnosis.

We offer that neuropsychological patterns and profiles of impairment (e.g., cortical vs. subcortical dementia profiles; see Salmon & Filoteo, 2007, for review) are well suited to examine the underlying cognitive manifestations of "pure" AD versus CVD versus "mixed" pathologies (e.g., see also Kramer et al., 2004). The fruits of such efforts will yield improvements in dementia detection, differential diagnosis, better targeted treatments, and a more sophisticated understanding of the presentation of mild forms of cognitive impairment when combined with information on cerebrovascular disease risk, imaging, genetics, and other biomarkers (e.g., amyloid imaging, CSF markers of Aβ and tau; APOE genotype and newly discovered genetic susceptibilities, see Naj et al., 2011). For example, studies have shown the combination of diabetes and the APOE ε4 allele to be more deleterious than either risk factor alone (Dore, Elias, Robbins, Elias, & Nagy, 2009; Irie, Fitzpatrick, Lopez, et al., 2008), or the presence of moderate-to-severe cerebral amyloid angiopathy—independent of AD pathology—results in poorer cognition (Arvanitakis et al., 2011).

Epidemiology and Neuropathology

Generally speaking, cerebrovascular pathology can be caused by acute events, such as a hemorrhagic stroke, or by slower cumulative processes, such as atherosclerotic or small vessel ischemic disease. Stroke itself is the second most common cause of death in the developed world after heart disease (Di Carlo, 2009); it is thought to be the second most common cause of dementia after AD (Salmon & Bondi, 2009); and a number of well-known risk factors exist for cerebrovascular disease (e.g., smoking, hypertension, hyperlipidemia, diabetes). Advancing age is among the most prominent of these risk factors and, despite the widespread use of antihypertensive and anticoagulant drug use in older adults, cerebrovascular disorders are on the rise due in part to the baby boom generation reaching retirement age (Jellinger, 2008a). The overall prevalence of dementia is about 5%–10% in persons 65 and older. For AD, the prevalence doubles about every 4.3 years, and for vascular dementia the prevalence doubles about every 5.3 years (Ganguli, Snitz, Saxton, et al., 2011).

Seidel et al. (Seidel, Tiovannetti, & Libon, 2011) note that cerebrovascular pathologies are uniformly associated with reductions in cerebral blood flow; otherwise, they are quite diverse in their effects. They may impact large and/or small vessels; they may result from acute events or may be associated with chronic conditions; and, they may be ischemic or hemorrhagic in nature. Furthermore, there is dispute about the role of various types of vascular lesions that contribute to cognitive impairments, including but not limited to, large cortical infarcts, lacunar infarcts, subcortical white matter disease, strategically placed subcortical infarcts, or their combinations. Delineating the myriad neuropathologies of cerebrovascular diseases and events is beyond the scope of this chapter. We will briefly highlight a few of the common pathologies that relate to vascular dementia, particularly subcortical ischemic vascular dementia; and the reader is referred to other sources for more complete coverage (see Gorelick et al., 2011; Seidel et al., 2011, for reviews).

Cerebral Infarctions

Cerebral infarcts are circumscribed areas of tissue loss of varying sizes, and they are quite common. For example, chronic *macroscopic* infarcts have been found to occur in roughly one-third to one-half of older adults (Schneider, Aggarwal, Barnes, Boyle, & Bennett, 2009; White et al., 2005) and, as one might expect, the greater number and/or volume of macroscopic infarcts is associated with an increased likelihood of dementia. Some studies suggest that multiple *microscopic* infarcts are associated with dementia—even after accounting for macroscopic infarcts (White et al., 2005). Gorelick et al. (2011) discuss that the presence of multiple microscopic infarcts implies that a more generalized neuropathologic process may be present, such as diffuse hypoxia, inflammation, oxidative stress, or disruption at the level of the blood-brain barrier. Seidel et al. (2011) discuss that derailment of the blood-brain barrier may lead to neuronal disruption by allowing toxins to reach neurons or by preventing the clearance of toxins from the brain, and may represent an important mechanism underlying small vessel white matter disease in older adults (see also Pantoni, 2010).

Primary Vessel Disease

Other common vascular pathologies include atherosclerosis, arteriolosclerosis, and cerebral amyloid angiopathy (CAA). Small vessel disease gives rise to chronic hypoperfusion and degeneration of white matter (Pantoni, 2010). Such white matter changes are observed as hyperintensities on T_2-weighted MRI scans, and they have been variously named over the years (e.g., "subcortical hyperintensities," "white matter lesions," "unidentified bright objects," "leukoaraiosis"). Their effects on cognition have been a source of great inconsistency across studies (e.g., recall Case Presentation in Chapter 3 of the individual with extensive white matter disease, but no evidence of cognitive dysfunction). Perhaps the most consistent findings have been little to no effects of periventricular white matter lesions on cognition, but specific effects between deep white matter lesions and neuropsychological mechanisms thought to be dependent on frontoparietal connectivity, such as executive function, processing speed, and visuospatial skills (Delano-Wood et al., 2008).

With the advent of newer MRI techniques, such as T_2*-weighted gradient-echo imaging that are sensitive to iron deposits, cerebral microbleeds are able to be imaged more reliably and look to be relatively common. Greenberg (Greenberg et al., 2009) notes that the cerebral microbleeds are typically due to two types of vascular pathologic changes: hypertensive vasculopathy and CAA. Hypertensive vasculopathy is typically associated with microbleeds in the basal ganglia, thalamus, brainstem, and cerebellum, whereas CAA is associated with a lobar distribution and predilection for the posterior cortical regions such as the occipital lobe. CAA seems to result from the accumulation of Aβ in cortical arterioles that in turn weakens the vessel wall and increases the chance of lobar microhemorrhages (Weller & Nicoll, 2009). This process appears to occur in roughly 10%–30% of unselected brain autopsies and is present in 80%–100% of "definite" or autopsy-confirmed AD (Jellinger, 2002). As Gorelick et al. (2011) summarize, CAA is most commonly diagnosed by the detection of hemorrhages confined to cortical or cortico-subcortical ("lobar") brain regions. Greenberg (1998) proposed clinical criteria for this presence of multiple hemorrhages restricted to lobar, cortical, or cortico-subcortical regions, in the absence of other definite causes such as head trauma or tumors, for the diagnosis of CAA (e.g., the Boston criteria for "probable" CAA). By contrast, the criteria for probable CAA cannot be made if any cerebral microbleeds are located in the basal ganglia, thalamus, or brainstem. These criteria have been validated against neuropathological (Knudsen, Rosand, Karluk, & Greenberg, 2001) or genetically diagnosed (van Rooden et al., 2009) CAA.

Neuroimaging

Neuroimaging procedures are foundational to the demonstration of cerebrovascular disease processes, although it is also clear that asymptomatic or "silent" brain infarction (SBI) is quite common and that the relative contributions of white matter lesions, microbleeds, and SBI to cognitive impairments remain uncertain. Gorelick et al. (2011), in their diagnostic statement on vascular contributions to cognitive impairment and dementia, define vascular cognitive impairment as a syndrome in which there is evidence of stroke or subclinical vascular brain injury based on clinical or neuroradiological features, and that is linked to impairment in at least one cognitive domain. They also note that the clinical presentation and course of cerebrovascular disease-related brain changes are highly variable, with the classic phenotype of stepwise decline in association with stroke being a relatively uncommon presentation for vascular cognitive impairment. Structural MRI of white matter lesions, microbleeds, and macroscopic and microscopic brain infarctions are judged to provide fairly sensitive and specific markers for cerebrovascular disease-related brain injury, although this relationship is confounded by the frequent presence of Alzheimer pathology (see Gorelick et al., 2011, for discussion). We will discuss a variety of these neuroimaging features in the context of the definitional schemes and clinical features associated with vascular cognitive impairment and dementia.

Genetics

As was known for years prior to its association with Alzheimer's disease, the apolipoprotein E ε4 allele is associated with an increase in risk for cardiovascular disease (see Eichner et al., 2002, for review). Despite the association between this susceptibility gene and cardiovascular disease, there is no apparent association between APOE and vascular dementia either in Caucasian (Kuller et al., 2005) or Asian populations (Kim et al., 2008). One of the difficulties in conducting this type of research is the high potential for "mixed" cerebrovascular and Alzheimer pathologies, thus blurring the distinctions between the APOE gene's effects on AD processes or cardiovascular disease risks. As discussed in the previous chapter, the recent findings of Bell et al. (2012) demonstrating APOE4's damaging effects at the level of the blood-brain barrier further reflects this potential complex interplay between cerebrovascular and Alzheimer pathologies.

There exist a variety of causative genes for vascular cognitive impairments, of which the most commonly encountered and best characterized condition is cerebral autosomal dominant arteriopathy with subcortical infarcts and leukoencephalopathy (CADASIL). Originally mapped to chromosome 19, and later refined to show it is caused by mutations in the *Notch3* gene (Joutel et al., 1996), CADASIL was the first to be genetically identified and is the most common single-gene disorder of the cerebral small arteries. Clinical features of the disorder, often appearing in mid-life and with clear-cut positive family histories in first-degree relatives, include migraine headaches, mood disturbances, recurrent stroke episodes, and cognitive decline—along with imaging evidence of extensive white matter lesions, lacunar infarcts, microbleeds, and overall atrophic changes. Recent work also has identified another variant, CARASIL (or cerebral autosomal recessive arteriopathy with subcortical infarcts and leukoencephalopathy) (Fukutake, 2011), that is caused by mutations in the HTRA1 gene encoding HtrA serine peptidase/protease 1 (HTRA1). A number of other single-gene disorders that have ischemic stroke as a major feature also include sickle cell disease, familial cerebral amyloid angiopathy, Fabry disease, and retinal vasculopathy with cerebral leukodystrophy (Meschia, Worrall, & Rich, 2011).

Diagnostic Criteria

Definitions and Clinical Features

Pathologically, vascular dementia (VaD) results in a cumulative decline in cognition due to strategically placed infarction, multiple infarctions, subcortical ischemic injury, hemorrhagic lesions, or combinations of some or all of the above. In general, the relationship between various vascular events and subsequent VaD appears to be additive in nature (Hayden et al., 2006; Kivipelto et al., 2006). Not surprisingly, the clinical and neuropathologic presentation of VaD can be quite heterogeneous, and a variety of conditions fall under the general rubric of VaD—which no doubt has led to some of the poorer diagnostic reliability rates when compared to AD (Jellinger, 2008b). Hodges and Graham (2001) discuss that these VaD-related processes typically fall into three general categories: (1) multiple large cortical infarctions (usually affecting 10cc or more of brain tissue) referred to as multi-infarct dementia; (2) dementia due to strategically placed infarction(s); and, (3) subcortical ischemic vascular dementia due to subcortical small vessel disease that results in multiple lacunar strokes, leukoaraiosis (Binswanger's disease), or diffuse white matter pathology.

Original Criteria

In previous decades, specific research criteria for the broadly defined diagnosis of VaD have been offered (e.g., see the work of Chui et al., 1992; Román et al., 1993; Tatemichi, Sacktor, & Mayeux, 1994). In general, these guidelines require deficits in multiple cognitive domains that occur in the presence of focal neurologic signs and symptoms and/or imaging (e.g., CT or MRI scan) evidence of cerebrovascular disease considered to be linked to the cognitive impairment. They go on to suggest that a relationship between dementia and cerebrovascular disease is indicated if the onset of dementia occurs soon after a recognized stroke, cognitive functioning declines sharply as opposed to gradually, or the course of cognitive deterioration is fluctuating or stepwise in its progressive decline.

Unfortunately, a number of studies have shown that some of the criteria, such as a stepwise course, do not appear to be especially sensitive to the presentation of VaD. In an interesting study that applied four different diagnostic criteria for VaD (e.g., Chui et al. 1992; Román et al., 1993; Bennett et al.'s 1990 criteria for Binswanger's disease, and the ICD-10 criteria for vascular dementia) to the same sample of patients, Cosentino et al. (2004) found that the criteria widely differed and were not necessarily interchangeable. The most common clinical characteristics associated with VaD, regardless of the diagnostic scheme used, were hypertension, extensive periventricular and deep white matter alterations on MRI, and differential impairment on executive function and visuospatial tests, with relatively higher scores on tests of delayed recognition memory (see also Hildebrandt, Haldenwanger, & Eling, 2009). Furthermore, the modified Hachinski Ischemia Scale (Rosen, Terry, Fuld, Katzman, & Peck, 1980) was shown to be low for most of the VaD patients, since cortical infarcts and a history of a sudden onset or stepwise progression of decline were rare.

In the criteria set forth by Roman et al. (1993), circumspection with regard to the level of certainty of presumed cerebrovascular pathology was built into the criteria. As a result, VaD was subtyped by the suspected pathology according to available clinical, radiologic, and neuropathologic features, and *possible* or *probable* VaD were further descriptors designed to note the relative certainty with which cerebrovascular disease was thought to contribute to the dementia syndrome. *Definite* VaD was diagnosed only when histopathologic evidence of cerebrovascular disease occurred in the absence of neurofibrillary tangles and neuritic plaques, exceeding those expected for age (i.e., no significant AD pathology) and without clinical evidence of other disorders capable of producing dementia (e.g., Pick's disease, LBD, etc.).

Poor Recognition of Multiple Pathologies among Revised Criteria

As Knopman and colleagues (2001) have pointed out in their important practice parameter article on the diagnosis of dementia, some vascular pathology exists in roughly 30%–40% of dementia cases that come to autopsy, and pure vascular pathology appears to account for dementia only about 10% of the time (see also autopsy study by Schneider, Arvanitakis, et al., 2009). A more recent epidemiologic study by Plassman et al. (2007) put the prevalence rate of pure VaD slightly higher at 16%, and Erkinjuntti and Gauthier (2009) state that some degree of cerebral small vessel disease is found in upward of 80% of AD patients. Jellinger (2008a) also noted that roughly 25%–80% of demented subjects across studies show both AD and cerebrovascular lesions, and the presence of multiple pathologies greatly increases the odds of dementia. Regardless of the best estimate of the percentage of pure VaD or mixed Alzheimer's and cerebrovascular disease, Knopman et al. (2001) sensibly recommended that future work have better recognition of the high degree of pathologic overlap of vascular and Alzheimer's dementias, and that diagnostic criteria ought to have a more realistic approach to clinical diagnosis given these high rates of comorbidities.

Unfortunately, this recommendation to provide more explicit recognition of such overlap has generally not been systematically examined in research over the previous decade; nor has it been incorporated into the recent revisions of the various diagnostic schemes (see Chapters 4 and 5). For example, the McKhann et al. (2011) workgroup chose to limit their focus to the diagnosis of AD, and all but one paragraph is devoted to etiologically mixed presentations in diagnosis. The workgroup provided a few different sets of criteria: one for an "all-cause" dementia; one specific for Alzheimer dementia (*probable* AD dementia); and, one if the course is atypical or has evidence of an etiologically mixed presentation (*possible* AD dementia). Presumably, the "all-cause" dementia would subsume vascular, DLB, FTD, and any mixed dementias, although this either/or scheme to differential diagnosis for AD vs. any other dementia (which potentially also includes co-occurring AD plus other etiologies) will likely fail to provide sufficient detail for co-occurring dementias or for targeted treatments when available. For example, one might wish to treat an individual thought to have comorbid AD and DLB differently from one with comorbid AD and VaD, although "all cause" dementia would not appear to be a helpful label when describing these two individuals with separable underlying pathologic processes.

Nor would the single paragraph devoted to etiologically mixed presentations (i.e., possible AD dementia) seem to be sufficient for characterizing this very common presentation. Recall the results of Schneider et al.'s (2009) finding that mixed cerebrovascular and AD pathology was nearly as common as "pure" AD. The prospect of co-occurring dementia pathologies is not a trivial one given the range of estimates noted above and in the other chapters (e.g., 30%–80% of AD patients will have significant cerebrovascular involvement; 20%–40% of AD patients will have significant neocortical Lewy body inclusions), and a better awareness of these concurrent underlying neuropatholgies—along with their base rates and typical patterns of neuropsychological impairment—is clearly needed.

New Criteria: AHA/ASA Workgroup on Vascular Contributions to Cognitive Impairment and Dementia

Despite the shortcomings of the McKhann et al. (2011) report in highlighting the common prospects for etiologically mixed presentations of dementia, another consensus workgroup has recently produced definitions and recommendations on the vascular contributions to cognitive impairment and dementia that appear to provide some of this much-needed focus. This article was sponsored by the American Heart Association and the American Stroke Association (AHA/ASA) and published by Gorelick et al. (2011). In this statement, Gorelick et al. introduce the construct of vascular cognitive impairment (VCI) to capture the entire spectrum of cognitive disorders associated with all forms of cerebral vascular brain injury, ranging from mild cognitive impairment (denoted as VaMCI) through fully developed dementia (denoted as VaD).

A number of important conclusions and recommendations were drawn in this 41-page report. For example, they offer that dysfunction of the neurovascular unit and mechanisms regulating cerebral blood flow are likely to be important components of the pathophysiological processes underlying VCI; and cerebral amyloid angiopathy is emerging as an important marker of risk for Alzheimer's disease, microinfarction, microhemorrhage and macrohemorrhage of the brain, and VCI. Perhaps most importantly, the authors suggest that the neuropathology of cognitive impairment in later life is often a mixture of Alzheimer's disease and microvascular brain damage that may overlap and synergize to heighten the risk of cognitive impairment. In this regard, MRI and other neuroimaging techniques are thought to play an important role in the definition and detection of VCI and provide evidence that subcortical forms of VCI with white matter hyperintensities and small deep infarcts are common. In many cases, risk markers for VCI are the same as traditional risk factors for stroke. These risks may include, but are not limited to, atrial fibrillation, hypertension, diabetes mellitus, and hypercholesterolemia. Furthermore, some of these same vascular risk factors may be risk markers for Alzheimer's disease (e.g., diabetes). Carotid intimal-medial thickness and arterial stiffness are emerging as markers of arterial aging and may serve as risk markers for VCI. The authors also point out that no specific treatments for VCI have been approved by the US Food and Drug Administration, although detection and control of the traditional risk factors for stroke and cardiovascular disease may be effective in the prevention of VCI.

The article also posits that assessment of patients with suspected VCI requires a comprehensive cognitive battery with operational definitions of cognitive impairment (e.g., 1 or 1.5 SDs below comparison groups) and is preferred over qualitative descriptions of cognitive symptoms (see Table 6.1 for details). In addition to ADL characterization, four domains of cognition must be assessed: executive function/attention, memory, language, and visuospatial functions. Table 6.1 details the criteria for VCI and subdivides it into dementia (that includes *probable* and *possible* VaD) and mild cognitive impairment (that includes *probable* VaMCI, *possible* VaMCI, and *unstable* VaMCI) due to vascular origin. The criteria also attempt to incorporate associated clinical and imaging features within each subcategory.

In the next section, we turn to the discussion of specific profiles and patterns of neuropsychological changes in vascular dementia and how they may differ from those of the dementia of AD.

Neuropsychological Profile of Vascular Dementia

The syndrome of vascular dementia (VaD) has often been heuristically characterized as a "subcortical" or frontal-subcortical dementia, similar to the dementia of Huntington's disease, and unlike the "cortical" dementia of AD described in the previous chapter. The contrasting neuropsychological features associated with cortical and subcortical dementias are useful in conceptualizing the profile of cognitive dysfunction typified in VaD—with some notable caveats like that noted in Case Presentation No. 2 presented at the beginning of this chapter of a strategically placed infarction leading to focal deficit. Distinctions drawn on tests of episodic and semantic memory, visuospatial skills, and specific aspects of executive function, are important considerations in the differential diagnosis of AD versus VaD. As stated in the previous chapter, the general profile of impairment in a cortical dementia like that of AD is characterized by deficits in episodic and semantic memory and "executive" functions, with perhaps later appearance of attention, constructional, and

Table 6.1 Gorelick et al. (2011) Criteria for Vascular Cognitive Impairment (VCI)

1. The term *VCI* characterizes all forms of cognitive deficits from VaD to MCI of vascular origin.
2. These criteria cannot be used for subjects who have an active diagnosis of drug or alcohol abuse/dependence. Subjects must be free of any type of substance for at least 3 months.
3. These criteria cannot be used for subjects with delirium.

Dementia

1. The diagnosis of dementia should be based on a decline in cognitive function from a prior baseline and a deficit in performance in two cognitive domains that are of sufficient severity to affect the subject's activities of daily living.
2. The diagnosis of dementia must be based on cognitive testing, and a minimum of four cognitive domains should be assessed: executive/ attention, memory, language, and visuospatial functions.
3. The deficits in activities of daily living are independent of the motor/ sensory sequelae of the vascular event.

Probable VaD

1. There is cognitive impairment and imaging evidence of cerebrovascular disease and,
   a. There is a clear temporal relationship between a vascular event (e.g., clinical stroke) and onset of cognitive deficits, or,
   b. There is a clear relationship in the severity and pattern of cognitive impairment and the presence of diffuse, subcortical cerebrovascular disease pathology (e.g., as in CADASIL).
2. There is no history of gradually progressive cognitive deficits before or after the stroke that suggests the presence of a nonvascular neurodegenerative disorder.

Possible VaD

There is cognitive impairment and imaging evidence of cerebrovascular disease but

1. There is no clear relationship (temporal, severity, or cognitive pattern) between the vascular disease (e.g., silent infarcts, subcortical small-vessel disease) and the cognitive impairment.
2. There is insufficient information for the diagnosis of VaD (e.g., clinical symptoms suggest the presence of vascular disease, but no CT/MRI studies are available).

3. Severity of aphasia precludes proper cognitive assessment. However, patients with documented evidence of normal cognitive function (e.g., annual cognitive evaluations) before the clinical event that caused aphasia *could* be classified as having probable VaD.
4. There is evidence of other neurodegenerative diseases or conditions in addition to cerebrovascular disease that may affect cognition, such as
   a. A history of other neurodegenerative disorders (e.g., Parkinson disease, progressive supranuclear palsy, dementia with Lewy bodies);
   b. The presence of Alzheimer disease biology is confirmed by biomarkers (e.g., PET, CSF, amyloid ligands) or genetic studies (e.g., *PS1* mutation); or
   c. A history of active cancer or psychiatric or metabolic disorders that may affect cognitive function.

VaMCI

1. VaMCI includes the four subtypes proposed for the classification of MCI: amnestic, amnestic plus other domains, nonamnestic single domain, and nonamnestic multiple domain.
2. The classification of VaMCI must be based on cognitive testing, and a minimum of four cognitive domains should be assessed: executive/attention, memory, language, and visuospatial functions. The classification should be based on an assumption of decline in cognitive function from a prior baseline and impairment in at least 1 cognitive domain.
3. Instrumental activities of daily living could be normal or mildly impaired, independent of the presence of motor/sensory symptoms.

Probable VaMCI

1. There is cognitive impairment and imaging evidence of cerebrovascular disease and
   a. There is a clear temporal relationship between a vascular event (e.g., clinical stroke) and onset of cognitive deficits, or,
   b. There is a clear relationship in the severity and pattern of cognitive impairment and the presence of diffuse, subcortical cerebrovascular disease pathology (e.g., as in CADASIL).
2. There is no history of gradually progressive cognitive deficits before or after the stroke that suggests the presence of a nonvascular neurodegenerative disorder.

Possible VaMCI

There is cognitive impairment and imaging evidence of cerebrovascular disease but,

1. There is no clear relationship (temporal, severity, or cognitive pattern) between the vascular disease (e.g., silent infarcts, subcortical small-vessel disease) and onset of cognitive deficits.

(continued)

Table 6.1 (Continued)

2. There is insufficient information for the diagnosis of VaMCI (e.g., clinical symptoms suggest the presence of vascular disease, but no CT/MRI studies are available).
3. Severity of aphasia precludes proper cognitive assessment. However, patients with documented evidence of normal cognitive function (e.g., annual cognitive evaluations) before the clinical event that caused aphasia *could* be classified as having probable VaMCI.
4. There is evidence of other neurodegenerative diseases or conditions in addition to cerebrovascular disease that may affect cognition, such as
   a. A history of other neurodegenerative disorders (e.g., Parkinson disease, progressive supranuclear palsy, dementia with Lewy bodies);
   b. The presence of Alzheimer disease biology is confirmed by biomarkers (e.g., PET, CSF, amyloid ligands) or genetic studies (e.g., *PS1* mutation); or,
   c. A history of active cancer or psychiatric or metabolic disorders that may affect cognitive function.

Unstable VaMCI

Subjects with the diagnosis of probable or possible VaMCI whose symptoms revert to normal should be classified as having "unstable VaMCI."

VCI indicates vascular cognitive impairment; VaD, vascular dementia; MCI, mild cognitive impairment; CADASIL, cerebral autosomal dominant arteriopathy with subcortical infarcts and leukoencephalopathy; CT/MRI, computed tomography/ magnetic resonance imaging; PET, positron emission tomography; CSF, cerebrospinal fluid; and VaMCI, vascular mild cognitive impairment.

visuospatial deficits. On the other hand, subcortical dementias such as HD, in addition to their motor disorder, usually demonstrate slowness of thought and early prominent deficits in executive functions, and visuoperceptual and constructional abilities, although they often show only mild or moderate memory and language impairments thought to have quantitative and qualitative distinctions from those of cortical dementia patients (see Table 6.2 for summary).

Some investigators express doubt that cognitive profiles are useful in separating AD from VaD (see Schneider, Boyle, Arvanitakis, Bienias, & Bennett, 2007; Schneider, Wilson, Bienias, Evans, & Bennett, 2004; Wilson et al., 2011), not only because cerebrovascular disease contributes to some of the same domains of cognitive impairment as in AD (e.g., executive function), but also because of the commonness of mixed pathologic processes. Some authors suggest that many cases of dementia meeting the original McKhann et al. (1984) criteria

Table 6.2 Neuropsychological Features Associated with Cortical and Subcortical Dementia

COGNITIVE DOMAIN	CORTICAL DEMENTIA	SUBCORTICAL DEMENTIA
Episodic Memory	*Consolidation deficit*	*Retrieval deficit*
1. Recall vs. Recognition	Equally impaired	Less impaired on recognition
2. Forgetting Rates	Rapid and severe	Slow and approaching normal
3. Intrusion Errors	Frequent	Infrequent
4. Serial Position	Decreased primacy effect	Normal serial position effects
5. Semantic encoding	Not beneficial	Beneficial
Language and Semantic Knowledge	*Prominent deficit*	*Mild to no deficit*
1. Verbal Fluency	Category < Letter	Category = Letter
2. Object Naming	Impaired	Less Impaired to Normal
2a. Error Types on Naming (pelican – bird)	Semantic/ superordinate errors (asparagus – pencil; acorn – peanut)	Perceptual/coordinate errors
2b. Consistency of Missed Items	High across tasks and sessions	Less consistent
Remote/Retrograde Memory	*Temporal gradient deficit*	*No temporal gradient deficit*
Visuospatial Abilities	*Deficits common*	*Deficits common*
1. Timing of Deficits	Affected later in course of decline	Affected early in course of decline
2. Visuoconstruction	Deficit in extrapersonal orientation	Deficit in personal orientation
3. Clock Drawing	Command < Copy	Command = Copy
3a. Basis of Errors	*Conceptual*	*Planning/Motoric*

(continued)

Table 6.2 (Continued)

COGNITIVE DOMAIN	CORTICAL DEMENTIA	SUBCORTICAL DEMENTIA
3b. Types	Leaving off the hands	Large gaps between numbers
	Frequent stimulus bound errors	Stimulus bound errors infrequent
Attention	*Mild to no deficit*	*Prominent deficit*
Working Memory	*Mild deficit*	*Prominent deficit*
Executive Functions	*Prominent deficit*	*Prominent deficit*
1. Possible Distinctions	Linked to lexical/ semantic losses	Pervasive and ubiquitous
1a. Perseverations	Mild and conceptually based	Severe and motorically hyperkinetic
1b. Pervasiveness and Timing	Circumscribed early; pervasive later	Pervasive early and throughout course

Note: Table was derived in part from the reviews of Duke and Kaszniak (2000), Salmon and Filoteo (2007), and Seidel, Giovannetti, and Libon (2011).

for the clinical diagnosis of probable AD have been shown to arise from mixed pathologies (Schneider, Arvanitakis, et al., 2009; Sonnen et al., 2007).

Unfortunately, the McKhann et al. (2011) criteria encourage, but do not require, the use of neuropsychological assessment in documenting specific cognitive impairments; rather, "either 'bedside' mental status examination or neuropsychological testing" is suggested as sufficient. In cases where a dementia has been clearly established, is of at least moderate severity, and the health care provider is concerned with tracking the course and progression of decline well past the mild stages and initial diagnosis, then mental status testing would certainly be indicated. However, we contend that "bedside" mental status testing, reliance on brief cognitive screening instruments, or the use of clinical dementia rating forms, is insufficient for early differential diagnosis and the profiling of mild forms of cognitive impairment. Such strategies are less sensitive and less reliable in documenting specific cognitive impairments or in predicting progression than neuropsychological assessements (see Saxton et al., 2009; Chang et al., 2011; Chang et al., 2010).

Nevertheless, some investigators assert that neuropsychological assessment is not effective in documenting the early cognitive declines in dementia (see

Storandt & Morris, 2010) and instead prefer the use of clinical judgment and reliance on rating forms, such as the Clinical Dementia Rating scale, that are designed to assess changes in function as determined by history or collateral report. However, the use of the global CDR score of 0.5—which connotes an MCI state—has been shown to suffer from a certain "granularity" (Petersen, 2010). Chang et al. (2011), for example, found that when MCI individuals, all of whom had global CDR scores of 0.5, were divided into two groups based on the three CDR subcategories assessing instrumental activities of daily living (IADL), those with any impaired IADL ratings showed a more widespread pattern of gray matter losses involving frontal and parietal regions, worse episodic memory and executive function scores, and progressed to AD more often than those with intact IADL ratings. These findings highlight that the conventional practice of relying on the global CDR score in diagnosis under-utilizes valuable IADL information readily available in the scale and likely delays the identification of an important subset of individuals either at higher risk of clinical decline or, worse, misses those with declines already sufficient for the diagnosis of mild dementia. In other words, one can argue that if individuals—with the existing instruments used in this Uniform Data Set from the Alzheimer's Disease Neuroimaging Initiative (ADNI)—demonstrated episodic memory, executive function, and IADL impairments, this constellation of findings is sufficient for the diagnosis of mild dementia in these individuals who were instead diagnosed with MCI by the more cursory ADNI criteria (e.g., subjective memory complaint; Logical Memory Story A delayed recall > 1.5 SD below norms; Global CDR = 0.5; MMSE > 23). Such widely used diagnostic criteria are arguably less sensitive to the early presentation of cognitive and functional declines exposed by these other neuropsychological measures and IADL ratings.

We contend that neuropsychological patterns and profiles of impairment (e.g., cortical vs. subcortical dementia profiles; see Salmon & Filoteo, 2007, for review) would seem particularly well suited to examine the underlying cognitive manifestations of "pure" AD versus CVD versus "mixed" pathologies (see also Kramer, et al., 2004). We also suggest that sufficient clinical, neuropsychological, imaging, and perhaps biomarker information is available to clearly describe mixed dementia patients, and that the neuropsychological assessment is an essential component to this differential diagnosis, whether the dementia is thought to be due to a single underlying process such as AD or due to multiple etiologies. Further, we suggest that the cursory examination of cognition across many research studies fails to appreciate some of the basic distinctions drawn from the classic neuropsychological studies contrasting cortical and subcortical dementias, such as that of forgetting rates or the contrast between recall and recognition memory performances. For example, to suggest that a cognitive domain like episodic memory is impaired in both AD and VaD, and thus concluded to be unhelpful in separating these dementias (see Wilson, et al., 2011), without specifically contrasting recall and recognition, fails to acknowledge much of the research on a simple difference drawn between impaired recall and recognition in the case of AD (i.e., rapid forgetting) versus impaired recall with improved recognition in the case of subcortical ischemic VaD (i.e., retrieval deficit).

In addition, many studies in this area either have used a "one test, one domain" approach to diagnosis (e.g., Trails B represents all of executive function; delayed recall of a story represents episodic memory, etc.) or summarily combined measures to create a single composite score that is then used to reflect a multifaceted domain of cognition like executive function. Collapsing multiple measures with multiple underlying processes—some of which may be impaired while others may not—dilutes the ability to detect specific components of cognitive dysfunction, especially for a broad domain like that of executive function (Clark et al., 2012). Likewise, as is often done in many MCI studies (e.g., Petersen et al., 2005), there is widespread use of a single measure like 20-minute delayed recall of Story A of Logical Memory to represent all of episodic memory in diagnosis, in lieu of using more measures or at least both LM stories (and its standardized 30-min delay interval) to obtain standard scores anchored to its normative reference values. Strategies that collapse rather than contrast critical measures (e.g., recall vs. recognition) or derail a test from its standardized administration, scoring, and normative referencing (e.g., dropping one of the stories, decreasing the delay interval, and applying delimited education corrections only; see Petersen, et al., 2005) are decisions that arguably render any measure less sensitive and less reliable.

Selection of the most sensitive measures is also important. For example, a number of investigators have shown that verbal list learning tests (e.g., Buschke Selective Reminding Test; California Verbal Learning Test; Rey Auditory Verbal Learning Test) are among the most sensitive in MCI (de Jager, Hogervorst, Combrinck, & Budge, 2003; Masur, Fuld, Blau, Crystal, & Aronson, 1990; Rabin, Pare, Saykin, et al., 2009) and to the earliest stages of an evolving dementia (Bondi, Salmon, Galasko, Thomas, & Thal, 1999; Lange et al., 2002; Tierney, Yao, Kiss, & McDowell, 2005). Finally, the statistical maxim that multiple measures tend to provide a more reliable estimate of a cognitive construct than any single measure (Anastasi & Urbina, 1997) is also relevant to those studies subsuming all of a given cognitive domain like episodic memory to a single measure like delayed recall of a story paragraph. As investigators have shown, measures of learning *or* recall provide comparable predictive utility of progression to AD (Chang et al., 2011), a finding that reinforces some of the original demonstrations of the utility of learning measures in preclinical AD (e.g., Bondi et al., 1999; Grober & Kawas, 1997; Masur, et al., 1990).

As we further discuss below, knowledge of the base rates of pure AD, pure VaD, and mixed dementia pathologies are also important considerations for the diagnostician, and large percentages of the dementias of late life will have AD, as well as vascular, Lewy body, and other co-occurring pathologies. Examining the prevalencies of specific cognitive deficit profiles in known groups will be very helpful as well. As the work of Filoteo and colleagues (Filoteo et al., 1997; Zizak et al., 2005) have shown, for example, clear retrieval deficit profiles (e.g., impaired recall with improved recognition) appear to be present in about half of HD patients (see also Weintraub, Moberg, Culbertson, et al., 2004, for similar findings in Parkinson's disease). Therefore, the prevalencies or base rates of these cognitive profiles, even in homogeneous subcortical dementia groups, are important considerations for the diagnostician to bear in mind.

Given the less-than-perfect prevalencies of prototypical cognitive profiles in dementia, one might ask whether the diagnostician should rely on the use of neuropsychological deficit patterns and profiles. We argue that clinical neuropsychology provides some of the best accuracy rates for the clinical diagnosis of various dementias, and either equals or exceeds other more relied upon clinical, imaging, or biomarker information (e.g., Gomar et al., 2011; Heister et al., 2011; Jedynak et al., 2012; Landau et al., 2010; Schmand, Huizenga, & van Gool, 2010; Tiraboschi et al., 2006); and these studies have found comparable or superior prediction with *individual* cognitive measures. Outcome studies using more comprehensive neuropsychological assessments—and actuarial examinations of patterns and profiles of neuropsychological dysfunction—have yet to be done. Clinical neuropsychology has a great deal of room for improvement in its own right, and more consistent use of empirically determined important measures in differential diagnosis is one area where improvements in "best practice models" can be made. For example, the inclusion of false positive errors on recognition memory testing has shown improvements in sensitivity and specificity rates for separating AD and VaD (Hildebrandt, et al., 2009). The work of Libon and colleagues (Eppig et al., 2011; Libon et al., 2011; Libon et al., 2010) suggests that more in-depth analysis of the relationships between neuropsychological scores can potentially enhance the diagnostic accuracy of MCI subtypes. An amnestic disorder characterized by a somewhat flattened learning curve, poor recall and recognition (i.e., evidence of rapid forgetting), and often with a proclivity for intrusion errors, typifies the profile seen in the classic single-domain amnestic MCI case and would be thought to represent an evolving cortical dementia syndrome with underlying AD pathology. Improvement on recognition memory relative to free recall, and perhaps lower rates of intrusion errors, in the context of imaging or other evidence of cerebrovascular disease, would be suggestive of underlying subcortical ischemic vascular disease.

Finally, clinical neuropsychology offers patients and their families much more than a diagnosis. It plays a unique and pivotal role in defining and describing the specific cognitive strengths and weaknesses confronted by individuals, and we are often in the best position to provide specific treatment recommendations to the patient, his or her family, and the patient's health care providers.

Cognitive dysfunction, secondary to stroke and its resulting strategic cortical and/or subcortical infarction, is a distinct and salient event, and the diagnostic process for the clinical neuropsychologist in this situation relies on the long tradition of localization and syndromal perspectives in which most neuropsychologists have been trained (e.g., aphasia, neglect, Gerstmann syndrome). By contrast, more recent work on the neuropsychological deficits associated with VaD has primarily focused on differentiating subcortical ischemic VaD from AD, and these efforts have generally shown features consistent with subcortical versus cortical dementia syndromes, respectively. Therefore, we will concentrate our discussion on this category of VaD resulting from subcortical small vessel ischemic disease. Accordingly, any assessment of the cognitive profile of subcortical ischemic VaD will begin with a canvassing of both episodic memory and executive function abilities, and much of the clinical research in this area has compared these two cognitive domains alongside one another, which we will do also.

Episodic Memory and Executive Functions

Neuropsychological studies largely demonstrate that patients with subcortical VaD are more impaired than those with AD on tests of *executive functions*, whereas patients with AD are more impaired than those with subcortical VaD on tests of *episodic memory* (Desmond, 2004; Graham, Emery, & Hodges, 2004; Kertesz & Clydesdale, 1994; Lafosse et al., 1997; Lamar et al., 1997; cf. Reed et al., 2004; Reed et al., 2007, for a differing conclusion). These studies also suggest that executive dysfunction is the most conspicuous deficit associated with subcortical VaD, perhaps because the subcortical pathology frequently interrupts frontosubcortical circuits that mediate this aspect of cognition (see the original work by Alexander, DeLong, & Strick, 1986; or, reviews by Cummings, 1993; DeLong & Wichmann, 2007; and Mega & Cummings, 1994, for details regarding basal ganglia thalamocortical neuronal circuitry). For example, Price and colleagues (2005) have shown that VaD patients with significant white matter abnormalities on imaging demonstrate a profile of greater executive function and visuoconstructive impairments than impairment of memory and language abilities, which concur with the findings of Cosentino et al. (2004) discussed earlier in the chapter; and another study by Carey et al. (2008) found that subcortical lacunes on MRI corresponded to poorer executive functions, even in otherwise cognitively normal older adults. Each of these studies is consistent with the notion of disrupted frontosubcortical pathways to varying degrees.

Libon and colleagues (2011) have further suggested that the executive dysfunction observed in small vessel ischemic VaD is not only quantitatively more severe than AD, but also qualitatively distinct. The executive control deficits seen in VaD tend to be ubiquitous or pervasive, whereas AD patients often show less severe executive deficits that appear to be restricted to the response selection of lexical/semantic information. For example, when observing graphomotor perseverations, patients with VaD produce not just a high volume of errors, but their errors reflect problems in desisting from a motor act. Thus, if asked to draw "three squares and five circles" patients with VaD might draw more figures that requested. By contrast, patients with AD produce fewer perseverations, and the types of graphomotor errors differ. If asked to draw "three squares and five circles," a patient with AD may write in words "three squares and five circles." This type of error suggests lexical access or semantic knowledge problems, and Lamar et al. (1997) have shown that the former motor perseverations in VaD are associated with executive dysfunction, whereas the latter lexical/semantic errors in AD have been shown to correlate with object naming and category fluency.

Conversely, VaD patients demonstrate better episodic memory performance relative to patients with AD. Duke and Kaszniak (2000) discuss similar notions, and further note that the time course of the deficit profiles are important to consider as well. That is, although executive function impairments are present in AD, they are less prominent than the episodic memory disorder in the neuropsychological profile of the mild stages of AD and tend to become more pronounced later in the course of the illness. In contrast, patients with frontal-subcortical dementia may demonstrate executive dysfunction, which occurs earlier in the disease progression and may be initially more severe. Others also have suggested that frank episodic memory impairment may not come until later in the course of VaD, although retrieval errors and source memory difficulties associated with executive dysfunction may appear early in the course (Cohen, 2009).

Although neuropsychological studies provide consistent evidence for distinct cognitive profiles of episodic memory and executive dysfunction in subcortical ischemic VaD and AD, some recent work has deemphasized the importance of this distinction, perhaps due in part to the increasing appreciation of executive dysfunction in MCI and early AD and the wide variety of cognitive deficit profiles associated with vascular cognitive impairment (Lamar, Price, Giovannetti, Swenson, & Libon, 2010). In addition, most studies comparing AD and VaD groups have recruited clinically diagnosed patients without subsequent autopsy verification of their diagnoses. Some misclassification of patients across groups is expected because AD and VaD can overlap in their clinical presentations as well as in their underlying pathologies (e.g., see Schneider, Arvanitakis, et al., 2009).

To avoid this situation, Reed and colleagues have compared the profiles of neuropsychological deficits exhibited by patients with autopsy-confirmed subcortical VaD or AD (Reed et al., 2004; Reed et al., 2007). Consistent with prior studies, patients with AD had a pronounced deficit in episodic memory that was significantly greater than their executive function deficit. This finding is consistent with the neuropathologic staging of Braak and Braak (1991) suggesting that that the typical progression of AD neurofibrillary tangle accumulation emanates from the medial temporal to the lateral temporal to the frontal cortices (see Figure 5.4 in Chapter 5). By contrast, patients with subcortical VaD had a deficit in executive functions that was greater than their deficit in episodic memory, although this difference was not statistically significant.

On further inspection of individual patient profiles, more than 70% of the AD patients exhibited a profile with memory impairment more prominent than executive dysfunction, although only about half of the patients with subcortical VaD exhibited a profile with more prominent executive dysfunction than memory impairment. Interestingly, severe cerebrovascular disease at autopsy was not necessarily associated with clinically significant cognitive impairment, although the profile analysis between subcortical VaD and AD patients was more pronounced when the analysis was restricted to those patients who exhibited significant cognitive impairment at their clinical assessment. That is, roughly 80% of AD patients exhibited a low memory profile and nearly 70% of subcortical VaD patients showed a low executive profile (see Figure 6.4). None of the VaD patients had a low memory profile, and only 5% of the AD patients had a low executive profile. Reed et al.'s (2007) study suggests that relatively distinct cognitive deficit profiles might be clinically useful in differentiating between subcortical VaD and AD, although additional research with autopsy-diagnosed patients is needed to further define the deficit profile that will be most useful in this regard.

Two additional points from this important study are worth considering. First, despite the appreciable dissociations in the percentages of executive dysfunction and episodic memory impairment between VaD and AD, the authors concluded that the cognitive effects of small vessel cerebrovascular disease are variable and not especially distinct; and thus they question the utility of executive dysfunction in the diagnosis of VaD. This interpretation

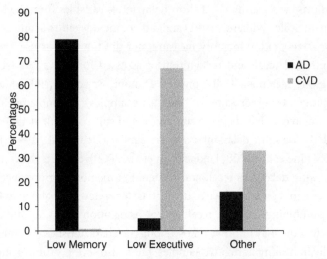

FIGURE 6.4 Distribution of neuropsychological test profiles by diagnostic group when cases were restricted to those with clinical cognitive impairment or dementia. AD = autopsy-confirmed Alzheimer's disease; CVD = autopsy-confirmed cerebrovascular disease (without AD pathology). Based on data from Reed et al., (2007).

of their findings would seem to be relatively conservative in light of the differing percentages noted above between the VaD and AD groups on executive function and episodic memory measures, especially for those analyses restricted to those with cognitive impairments; and it implies that executive function and episodic memory dissociations would need to approach accuracy levels well above 80% to be regarded as useful—a criterion level that would seem to be highly conservative. To provide a broader context, the high percentages of distinct neuropsychological profiles between VaD and AD noted by Reed et al. (2007) are better than a number of other markers for various other disorders. For example, visual hallucinations (VH) and extrapyramidal symptoms (EPS) are among the core diagnostic features in the diagnosis of DLB (see Chapter 7; McKeith et al., 2005), yet the prevalence rate of VH is well below 50%, and EPS is present in only one- to two-thirds of DLB cases (Aarsland, Ballard, McKeith, Perry, & Larsen, 2001; Tiraboschi et al., 2006).

The second point regarding Reed et al.'s (2007) conclusions is that the cognitive variables used to define the constructs of episodic memory and executive function were single composite measures that either did not employ many of the specific contrasting distinctions related to cortical versus subcortical dementia or, worse, combined rather than contrasted important measures. For example, the verbal episodic memory composite used by Reed et al. was comprised of learning and short delay recall variables from the Memory Assessment Scale (Williams, 1991) and did not include either a long delay free recall or a recognition memory measure; nor did the authors use a measure that contrasted recall and recognition or assessed forgetting rate (see Delis et al., 1991; Massman, Delis, Butters, Dupont, & Gillin, 1992; Massman, Delis, Butters, Levin, & Salmon, 1990, for examples). As ample research has shown, free recall deficits between cortical and subcortical dementia groups, particularly for short delay intervals, are similar (Delis et al., 1991; Delis et al., 2005; Fine et al., 2008; Hildebrandt et al., 2009), and it is the distinction between long delay free recall and recognition memory performance that is more useful in separating the two dementias (for review, see Salmon & Filoteo, 2007). Combining learning, recall and/or recognition measures into a single composite score may improve on psychometric characteristics to some extent, especially in healthy normative samples, but it also severely dilutes important pattern distinctions one can draw between these measures in clinical situations, and it diminishes a measure's sensitivity to subtle change because these individually important scores are summarily combined with other insensitive measures (see also Delis, Jacobson, Bondi, Hamilton, & Salmon, 2003, for discussion). Regardless of the conservative conclusions drawn and the use of single episodic memory and executive function composite scores, Reed et al. (2007) nevertheless showed distinct profiles between autopsy-confirmed groups of subcortical ischemic VaD and AD. Future studies that more sharply contrast the neuropsychological features of cortical and subcortical dementia groups should be able to build on this important work.

Other important components to episodic memory processes such as the *rate of forgetting* or the presence of *intrusion errors* (Butters, Salmon, & Butters, 1994) may further help to differentiate cortical from subcortical dementia but are rarely examined. It is interesting to note that Reed and colleagues (Kramer et al., 2004) in an earlier study examined forgetting rates and found that AD patients had more severe forgetting than VaD. Among the VaD group, interesting subgroups emerged in which some showed rapid forgetting and others exhibited good retention rates. Those VaD patients with good retention showed a trend for greater executive impairments relative to either the AD group or the VaD subgroup with rapid forgetting. These authors suggested that the finding of rapid forgetting in the context of subcortical ischemic vascular disease implies concomitant AD pathology, whereas dementia in patients with good retention may be more vascular in origin. Finally, the authors noted that, in the subsample of VaD patients with rapid forgetting who were followed to autopsy, all in this small sample had AD pathology—further linking this pattern of memory deficit to AD even against the backdrop of subcortical small vessel ischemic disease.

In a companion paper with autopsy-confirmed AD and VaD patients, Reed et al. (2004) reached a similar conclusion wherein they showed good accuracy for the neuropsychological diagnosis of either pure AD or mixed AD and VaD, although neuropsychological diagnoses missed the presence of ischemic VaD in over half the cases. Results further showed that some of the usual clinical features often considered to be associated with VaD (e.g., elevated Hachinski Ischemia Scale scores, abrupt onset or stepwise progression of cognitive decline) were unhelpful, similar to findings noted by Cosentino and colleagues (2004). The constellation of studies from this group suggests that the episodic memory failure is worse in AD than in VaD, although the executive dysfunction—and many of the "standard" clinical features (e.g., elevated stroke risk factors; stepwise progression)—may not be worse in many cases of VaD.

The concept of "executive function" is broad and encompasses many tasks and abilities (e.g., set-shifting, planning, inhibition, problem-solving), and specific aspects of executive function may be differentially affected by VaD and AD. Coming back to the study by Reed et al. (2007), much like their composite episodic memory measure, the executive function composite score may not have been optimal in its ability to separate VaD from AD since it was comprised in part of letter fluency ("FAS") scores, which, again, are not especially distinct between cortical and subcortical dementia. Category fluency (e.g., animals, fruits, and vegetables; or AFV), and more specifically the differences between letter and category fluency (Monsch et al., 1994), is preferable in demonstrating such distinctions between cortical and subcortical dementia on verbal fluency (see Salmon & Bondi, 2009). The disproportionately severe fluency impairment exhibited by AD when generating exemplars from a specific semantic category, compared with generation of words beginning with a particular letter, is indicative of a loss of semantic knowledge or, at least, a breakdown in the organization of semantic memory and separates it from the lexical search or retrieval based difficulties—but intact semantic knowledge—thought to underlie the equally poor letter and category fluency performances typically seen in subcortical dementia (see Salmon & Bondi, 2009).

An important caveat of this contrast between letter and category fluency is that it is drawn from research that specifically contrasted F, A, and S words to AFV (animals, fruits, vegetables) categories (Monsch et al., 1994). Other letter versus category fluency contrasts either have not been as extensively examined and require empirical support of their dissociations between cortical and subcortical dementias (e.g., D-KEFS verbal fluency) or have shown poorer sensitivity and specificity rates in AD relative to AFV (e.g., supermarket fluency on DRS or first names fluency; Monsch et al., 1994). Many of the recent studies contrasting letter and category fluency have used only portions (e.g., F- or S-words vs. animals), again potentially decreasing the reliability of such contrasts (Anastasi & Urbina, 1997). Even further, decisions regarding selection of tests comprising the Uniform Data Set of neuropsychological tests across all the NIH-funded Alzheimer's Disease Centers included only category fluency measures (e.g., only animals and vegetables; Weintraub, et al., 2009), thereby negating any potential for examining the contrast between letter and category fluency.

To summarize, we reiterate from the AD chapter that an episodic memory disorder characterized by a somewhat flattened learning curve, poor recall and recognition (i.e., evidence of rapid forgetting), and often a proclivity for intrusion errors, typifies the profile seen in a cortical dementia syndrome and suggests underlying AD pathology (see Table 6.2). Improved recognition relative to free recall, perhaps lower rates of intrusion errors, in the context of imaging or other evidence of cerebrovascular disease, would be suggestive of subcortical ischemic VaD. Executive dysfunction may be present in both dementias, although we would echo the conclusions of Duke and Kaszniak (2000) and of Seidel, Giovannetti, and Libon (2011) in suggesting that executive function impairments in AD may be less prominent or pervasive than the memory disorder; whereas in VaD the executive function impairment is more prominent and severe than the memory deficit. It may be possible that specific aspects of executive dysfunction are more common in AD than VaD, but few if any studies have widely canvassed executive functions in both dementias, and this would seem to be an interesting direction for future research (e.g., see Clark et al., 2012). When both episodic memory and executive function impairments are present and of similar severity, mixed AD and cerebrovascular pathology is possible.

It bears reemphasizing that the distinctions drawn between AD and subcortical ischemic VaD, on the basis of executive function versus episodic memory impairments, are likely due to the prominent frontal-subcortical dysfunction in VaD relative to the pathology of AD that is predominantly cortical (Pantoni, 2010). The subgroup of VaD patients characterized by extensive subcortical ischemic vascular disease is perhaps more neuropsychologically distinct from AD than some of the other vascular pathologies. For example, multi-infarct dementia, or subgroups of VaD due to strategic cortical infarctions, may share similarities with cortical dementia syndromes, including but not limited to the episodic memory impairment characteristic of AD. In addition to the pattern of episodic memory loss seen in AD, a large number of possible other cortical syndromes may be present in any given case of MID. This is due to the fact that cortical infarcts may occur in nearly any cortical region that results in impairment of those associated cognitive abilities. For example, aphasias characteristic of frontotemporal dementia may result from strategic infarctions of frontal and/or temporal regions, behavioral syndromes found in the behavioral variant of FTD and AD (e.g., disinhibition, inertia) may result from orbitofrontal or medial frontal cortical infarctions, and various forms of visual agnosia (e.g., Balint's syndrome, object recognition deficits) found in posterior cortical atrophy and visual variants of AD may result from posterior cerebral artery infarctions. This high potential for heterogeneity in the pathologies of VaD underscores the difficulty in describing a modal profile of impairment in VaD due to MID or other strategic infarctions. Integration of the neuropsychological presentation of a particular individual with his or her imaging findings is helpful to differentiate between possible underlying neurodegenerative versus cerebro-vascular syndromes.

Of course, episodic memory and executive functions are but two cognitive domains, and other domains may further help to characterize the subcortical dementia of small vessel ischemic VaD.

Language and Semantic Knowledge

Another important point to the above discussion is that perhaps the two types of verbal fluency measures typically used by neuropsychologists ought not to be thought of together as executive function measures—as is often done (e.g., see Reed et al., 2007). Research has shown that letter and category fluency measures tend to load on different factors and have appreciably different brain substrates. In the case of letter fluency, it is more often associated with other executive function measures, whereas category fluency tends to associate with other language tasks. Meta-analytic work by Henry, Crawford, and Phillips (2004) suggests that performance on letter fluency is differentially sensitive to frontal impairment; and studies have shown that the output on tests of letter fluency produced by VaD patients is reduced relative to AD patients (Carew, Lamar, Cloud, Grossman, & Libon, 1997; Lafosse et al., 1997). By contrast, performance on category fluency is affected by damage to the lateral temporal lobes, presumably because successful performance on this test depends on semantic knowledge, and semantic operations have heavy input from the lateral temporal lobes (e.g., Levy, Bayley, & Squire, 2004; Wierenga et al., 2010). Interestingly, the study by Carew et al. (1997) showed that VaD patients' output on category (animal) fluency was similar to AD patients, although their semantic associations between items produced was significantly higher than the AD group and comparable to that of the healthy control group. Thus, the reduced output on animal fluency in VaD patients was thought to reflect difficulty with search-retrieval strategies, whereas the reduced output in AD was thought to be reflective of a degradation of semantic knowledge. Henry et al. (2004) further confirmed in their meta-analyses that AD patients exhibit a more pronounced impairment on category fluency than letter fluency, again suggesting a breakdown in semantic knowledge, or its successful access to semantic information, in AD. Recall too that AD patients show greater impairment on the Boston Naming Test (Bayles & Tomoeda, 1983; Bowles, Obler, & Albert, 1987) than patients with Huntington's disease (Hodges, Salmon,

& Butters, 1991); and AD patients make more semantic errors whereas HD patients make more perceptually based errors.

Unfortunately, language disturbance is rarely specifically characterized in many studies of VaD, although one study by Lukatela et al. (1998) showed that VaD patients outperformed AD patients and made distinct types of errors. AD patients made more superordinate naming errors, whereas the VaD patients committed more coordinate errors (e.g., naming an acorn a "peanut"), again implying differences in the organization of semantic knowledge between the two types of dementia. Although another study by Laine et al. (1997) failed to show group differences between AD and VaD on the BNT, they continued to show that AD patients made more semantic errors.

We would therefore offer the same type of recommendation as in the prior section on episodic memory and executive functions. That is, in the absence of a strategic infarction affecting language function, subcortical ischemic VaD would not be expected to impair object naming, nor would we expect the disproportionate impairment on category fluency relative to letter fluency, to the same degree as that seen in AD. When quantitative impairment on these measures is of comparable magnitude to that of AD, inspection of the quality of naming errors will be helpful to further differentiate the integrity of semantic operations.

Attention and Working Memory

Although declines in attention and working memory occur in both cortical and subcortical dementias, they tend to show more prominent impairment in subcortical dementia syndromes. Early studies with HD patients, for example, showed comparatively worse performances than AD patients on attention items of the MMSE (Brandt, Folstein, & Folstein, 1988), the attention subscale of the DRS (Salmon, Kwo-on-Yuen, Heindel, Butters, & Thal, 1989), and on digit span, visual memory span, or mental control items of the WMS-R (Tröster, Jacobs, Butters, Cullum, & Salmon, 1989). More experimentally derived measures related to orienting, allocating, or shifting of attention have also been shown to be impaired in a variety of subcortical dementia groups (e.g., HD, PD, progressive supranuclear palsy) relative to patients with AD (see Salmon & Filoteo, 2007). Similar findings have been observed with measures of working memory, such that the subcortical dementia syndrome of patients with HD or PD shows early and pervasive impairment in all aspects of working memory, whereas for AD it may be more circumscribed to impairment of the central executive with sparing of the phonological loop and visuospatial sketchpad (Baddeley, Bressi, Della Sala, Logie, & Spinnler, 1991; Collette, Van der Linden, Bechet, & Salmon, 1999).

Studies of attention and working memory specific to VaD confirm that many of the declines noted in other subcortical dementia syndromes are observed in VaD patients as well. For example, Libon and colleagues (1997) showed that patients with small vessel ischemic VaD as well as patients with Parkinson's disease performed less accurately on the Boston revision of the Mental Control subtest of the WMS than AD patients. This test was designed to measure the capacity to establish and maintain a mental set through a series of tasks (e.g., recite the months of the year backward). Lamar et al. (2002) further revealed that the VaD and AD patients perform differently over time as well. The VaD patients made fewer and fewer correct responses over time, whereas performance of AD patients leveled off by the midway point with no further decline, which was thought to be indicative of a differential impairment in maintaining mental set in the VaD group. A pair of studies by Lamar et al. (2007; 2008) also examined working memory using a Backwards Digit Span test and found that individuals with moderate-to-severe white matter disease performed below those with minimal-to-mild white matter disease on the serial-ordering component of this test, suggesting differential impairment for mental manipulation and temporal reordering. Furthermore, serial order performance was explained by both dementia severity and executive functioning.

Visuospatial Abilities

Visuospatial deficits have been described in both cortical and subcortical dementia syndromes, although few studies have directly compared the two types of dementia on tests of visuospatial skills. In the subcortical dementia syndrome of HD, performance on many different tests of visuospatial abilities (e.g., Block Design; Clock Drawing Test) is often impaired early in the course and continues to decline as the dementia worsens (Lawrence, Watkins, Sahakian, Hodges, & Robbins, 2000; Ward et al., 2006). AD patients also tend to demonstrate impairments on many of these same measures (see Cronin-Golomb & Amick, 2001), although it is unclear whether the visuospatial processing features giving rise to such impairments in two dementia syndromes are similar. For example, Rouleau et al. (1992) showed that, despite equal impairments on clock drawing between AD and HD patient groups, the two groups made distinct types of errors. AD patients tended to make conceptual errors, whereas HD patients tended to make graphomotor and planning errors. Some evidence also exists that AD and HD patients show dissociations between personal and extrapersonal spatial orientation abilities (Brouwers, Cox, Martin, Chase, & Fedio, 1984; Lineweaver, Salmon, Bondi, & Corey-Bloom, 2005) and visual sensory integration (Festa et al., 2005). The deficits shown by HD patients on visuospatial tasks have generally been attributed to planning, motor, and bradyphrenic difficulties that accompany disruption of frontal-subcortical circuits, whereas the difficulties noted in AD patients seem to arise from deficits in accessing knowledge of the attributes, features, and meaning of visuospatial stimuli.

When applying some of these purported dissociable component processes of visuospatial functioning specifically to VaD, some interesting dissociations have emerged. Freeman et al. (2000), for example, showed that AD patients generally outperformed VaD patients on a modification of the Rey-Osterrieth Complex Figure Test (ROCF). The drawings of the VaD patients were more fragmented and contained numerous perseverations and omissions. Despite these errors, patients with VaD obtained higher delayed recognition memory for the various cluster elements of the ROCF than AD patients. Recall also that the studies of Cosentino et al. (2004) and Price et al. (2005), discussed above, demonstrated greater visuospatial impairments in their groups of VaD patients relative to AD. In both studies, VaD patients made more clock drawing errors than AD patients. Prior research from this group has shown that the total of errors summed across the command and copy conditions is highly correlated with performance on tests of executive control and visuospatial ability, and the clock drawing test appears to be a diagnostically sensitive measure for subcortical VaD (Cosentino et al., 2004; Libon, Swenson, Barnoski, & Sands, 1993).

Motor, Psychomotor, and Other Skills
Very few studies have directly compared AD and VaD groups on tests of motor and psychomotor skills. One study by Zhou and Jia (2009) examined two groups of MCI patients with either cerebral small vessel disease or with prodromal Alzheimer's disease and found that the latter group performed worse on memory tasks but better on processing speed measures (e.g., Digit Symbol). By contrast, Mathias and Burke (2009) summarize that the few studies examining motor or psychomotor performances have not been helpful in discriminating between AD and VaD (e.g., Digit Symbol, sequential operations, reaction time, ideomotor apraxia). Although this meta-analytic study showed that a number of cognitive measures were limited in their ability to discriminate between the two dementia groups, Mathias and Burke did

highlight that patients with VaD were more impaired than patients with AD on one test of perception (Emotional Recognition; Shimokawa et al., 2003), whereas patients with AD were more impaired than those with VaD on tests of episodic memory. Specifically, compared to VaD, persons with AD were better able to identify facial expressions and appropriately match emotional expressions to situations, but were less able to recall verbal material after a delay. Future research on this dissociation in emotion processing between VaD and AD is clearly needed to follow up on these intriguing initial findings.

Finally, an exciting new area of research on psychomotor skills in MCI and dementia involves the use of computerized virtual environments (VE) in order to simulate a number of real-world tasks such as driving (Marcotte et al., 2004; Shechtman et al., 2007), shopping (Whitney et al., 2006), or navigating through streets while on foot (Tippett et al., 2009). One representative study by Tippett et al. (2009) showed that an MCI group demonstrated a similar spatial-navigation ability to that of control participants, although the MCI participants' speed of movement within the city environment was reduced and they took longer to respond to changes in maze direction. Zakzanis et al. (2009), using the same VE task, also showed that when compared to older adults, patients with AD made more mistakes on the recognition task, being more likely to commit false positive scene errors (i.e., mistakenly affirm having seen an element in the city when it was in fact a foil). The performances of VaD patients on VE tasks—such as scene recognition—would be particularly interesting as well. In a single VE task such as this, a number of interesting measures can be obtained that relate to learning and memory, movement, and timing. More generally, given the recent advent of computer "tablets" such as Apple's iPad and the great potential for administering a wide array of tasks on such a platform, it will be interesting to see the translation of neuropsychological tests, including the use of virtual environments, in these new ways. Perhaps even more potential with such a platform or with smartphones or other assistive technologies might be realized with the advent of performance-based assessments of instrumental ADL functions such as shopping, medication adherence, transportation, handling finances, and telephone use, to name but a few.

Treatments

Given the continued growth of the aging population in the coming decades, the prevalence of dementia will also grow. As stated in Chapter 5, the prevalence of AD is expected to top 14 million or more in the United States by

2050. Given the possibility that vascular risk factors may increase the risk and promote the development of both VaD and perhaps AD, greater emphasis is being placed on the detection of prodromal changes related to the development of dementia. In one community study reported by Dodge et al. (2011), the authors concluded that the risk of dementia could be reduced by more than 10% simply by eliminating overt cerebrovascular disease. Future work is needed to help clarify whether vascular disease exerts an additive or synergistic effect on AD clinical expression. What is increasingly clear, however, is the finding that vascular factors influence the incidence of AD, and identification of the respective underlying neuropathologies of AD and VaD will help to discern the pathophysiologic underpinnings responsible for progressive cognitive and functional decline.

This pursuit is important because risk factors for cerebrovascular disease are among the most amenable to modification and effectively treated. Hypertension, hyperlipidemia, diabetes, obesity, and the like are easily targeted for intervention with a variety of pharmacologic and other interventions. Even among AD patients, small vessel cerebrovascular disease is common and has been closely linked to hypertension (Pantoni, 2010). This high comorbidity has led to some speculation that small vessel CVD may account for some proportion of the increased risk of AD development in hypertensive patients, and some investigators assert that cognitive impairment associated with blood pressure elevation may have an additive effect on declines related to Alzheimer pathology (Knopman & Roberts, 2010). In such a scenario, less underlying Alzheimer pathology would be needed to express dementia in an individual with concomitant small vessel ischemic disease due to hypertension, and the implications would be such that with earlier detection and treatment of CVD risk factors, one might achieve an eventual decrease in the development of dementia.

It may be that the combination of AD and vascular pathologies results in, or accelerates the expression of, cognitive impairment in some individuals. This interactive model of Alzheimer's and vascular diseases implies that a more sophisticated utilization of existing treatments—particularly with respect to cerebrovascular disease risks—may effect reductions in the overall incidence rates of dementia. Early detection and treatment of overlying vascular disease may significantly reduce the incidence of dementia even in the absence of major advances in our ability to detect and treat underlying Alzheimer's pathology. This underscores the need for further research examining the ability of existing clinical (e.g., blood pressure), imaging, genetic, and neuropsychological assessment techniques to identify individuals at greatest risk for dementia due to potentially treatable causes (see Nation et al., 2011, for discussion).

While a full review of treatments for CVD is beyond the scope of this chapter (see Gorelick et al., 2011, for broader review), there are a whole host of lifestyle (diet and obesity, physical activity, mental activities, alcohol and drug intake, smoking and social supports), mood, and physiological factors (blood pressure, lipids, inflammation, hyperglycemia, insulin resistance, metabolic syndrome, and diabetes) that impact vascular-related cognitive impairments and are amenable to treatment. We will highlight but two of these latter factors and discuss some of their complex relationships with vascular cognitive impairments: blood pressure and diabetes.

Blood Pressure and Hypertension
Blood pressure (BP) elevation is a well-established risk factor for dementia, although studies examining antihypertensive medication use in the prevention of dementia in older adults have been mixed (Duron & Hanon, 2010). For example, most longitudinal studies have repeatedly found that elevated BP in midlife is predictive of cognitive decline in late life, although cross-sectional studies indicate that both high and low BP are associated with cognitive decline and dementia in older adults (Qiu, Winblad, & Fratiglioni, 2005). Nation et al. (2011) discusses that these mixed results highlight that the mechanisms responsible for the increased risk of dementia associated with hypertension are not fully understood. Admittedly, the relationship between BP and cognition is complex (e.g., perhaps curvilinear) and age-dependent (Qiu, et al., 2005).

Evidence also indicates that separate components of the BP curve show differential relationships with cognition across the life span. For example, systolic blood pressure (SBP) tends to increase with age, mean arterial pressure remains relatively static, and diastolic blood pressure (DBP) tends to decrease to some degree (Mitchell, 2008). These differences are thought to be due to loss of compliance within the large elastic arteries, particularly the aorta, secondary to the breakdown of elastin and deposition of collagen as a result of aging and atherosclerosis (Safar, 2010). These changes alter the timing of pressure wave reflections returning to the heart, causing augmentation of SBP and decreased buffering of pressure fluctuations during the cardiac cycle. The result is high rates of systolic hypertension in the elderly and increases in pulse pressure, which is a term denoting the arithmetic subtraction of SBP from DBP (Nation et al., 2010).

The steady component of BP (i.e., mean arterial pressure) is determined by cardiac output and total peripheral resistance, whereas pulse pressure (PP = SBP − DBP) is determined by a more complex combination of factors, including SBP, arterial compliance, and wave reflection, all of which increase with age and vascular disease (Nichols & O'Rourke, 2006). PP elevation has been associated with cognitive decline and increased risk of Alzheimer's disease (Nation et al., 2010; Qiu, Winblad, Viitanen, & Fratiglioni, 2003; Waldstein et al., 2008). The mechanism responsible for the cognitive effects of PP elevation are not known, but Nation et al. (2011) discuss that it may be related to the increased pulse wave velocity associated with large vessel stiffening as we get older. As the aorta and carotid arteries lose their elasticity with age, there is an increase in the speed with which the pulse wave is propagated throughout the vascular tree (Safar, 2008). The increased impedance encountered by the pulse wave as it travels from the aortic arch to the carotid artery is largely responsible for reflecting much of the pulse wave prior to its entry into the brain. This impedance mismatch may prevent high velocity pulse waves from penetrating all the way to the brain's microvasculature. Arterial stiffening causes a decrease in impedance mismatching at the carotid artery as the aorta becomes less compliant. The rich, autoregulated microvasculature of the brain is dependent on torrential blood flow to meet its high metabolic demands. Consequently, pulse waves traveling relatively unimpeded deep into the microvasculature of the brain may place excessive mechanical strain on the cerebral arterioles that form the primary source of vascular resistance in the brain. In the context of chronic PP elevation, this increase in mechanical strain has been posited to cause adaptive hypertrophic changes in the arteriolar resistance vessels leading to cerebral small vessel disease or arteriolosclerosis (Mitchell, 2008; Safar, 2010). In older adults, SBP and PP have been more consistently associated with cognitive decline and increased risk of Alzheimer's and small vessel ischemic disease, whereas results from examining DBP and mean arterial pressure are more mixed (see Nation et al., 2011, for review). Elevated PP may represent a particularly useful variable for examining the increased risk of dementia in patients with hypertension. Indeed, PP elevation has been associated with white matter hyperintensities in patients with hypertension and in patients with AD (Kearney-Schwartz et al., 2009; Lee, Jeong, Choi, Sohn, & Chui, 2006) as well as with the autopsy presence of cerebrovascular disease in pathologically confirmed AD patients (Nation et al., 2012).

It remains unclear which aspect of arterial stiffening is primarily responsible for damaging the brain's vasculature and causes cognitive impairment.

Possibilities include the increased velocity of the pulse wave, increased central or aortic pulse pressure, augmentation of systolic blood pressure, and decreased impedance mismatch at the carotid artery. Each of these hemodynamic changes that accompany aortic stiffening can be measured and may have differential impacts on brain function. One study reported the results of a comprehensive assessment of the effects of wave pulsatility on brain structure and cognition in older adults (Mitchell et al., 2011) and found that carotid-femoral pulse wave velocity (PWV) was associated with memory declines, subcortical infarctions, and white matter lesions. Central or aortic pulse pressure was also related to poor memory and subcortical infarctions, but not white matter lesions. Carotid pulsatility index (a measure of the mismatch between aortic and carotid impedance) was more broadly associated with memory, speed of processing, executive dysfunction, subcortical infarctions, and both white and grey matter total volume losses, but not white matter lesions.

These findings suggest that different hemodynamic consequences of arterial stiffening may be responsible for a variety of structural brain changes and decline in specific cognitive domains, likely due to differences in cerebrovascular structures supplying different areas of the brain. For example, small terminal vessels supplying subcortical regions may be affected differently by the same hemodynamic strain applied to the pial vessels of the cortical mantle. These data suggest that indices of impedance mismatch at the carotid artery may be related to both cortical and subcortical injury and global cognition, whereas pulse wave velocity and central pulse pressure may have more specific effects on subcortical structures and memory. PWV also seemed to be the only index associated with white matter lesions, suggesting a specific impact on small vessel disease. Future detailed studies such as these are needed to separate the effects of these various pulsatile factors on different brain regions and specific cognitive operations. For example, it is unclear whether these measures were related to poor recall and recognition or recall alone, and whether they were associated with hippocampal atrophy in addition to subcortical lesions.

Although these more sophisticated studies are valuable in determining the mechanism of impairment associated with arterial stiffening, studies that simply use brachial artery PP are also critical for several reasons. Brachial artery PP elevation has been associated with impairment and decline in a variety of cognitive domains (Nation et al., 2010; Waldstein et al., 2008) and is highly correlated with other measures of central pulsatility (Mitchell, McMahon, Beck, & Sarazan, 2010). In fact, a recent study found that brachial PP was more highly correlated with CBF in the middle cerebral artery than any other measure of central pulsatility, including PWV and central PP (Xu et al., 2011). Importantly, brachial PP is easily obtained, available on nearly any patient, and does not require sophisticated equipment and specially trained staff. Future studies examining the neuropsychological sequelae of brachial PP elevation could yield valuable data that may be immediately applicable in the clinic or at bedside.

It is well established that elevated BP is associated with reduced cerebral blood flow (CBF), although few studies have examined the relationship between PP elevation and decreased CBF to specific brain regions impacted by small vessel ischemic disease. Even fewer studies have employed sensitive, noninvasive techniques, such as MRI, to examine these relationships. Such studies are needed in order to establish the specific BP and neuroimaging measures most closely associated with increased risk of small vessel ischemic disease as well as vascular-related cognitive impairment in older adults. Once these indices are established, treatments may be selected to specifically target the underlying pathophysiology.

Antihypertensive Pharmacologic Treatments

Nation et al. (2010) discuss that no currently available pharmacologic treatments directly target arterial stiffness, but the various classes of antihypertensive medication are known to have differential effects on arterial compliance. For example, most antihypertensive medications target cardiac contractility, peripheral resistance, or blood volume, which may not address large artery compliance (Safar, 2008). Interestingly, antihypertensive medications known to produce some improvement in arterial compliance, including angiotensin-converting-enzyme inhibitors and calcium channel blockers, are the same medications that have shown the greatest efficacy in the prevention of cognitive impairment in older adults (Amenta, Mignini, Rabbia, Tomassoni, & Veglio, 2002). Conversely, medications that lower BP through sympathetic nervous system and blood volume mechanisms, such as beta-blockers and diuretics, may not specifically impact the pulsatile component of BP because they do not alter arterial compliance. These medications have shown more limited results in their ability to reduce the incidence of dementia in older adults. This discrepancy between classes of medications suggests that the differential effects of these medications on arterial compliance may play a role in their beneficial effects on cognition (Safar & Jankowski, 2010). Studies examining the different components of blood pressure and how they relate to cerebrovascular disease, cognitive impairment, and dementia risk could have important treatment implications in terms of medication selection, as different classes of antihypertensive medications differentially impact the various components of blood pressure.

Diabetes

Diabetes is a risk factor for dementia and is one of the conditions listed on a number of vascular risk profile questionnaires (e.g., Hachinski Ischemia Scale; Framingham Stroke Risk Profile). The mechanisms of this relationship between diabetes and dementia, although speculative, may relate to the metabolism of the beta amyloid protein (Craft, 2007) or to vascular ischemic disease (Launer, 2009), or both. Even in the absence of diagnosed diabetes, a study by Mortimer et al. (2010) demonstrated that high normal fasting blood glucose is associated with dementia among Chinese elderly. Furthermore, higher fasting blood glucose was associated with dementia independent of vascular risk factors and MRI indicators of vascular disease, and remained a significant risk factor when analyses were restricted to subjects with fasting blood glucose within the normal range. In other words, this study is the first to document that variation of fasting blood glucose in the normal range may be associated with dementia.

In addition, combinations of risk factors that include, for example, diabetes and the presence of the APOE ε4 allele have been shown to be more deleterious than either risk factor alone. A study by Dore et al. (2009) showed that the presence of both risk factors interacted to create a more deleterious impact on cognitive function than that conferred by either risk factor alone, and a second study by Irie et al. (2008) found that having both diabetes and the APOE ε4 allele approximately doubled the risk of dementia beyond either risk factor alone. Both findings suggest that the presence of the APOE ε4 allele modifies the risk for either AD or mixed AD/CVD dementias and that diabetes may directly or indirectly cause the neuronal and vessel damage.

Conclusion

Dementias due to cerebrovascular disease are heterogeneous and likely represent the second most common underlying cause of dementia behind that of Alzheimer's disease. Even among those clinically diagnosed with "probable" AD, autopsy studies reveal mixed AD and CVD pathology to be present as frequently as "pure" AD (Schneider et al., 2009), which behooves us to better recognize and understand the contributions of cerebrovascular disorders on cognition and daily function—whether in isolation or in combination with other pathologies. As shown in Table 6.2, the heuristic distinctions between cortical and subcortical dementia patterns of neuropsychological impairment (Salmon & Bondi, 2009; Salmon & Filoteo, 2007) represent important starting points for clinical diagnosis and research efforts to link these neuropsychological profiles to underlying brain substrates. Characteristic patterns of neuropsychological impairment in subcortical ischemic VaD include extensive executive dysfunction, visuospatial impairments, and more mild impairments in memory. Relative to AD, those with subcortical ischemic VaD demonstrate improvements in recognition memory relative to free recall, proportionately equal impairments on letter and category fluency, and qualitative distinctions in the types of errors produced across tests and in the timing of their appearance. Echoing the sentiments of Knopman et al. (2001) made more than a decade ago, a more realistic approach to clinical diagnosis (e.g., the common condition of "mixed" dementia due to comorbid AD and CVD pathology) remains an important goal for neuropsychology. Achieving such goals is salient given the availability of treatments for cerebrovascular disease and for lessening its risks.

References

Aarsland, D., Ballard, C., McKeith, I., Perry, R., & Larsen, J. (2001). Comparison of extrapyramidal signs in dementia with Lewy bodies and Parkinson's disease. *Journal of Neuropsychiatry and Clinical Neuroscience*, 13(3), 374–379.

Alexander, G., DeLong, M., & Strick, P. (1986). Parallel organization of functionally segregated circuits linking basal ganglia and cortex. *Annual Review of Neuroscience*, 9, 357–381.

Amenta, F., Mignini, F., Rabbia, F., Tomassoni, D., & Veglio, F. (2002). Protective effect of anti-hypertensive treatment on cognitive function in essential hypertension: analysis of published clinical data. *Journal of Neurological Sciences*, 203–204, 147–151.

Anastasi, A., & Urbina, S. (1997). *Psychological testing* (7th ed.). Upper Saddle River, NJ: Prentice Hall.

Arvanitakis, Z., Leurgans, S., Wang, Z., Wilson, R., Bennett, D., & Schneider, J. (2011). Cerebral amyloid angiopathy pathology and cognitive domains in older persons. *Annals of Neurology*, 69, 320–327.

Baddeley, A., Bressi, S., Della Sala, S., Logie, R., & Spinnler, H. (1991). The decline of working memory in Alzheimer's disease: a longitudinal study. *Brain*, 114, 2521–2542.

Bayles, K., & Tomoeda, C. (1983). Confrontation naming impairment in dementia. *Brain and Language*, 19, 98–114.

Bell, R. D., Winkler, E. A., Singh, I., Sagare, A. P., Deane, R., Wu, Z.,... Zlokovic, B. V. (2012). Apolipoprotein E controls cerebrovascular integrity via cyclophilin A. *Nature, 485*, 512–16.

Bennett, D. A., Wilson, R. S., Gilley, D. W., & Fox, J. H. (1990). Clinical diagnosis of Binswanger's disease. *Journal of Neurology, Neurosurgery and Psychiatry, 53*(11), 961–965.

Bondi, M., Salmon, D., Galasko, D., Thomas, R., & Thal, L. (1999). Neuropsychological function and apolipoprotein E genotype in the preclinical detection of Alzheimer's disease. *Psychology and Aging, 14*(2), 295–303.

Bowles, N., Obler, L., & Albert, M. (1987). Naming errors in healthy aging and dementia of the Alzheimer type. *Cortex, 23*(3), 519–524.

Braak, H., & Braak, E. (1991). Neuropathological staging of Alzheimer-related changes. *Acta Neuropathologica, 82*, 239–259.

Brandt, J., Folstein, S., & Folstein, M. (1988). Differential cognitive impairment in Alzheimer's and Huntington's disease. *Annals of Neurology, 23*, 555–561.

Brouwers, P., Cox, C., Martin, A., Chase, T., & Fedio, P. (1984). Differential perceptual-spatial impairment in Huntington's and Alzheimer's dementias. *Archives of Neurology, 41*, 1073–1076.

Butters, M., Salmon, D., & Butters, N. (1994). Neuropsychological assessment of dementia. In M. Storandt & G. VandenBox (Eds.), *Neuropsychological assessment of dementia and depression in older adults: A clinician's guide* (pp. 33–60). Washington, DC: American Psychological Association.

Carew, T. G., Lamar, M., Cloud, B. S., Grossman, M., & Libon, D. J. (1997). Impairment in category fluency in ischemic vascular dementia. *Neuropsychology, 11*(3), 400–412.

Carey, C., Kramer, J., Josephson, S., Mungas, D., Reed, B., Schuff, N.,...Chui, H. (2008). Subcortical lacunes are associated with executive dysfunction in cognitively normal elderly. *Stroke, 39*(2), 397–402.

Chang, Y., Bondi, M., McEvoy, L., Fennema-Notestine, C., Salmon, D., Galasko, D.,...Dale, A. (2011). Global clinical dementia rating of 0.5 in MCI masks variability related to level of function. *Neurology, 76*(7), 652–659.

Chang, Y. L., Bondi, M. W., Fennema-Notestine, C., McEvoy, L. K., Hagler, D. J., Jr., Jacobson, M. W., & Dale, A. M. (2010). Brain substrates of learning and retention in mild cognitive impairment diagnosis and progression to Alzheimer's disease *Neuropsychologia, 48*(5), 1237–1247.

Chui, H., Victoroff, J., Margolin, D., Jagust, W., Shankle, R., & Katzman, R. (1992). Criteria for the diagnosis of ischemic vascular dementia proposed by the State of California Alzheimer's Disease Diagnostic and Treatment Centers. *Neurology*, 43, 250–260.

Clark, L., Schiehser, D., Weissberger, G., Salmon, D., Delis, D., & Bondi, M. (2012). Specific measures of executive function predict cognitive decline in older adults. *Journal of the International Neuropsychological Society*, 18, 118–127.

Cohen, R. (2009). Neuropsychology of cardiovascular disease. In R. Cohen & J. Gunstad (Eds.), *Neuropsychology and cardiovascular disease* (pp. 3–18). New York: Oxford University Press.

Collette, F., Van der Linden, M., Bechet, S., & Salmon, E. (1999). Phonological loop and central executive functioning in Alzheimer's disease. *Neuropsychologia*, 37(8), 905–918.

Cosentino, S., Jefferson, A., Carey, M., Price, C., Davis-Garrett, K., Swenson, R., & Libon, D. (2004). The clinical diagnosis of vascular dementia: A comparison among four classification systems and a proposal for a new paradigm. *The Clinical Neuropsychologist*, 18(1), 6–21.

Cosentino, S., Jefferson, A., Chute, D., Kaplan, E., & Libon, D. (2004). Clock drawing errors in dementia: neuropsychological and neuroanatomical considerations. *Cognitive and Behavioral Neurology*, 17(2), 74–84.

Craft, S. (2007). Insulin resistance and Alzheimer's disease pathogenesis: potential mechanisms and implications for treatment. *Current Alzheimer Research*, 4, 147–152.

Cronin-Golomb, A., & Amick, M. (2001). Spatial abilities in aging, Alzheimer's disease, and Parkinson's disease. In F. Boller & S. Cappa (Eds.), *Handbook of neuropsychology, Vol. 6: Aging and dementia* (2nd ed., pp. 119–143). Amsterdam: Elsevier.

Cummings, J. (1993). Frontal-subcortical circuits and human behavior. *Archives of Neurology*, 50(8), 873–880.

de Jager, C., Hogervorst, E., Combrinck, M., & Budge, M. (2003). Sensitivity and specificity of neuropsychological tests for mild cognitive impairment, vascular cognitive impairment and Alzheimer's disease. *Psychological Medicine*, 33, 1039–1050.

Delano-Wood, L., Houston, W. S., Emond, J. A., Marchant, N. L., Salmon, D. P., Jeste, D. V.,...Bondi, M. W. (2008). APOE genotype predicts depression in women with Alzheimer's disease: a retrospective study. *International Journal of Geriatric Psychiatry*, 23(6), 632–636.

Delis, D., Jacobson, M., Bondi, M., Hamilton, J., & Salmon, D. (2003). The myth of testing construct validity using factor analysis or correlations with normal or mixed clinical populations: lessons from memory assessment. *Journal of the International Neuropsychological Society, 9*(6), 936–946.

Delis, D., Massman, P., Butters, N., Salmon, D., Cermak, L., & Kramer, J. (1991). Profiles of demented and amnesic patients on the California Verbal Learning Test: implications for the assessment of memory disorders. *Psychological Assessment, 3*, 19–26.

Delis, D., Wetter, S., Jacobson, M., Peavy, G., Hamilton, J., Gongvatana, A.,…Salmon, D. (2005). Recall discriminability: utility of a new CVLT-II measure in the differential diagnosis of dementia. *Journal of the International Neuropsychological Society, 11*(6), 708–715.

Delis, D. C., Kaplan, E., & Kramer, J. H. (2001). *Delis-Kaplan executive function system*. San Antonio, TX: The Psychological Corporation.

Delis, D. C., Kramer, J. H., Kaplan, E., & Ober, B. A. (2000). *California Verbal Learning Test: Second edition*. San Antonio, TX: Psychological Corporation.

DeLong, M., & Wichmann, T. (2007). Circuits and circuit disorders of the basal ganglia. *Archives of Neurology, 64*(1), 20–24.

Desmond, D. (2004). The neuropsychology of vascular cognitive impairment: is there a specific cognitive deficit? *Journal of the Neurological Sciences, 226*(1–2), 3–7.

Di Carlo, A. (2009). The human and economic burden of stroke. *Age and Ageing, 38*, 4–5.

Dodge, H., Chang, C., Kamboh, I., & Ganguli, M. (2011). Risk of Alzheimer's disease incidence attributable to vascular disease in the population. *Alzheimer's and Dementia, 7*(3), 356–360.

Dore, G., Elias, M., Robbins, M., Elias, P., & Nagy, Z. (2009). Presence of APOE e4 allele modifies the relationship between type 2 diabetes and cognitive performance: The Maine-Syracuse study. *Diabetologia, 52*, 255`–2560.

Duke, L., & Kaszniak, A. (2000). Executive control functions in degenerative dementias: a comparative review. *Neuropsychology Review, 10*(2), 75–99.

Duron, E., & Hanon, O. (2010). Antihypertensive treatments, cognitive decline, and dementia. *Journal of Alzheimer's Disease, 20*(3), 903–914.

Eichner, J., Dunn, S., Perveen, G., Thompson, D., Stewart, K., & Stroehla, B. (2002). Apolipoprotein E polymorphism and cardiovascular disease: a HuGE review. *American Journal of Epidemiology, 155*, 487–495.

Eppig, J., Wambach, D., Nieves, C., Price, C., Lamar, M., Delano-Wood, L.,…Libon, D. (2011). Dysexecutive functioning in mild cognitive impairment: derailment in temporal gradients. *Journal of the International Neuropsychological Society*, 1–9.

Erkinjuntti, T., & Gauthier, S. (2009). The concept of vascular cognitive impairment. *Frontiers of Neurology and Neuroscience*, 24, 79–85.

Festa, E., Inseler, R., Salmon, D., Paxton, J., Hamilton, J., & Heindel, W. (2005). Neocortical disconnectivity disrupts sensory integration in Alzheimer's disease. *Neuropsychology*, 19(6), 728–738.

Filoteo, J., Rilling, L., Cole, B., Williams, B., Davis, J., & Roberts, J. (1997). Variable memory profiles in Parkinson's disease. *Journal of Clinical and Experimental Neuropsychology*, 19(6), 878–888.

Fine, E., Delis, D., Wetter, S., Jacobson, M., Hamilton, J., Peavy, G., ... Salmon, D. (2008). Identifying the "source" of recognition memory deficits in patients with Huntington's disease or Alzheimer's disease: evidence from the CVLT-II. [Research Support, N.I.H., Extramural Research Support, U.S. Gov't, Non-P.H.S.]. *Journal of Clinical and Experimental Neuropsychology*, 30(4), 463–470.

Freeman, R., Giovannetti, T., Lamar, M., Cloud, B., Stern, R., Kaplan, E., & Libon, D. (2000). Visuoconstructional problems in dementia: contribution of executive systems functions. *Neuropsychology*, 14(3), 415–426.

Fukutake, T. (2011). Cerebral autosomal recessive arteriopathy with subcortical infarcts and leukoencephalopathy (CARASIL): from discovery to gene identification. *Journal of Stroke and Cerebrovascular Disease*, 20(2), 85–93.

Ganguli, M., Snitz, B., Saxton, J., et al. (2011). Outcomes of mild cognitive impairment by definition: A population study. *Archives of Neurology*, 68, 761–767.

Gomar, J., Bobes-Bascaran, M., Conejero-Goldberg, C., Davies, P., Goldberg, T., & for the Alzheimer's Disease Neuroimaging Initiative. (2011). Utility of combinations of biomarkers, cognitive markers, and risk factors to predict conversion from mild cognitive impairment to Alzheimer disease in the Alzheimer's Disease Neuroimaging Initiative. *Archives of General Psychiatry*, 68, 961–969.

Gorelick, P., Scuteri, A., Black, S., DeCarli, C., Greenberg, S., Iadecola, C., ... et al. (2011). Vascular contributions to cognitive impairment and dementia: A statement for healthcare professionals from the American Heart Association/American Stroke Association. *Stroke*, 42, 2672–2713.

Graham, N., Emery, T., & Hodges, J. (2004). Distinctive cognitive profiles in Alzheimer's disease and subcortical vascular dementia. *Journal of Neurology, Neurosurgery, and Psychiatry*, 75(1), 61–71.

Greenberg, S. (1998). Cerebral amyloid angiopathy: prospects for clinical diagnosis and treatment. *Neurology*, *51*(3), 690–694.

Greenberg, S., Vernooij, M., Cordonnier, C., Viswanathan, A., Al-Shahi Salman, R., Warach, S., ... Van Buchem, M. (2009). Cerebral microbleeds: a guide to detection and interpretation. *Lancet Neurology*, *8*(2), 165–174.

Grober, E., & Kawas, C. (1997). Learning and retention in preclinical and early Alzheimer's disease. *Psychology and Aging*, *12*(1), 183–188.

Hayden, K., Zandi, P., Lyketsos, C., Khachaturian, A., Bastian, L., Charoonruk, G., ... Cache County Investigators. (2006). Vascular risk factors for incident Alzheimer disease and vascular dementia: the Cache County study. *Alzheimer Disease and Associated Disorders*, *20*(2), 93–100.

Heaton, R., Miller, S., Taylor, M., & Grant, I. (Eds.). (2004). *Revised comprehensive norms for an Expanded Halstead-Reitan Battery: Demographically Adjusted neuropsychological norms for African American and Caucasian adults – professional manual* (3rd ed.). Lutz, FL: Psychological Assessment Resources, Inc.

Heister, D., Brewer, J., Magda, S., Blennow, K., McEvoy, L., & for the Alzheimer's Disease Neuroimaging Initiative. (2011). Predicting MCI outcome with clinically available MRI and CSF biomarkers. *Neurology*, *77*, 1619–1628.

Henry, J., Crawford, J., & Phillips, L. (2004). Verbal fluency performance in dementia of the Alzheimer's type: a meta-analysis. [Meta-Analysis Review]. *Neuropsychologia*, *42*(9), 1212–1222.

Henry, J., MacLeod, M., Phillips, L., & Crawford, J. (2004). A meta-analytic review of prospective memory and aging. [Meta-Analysis Review]. *Psychology and Aging*, *19*(1), 27–39.

Hildebrandt, H., Haldenwanger, A., & Eling, P. (2009). False recognition helps to distinguish patients with Alzheimer's disease and amnestic MCI from patients with other kinds of dementia. *Dementia and Geriatric Cognitive Disorders*, *28*(2), 159–167.

Hodges, J., & Graham, N. (2001). Vascular dementias. In J. Hodges (Ed.), *Early onset dementia: A multidisciplinary approach* (pp. 319–337). Oxford: Oxford University Press.

Hodges, J., Salmon, D., & Butters, N. (1991). The nature of the naming deficit in Alzheimer's and Huntington's disease. *Brain, 114*, 1547–1558.

Irie, F., Fitzpatrick, A., Lopez, O., et al. (2008). Enhanced risk for Alzheimer disease in persons with type 2 diabetes and APOE E4. *Archives of Neurology*, *65*, 89–93.

Jedynak, B. M., Lang, A., Liu, B., Katz, E., Zhang, Y., Wyman, B. T., Raunig, D., Jedynak, C. P., Caffo, B., Prince, J. L. for the Alzheimer's Disease Neuroimaging Initiative. (2012). A computational neurodegenerative disease progression score: Method and results with the Alzheimer's disease neuroimaging initiative cohort. *Neuroimage, 63*(3), 1478–1486.

Jellinger, K. (2002). Alzheimer disease and cerebrovascular pathology: An update. *Journal of Neural Transmission, 109*, 813–836.

Jellinger, K. (2008a). Morphologic diagnosis of "vascular dementia": A critical update. *Journal of the Neurological Sciences, 270*, 1–12 [Epub].

Jellinger, K. (2008b). The pathology of "vascular dementia": a critical update. *Journal of Alzheimer's Disease, 14*(1), 107–123.

Joutel, A., Corpechot, C., Ducros, A., Vahedi, K., Chabriat, H., Mouton, P.,...Tournier-Lasserve, E. (1996). Notch3 mutations in CADASIL, a hereditary adult-onset condition causing stroke and dementia. *Nature, 383*, 707–710.

Kearney-Schwartz, A., Rossignol, P., Bracard, S., Felblinger, J., Fay, R., Boivin, J.,...Zannad, F. (2009). Vascular structure and function is correlated to cognitive performance and white matter hyperintensities in older hypertensive patients with subjective memory complaints. *Stroke, 40*(4), 1229–1236.

Kertesz, A., & Clydesdale, S. (1994). Neuropsychological deficits in vascular dementia vs Alzheimer's disease: frontal lobe deficits prominent in vascular dementia. *Archives of Neurology, 51*, 1226–1231.

Kim, K., Youn, J., Han, M., Paik, N., Lee, T., Park, J.,...Woo, J. (2008). Lack of association between apolipo- protein E polymorphism and vascular dementia in Koreans. *Journal of Geriatric Psychiatry and Neurology, 21*, 12–17.

Kivipelto, M., Ngandu, T., Laatikainen, T., Winblad, B., Soininen, H., & Tuomilehto, J. (2006). Risk score for the prediction of dementia risk in 20 years among middle aged people: a longitudinal, population-based study. *Lancet Neurology, 5*(9), 735–741.

Knopman, D., DeKosky, S., Cummings, J., Chui, H., Corey-Bloom, J., Relkin, N.,...Stevens, J. (2001). Practice parameter: Diagnosis of dementia (an evidence-based review): Report of the Quality Standards Subcommittee of the American Academy of Neurology. *Neurology, 56*, 1143–1153.

Knopman, D., & Roberts, R. (2010). Vascular risk factors: imaging and neuropathologic correlates. *Journal of Alzheimer's Disease, 20*(3), 699–709.

Knudsen, K., Rosand, J., Karluk, D., & Greenberg, S. (2001). Clinical diagnosis of cerebral amyloid angiopathy: validation of the Boston Criteria. *Neurology, 56,* 537–539.

Kongs, S. K., Thompson, L. L., Iverson, G. L., & Heaton, R. K. (2000). *The Wisconsin Card Sorting Test – 64 card version professional manual.* Odessa, FL: Psychological Assessment Resources.

Kramer, J., Mungas, D., Reed, B., Schuff, N., Weiner, M., Miller, B., & Chui, H. (2004). Forgetting in dementia with and without subcortical lesions. *The Clinical Neuropsychologist, 18,* 32–40.

Kuller, L., Lopez, O., Jagust, W., Becker, J., DeKosky, S., Lyketsos, C., . . . Dulberg, C. (2005). Determinants of vascular dementia in the Cardiovascular Health Cognition Study. *Neurology, 64,* 1548–1552.

Lafosse, J., Reed, B., Mungas, D., Sterling, S., Wahbeh, H., & Jagust, W. (1997). Fluency and memory differences between ischemic vascular dementia and Alzheimer's disease. *Neuropsychology 11,* 514–522.

Laine, M., Vuorinen, E., & Rinne, J. (1997). Picture naming deficits in vascular dementia and Alzheimer's disease. *Journal of Clinical and Experimental Neuropsychology, 19*(1), 126–140.

Lamar, M., Catani, M., Price, C., Heilman, K., & Libon, D. (2008). The impact of region-specific leukoaraiosis on working memory deficits in dementia. *Neuropsychologia, 46*(10), 2597–2601.

Lamar, M., Podell, K., Carew, T., Cloud, B., Resh, R., Kennedy, C., . . . Libon, D. (1997). Perseverative behavior in Alzheimer's disease and subcortical ischemic vascular dementia. *Neuropsychology, 11,* 523–534.

Lamar, M., Price, C., Davis, K., Kaplan, E., & Libon, D. (2002). Capacity to maintain mental set in dementia. *Neuropsychologia, 40*(4), 435–445.

Lamar, M., Price, C., Giovannetti, T., Swenson, R., & Libon, D. (2010). The dysexecutive syndrome associated with ischaemic vascular disease and related subcortical neuropathology: a Boston process approach. *Behavioral Neurology, 22*(1–2), 53–62.

Lamar, M., Price, C., Libon, D., Penney, D., Kaplan, E., Grossman, M., & Heilman, K. (2007). Alterations in working memory as a function of leukoaraiosis in dementia. *Neuropsychologia, 45,* 245–254.

Landau, S., Harvey, D., Madison, C., Reiman, E., Foster, N., Aisen, P., . . . Jagust, W. (2010). Comparing predictors of conversion and decline in mild cognitive impairment. *Neurology, 75*(3), 230–238.

Lange, K., Bondi, M., Salmon, D., Galasko, D., Delis, D., Thomas, R., & Thal, L. (2002). Decline in verbal memory during preclinical Alzheimer's disease:

examination of the effect of APOE genotype. *Journal of the International Neuropsychological Society, 8*(7), 943–955.

Launer, L. (2009). Diabetes: vascular or neurodegenerative. An epidemiologic perspective. *Stroke, 40*(Suppl), S53–S55.

Lawrence, A., Watkins, L., Sahakian, B., Hodges, J., & Robbins, T. (2000). Visual object and visuospatial cognition in Huntington's disease: implications for information processing in corticostriatal circuits. *Brain, 123*(Pt 7), 1349–1364.

Lee, A., Jeong, S., Choi, B., Sohn, E., & Chui, H. (2006). Pulse pressure correlates with leukoaraiosis in Alzheimer disease. *Archives of Gerontology and Geriatrics, 42*(2), 157–166.

Levy, D., Bayley, P., & Squire, L. (2004). The anatomy of semantic knowledge: medial vs. lateral temporal lobe. *Proceedings of the National Academy of Sciences, 101*(17), 6710–6715.

Libon, D., Bogdanoff, B., Bonavita, J., Skalina, S., Cloud, B., Resh, R., ... Ball, S. (1997). Dementia associated with periventricular and deep white matter alterations: a subtype of subcortical dementia. *Archives of Clinical Neuropsychology, 12*(3), 239–250.

Libon, D., Bondi, M., Price, C., Lamar, M., Eppig, J., Wambach, D., ... Penney, D. (2011). Verbal serial list learning in mild cognitive impairment: a profile analysis of interference, forgetting, and errors. *Journal of the International Neuropsychological Society, 17*(5), 905–914.

Libon, D., Eppig, J., Xie, S., Wicas, G., Lippa, C., Bettcher, B., & Wambach, D. (2010). The heterogeneity of mild cognitive impairment: A neuropsychological analysis. *Journal of the International Neuropsychological Society, 16*, 84–93.

Libon, D., Swenson, R., Barnoski, E., & Sands, L. (1993). Clock drawing as an assessment tool for dementia. *Archives of Clinical Neuropsychology, 8*(5), 405–415.

Lineweaver, T. T., Salmon, D. P., Bondi, M. W., & Corey-Bloom, J. (2005). Differential effects of Alzheimer's disease and Huntington's disease on the performance of mental rotation. *Journal of the International Neuropsychological Society, 11*(1), 30–39.

Lukatela, K., Malloy, P., Jenkins, M., & Cohen, R. (1998). The naming deficit in early Alzheimer's and vascular dementia. *Neuropsychology, 12*(4), 565–572.

Marcotte, T., Wolfson, T., Rosenthal, T., Heaton, R., Gonzalez, R., Ellis, R., ... HIV Neurobehavioral Research Center Group. (2004). A multimodal assessment of driving performance in HIV infection. *Neurology, 63*(8), 1417–1422.

Massman, P., Delis, D., Butters, N., Dupont, R., & Gillin, J. (1992). The subcortical dysfunction hypothesis of memory deficits in depression: neuropsychological validation in a subgroup of patients. *Journal of Clinical and Experimental Neuropsychology, 14*(5), 687–706.

Massman, P., Delis, D., Butters, N., Levin, B., & Salmon, D. (1990). Are all subcortical dementias alike? Verbal learning and memory in Parkinson's and Huntington's disease patients. *Journal of Clinical and Experimental Neuropsychology, 12*(5), 729–744.

Masur, D., Fuld, P., Blau, A., Crystal, H., & Aronson, M. (1990). Predicting development of dementia in the elderly with the Selective Reminding Test. *Journal of Clinical and Experimental Neuropsychology, 12*(4), 529–538.

Mathias, J., & Burke, J. (2009). Cognitive functioning in Alzheimer's and vascular dementia: a meta-analysis. *Neuropsychology, 23*(4), 411–423.

McKeith, I., Dickson, D., Lowe, J., Emre, M., O' Brien, J., Feldman, H.,...for the consortium on DLB. (2005). Diagnosis and management of dementia with Lewy bodies: Third report of the DLB Consortium (review). *Neurology, 65*(12), 1863–1872.

McKhann, G., Drachman, D., Folstein, M., Katzman, R., Price, D., & Stadlan, E. (1984). Clinical diagnosis of Alzheimer's disease: Report of the NINCDS-ADRDA work group under the auspices of Department of Health and Human Services Task Force on Alzheimer's Disease. *Neurology, 34*, 939–944.

McKhann, G., Knopman, D., Chertkow, H., Hyman, B., Jack, C., Jr., Kawas, C.,...Phelps, C. (2011). The diagnosis of dementia due to Alzheimer's disease: recommendations from the National Institute on Aging-Alzheimer's Association workgroups on diagnostic guidelines for Alzheimer's disease. *Alzheimer's and Dementia, 7*(3), 263–269.

Mega, M., & Cummings, J. (1994). Frontal-subcortical circuits and neuropsychiatric disorders. *Journal of Neuropsychiatry and Clinical Neuroscience, 6*(4), 358–370.

Meschia, J., Worrall, B., & Rich, S. (2011). Genetic susceptibility to ischemic stroke. *Nature Reviews. Neurology, 7*(7), 369–378.

Mitchell, A., McMahon, C., Beck, T., & Sarazan, R. (2010). Sensitivity of two noninvasive blood pressure measurement techniques compared to telemetry in cynomolgus monkeys and beagle dogs. *Journal of Pharmacological and Toxicological Methods, 62*(1), 54–63.

Mitchell, G. (2008). Effects of central arterial aging on the structure and function of the peripheral vasculature: implications for end-organ damage. *Journal of Applied Physiology, 105*(5), 1652–1660.

Mitchell, G., van Buchem, M., Sigurdsson, S., Gotal, J., Jonsdottir, M., Kjartansson, O.,...Launer, L. (2011). Arterial stiffness, pressure and flow pulsatility and brain structure and function: the Age, Gene/Environment Susceptibility – Reykjavik study. *Brain, 134*(Pt 11), 3398–3407.

Monsch, A., Bondi, M., Butters, N., Paulsen, J., Salmon, D., Brugger, P., & Swenson, M. (1994). A comparison of category and letter fluency in Alzheimer's disease and Huntington's disease. *Neuropsychology, 8,* 25–30.

Mortimer, J., Borenstein, A., Ding, D., Decarli, C., Zhao, Q., Copenhaver, C.,...Hong, Z. (2010). High normal fasting blood glucose is associated with dementia in Chinese elderly. *Alzheimer's and Dementia, 6*(6), 440–447.

Naj, A., Jun, G., Beecham, G., Wang, L., Vardarajan, B., Buros, J.,...Schellenberg, G. D. (2011). Common variants at MS4A4/MS4A6E, CD2AP, CD33 and EPHA1 are associated with late-onset Alzheimer's disease. *Nature Genetics, 43*(5), 436–441.

Nation, D., Hong, S., Jak, A., Delano-Wood, L., Mills, P., Bondi, M., & Dimsdale, J. (2011). Stress, exercise, and Alzheimer's disease: a neurovascular pathway. *Medical Hypotheses, 76*(6), 847–854.

Nation D. A., Delano-Wood, L., Bangen, K. J., Wierenga, C. E., Jak, A. J., Hansen, L. A., Galasko, D. R., Salmon, D. P., & Bondi, M. W. (2012). Antemortem pulse pressure elevation predicts cerebrovascular disease in autopsy-confirmed Alzheimer's disease. *Journal of Alzheimer's Disease, 30,* 595–603.

Nation, D. A., Wierenga, C. E., Delano-Wood, L., Jak, A. J., Delis, D. C., Salmon, D. P., & Bondi, M. W. (2010). Elevated pulse pressure is associated with age-related decline in language ability. *Journal of the International Neuropsychological Society, 16*(5), 933–938.

Nichols, W., & O' Rourke, M. (2006). *McDonald's blood flow in arteries: Theoretical, experimental and clinical principles* (4th ed.). London: Edward Arnold.

Pantoni, L. (2010). Cerebral small vessel disease: from pathogenesis and clinical characteristics to therapeutic challenges. *Lancet Neurology, 9,* 689–701.

Petersen, R. (2010). Alzheimer's disease: progress in prediction. *Lancet Neurology, 9*(1), 4–5.

Petersen, R., Thomas, R., Grundman, M., Bennett, D., Doody, R., Ferris, S.,...Thal, L. (2005). Vitamin E and donepezil for the treatment of mild cognitive impairment. *New England Journal of Medicine, 352*(23), 2379–2388.

Plassman, B., Langa, K., Fisher, G., Heeringa, S., Weir, D., Ofstedal, M.,...Wallace, R. (2007). Prevalence of dementia in the United States: the aging, demographics, and memory study. *Neuroepidemiology, 29*(1–2), 125–132.

Price, C., Jefferson, A., Merino, J., Heilman, K., & Libon, D. (2005). Subcortical vascular dementia: integrating neuropsychological and neuroradiologic data. *Neurology, 65*(3), 376–382.

Qiu, C., Winblad, B., & Fratiglioni, L. (2005). The age-dependent relation of blood pressure to cognitive function and dementia. *Lancet Neurology, 4*(8), 487–499.

Qiu, C., Winblad, B., Viitanen, M., & Fratiglioni, L. (2003). Pulse pressure and risk of Alzheimer disease in persons aged 75 years and older: a community-based, longitudinal study. *Stroke, 34*(3), 594–599.

Rabin, L., Pare, N., Saykin, A., et al. (2009). Differential memory test sensitivity for diagnosing amnestic mild cognitive impairment and predicting conversion to Alzheimer's disease. *Aging, Neuropsychology, and Cognition, 16*, 357–376.

Reed, B., Mungas, D., Kramer, J., Betz, B., Ellis, W., Vinters, H.,...Chui, H. (2004). Clinical and neuropsychological features in autopsy-defined vascular dementia. *The Clinical Neuropsychologist, 18*(1), 63–74.

Reed, B., Mungas, D., Kramer, J., Ellis, W., Vinters, H., Zarow, C.,...Chui, H. (2007). Profiles of neuropsychological impairment in autopsy-defined Alzheimer's disease and cerebrovascular disease. *Brain, 130*(Pt 3), 731–739.

Román, G., Tatemichi, T., Erkinjuntti, T., Cummings, J., Masdeu, J., Garcia, J.,...et al. (1993). Vascular dementia: diagnostic criteria for research studies. Report of the NINDS-AIREN International Workshop. *Neurology, 43*(2), 250–260.

Rosen, W., Terry, R., Fuld, P., Katzman, R., & Peck, A. (1980). Pathological verification of ischemic score in differentiation of dementias. *Annals of Neurology, 7*, 486–488.

Rouleau, I., Salmon, D., Butters, N., Kennedy, C., & McGuire, K. (1992). Quantitative and qualitative analyses of clock drawings in Alzheimer's and Huntington's disease. *Brain and Cognition, 18*, 70–87.

Safar, M. (2008). Pulse pressure, arterial stiffness and wave reflections (augmentation index) as cardiovascular risk factors in hypertension. *Therapeutic Advances in Cardiovascular Disease, 2*(1), 13–24.

Safar, M. (2010). Arterial aging–hemodynamic changes and therapeutic options. *Nature Reviews. Cardiology*, 7(8), 442–449.

Safar, M., & Jankowski, P. (2010). Antihypertensive therapy and de-stiffening of the arteries. *Expert Opinion on Pharmacotherapy*, 11(16), 2625–2634.

Salmon, D., & Bondi, M. (2009). Neuropsychological assessment of dementia. *Annual Review of Psychology*, 60, 257–282.

Salmon, D., & Butters, N. (1992). Neuropsychologic assessment of dementia in the elderly. In R. Katzman & J. Rowe (Eds.), *Principles of geriatric neurology* (pp. 144–163). Philadelphia: F. A. Davis.

Salmon, D., & Filoteo, J. (2007). Neuropsychology of cortical vs subcortical dementia. *Seminars in Neurology*, 27, 7–21.

Salmon, D., Kwo-on-Yuen, P., Heindel, W., Butters, N., & Thal, L. (1989). Differentiation of Alzheimer's disease and Huntington's disease with the Dementia Rating Scale. *Archives of Neurology*, 46(11), 1204–1208.

Saxton, J., Snitz, B. E., Lopez, O. L., Ives, D. G., Dunn, L. O., Fitzpatrick, A., Carlson, M. C., Dekosky, S. T.; GEM Study Investigators (2009). Functional and cognitive criteria produce different rates of mild cognitive impairment and conversion to dementia. *Journal of Neurology, Neurosurgery and Psychiatry*, 80(7), 737–743.

Schmand, B., Huizenga, H., & van Gool, W. (2010). Meta-analysis of CSF and MRI biomarkers for detecting preclinical Alzheimer's disease. *Psychological Medicine*, 40, 135–145.

Schneider, J., Aggarwal, N., Barnes, L., Boyle, P., & Bennett, D. (2009). The neuropathology of older persons with and without dementia from community versus clinic cohorts. *Journal of Alzheimer's Disease*, 18, 691–701.

Schneider, J., Arvanitakis, Z., Leurgans, S., & Bennett, D. (2009). The neuropathology of probable Alzheimer disease and mild cognitive impairment. *Annals of Neurology*, 66, 200–208.

Schneider, J., Boyle, P., Arvanitakis, Z., Bienias, J., & Bennett, D. (2007). Subcortical cerebral infarcts, episodic memory, and AD pathology in older persons. *Annals of Neurology*, 62, 59–66.

Schneider, J., Wilson, R., Bienias, J., Evans, D., & Bennett, D. (2004). Cerebral infarctions and the likelihood of dementia from Alzheimer disease pathology. *Neurology*, 62, 1148–1155.

Seidel, G., Giovannetti, T., & Libon, D. (2011). Cerebrovascular disease and cognition in older adults. In M. Pardon & M. Bondi (Eds.), *Current topics in behavioral neuroscience: Behavioral of neurobiology of aging* (pp. Epub ahead of print). New York: Springer-Verlag.

Shechtman, O., Classen, S., Stephens, B., Bendixen, R., Belchior, P., Sandhu, M.,...Davis, E. (2007). The impact of intersection design on simulated driving performance of young and senior adults. *Traffic Injury Prevention*, 8(1), 78–86.

Shimokawa, A., Yatomi, N., Anamizu, S., Torii, S., Isono, H., & Sugai, Y. (2003). Recognition of facial expressions and emotional situations in patients with dementia of the Alzheimer and vascular types. *Dementia and Geriatric Cognitive Disorders*, 15(3), 163–168.

Sonnen, J., Larson, E., Crane, P., Haneuse, S., Li, G., Schellenberg, G., et al. (2007). Pathological correlates of dementia in a longitudinal, population-based sample of aging. *Annals of Neurology*, 62, 406–413.

Storandt, M., & Morris, J. (2010). Ascertainment bias in the clinical diagnosis of Alzheimer disease. *Archives of Neurology*, 67(11), 1364–1369.

Tatemichi, T., Sacktor, N., & Mayeux, R. (1994). Dementia associated with cerebrovascular disease, other degenerative deiseases, and metabolic disorders. In R. Terry, R. Katzman & K. Bick (Eds.), *Alzheimer's disease* (pp. 123–166). New York: Raven Press.

Tierney, M., Yao, C., Kiss, A., & McDowell, I. (2005). Neuropsychological tests accurately predict incident Alzheimer disease after 5 and 10 years. *Neurology*, 64, 1853–1859.

Tippett, W., Lee, J., Zakzanis, K., Black, S., Mraz, R., & Graham, S. (2009). Visually navigating a virtual world with real-world impairments: a study of visually and spatially guided performance in individuals with mild cognitive impairments. *Journal of Clinical and Experimental Neuropsychology*, 31(4), 447–454.

Tiraboschi, P., Salmon, D., Hansen, L., Hofstetter, R., Thal, L., & Corey-Bloom, J. (2006). What best differentiates Lewy body from Alzheimer's disease in early-stage dementia? *Brain*, 129(Pt 3), 729–735.

Tröster, A., Jacobs, D., Butters, N., Cullum, C., & Salmon, D. (1989). Differentiation of Alzheimer's disease from Huntington's disease with the Wechsler Memory Scale – Revised. *Clinics in Geriatric Medicine*, 5, 611–632.

van Rooden, S., van der Grond, J., van den Boom, R., Haan, J., Linn, J., Greenberg, S., & van Buchem, M. (2009). Descriptive analysis of the Boston criteria applied to a Dutch-type cerebral amyloid angiopathy population. *Stroke*, 40, 3022–3027.

Waldstein, S., Rice, S., Thayer, J., Najjar, S., Scuteri, A., & Zonderman, A. (2008). Pulse pressure and pulse wave velocity are related to cognitive decline in the Baltimore Longitudinal Study of Aging. *Hypertension*, 51(1), 99–104.

Ward, J., Sheppard, J., Shpritz, B., Margolis, R., Rosenblatt, A., & Brandt, J. (2006). A four-year study of cognitive functioning in Huntington's disease. *Journal of the International Neuropsychological Society, 12*, 445–454.

Weintraub, S., Moberg, P., Culbertson, W., et al. (2004). Evidence for impaired encoding and retrieval memory profiles in Parkinson's disease. *Cognitive and Behavioral Neurology, 17*, 195–200.

Weintraub, S., Salmon, D., Mercaldo, N., Ferris, S., Graff-Radford, N., Chui, H.,...Morris, J. (2009). The Alzheimer's Disease Centers' Uniform Data Set (UDS): the neuropsychologic test battery. *Alzheimer Disease and Associated Disorders, 23*(2), 91–101.

Weller, R. O., Boche, D., Nicoll, J. A. (2009). Microvasculature changes and cerebral amyloid angiopathy in Alzheimer's disease and their potential impact on therapy. *Acta Neuropathologica, 118*, 87–102.

White, L., Small, B., Petrovitch, H., Ross, G., Masaki, K., Abbott, R.,...Markesbery, W. (2005). Recent clinical-pathologic research on the causes of dementia in late life: update from the Honolulu-Asia Aging Study. *Journal of Geriatric Psychiatry and Neurology, 18*, 224–227.

Whitney, S., Sparto, P., Hodges, L., Babu, S., Furman, J., & Redfern, M. (2006). Responses to a virtual reality grocery store in persons with and without vestibular dysfunction. *Cyberpsychology, Behavior, and Social Networking, 9*(2), 152–156.

Wierenga, C., Stricker, N., McCauley, A., Simmons, A., Jak, A., Chang, Y.,...Bondi, M. (2010). Increased functional brain response during word retrieval in cognitively intact older adults at genetic risk for Alzheimer's disease. *Neuroimage, 51*(3), 1222–1233.

Williams, J. (1991). *Memory Assessment Scales professional manual.* Odessa, FL: Psychological Assessment Resources.

Wilson, R., Weir, D., Leurgans, S., Evans, D., Hebert, L., Langa, K.,...Bennett, D. (2011). Sources of variability in estimates of the prevalence of Alzheimer's disease in the United States. *Alzheimer's and Dementia, 7*(1), 74–79.

Xu, T., Staessen, J., Wei, F., Xu, J., Li, F., Fan, W.,...Li, Y. (2011). Blood flow pattern in the middle cerebral artery in relation to indices of arterial stiffness in the systemic circulation. *American Journal of Hypertension, 25*(3), 319–324.

Zakzanis, K., Quintin, G., Graham, S., & Mraz, R. (2009). Age and dementia related differences in spatial navigation within an immersive virtual environment. *Medical Science Monitor, 15*(4), CR140–150.

Zhou, A., & Jia, J. (2009). Different cognitive profiles between mild cognitive impairment due to cerebral small vessel disease and mild cognitive impairment of Alzheimer's disease origin. *Journal of the International Neuropsychological Society*, *15*, 898–905.

Zizak, V., Filoteo, J., Possin, K., Lucas, J., Rilling, L., Davis, J.,...Salmon, D. (2005). The ubiquity of memory retrieval deficits in patients with frontal-striatal dysfunction. *Cognitive and Behavioral Neurology*, *18*(4), 198–205.

7

■ ■ ■

Dementia with Lewy Bodies

With Guest Author Tanis J. Ferman, PhD

Case Presentation

History

The patient, a right-handed retired physician, was first seen at the clinic at the age of 75. He had experienced an insidious and progressive decline in cognition over the preceding 3 years, with difficulties in concentration, keeping track of details, word finding, and forgetfulness. He stopped working at age 74 and, at that time, was having trouble working the dictation system, and he had developed some trouble with directional-sense.

He developed cognitive fluctuations with episodes where he was strikingly lucid and eloquent, and other times where he appeared more confused and his comments were out of context. He also developed daytime hypersomnolence that seemed to fluctuate during the day. Despite these difficulties, he had learned how to use a computer, and several aspects of recent memory were relatively preserved. He also showed a rather dramatic initial improvement with donepezil.

In the year prior to his initial evaluation, he had developed shuffling gait, falls, micrographia, and slowness of movement. On some mornings he walked remarkably well, but most of the time he had great difficulties with balance. His motor difficulties responded well to carbidopa/levodopa. He

(continued)

also developed autonomic dysfunction with orthostatic hypotension and complained of lightheadedness and near-syncopal episodes. There were instances in which his systolic blood pressure was recorded to reach below 90 and diastolic BP below 60. He was treated with fludrocortisone and later with midodrine hydrochloride, which was helpful but did not completely eliminate the problem.

He also had an interesting sleep history. At around age 66, he began to exhibit dream enactment behavior during sleep in which he vocalized, yelled, vigorously shook a limb, and acted as if he were running in bed. When awakened, he often described being chased by something, and the movements mirrored dream content. These episodes occurred an average of one night per week. His spouse had learned to awaken quickly and either wake him up or move out of the way so as not to be injured. He also snored loudly and apneic pauses were witnessed when he slept on his back. He underwent an overnight sleep study that revealed an Apnea/Hypopnea index of 5 (within normal limits) with disordered breathing episodes reflecting strictly hypopneas that only occurred in the supine position, with oxygen saturation nadir of 89%. The arousal index was 25 per hour, the majority of which were not related to disordered breathing or periodic limb movements. The sleep study also demonstrated REM sleep without atonia and two behavioral episodes of vigorous movements that clearly emerged out of REM sleep, indicating physiologic evidence for REM sleep behavior disorder (RBD). There was no epileptiform activity on the recording. He had night terrors as a child and experienced occasional hypnogogic hallucinations as a freshman in college. There was no history of cataplexy.

His mood was minimally affected. A local psychiatrist spent considerable time with him and did not feel clinically significant depression was present. Visual hallucinations developed at the age of 76, and occurred essentially every day, and included images of people as well as objects. He tended to use his hands as if tying knots or other manipulations when no such objects were there. He sometimes believed there was a hole in the floor and strongly suggested not to continue proceeding forward. He was given low dose quetiapine, tolerating it reasonably well (higher doses >50mg worsened somnolence and needed to be titrated downward). The use of quetiapine did not eliminate the hallucinations, but reduced his anxiety and fearfulness about them. There was no delusional ideation and no Capgras phenomenon.

He underwent an EEG at age 75 and again at age 76; both revealed dysrhythmia grade 2–3 generalized, nonspecific but maximal to posterior head regions.

Family History
He had a half sister with cognitive difficulties at age 70, and a maternal uncle with similar problems that began after age 60.

Physical Examination
Neurologic: Focused examination revealed an alert, attentive gentleman who provided a lucid history of his clinical course. He had clear constructional dyspraxia. There was mild bradykinesia, decreased arm swing while walking, mildly decreased facial animation, mild hypokinetic dysarthia, mild rigidity (worse on right), mild postural tremor but no resting tremor. Palmomental reflex present, snout and glabellar were absent. He scored 31 out of 38 on the short test of mental status.

Neuroimaging Studies
He underwent five MRI scans as part of a research imaging project. His initial diagnostic MRI scan (see Figure 7.1a) was read as:

> Mild to moderate cerebral atrophy. The ventricular system may be slightly larger than expected for the degree of sulcal widening. Findings may be related to primarily central cerebral atrophy; however, a component of communicating hydrocephalus/NPH is a consideration as well. Focal and confluent areas of increased T2 signal are present in the subcortical and periventricular white matter of both cerebral hemispheres, as well as within the pons. The appearance is most compatible with small vessel ischemic or degenerative change. The remainder of the intracranial contents are unremarkable.

Four years later, follow-up scanning (Figure 7.1b) showed a stable MRI with slight ventricular enlargement consistent with diffuse cerebral atrophy. Patchy T2 signal in the white matter of both cerebral hemispheres, consistent with chronic small vessel ischemic changes which are moderate to advanced allowing for patient age. There was no significant hippocampal atrophy.

Course of Illness
The patient returned for a series of follow-up visits after the initial consult. He was seen by Neurology, Psychiatry, and Internal Medicine over

(continued)

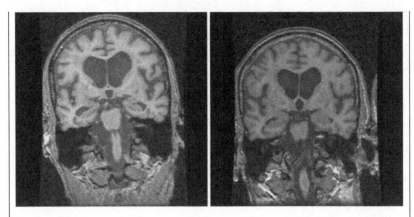

FIGURE 7.1 MRI scans of the patient at the year of diagnosis (Panel A) and again four years later (Panel B).

time. About 3 years post initial evaluation and 18 months prior to his death, he was seen again by Neurology. The neurologist documented that over time there had been obvious progression in his cognitive difficulties, including marked visual spatial difficulties, verbal blocking and forgetfulness. He continued to demonstrate cognitive fluctuations, and at times he seemed to follow questions and answer appropriately, while at other times not. He continued on Aricept, having increased to 15 mg daily, perhaps very slightly improved, but not markedly so. His RBD became quiescent over time. He continued to exhibit worsening daytime sleepiness and dozed frequently during the day, but tended to sleep reasonably well at night.

His mood was minimally affected; he continued to remain generally in good spirits. Visual hallucinations persisted essentially every day and continued to include the same quality of people as well as objects. He continued to modestly benefit from quetiapine. Also as stated, he received low dose carbidopa/levodopa as well as Lodosyn, experiencing minimal tremor, but his greatest difficulties remained with gait—with continued fluctuations in severity. He tended to lean backward while sitting, and fall backward while standing or walking.

At 5 years post initial evaluation (8 years since symptom onset), the patient died. He succumbed while residing in an adult foster care facility. He had actually been doing reasonably well over the prior week and had his usual remarkably lucid moments.

Autopsy Findings

1. Lewy body disease, diffuse Neocortical type, characterized by:
   a. Frequent brainstem, limbic, and neocortical alpha-synuclein-positive Lewy neurites, Lewy bodies, and pale bodies.
   b. Profound pallor of substantia nigra and locus ceruleus, marked, with moderate pigmentary incontinence, neuronal loss and gliosis (lateral > medial), with frequent alpha-synuclein-positive Lewy bodies, pale bodies, and Lewy neurites, and absent neurofibrillary tangles.
   c. Neocortical neuronal loss and gliosis, mild, with mild superficial spongiosis.
   d. Scattered alpha-synuclein-positive deposits, spinal gray.
2. Braak neurofibrillary tangle stage III; NIA-Reagan: low to intermediate likelihood of AD; CERAD possible AD, with:
   a. Neocortex: frequent diffuse plaques; sparse neuritic plaques, absent tau-positive neuritic plaques, and absent neurofibrillary tangles.
   b. Amygdala, entorhinal cortex, subiculum, and hippocampus: sparse to moderate neuritic plaques and frequent neurofibrillary tangles.
   c. Amyloid angiopathy leptomeningeal > cortical, patchy with focal myelin pallor, and related perivascular chronic inflammation, and hemosiderin deposition, but no evidence for lobal hemorrhage.
3. Argyrophilic grains with frequent medial-temporal silver- and tau-positive grains, sparse coiled bodies and amygdaloid ballooned neurons.
4. Cerebral atrophy, generalized, mild; left hemibrain weight 741 g.
5. Cranial arteriolosclerosis with patchy white matter pallor and rarefaction.
6. Cranial atherosclerosis: right middle cerebral (M1), grade 1 of 4; left middle cerebral focal grade 3 at origin, M1 and M2 grade 1.

Neuropsychological Studies

As shown in Figure 7.2, although this patient presented initially with challenges on one or two memory measures, these were mild and largely limited

(continued)

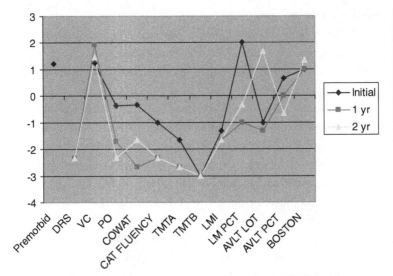

FIGURE 7.2 Neuropsychological profile. All scores are age adjusted z scores. Premorbid = Wide Range Achievement Test (3rd edition; Wilkinson, 1993); Reading score, DRS = Mattis Dementia Rating Scale (Mattis, 1988); total scores, VC = Verbal comprehension, PO = perceptual organization, WMI = Working Memory Index, all from Wechsler Adult Intelligence Scale-Third edition (Wechsler, 1997); COWAT = Controlled Oral Word Association Test (Benton & Hamsher, 1978); Cat Fluency = Category Fluency test; LM1 = Wechsler Memory Scale Revised (WMS-R; Wechsler, 1987); Logical Memory Immediate Recall, LMPCT = WMS-R Logical Memory Delay divided by LM1. AVLTLOT = Rey Auditory Verbal Learning Test (AVLT; Rey, 1964) total of trials 1–5 minus 5*trial 1 (see Ivnik et al., 1992); AVLTPCT = AVLT 30-minute delay divided by AVLT trial 5. Boston = Boston Naming Test (Kaplan, Goodglass, & Weintraub, 1983). DRS, COWAT, Category Fluency, WMS-R, AVLT and Boston scores are based on Mayo Older American's Normative Studies (MOANS) norms.

to encoding or acquisition problems. More noteworthy were the severely compromised Trail Making B and modestly compromised Trail Making A scores. Over time, perceptual organizational function dropped rapidly as did other timed and speeded measures. The early speeded and visual perceptual deficits and relatively preserved delayed recall skills are common in DLB.

Diagnostic Criteria

In 1996, consensus criteria for the clinical diagnosis of DLB were put forth that require dementia plus one or two of the following core features (2 for probable DLB, 1 for possible DLB): Recurrent, fully formed visual hallucinations (VH), parkinsonism, and fluctuating cognition (McKeith et al., 1996). Using these criteria, diagnostic accuracy varies from poor to excellent (Aarsland et al., 2008; McKeith et al., 2000; Nelson et al., 2010). Problems with reliable assessment of fluctuations, a lack of empiric data regarding when core features should occur relative to dementia onset, and limitations to study design (e.g., circularity, absence of standardized assessment, inclusion of cases with advanced dementia) contribute to this discrepancy (Klatka, Louis, & Schiffer, 1996; Kuzuhara & Yoshimura, 1993; Lippa, Smith, & Swearer, 1994; Mega et al., 1996; Walker et al., 2000). The third international workshop on DLB and Parkinson's disease dementia (PDD) convened in 2003 and revised the consensus diagnostic criteria in 2005 (McKeith et al., 2005). As shown in Table 7.1, these criteria differed from the original with the inclusion of suggested features, which include REM sleep behavior disorder. In an autopsy validation study, each of the three core features increased the odds of autopsy-confirmed DLB up to two-fold, and RBD increased the odds six-fold (Ferman et al., 2011).

Epidemiology

Neocortical Lewy bodies are found in about 20%–35% of elderly persons with dementia (Galasko et al., 1994; Hansen et al., 1990; Hulette et al., 1995; Joachim, Morris, & Selkoe, 1988) and do not commonly occur in normal brains (E. Perry et al., 1990). Based on sensitive immunostaining techniques, dementia with Lewy bodies (DLB) was considered the second most common cause of neurodegenerative dementia following Alzheimer's disease (AD) (Lennox et al., 1989; E. Perry et al., 1990), although more recent autopsy studies demonstrate infarcts to be more common than Lewy bodies—at least among those with MCI (Schneider, Arvanitakis, Leurgans, & Bennett, 2009). Unlike AD, DLB prevalence does not seem to increase with advancing age in the elderly. In a consecutive series of 1,100 autopsy cases of patients with dementia over age 70, there was a significant increase in the relative prevalence of AD with cerebrovascular disease associated with age, but only a slight increase in DLB with AD, and an age-associated decrease in the prevalence of DLB without AD (Jellinger & Attems, 2011).

Neuropathology

Description and Distribution of Cortical and Subcortical Lewy Bodies in DLB

The relationship between the presence of Lewy type neuronal inclusions and dementia was first identified in 1961 by Okazaki and colleagues

Table 7.1 Revised Criteria for the Clinical Diagnosis of Dementia with Lewy Bodies (DLB)

1. *Central feature* (essential for a diagnosis of possible or probable DLB)
   - Dementia defined as progressive cognitive decline of sufficient magnitude to interfere with normal social or occupational function
   - Prominent or persistent memory impairment may not necessarily occur in the early stages but is usually evident with progression
   - Deficits on tests of attention, executive function, and visuospatial ability may be especially prominent
2. *Core features* (2 core features are sufficient for a diagnosis of probable DLB, 1 for possible DLB)
   - Fluctuating cognition with pronounced variation in attention and alertness
   - Recurrent visual hallucinations that are typically well formed and detailed
   - Spontaneous features of parkinsonism
3. *Suggestive features* (if 1 or more of these is present in the presence of one or more core features, a diagnosis of probable DLB can be made. In the absence of any core features, one or more suggestive features is sufficient for possible DLB. Probable DLB should not be diagnosed on the basis of suggestive features alone.)
   - REM sleep behavior disorder
   - Severe neuroleptic sensitivity
   - Low dopamine transporter uptake in the basal ganglia demonstrated by SPECT or PET imaging
4. *Supportive features* (commonly present but not proven to have diagnostic specificity)
   - Repeated falls and syncope
   - Transient, unexplained loss of consciousness
   - Severe autonomic dysfunction, e.g., orthostatic hypotension, urinary incontinence
   - Hallucinations in other modalities
   - Systematized delusions

(continued)

Depression
- Relative preservation of medial temporal lobe structures on CT/MRI scan
- Generalized low uptake on SPECT/PET perfusion scan with reduced occipital activity
- Abnormal (low uptake) MIBD myocardial scintigraphy
- Prominent slow wave activity on EEG with temporal lobe transient sharp waves

5. A diagnosis of DLB is less likely
- In the presence of cerebrovascular disease evident as focal neurologic signs or on brain imaging
- In the presence of any other physical illness or brain disorder sufficient to account in part, or in total for the clinical picture
- If the parkinsonism only appears for the first time at a stage of severe dementia.

6. *Temporal sequence* of symptoms
- DLB should be diagnosed when dementia occurs before or concurrently with parkinsonism (if it is present). The term Parkinson's disease dementia (PDD) should be used to describe dementia that occurs in the context of well-established Parkinson's disease. In a practice setting, the term that is most appropriate to the clinical situation should be used, and generic terms such as LB disease are often helpful. In research studies in which distinction needs to be made between DLB and PDD, the existing 1-year rule between the onset of dementia and parkinsonism in DLB continues to be recommended. Adoption of other time periods will simply confound the data pooling or comparison between studies. In other research settings that may include clinicopathologic studies and clinical trials, both clinical phenotypes may be considered collectively under categories such as LB disease or alpha-synucleinopathy.

Source: McKeith et al. (2005).

(Okazaki, Lipkin, & Aronson, 1961). Lewy bodies are concentric, intra-cytoplasmic neuronal inclusions that have long been a recognized pathology of brainstem monoaminergic and cholinergic nuclei in idiopathic Parkinson's disease (PD) (Dickson, 2002; Pollanen, Dickson, & Bergeron, 1993). Subcortical Lewy bodies are distributed in the dorsal motor nucleus of the vagus, medullary gigantocellular nuclei, locus coeruleus, raphé nucleus, midbrain tegmentum, hypothalamus and basal forebrain (Braak et al., 2003; Dickson et al., 1987; Dickson, Feany, Yen, Mattiace, & Davies, 1996). Neocortical Lewy bodies are less eosinophilic, less circumscribed, and are better detected by ubiquitin and particularly by α-synuclein immunohistochemistry (Dickson, 2002; Lennox et al., 1989; Mega et al., 1996). The limbic (anterior cingulate, entorhinal, amygdala) and temporal regions are specifically vulnerable to cortical Lewy bodies, with lesser involvement of frontal and posterior cortical regions (Braak et al., 2003; Kosaka, 1990; Kosaka, Yoshimura, Ikeda, & Budka, 1984). Spongiosis is also observed in the amygdala and basal forebrain. Lewy neurites (LN) are widespread α-synuclein positive inclusions that are located in neural processes, and preferentially affect limbic and temporal lobe structures (Dickson, 2002; Dickson et al., 1996; Dickson et al., 1991; Dickson et al., 1994). In addition to α-synuclein and ubiquitin, there are other proteins that exist in neurons with Lewy bodies that depend on the specific neuron where the Lewy body forms. Tyrosine hydroxylase, a rate-limiting enzyme for dopamine and norepinephrine was detected and increased in catecholaminergic neurons with Lewy bodies in the locus coeruleus and substantia nigra, and choline acetyltransferase was found and increased in Lewy bodies of cholinergic-rich neurons of the pedunculopontine nucleus and the nucleus basalis of Meynert (Dugger & Dickson, 2010). These findings suggest a potential effect of LB pathology, which is sequestration of rate-limiting enzymes responsible for neurotransmitter production, and this may contribute to neurotransmitter deficiencies.

AD-Type Pathology in DLB

A proportion of DLB cases have AD-type pathology that includes neurofibrillary tangles (NFTs) and neuritic plaques (Hansen et al., 1990; Hulette et al., 1995; Lippa et al., 1994). As discussed in Chapter 5, neuritic plaques are composed of extracellular beta-amyloid (Aβ) protein deposits comprised of 40 and 42 amino acid peptides. The neuritic plaques that accompany AD include a dense core of Aβ40 with neuritic processes composed of the protein tau (Dickson, 1997b). In contrast, plaques in Lewy body disease are typically diffuse (though some may contain a core), and are primarily composed of Aβ42 with a paucity or absence of tau-positive neurites (R. Armstrong, Cairns, & Lantos, 2000; Dickson, 1997a; Dickson et al., 1989; Jellinger, 2000; Lippa, Smith, & Perry, 1999). Diffuse plaques are also numerous in brains of cognitively normal elderly (Dickson, 1991; Dickson et al., 1992; Katzman et al., 1988). Most clinicopathologic studies of DLB and AD do not take this distinction into account and, as such, it is not known whether differences in plaque-type influence clinical presentation. When NFTs are present in Lewy body disease, they are often infrequent but the count can be high (Crystal, Dickson, Lizardi, Davies, & Wolfson, 1990; Hansen, Masliah, Galasko, & Terry, 1993; Hansen et al., 1990; W Samuel, Galasko, Masliah, & Hansen, 1996), and regional distribution using Braak staging is typically lower in DLB than AD, indicating confinement to limbic regions (Braak & Braak, 1991; Samuel, Alford, Hofstetter, & Hansen, 1997). In an autopsy sample of 113 DLB cases, over half (56%) had a Braak NFT stage that was ≤IV (Ferman et al., 2011). Diagnostic accuracy of DLB is significantly better in those with low Braak stages and lower tangle density pathology (Del Ser, Hachinski, Merskey, & Munoz, 2001; Merdes et al., 2003). That is, patients with low Braak stages were more likely to have been correctly diagnosed as having DLB during life, and there is good specificity but poor sensitivity for patients with Braak stage IV and above. Nonetheless, including RBD in the diagnostic criteria results in an improved sensitivity rate to 88% without compromising the specificity rate of 73% (Ferman et al., 2011), even in cases with Braak stages greater than IV.

Dickson and colleagues (Fujishiro et al., 2008) undertook a clinico-pathological validation of the pathologic criteria included in the McKeith et al. (2005) revision to DLB diagnostic criteria (McKeith et al., 2005). Based on a prospectively recruited, longitudinally followed sample that came to autopsy, they proposed a minor adaptation to the original neuropathological scheme. Specifically, the authors suggested distinguishing between Braak Stage V and VI, and to consider those with Braak stage VI and neocortical Lewy bodies to have low likelihood DLB instead of intermediate likelihood DLB, and to also consider including those with AD and amygdala-only Lewy bodies as low likelihood DLB. This scheme, listed in Table 7.2 below, recognizes that, as Lewy body pathology increases in the brain, the likelihood that the DLB clinical syndrome is present also increases. Conversely,

Table 7.2 Proposed DLB Pathological Criteria Based on Results from Prospective Cases

LEWY BODIES	ALZHEIMER-TYPE PATHOLOGY			
	NIA LOW LIKELIHOOD AD (BRAAK STAGE 0-II)	NIA INTERMEDIATE LIKELIHOOD AD (BRAAK STAGE III-IV)	NIA HIGH LIKELIHOOD AD (BRAAK STAGE V)	NIA HIGH LIKELIHOOD AD (BRAAK STAGE VI)
No Lewy bodies	Low Likelihood DLB 0/3	Low Likelihood DLB 0/9	Low Likelihood DLB 0/3	Low Likelihood DLB 1/7
Amygdala	Low Likelihood DLB 0	Low Likelihood DLB 0	Low Likelihood DLB 0	Low Likelihood DLB 0/2
Brainstem	Low Likelihood DLB 0	Low Likelihood DLB 0	Low Likelihood DLB 0	Low Likelihood DLB 0
Limbic	High Likelihood DLB 2/2	Intermediate Likelihood DLB 2/2	Intermediate Likelihood DLB 0/1	Low Likelihood DLB 2/4
Diffuse	High Likelihood DLB 6/6	High Likelihood DLB 20/21	Intermediate Likelihood DLB 9/10	Low Likelihood DB 1/5

Each box shows the ratio of clinically probable DLB to the total number of cases in that pathologic category for all 76 prospectively diagnosed DLB and AD cases. It refers to the clinical likelihood of DLB based on CDLB pathologic criteria that include distribution of Lewy bodies and neurofibrillary tangles based on Braak stage.

Source: From Fujishiro et al. (2008). Reproduced with permission.

as Alzheimer pathology increases in the brain, the likelihood of clinically probable DLB decreases.

Clinicopathologic Correlates in DLB and AD

In AD, dementia severity is not associated with neocortical plaque density but is related to NFT burden (Arriagada, Growdon, Hedley-Whyte, & Hyman, 1992; Samuel et al., 1996; Samuel, Henderson, & Miller, 1991). In DLB, LB density but not plaque or NFT density is correlated with dementia severity (Haroutunian et al., 2000; Hurtig et al., 2000; Samuel, et al., 1996). In a community based sample of patients with PDD, Aarsland and colleagues showed an association between LB score and annual decline on the MMSE after controlling for age, gender, and education (Aarsland, Perry, Brown, Larsen, & Ballard, 2005). Lewy neurite density has also been associated with the degree of cognitive impairment in DLB (Churchyard & Lees, 1997), suggesting that these inclusions may interfere with neuronal function, but further investigation is needed.

In AD, the CA1 region and subiculum of the hippocampus are severely affected, while the CA2/3 region is considered the "resistant zone" and is typically spared (Nagy et al., 1996; Ransmayr et al., 1992; West, Coleman, Flood, & Tronosco, 1994). In DLB, it is the CA2/3 region that is affected, while the CA1 and subiculum regions are typically spared (Dickson, 1991; Harding, Lakay, & Halliday, 2002). Similarly, AD is associated with a near total loss of perforant pathway neurons, whereas in DLB the perforant pathway is more comparable to that of normal controls (Lippa, Pulaski-Salo, Dickson, & Smith, 1997). Although damage to the CA1 region has been associated with memory impairment, it is not known whether CA2/3 pathology affects memory function. It also remains to be seen whether those DLB patients with some CA1 involvement are more likely to show the pattern of rapid forgetting, the type of memory disturbance that is observed in AD.

The ventral temporal lobe is heavily burdened by prominent Lewy body pathology and spongiosis (Byrne, Lennox, Lowe, & Godwin-Austen, 1989; Dickson et al., 1987). This neuroanatomic pattern occurs early and well before the onset of Lewy body pathology in other cortical regions, including the parietal lobe (Braak et al., 2003). This raises the possibility of early specific visual perceptual deficits of the ventral processing visual stream, due to disruption of the pattern/object recognition pathway. Patients with visual hallucinations (VH) have higher LB densities in amygdala, parahippocampus and inferior temporal cortex (Harding, Broe, & Halliday, 2002), suggesting the involvement of these regions in the development of VH. Nonetheless, VH can and do occur in patients without cortical pathology. In an autopsy study by our group, VH occurred with equal frequency in those with limbic versus cortical Lewy bodies (Ferman et al., 2003). DLB patients with early VH onset had heavier limbic LB deposition, whereas earlier VH onset in AD was associated with greater combined limbic and cortical NFT pathology. This suggests that VH in AD is related to an advanced stage of the disease, but in DLB it is related to early selective limbic vulnerability.

A recent study examined whether autopsy-confirmed DLB with or without RBD differed clinically or pathologically (Dugger et al., 2011). Results showed that individuals with probable RBD were more likely male, had a shorter duration of dementia (8 vs. 10 years), earlier onset of parkinsonism (2 vs. 5 years), and earlier onset of visual hallucinations (3 vs. 6 years). Moreover, autopsy-confirmed DLB with RBD had a lower Braak neurofibrillary tangle stage and lower neuritic plaque scores, but no difference in Lewy body distribution. Furthermore, women with autopsy-confirmed DLB without a history of RBD had a later onset of hallucinations and parkinsonism, and a higher Braak stage. These results indicate that RBD in the context of Lewy body disease appears to be associated with a distinct clinical and pathologic pattern.

The Cholinergic Hypothesis Fits DLB Better Than AD

Profound cholinergic neuronal loss and severely depleted choline acetyltransferase levels occur early in DLB disease course, whereas normally aging individuals show little difference—as does AD until the advanced stage of dementia (Dickson, et al., 1987; E. Perry et al., 1994; Perry et al., 1993; Tiraboschi et al., 2002). As stated in Chapter 5, significant cholinergic cell loss is actually *not* an early feature of AD, though it does become prominent in late AD. Moreover, the use of cholinergic toxins to selectively target the nucleus basalis of Meynert (which is 90% cholinergic and widely projects to the cortex) (Mesulam, Mufson, Levey, & Wainer, 1983) actually reveals no impairment of memory but, rather, results in deficient sustained and divided attention. The damage to the basal forebrain may, therefore, interfere more substantially with attention than memory. Furthermore, anticholinergic agents can elicit visual hallucinations and disturbed consciousness, and the degree of this disruption varies as a function of cholinergic deficiency (Flacker et al., 1998; E. Perry & Perry, 1995; E. Perry, Walker, Grace, & Perry, 1999; Tune et al., 1981). Again, patients with DLB are more likely to have early visual hallucinations and problems with daytime arousal and fluctuating cognition, compared to age- and dementia-matched peers (Ballard et al., 1997; Ferman et al., 2011; Ferman et al., 2004).

One hypothesized mechanism for VH in DLB includes cholinergic depletion of the basal forebrain alone or with the inferior temporal lobe (Harding, Broe, et al., 2002; E. Perry et al., 1993; E. Perry et al., 1990; R. Perry, McKeith, & Perry, 1997). Increasing acetylcholine availability with cholinesterase inhibitors improves attention and alertness and lessens hallucinations in early DLB (Bergman & Lerner, 2002; Lebert, Pasquier, Souliez, & Petit, 1998; Maclean, Collins, & Byrne, 2001; Samuel et al., 2000a; Shea, MacKnight, & Rockwood, 1998; Wengel, Roccaforte, & Burke, 1998). Thus, cholinergic depletion is a critical factor in the symptom manifestation of early DLB but appears to be less so in early AD. This finding highlights the importance of differentiating between early versus late stages of different dementias, since patients with advanced AD may have similar clinical features to those with early DLB.

Genetics

No genes have been specifically identified for dementia with Lewy bodies. Nonetheless, over the past few years, 11 genes have been cloned for Parkinson's disease (PD). This is remarkable considering that it used to be believed that PD was not heritable due to low concordance rates in monozygotic twins. It is now known that the twin studies simply did not have enough power (due to factors such as reduced penetrance), and the risk of PD in a first-degree relative is 2.5 times that of controls (Rocca et al., 2004). One study found an identical twin pair, previously reported to be discordant, but later revealed that one twin had a 30-year disease course and the other developed his symptoms 20 years later and had a 14-year disease course (Dickson et al., 2001). Neuropathology of each twin revealed Lewy bodies in the brainstem and limbic regions in both cases (Dickson et al., 2001). The first gene associated with PD was a point-mutation of alpha-synuclein (Polymeropoulos et al., 1997). Alpha-synuclein has since been shown to be a major component of Lewy bodies and Lewy neurites. Studies of several large families have also revealed that multiplications of the alpha-synuclein gene can cause autosomal-dominant parkinsonism with or without an associated dementia (Zimprich et al., 2004). Mutations have also been identified in a large, multifunctional protein, LRRK2 (leucine-rich repeat kinase 2) (Zimprich et al., 2004). Within affected carriers, autopsies have revealed Lewy body pathology, tau pathology, or nigral degeneration without distinctive histopathology. LRRK2 is an enormous gene with 39 coding variants, but it is surprising that different pathologies can be caused by mutation of the same gene. It has been suggested that LRRK2 may be responsible for the phosphorylation of both alpha-synuclein and tau.

Neuropsychological Profile of Lewy Body Disease

The dementias of DLB and AD are similar in insidious onset and progressive course, and prior to autopsy many patients with Lewy body disease had been given the antemortem diagnosis of AD (Hansen et al., 1990; Lippa et al., 1994). Despite some similarities, several studies have demonstrated differences in neurocognitive performance between DLB and AD. Hansen and colleagues revealed significantly greater deficits for DLB compared to AD in attention, letter fluency, visual perceptual organization, and visual constructional skills (Hansen et al., 1990). Compared to AD, DLB was associated with worse performance on the construction subscale of the Dementia Rating Scale (DRS) while the AD group produced lower scores on the memory subscale (Salmon et al., 1996). Our studies show that, compared to autopsy-confirmed pure AD, clinically diagnosed DLB patients demonstrate a pattern of disproportionate deficits in visual perceptual skills, attention, and fluency with significantly better memory and object naming performance (Ferman et al., 1999; Ferman et al., 2002; Ferman et al., 2006). Logistic regression modeling was done to determine the diagnostic utility of these measures in the differentiation of separate, prospective sample of persons with DLB (n = 87) from those with AD (n = 138) and normal aging (n = 103) (Ferman et al., 2006). Patient groups did not differ in age, education, or dementia severity (based on the Global Deterioration Scale [GLDS] and Clinical Dementia Rating Scale [CDR]). The logistic models revealed that impairment in basic attention, visual perception, visual construction, and memory distinguish DLB from normal aging (sensitivity of 88.6%, specificity of 96.1%). In contrast, impaired visual construction and attention plus preserved memory and naming skills distinguished DLB from AD (sensitivity of 83.3% and a specificity of 91.4%). These results confirm our prior findings of a double dissociation in neurocognitive function between early DLB and AD.

Visual Spatial Ability

DLB is associated with significant deficits in higher order visual processing, a finding that is not attributable to motor slowness associated with parkinsonism. Interestingly, DLB patients with VH tend to do more poorly on visual tasks (Calderon et al., 2001; Ferman et al., 1999; Ferman et al., 2002; Simard, van Reekum, & Myran, 2003). Nonetheless, some studies have not found differences between AD and DLB on visual tasks (Forstl, Burns, Luthert, Ciarns, & Levy, 1993; Gnanalingham, Byrne, Thornton, Sambrook, & Bannister, 1997). One explanation is that the inclusion of patients in the advanced stages of dementia can obfuscate group differences due to generalized impairment. Alternately, impaired performance may be the result of differential impairment of other task demands. For example, visual problem solving may be negatively affected by executive difficulties in AD, and by perceptual difficulties in DLB. Mori and colleagues examined this issue and revealed deficits in DLB but not AD on basic visual tasks that did not require executive function (Mori et al., 2000). Reflexive saccadic eye movements responsible for shifting the fovea toward visual targets show greater impairment for the PDD and DLB groups compared to AD, PD, and normal controls (Mosimann et al., 2005). Also, flash electroretinography reveals abnormalities of the photoreceptors in the retina that may interfere with signal transmission to the bipolar cells (Devos et al., 2005). Regional blood flow has been shown to be lower in occipital regions in DLB but not AD (Imamura et al., 2001; Lobotesis et al., 2001). Overall, these findings suggest that the etiology of the visual impairment in DLB may not be entirely due to disruption of the cortical extrastriate association areas, but may also have an afferent or earlier neural contribution before reaching the cortex for further processing.

Episodic Memory
Memory difficulties, when present in early DLB, appear to be fairly mild and stand in direct contrast to the pronounced amnestic disturbance of AD. Neuropathologic and imaging studies also show significant atrophy in the hippocampus in AD, while patients with DLB show little difference from normal controls (Barber et al., 1999; Dickson et al., 1991; D. W. Dickson et al., 1994; Hashimoto et al., 1998; Ishii et al., 1998; Lobotesis et al., 2001). Salmon and colleagues demonstrated a pattern of poor initial learning and recall in four of five patients with DLB without the rapid forgetting that is typically observed in AD. In a sample of 9 pure DLB, 57 mixed DLB/AD, and 66 pure AD, patients with AD pathology performed worse on tasks of verbal memory, while patients with LB pathology performed worse on tasks of visuospatial skills, and combined pathology affected visuospatial performance but not verbal memory (Johnson, Morris, & Galvin, 2005).

A follow-up study by Salmon and colleagues (Hamilton et al., 2004) confirmed that the memory deficit associated with early DLB is characterized by poor learning and delayed free recall but improvement in retention and recognition memory rates. For example, groups of neuropathologically confirmed DLB and AD were shown to produce consistent decrements in the patterns of episodic memory deficits in the early stages of the disease (e.g., comparably impaired scores on CVLT Trials 1–5 Total Learning; Logical Memory Immediate Recall; CVLT Long Delay Free Recall; Logical Memory Delayed Recall). However, as shown in Figure 7.3, patients with autopsy-confirmed DLB demonstrated better retention (or savings) scores, as well as better recognition memory than patients with autopsy-confirmed AD. This difference in the pattern of memory performance occurred in the context of equivalent severity of dementia in the two groups (mean DRS scores of both groups ≈ 114; mean MMSE scores of both groups ≈ 23), equivalent naming (mean BNT scores of both groups ≈ 22/30), and functional and clinical measures of disease course. Furthermore, the DLB patients had more severe visuospatial deficits than the AD patients, arguing against the possibility that the DLB patients were simply less demented than the AD patients (see Figure 7.3). Therefore, as was discussed in the prior chapter on vascular dementia, the addition of a recognition memory component to episodic memory testing is a valuable complement to assess for the

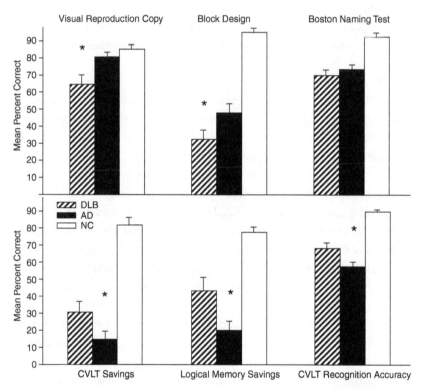

FIGURE 7.3 Mean scores of normal control (NC; *n* = 24) participants and autopsy-confirmed Alzheimer's disease (AD; *n* = 24), and dementia with Lewy bodies (DLB; *n* = 24) groups on several neuropsychological tests. The DLB patients were significantly more impaired than AD patients on tests of visuospatial ability, less impaired on verbal memory savings and recognition memory, not shown, and did not differ on naming.
Figure adapted from Hamilton et al. (2004), with permission.

extent of forgetting and to determine whether the memory deficit may be more related to an encoding/storage or a retrieval-based difficulty.

Differential Diagnosis with Alzheimer's Disease

AD patients can also develop parkinsonism and visual hallucinations, although this is far less common than in DLB. Visual hallucinations occur in 22% to 89% of autopsy-confirmed DLB samples, and in 11% to 28% of autopsy-confirmed AD samples (Harding, Broe, et al., 2002; Hope, Keene, Fairburn, Jacoby, & McShane, 1999; Klatka, et al., 1996; E. Perry et al., 1990; Rockwell, Choure, Galasko, Olichney, & Jeste, 2000; Tiraboschi et al., 2002). Moreover, the mean time from onset of cognitive changes to these symptoms in AD is 5.7 and 6.8 years, respectively. In DLB, however, the mean interval from onset of cognitive changes to parkinsonism and hallucinations is 1.5 and 2 years, respectively, and in some cases these neuropsychiatric symptoms will predate the cognitive changes (e.g., recall the case at the beginning of the chapter, wherein RBD appeared some years prior to the cognitive symptoms).

The dementias of DLB and AD are similar in insidious onset and progressive course, and many patients given the antemortem diagnosis of AD will have Lewy body disease on autopsy (Hansen, et al., 1990; Lippa, et al., 1994). Despite some similarities, several studies have demonstrated differences in neurocognitive performance between DLB and AD. Compared to AD, patients with clinically diagnosed DLB demonstrate a pattern of disproportionate deficits in visuoperceptual skills, attention, and fluency with disproportionately better memory (particularly recall savings or recognition memory) and either comparable or better object naming performance (Ferman et al., 1999; Ferman et al., 2002; Ferman et al., 2004). Poorer baseline performances on tests of visuospatial skills appear to be associated with a more rapid rate of cognitive decline in DLB but not AD (Hamilton et al. 2008) and may presage a particularly malignant disease course of DLB. As discussed, memory disturbance is a critical precursor to AD; however, memory difficulties, when present in early DLB, appear to be fairly mild (Ferman et al., 1999; Ferman et al., 2002; Salmon et al., 1996).

Neuroimaging Studies

Neuropathologic and imaging studies also show significant atrophy and reduced regional cerebral blood flow to the hippocampus in AD, whereas patients with DLB show little difference from normal control groups (Barber et al., 1999; Dickson et al., 1991; D. W. Dickson et al., 1994; Hashimoto et al., 1998; Ishii et al., 1998; Lobotesis et al., 2001). There is a signature pattern of atrophy in DLB characterized by gray matter losses in the dorsal midbrain, basal forebrain, and hypothalamus compared to the widespread gray matter losses involving temporoparietal association cortices and medial temporal lobes in AD (Whitwell et al., 2007). The DLB pattern of gray matter loss results in very good sensitivity (79%) and specificity (99%) compared to AD and FTLD (Vemuri et al., 2011). Rates of atrophy also differentiate DLB from AD. Specifically, the rates of whole brain atrophy and ventricular expansion in AD was significantly increased in AD compared to normal controls, while rates of atrophy in DLB over the same time period did not differ from normal controls (Whitwell et al., 2007).

The Mild Cognitive Impairment (MCI) of DLB

Current studies suggest the "MCI" of DLB to be early visuoperceptual and/or attention deficits. The data from our groups and others reveal disproportionate deficits in higher order visual processing, a finding that is not attributable to motor slowness associated with parkinsonism (Ala, Hughes, Kyrouac, Ghobrial, & Elbie, 2001; Boeve et al., 1998; Calderon et al., 2001; Ferman et al., 1999; Hansen et al., 1990). A clinical history of RBD in the context of dementia with disproportionate visual deficits and relatively preserved memory and naming is likely to represent the earliest stages of DLB (Ferman et al., 2002). In a sample of 8 patients followed prospectively with MCI who subsequently were found to have Lewy body disease at autopsy, cognitive findings revealed attention and/ or visuoperceptual deficits as the earliest cognitive manifestations (Molano et al., 2010). The pattern of atrophy in nonamnestic MCI with attention/executive deficits showed gray matter loss in the basal forebrain and hypothalamus, very similar to that which is observed in the imaging studies of DLB. The combination of imaging and neuropsychological assessment to characterize this clinical phenotype may help with early differential diagnosis of DLB from AD.

Associated Clinical Features

The cardinal clinical features of DLB are parkinsonism, hallucinations, fluctuations, and (to our thinking) RBD. The features are not uniformly present in all cases. The frequency of these features in our consecutive clinical series is presented in Figure 7.4. For example, 46% of patients in the sample demonstrated VH at initial diagnosis. The estimated age of onset of these symptoms is presented in Figure 7.5. Note that 21% of patients had only cognitive symptoms at initial evaluation. Cardinal symptoms leading to the DLB diagnosis developed subsequent to initial evaluation. These data suggest that the appearance of RBD is associated with an earlier age of onset.

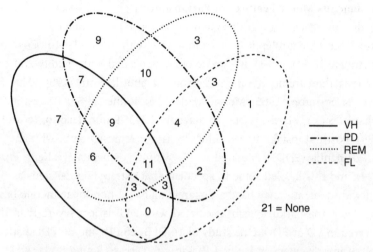

FIGURE 7.4 Percent of patients at initial diagnosis in Mayo DLB cohort with cardinal symptoms based on rigorous criteria, e.g., fluctuations present only if patient scored >2 on Mayo Fluctuations Score. N = 287. VH = Visual Hallucination, PD = Parkinsonism, REM = REM sleep behavior disorder, FL = Fluctuations.

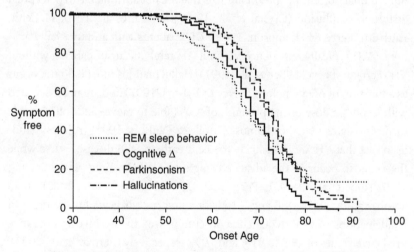

FIGURE 7.5 Age of onset of cardinal symptoms of Lewy Body disease. Fluctuations excluded due to unreliability in reporting age of onset.

Spontaneous Motor Features of Parkinsonism

For diagnostic clarity, parkinsonian signs must be spontaneous and not attributable to neuroleptic medications (McKeith et al., 1996). Cognitive impairment in PD and DLB is more often associated with rigidity and bradykinesia than tremor (Huber, Paulson, & Shuttleworth, 1988; Mayeux, Stern, & Spanton, 1985; Molsa, Marttila, & Rinne, 1984; Pearce, 1974; Richards, Stern, Marder, Cote, & Mayeux, 1993; Rinne, Laakso, & Molsa, 1984). Postural instability/gait difficulty is overrepresented in DLB and PD with dementia (PDD) compared to PD without dementia (McKeith et al., 2004), and this has led some to speculate that extrapyramidal signs associated with dementia may have a dopaminergic and nondopaminergic basis. In general, the parkinsonism associated with DLB is less severe than that observed in PD or PDD. One study of 14 DLB, 28 PD, and 30 PDD patients showed improvement in Unified Parkinson's Disease Rating Scale (UPDRS) score for all three groups in response to l-dopa, but less so for the DLB patients (Molloy, McKeith, O'Brien, & Burn, 2005). The possibility that this effect may be mediated by greater initial motor deficits in the PDD and PD groups should be considered.

Visual Hallucinations

Visual hallucinations (VH) in DLB consist of fully formed, detailed, three-dimensional objects, people, or animals that are not attributable to perceptual distortion or illusion (Crystal et al., 1990; Hansen, et al., 1990; McKeith, Fairbairn, Perry, & Thompson, 1994). DLB patients with auditory hallucinations (AH) typically experience VH, but AH rarely occur in patients without VH (Ferman, Boeve, Silber, et al., 1997). Hallucinations in DLB do not occur as a function of AD pathology (Cercy & Bylsma, 1997) and are not associated with levodopa dose or the presence of "on" (able to move) and "off" (unable to move) states (Sanchez-Ramos, Ortoll, & Paulson, 1996). Autopsy studies reveal that VH are most likely to occur early in DLB disease course while they tend to occur in the advanced stages of AD (Ala, Yang, Sung, & Frey, 1997; Hope et al., 1999; E. Perry et al., 1990; Rockwell et al., 2000). In an autopsy study of 41 DLB and 70 AD, a cutoff of four years for the onset of hallucinations relative to dementia onset improved the positive and negative predictive values of DLB to 81% and 79%, respectively (Ferman et al., 2003). Patients with VH typically have greater cognitive and functional impairment, but whether the presence of VH in DLB is associated with faster rate of disease progression has yet to be determined.

Fluctuations

The fluctuations of DLB resemble signs of delirium without identifiable precipitants of such mental status changes. This phenomenon involves a waxing and waning of cognition, abilities, and arousal. It has been described as variable attention, incoherent speech, hypersomnolence, impaired awareness of surroundings, staring into space, or appearing "glazed" or "switched off." The prevalence of fluctuations in DLB samples is widely discrepant and ranges from 10% to 80% with poor interrater reliability. Studies typically do not specify how the presence of fluctuations was determined, and the usefulness of this core clinical feature has been highly criticized. Ferman and colleagues developed a fluctuations questionnaire to determine whether there are salient features of fluctuations that reliably differentiate DLB (n = 70) from AD (n = 70) and normal elderly (n = 200) (Ferman et al., 2004). A 19-item questionnaire was administered to informants and included items describing delirium (Inouye et al., 1990) and aspects of DLB fluctuations reported in the literature (McKeith, Fairbairn, Perry, Thompson, & Perry, 1992; McKeith et al., 1996). Results showed that four items significantly differentiated DLB from AD. These features include: (1) daytime drowsiness and lethargy; (2) daytime sleep of two or more hours; (3) staring into space for long periods; and (4) times when the patient's flow of ideas seem disorganized, unclear, or not logical. The presence of three or four features of this composite occurred in 63% of DLB compared to 12% of AD and 0.5% normal elderly (p < 0.01). Acceptable test-retest reliability is demonstrated for each group (r > 0.70). A fluctuations score of 3 or 4 out of the 4 possible items yields a positive predictive value of 83% for the clinical diagnosis of DLB against an alternate diagnosis of AD. A score of less than 3 yields a negative predictive value of 70% for the absence of a clinical diagnosis of DLB in favor of AD. Since not all patients with DLB have fluctuations, these values suggest reasonable diagnostic utility. In the DLB group, chi-square analyses showed that no particular combination of visual hallucinations, parkinsonism, or RBD is associated with a fluctuations composite score of 3 or 4 (p > 0.05). The Fluctuations Score is not correlated with the UPDRS motor score for either the DLB (r = +0.22, p > 0.05) or AD (r = +0.20, p > 0.05) groups, revealing that fluctuations are not significantly related to the extent of underlying parkinsonism. These data indicate that an informant-based questionnaire is sensitive to fluctuations in alertness and speech, but fails to differentiate fluctuations in ability or cognition between DLB and AD. It may be worthwhile to distinguish between fluctuations in arousal and cognition, whereby the latter may be best evaluated with neuropsychological tests. This is supported by findings that attention, vigilance, and reaction time show greater impairment and variability in DLB than in AD.

REM Sleep Behavior Disorder (RBD)

The loss of normal muscle atonia during rapid eye movement (REM) sleep refers to the parasomnia of REM Sleep Behavior Disorder (RBD). In RBD, augmented muscle activity during REM sleep mimics dream content and can range from elevated muscle tone to complex behavioral sequences such as pantomiming various activities that may be subdued or quite vigorous (American Sleep Disorders Association, 1997; Boeve et al., 1998). The presumed pathophysiologic mechanism of RBD, based on the cat model, involves damage to the descending pontine-medullary reticular formation (including the gigantocellular medullary nuclei) that leads to a loss of the normal REM sleep inhibition of the spinal alpha-motoneurons (Jouvet & Delorme, 1965; Lai & Siegel, 2003). Smaller lesions in this region produce REM sleep without atonia, while larger lesions result in more elaborate motor behavior during REM sleep (Hendricks, Morrison, & Mann, 1982). In humans, polysomnographic evidence of REM sleep without atonia is considered the electrophysiologic substrate of RBD and has been found in patients with and without florid RBD (Gagnon et al., 2002; Plazzi et al., 1997).

As shown in the case at the beginning of this chapter, RBD can precede the onset of neurodegenerative diseases with alpha-synuclein inclusions (i.e., DLB, Parkinson's disease, multiple system atrophy) by years and even decades (Boeve et al., 1998; Plazzi et al., 1997; Schenck, Bundlie, & Mahowald, 1996; Turner, Chervin, Frey, Minoshima, & Kuhl, 1997). In DLB, the frequency of RBD has been reported to be about 75% in autopsy-confirmed DLB (Ferman et al., 2011). It rarely occurs in tau-predominant neurodegenerative conditions, such as Alzheimer's disease (Boeve, Silber, Ferman, Lucas, & Parisi, 2001). The estimated 5-year risk of developing PD or DLB in a cohort with idiopathic RBD is 17.7%, and the 12-year risk is 52.4% (Postuma et al., 2009). When RBD is present with dementia, but not parkinsonism or visual hallucinations, the cognitive pattern is indistinguishable from DLB, and both groups significantly differ from AD (Ferman et al., 2002). In Schenck and Mahowald's original DLB cohort, 65% showed the development of parkinsonism or dementia after 7 years of follow-up (Schenck & Mahowald, 2002). Results to date suggest that RBD and cognitive impairment may be an early harbinger of DLB, and may be predictive of Parkinson's disease with dementia as well (Marion, Qurashi, Marshall, & Foster, 2008; Molano et al., 2010; Vendette et al., 2007).

Neuropathologic confirmation of Lewy body disease has been demonstrated in a patient with a 20-year history of idiopathic RBD (Uchiyama et al., 1995) and another with a 15-year history of idiopathic RBD (Boeve et al., 2007). It was also demonstrated in a patient with a 17-year history of RBD who later developed DLB (Turner, D'Amato, Chervin, & Blaivas, 2000). In an autopsy series of 15 patients holding a diagnosis of RBD and a neurodegenerative disorder, 12 had Lewy body disease and 3 had multiple system atrophy (MSA), providing further evidence that RBD reflects an underlying synucleinopathy (Boeve, Silber, et al., 2003; Hulette et al., 1995). The relationship between RBD and the synucleinopathies has clear clinical implications for the early prediction of DLB, differential diagnosis, and for the refinement of the DLB diagnostic criteria.

Excessive Daytime Sleepiness

Patients with DLB often have daytime drowsiness, but the cause of the somnolence/drowsiness is not known. A clinical referral sample of 78 patients with DLB underwent overnight polysomnography, and we examined indices of sleep continuity (Boeve, Ferman, et al., 2003). The mean age was 71 ± 8 years, and severity of dementia ranged from mild to moderate (mean Dementia Rating Scale [DRS] Score = 115 ± 18). About three-quarters of the sample had a significant number of arousals not accounted for by a movement or breathing disturbance. In half of the DLB sample, sleep efficiency fell well below the expected 80% for this age group (Bliwise, 1993; Kales, Ansel, Markham, Scharf, & Tan, 1971; Wetter, Collado-Seidel, Pollmacher, Yassouridis, & Trenkwalder, 2000). REM sleep without atonia was evident in 83% of the entire sample. Full night studies were done in 47 DLB patients (AH ≤ 10) who did not qualify for a split night study with a Continuous Positive Airway Pressure (CPAP) trial. In that group, mean sleep efficiency was still poor 71.4% ± 14.8%, and 45% had sleep efficiency below 70%. Taken together, patients with DLB have poor sleep efficiency that is not entirely accounted for by periodic limb movements of sleep or sleep apnea. Further studies are needed that represent a random selection of DLB patients and an AD group matched for age, gender, and dementia severity.

Dysautonomia

Autonomic abnormalities, in particular orthostatic hypotension and carotid sinus sensitivity, are more common in DLB than AD or elderly control groups

---

(Ballard, Shaw, McKeith, & Kenny, 1998). A comparison of dysautonomia in DLB, PD, and MSA shows that orthostatic hypotension is quite common in all three groups but MSA is the most severely affected, PD is least severely affected, and DLB has intermediate severity (Thaisetthawatkul et al., 2004). The DLB group tended to respond better to medications than those with MSA. The frequency of urinary symptoms and pattern of sweat loss in DLB was comparable to that of PD but much less than MSA. Lewy bodies and Lewy neurites have been found in the enteric nervous system, cardiac sympathetic system and intermediolateral cell column (Braak, de Vos, Bohl, & Del Tredici, 2006; Wakabayashi & Takahashi, 1997). Neuroimaging studies of the postganglionic axons of the heart reveals reduced [123]MIGB uptake in DLB and RBD, but not in MSA or AD (Kobayashi, Tateno, Morii, Utsumi, & Saito, 2009; Miyamoto, Miyamoto, Iwanami, & Hirata, 2009). When found in Parkinson disease, dysautonomia is associated with cognitive impairment (Kim et al., 2009).

Rate of Decline

In studies of dementia, the variables comprising independent predictors of (1) cognitive decline, (2) time to nursing home care, and (3) death, consisted of parkinsonism, psychosis, and younger age of onset (Mayeux, Stern, & Sano, 1985; Mortimer, Ebbitt, Jun, & Finch, 1992; Stern et al., 1994; Stern et al., 1997; Stern, Mayeux, Sano, Hauser, & Bush, 1987). It is not known whether patients with DLB were included in these older studies. Several studies of DLB indicate a more rapid progression than that of pure AD (T. Armstrong et al., 1991; Ballard, Patel, Oyebode, & Wilcock, 1996; Byrne et al., 1989; Dickson et al., 1987; Lippa et al., 1994; McKeith et al., 1992; Olichney et al., 1998), especially among those DLB patients with more severe visuospatial deficits initially (Hamilton et al. 2008). Some data, however, show no difference in rate of cognitive decline between DLB and AD (Ballard et al., 2001; Helmes, Bowler, Merskey, Munoz, & Hachinski, 2003). In an autopsy study with patients who were part of the Florida Alzheimer's Disease Initiative (ADI) Brain Bank, there was a shorter duration of illness (p < 0.03) for DLB compared to AD (Ferman, et al., 2003). It is unclear as to whether this discrepancy in disease progression reflects a shift in treatment paradigms, methodologic differences, or the compilation of mean values from large samples that may obscure a subgroup of patients with rapid decline. It is our clinical experience that there is a subgroup of patients with DLB who have an unusually rapid decline. It is not yet known whether specific features are associated with more rapid disease progression.

Treatment of DLB

Pharmacologic Treatments

It is generally agreed that neurodegenerative conditions are the result of neuronal degeneration that has evolved years before the emergence of clinical signs (Agid et al., 1989; Koller et al., 1991). Given this prodromal window, we should focus on improving our ability to detect the earliest features of DLB, because it is in the initial stage of the disease that the application of future potential therapies will be most useful in halting or slowing disease progression. Also, distinguishing early DLB from AD has implications for symptom management including avoiding iatrogenic treatment complications and reducing excess disability from medical comorbidities.

Neuroleptic medication is frequently administered to dementia patients for episodic confusion, hallucinations, delusions, and agitation (Francis, Martin, & Kapoor, 1990; Moore, 1977). These clinical features are commonly observed in DLB, but there is convincing evidence that patients with DLB can harbor neuroleptic sensitivity to traditional and to some atypical neuroleptics (Allen, Walker, D'Ath, & Katona, 1995; Burke, Pfeiffer, & McComb, 1998; McKeith et al., 1992; Miller et al., 1998; Rosebush & Mazurek, 1999; Sechi et al., 2000). Specifically, antipsychotic agents with D2 antagonism and anticholinergic properties precipitate and/or exacerbate extrapyramidal signs and cognitive impairment, respectively (Court et al., 2000; Piggott et al., 1998). Unfortunately, discontinuation of the neuroleptic does not necessarily lead to a reversal of the adverse reaction (McKeith et al., 1992). There is a mixed literature on the relationship between atypical antipsychotics and cognition, though the effects of quetiapine appear to be better in DLB than in AD (Aarsland, Larsen, Lim, & Tandberg, 1999; Ballard et al., 2005; Cummings, Street, Masterman, & Clark, 2002; Ellingrod et al., 2002; Juncos et al., 2004; Mulsant et al., 2004). Olanzepine does not seem to worsen parkinsonism (Cummings et al., 2002), though its anticholinergic properties may exacerbate cognitive impairment (Mulsant et al., 2004).

Levodopa-carbidopa is well tolerated in DLB, with a beneficial effect on motor function (Bonelli et al., 2004) and no reported adverse cognitive, neuropsychiatric, or sleep effects (Molloy, Minett, O'Brien, McKeith, & Burn, 2009; Molloy et al., 2006). In some patients, response may not be at the magnitude of that seen in patients with PDD or PD (McKeith et al., 2004). There are reports of levodopa-carbidopa having a positive impact on cognition

(Kulisevsky et al., 2000; Morrison, Borod, Brin, Halbig, & Olanow, 2004). Dopamine agonists, such as pramipexole and ropinirole tend to exacerbate DLB visual hallucinations, drowsiness, and cognitive impairment.

Another treatment issue concerns the profoundly depleted levels of brain acetylcholine in DLB compared to AD (Levy et al., 1994; E. Perry et al., 1993; E. Perry et al., 1990; R. Perry et al., 1997). Drugs with anticholinergic properties are often prescribed to the elderly to treat mood, psychosis, parkinsonism, incontinence, and pulmonary disease (Tune & Egeli, 1999). Several studies have demonstrated adverse reactions to anticholinergic agents that mimic delirium (Bedard et al., 1999; Flacker et al., 1998; Han et al., 2001; Tune et al., 1981). Alternately, improvement (sometimes dramatic) in delirium-like symptoms (including VH) can occur with the use of cholinesterase inhibitors (Kaufer, Catt, Lopez, & DeKosky, 1998; Levy et al., 1994; McKeith et al., 2000; E. Perry et al., 1994; Shea et al., 1998; Wilcock & Scott, 1994). Studies of cholinesterase inhibitors (Bosboom, Stoffers, & Wolters, 2004; Grace et al., 2001; Samuel et al., 2000b) reveal improved cognition in DLB and AD, and detrimental effects when suddenly withdrawn (Minett et al., 2003). A comparison of 30 DLB and 40 PDD with donepezil revealed improved MMSE scores by a mean of 3.9 points in the DLB group and by 3.2 points in PDD by 20 weeks (Thomas et al., 2005). Extrapyramidal side effects of cholinesterase inhibitors are actually quite low, and it is recommended as a first-line treatment for DLB (Cummings, 2004).

Nonpharmacologic Treatments
See Chapter 10 for a detailed discussion of generic nonpharmacologic approaches to disruptive behavior associated with dementia. For DLB, several specific behavior issues are associated with the cardinal features of hallucinations and REM sleep behavior disorder.

Before treating hallucinations or delusions, it must be determined whether these symptoms are actually distressing or harmful to the patient, or both. It is not uncommon for the family member to be more alarmed by the behavior than the patient. When dealing with delusions, it is important to beware that the DLB patient's ability to distinguish dream content from wakeful experience may be diminished. Such DLB patients may earnestly describe experiencing events that never happened. Trying to convince them of the unreality of these events may prove frustrating and unsuccessful. Educating the family member about ways to cope with these behaviors include encouraging them to validate the patient's feelings, helping to devise strategies that "go along" with the behavior (e.g., checking the house for intruders), that provide reassurance, and that refrain from arguing or trying to reason with the patient.

Providing information for the caregiver is an important part of helping to manage challenging behaviors. Psychoeducation intervention groups for caregivers have been associated with significant improvements in agitation and anxiety for dementia patients (Haupt, Karger, & Janner, 2000). Utilizing available support services, including adult day programs and companion services, has also been shown to reduce caregiver related stress and reported feelings of overload, strain, depression, and anger (Zarit, Stephens, Townsend, & Greene, 1998). Caregivers and health professionals may be interested in obtaining additional information about caregiving or services through the following websites: www.lewybodydementia.org and www.alz.org.

Conclusions

Along with Alzheimer's disease and vascular dementia, Lewy body disease is considered one of the three most common forms of dementia. It is more common in men. The clinical presentation is often striking not only for the parkinsonism but the also for the dramatic fluctuations in patients' level of arousal and cognitive integrity, the vivid hallucinations that they report and the histories of dream enactment behavior during sleep. Autonomic dysfunction is also often present. It is noteworthy that any given patient with DLB may have any combination of these features (e.g., parkinsonism is not a requirement for a diagnosis of DLB). The pathology is complex with neuritic plaque and neurofibrillary tangle pathology often co-occurring with Lewy bodies. Early in the disease course, many DLB patients may have complaints of memory difficulty, but often this is an attentional or processing speed issue. The prominent clinical presentation involves deficits in attention and concentration and problems in complex visual perceptual processing. A significant subset of DLB patients is at risk to display neuroleptic malignant syndrome if exposed to antipsychotic medications. Conversely a significant subset will show a remarkable improvement when treated with a cholinesterase inhibitor. Patients are typically responsive to antiparkinsonian treatment with carbidopa-levodopa, but have adverse reactions to the dopamine agonists. Recognition and understanding of this condition has increased rapidly in the past two decades, but there is still much to be learned.

References

Aarsland, D., Larsen, J., Lim, N., & Tandberg, E. (1999). Olanzapine for psychosis in patients with Parkinson's disease with and without dementia. *Journal of Neuropsychology and Clinical Neuroscience, 11*, 392–394.

Aarsland, D., Perry, R., Brown, A., Larsen, J., & Ballard, C. (2005). Neuropathology of dementia in Parkinson's disease: A prospective community based study. *Annals of Neurology, 58*, 773–776.

Aarsland, D., Rongve, A., Nore, S., Skogseth, R., Skulstad, S., Ehrt, . . . Ballard, C. (2008). Frequency and case identification of dementia with Lewy bodies using the revised consensus criteria. *Dementia and Geriatric Cognitive Disorders, 26*(5), 445–452.

Agid, Y., Cervera, P., Hirsch, E., Javoy-Agid, F., Lehericy, S., Raisman, R., & Ruberg, M. (1989). Biochemistry of Parkinson's disease 28 years later: A critical review. *Movement Disorders, 4*(Suppl 1), S126–S144.

Ala, T. A., Hughes, L. F., Kyrouac, G. A., Ghobrial, M. W., & Elble, R. J. (2001). Pentagon copying is more impaired in dementia with Lewy bodies than in Alzheimer's disease. *Journal of Neurology, Neurosurgery, and Psychiatry, 70*(4), 483–488.

Ala, T., Yang, K., Sung, J., & Frey, W., 2nd. (1997). Hallucinations and signs of parkinsonism help distinguish patients with dementia and cortical Lewy bodies from patients with Alzheimer's disease at presentation: A clinicopathological study. *Journal of Neurology, Neurosurgery, and Psychiatry, 62*, 16–21.

Allen, R., Walker, Z., D' Ath, P., & Katona, C. (1995). Risperidone for psychotic and behavioural symptoms in Lewy body dementia. *Lancet, 346*(8968), 185.

American Sleep Disorders Association. (1997). *The international classification of sleep disorders diagnostic and coding manual*. Rochester, Minnesota: American Sleep Disorders Association.

Armstrong, R., Cairns, N., & Lantos, P. (2000). Beta-amyloid deposition in the temporal lobe of patients with dementia with Lewy bodies: Comparison with non-demented cases and Alzheimer's disease. *Dementia and Geriatric Cognitive Disorders, 11*(4), 187–192.

Armstrong, T., Hansen, L., Salmon, D., Masliah, E., Pay, M., Kunin, J., & Katzman, R. (1991). Rapidly progressive dementia in a patient with the Lewy body variant of Alzheimer's disease. *Neurology, 41*(8), 1178–1180.

Arriagada, P., Growdon, J., Hedley-Whyte, E., & Hyman, B. (1992). Neurofibrillary tangles but not senile plaques parallel duration and severity of Alzheimer's disease. *Neurology, 42*(3 Pt 1), 631–639.

Ballard, C., Margallo-Lana, M., Juszczak, E., Swann, D., O' Brien, T., Everratt, A.,...Jacoby, R. (2005). Quetiapine and rivastigmine and cognitive decline in Alzheimer's disease: Randomised double blind placebo controlled trial. *BMJ, 333,* 857–858.

Ballard, C., McKeith, I., Harrison, R., O' Brien, J., Thompson, P., Lowery, K.,...Ince, P. (1997). A detailed phenomenological comparison of complex visual hallucinations in dementia with Lewy bodies and Alzheimer's disease. *International Psychogeriatrics, 9*(4), 381–388.

Ballard, C., O' Brien, J., Morris, C., Barber, R., Swann, A., Neill, D., & McKeith, I. (2001). The progression of cognitive impairment in dementia with Lewy bodies, vascular dementia and Alzheimer's disease. *International Journal of Geriatric Psychiatry, 16*(5), 499–503.

Ballard, C., Patel, A., Oyebode, F., & Wilcock, G. (1996). Cognitive decline in patients with Alzheimer's disease, vascular dementia and senile dementia of Lewy body type. *Age and Ageing, 25*(3), 209–213.

Ballard, C., Shaw, F., McKeith, I., & Kenny, R. (1998). High prevalence of neurovascular instability in neurodegenerative dementias. *Neurology, 51,* 1760–1762.

Barber, R., Gholkar, A., Scheltens, P., Ballard, C., McKeith, I., & O' Brien, J. (1999). Medial temporal lobe atrophy on MRI in dementia with Lewy bodies. *Neurology, 52,* 1153–1158.

Bedard, M., Pillon, B., Dubois, B., Duchesne, N., Masson, H., & Agid, Y. (1999). Acute and long-term administration of anticholinergics in Parkinson's disease: specific effects on the subcortico-frontal syndrome. *Brain and Cognition, 40*(2), 289–313.

Benton, A., & Hamsher, K. (1978). *Multilingual Aphasia Examination: Manual.* Iowa City: University of Iowa.

Bergman, J., & Lerner, V. (2002). Successful use of donepezil for the treatment of psychotic symptoms in patients with Parkinson's disease. *Clinical Neuropharmacology, 25*(2), 107.

Bliwise, D. (1993). Sleep in normal aging and dementia. *Sleep, 16*(1), 40–81.

Boeve, B., Ferman, T., Silber, M., Lin, S., Fredrickson, P., Smith, G.,...Petersen, R. (2003). Sleep disturbances in dementia with Lewy bodies involve more than REM sleep behavior disorder. *Neurology, 60*(Suppl 1), A79.

Boeve, B., Silber, M., Ferman, T., Kokmen, E., Smith, G., Ivnik, R.,...Petersen, R. (1998). REM sleep behavior disorder and degenerative dementia: An association likely reflecting Lewy body disease. *Neurology, 51,* 363–370.

Boeve, B., Silber, M., Ferman, T., Lucas, J., & Parisi, J. (2001). Association of REM sleep behavior disorder and neurodegenerative disease may reflect an underlying synucleinopathy. *Movement Disorders, 16*(4), 622–630.

Boeve, B., Silber, M., Parisi, J., Dickson, D., Ferman, T., & et al. (2003). Synucleinopathy pathology and REM sleep behavior disorder plus dementia or parkinsonism. *Neurology, 61*(1), 40–45.

Boeve, B., Silber, M., Saper, C., Ferman, T., Dickson, D., Parisi, J., . . . Braak, H. (2007). Pathophysiology of REM sleep behaviour disorder and relevance to neurodegenerative disease. *Brain, 130*(Pt 11), 2770–2788.

Bonelli, S., Ransmayr, G., Steffelbauer, M., Lukas, T., Lampl, C., & Deibl, M. (2004). L-Dopa responsiveness in dementia with Lewy bodies, Parkinson disease with and without dementia. *Neurology, 63,* 376–378.

Bosboom, J., Stoffers, D., & Wolters, E. (2004). Cognitive dysfunction and dementia in Parkinson's disease. *Journal of Neural Transmission, 111,* 1303–1315.

Braak, H., & Braak, E. (1991). Neuropathological staging of Alzheimer-related changes. *Acta Neuropathologica, 82,* 239–259.

Braak, H., de Vos, R., Bohl, J., & Del Tredici, K. (2006). Gastric alpha-synuclein immunoreactive inclusions in Meissner's and Auerbach's plexuses in cases staged for Parkinson's disease-related brain pathology. *Neuroscience Letters, 396,* 67–72.

Braak, H., Del Tredici, K., Rub, U., de Vos, R., Jansen Steur, E., & Braak, E. (2003). Staging of brain pathology related to sporadic Parkinson's disease. *Neurobiology of Aging, 24*(2), 197–211.

Burke, W., Pfeiffer, R., & McComb, R. (1998). Neuroleptic sensitivity to clozapine in dementia with Lewy bodies. *Journal of Neuropsychiatry and Clinical Neurosciences, 10*(2), 227–229.

Byrne, E., Lennox, G., Lowe, J., & Godwin-Austen, R. (1989). Diffuse Lewy body disease: clinical features in 15 cases. *Journal of Neurology, Neurosurgery, and Psychiatry, 52*(6), 709–717.

Calderon, J., Perry, R., Erzinclioglu, S., Berrios, G., Dening, T., & Hodges, J. (2001). Perception, attention, and working memory are disproportionately impaired in dementia with Lewy bodies compared with Alzheimer's disease. *Journal of Neurology, Neurosurgery, and Psychiatry, 70,* 157–164.

Cercy, S., & Bylsma, F. (1997). Lewy bodies and progressive dementia: a critical review and meta-analysis. *Journal of the International Neuropsychological Society, 3*(2), 179–194.

Churchyard, A., & Lees, A. (1997). The relationship between dementia and direct involvement of the hippocampus and amygdala in Parkinson's disease. *Neurology, 49*(6), 1570–1576.

Court, J., Piggott, M., Lloyd, S., Cookson, N., Ballard, C., McKeith, I., ... Perry, E. (2000). Nicotine binding in human striatum: elevation in schizophrenia and reductions in dementia with Lewy bodies, Parkinson's disease and Alzheimer's disease and in relation to neuroleptic medication. *Neuroscience, 98*(1), 79–87.

Crystal, H., Dickson, D., Lizardi, J., Davies, P., & Wolfson, L. (1990). Antemortem diagnosis of diffuse Lewy body disease. *Neurology, 40*(10), 1523–1528.

Cummings, J. (2004). Reconsidering diagnostic criteria for dementia with Lewy bodies. Highlights from the Third International Workshop on Dementia with Lewy bodies and Parkinson's disease dementia. *Reviews in Neurological Diseases, 1*(1), 31–34.

Cummings, J., Street, J., Masterman, D., & Clark, W. (2002). Efficacy of olanzapine in the treatment of psychosis in dementia with Lewy bodies. *Dementia and Geriatric Cognitive Disorders, 13*, 67–73.

Del Ser, T., Hachinski, V., Merskey, H., & Munoz, D. (2001). Clinical and pathologic features of two groups of patients with Dementia with Lewy bodies: Effect of coexisting Alzheimer-type lesion load. *Alzheimer Disease and Associated Disorders, 15*, 31–44.

Devos, D., Tir, M., Maurage, C., Waucquier, N., Defebvre, L., Defoort-Dhellemmes, S., & Destee, A. (2005). ERG and anatomical abnormalities suggesting retinopathy in dementia with Lewy bodies. *Neurology, 65*, 1107–1110.

Dickson, D. (1991). Neuropathological diagnosis of Alzheimer's disease: a perspective from longitudinal clinicopathological studies. *Neurobiology of Aging, 13*, 179–789.

Dickson, D. (1997a). Neuropathological diagnosis of Alzheimer's disease: a perspective from longitudinal clinicopathological studies. *Neurobiology of Aging, 18*(4 Suppl), S21–S26.

Dickson, D. (1997b). The pathogenesis of senile plaques. *Journal of Neuropathology and Experimental Neurology, 56*(4), 321–339.

Dickson, D. (2002). Dementia with Lewy bodies: neuropathology. *Journal of Geriatric Psychiatry and Neurology, 15*(4), 210–216.

Dickson, D., Crystal, H., Mattiace, L., Kress, Y., Schwagerl, A., Ksiezak-Reding, H., ... Yen, S. (1989). Diffuse Lewy body disease: light and electron microscopic immunocytochemistry of senile plaques. *Acta Neuropathologica (Berl), 78*(6), 572–584.

Dickson, D., Crystal, H., Mattiace, L., Masure, D., Blau, A., Davies, P., ... Aronson, M. (1992). Identification of normal and pathological aging in prospectively studied nondemented elderly humans. *Neurobiology of Aging, 13,* 179–189.

Dickson, D., Davies, P., Mayeux, R., Crystal, H., Horoupian, D., Thompson, A., & Goldman, J. (1987). Diffuse Lewy body disease: Neuropathological and biochemical studies of six patients. *Acta Neuropathologica (Berl), 75*(1), 8–15.

Dickson, D., Farrer, M., Lincoln, B., Mason, R., Zimmerman, T., Golbe, L., & Hardy, J. (2001). Pathology of PD in monozygotic twins with a 20-year discordance interval. *Neurology, 56,* 981–982.

Dickson, D., Feany, M., Yen, S., Mattiace, L., & Davies, P. (1996). Cytoskeletal pathology in non-Alzheimer degenerative dementia: new lesions in diffuse Lewy body disease, Pick's disease, and corticobasal degeneration. *Journal of Neural Transmission. Supplementum, 47,* 31–46.

Dickson, D., Ruan, D., Crystal, H., Mark, M., Davies, P., Kress, Y., & Yen, S.-H. (1991). Hippocampal degeneration differentiates diffuse Lewy body disease (DLBD) from Alzheimer's disease. *Neurology, 41,* 1402–1409.

Dickson, D., Schmidt, M., Lee, V., Zhao, M., Yen, S., & Trojanowski, J. (1994). Immunoreactivity profile of hippocampal CA2/3 neurites in diffuse Lewy body disease. *Acta Neuropathologica (Berl), 87*(3), 269–276.

Dickson, D. W., Davies, P., Bevona, C., Van Hoeven, K. H., Factor, S. M., Grober, E., . . . Crystal, H. A. (1994). Hippocampal sclerosis: a common pathological feature of dementia in very old (> or = 80 years of age) humans. *Acta Neuropathologica, 88,* 212–221.

Dugger, B., Boeve, B., Murray, M., Parisi, J., Fujishiro, H., Dickson, D., & Ferman, T. (2011). Rapid eye movement sleep behavior disorder and subtypes in autopsy-confirmed dementia with Lewy bodies. *Movement Disorders,* in press.

Dugger, B., & Dickson, D. (2010). Cell type specific sequestration of choline acetyltransferase and tyrosine hydroxylase within Lewy bodies. *Acta Neuropathologica, 120,* 633–639.

Ellingrod, V., Schultz, S., Ekstam-Smith, K., Kutscher, E., Turvey, C., & Arndt, S. (2002). Comparison of risperidone with olanzepine in elderly patients with dementia and psychosis. *Pharmacotherapy, 22,* 1–5.

Ferman, T., Boeve, B., Silber, M., et al. (1997). Hallucinations and delusions associated with the REM sleep behavior disorder/dementia syndrome. *Journal of Neuropsychiatry and Clinical Neurosciences, 9,* 692.

Ferman, T., Boeve, B., Smith, G., Lin, S., Silber, M., Pedraza, O., . . . Dickson, D. (2011). Inclusion of RBD improves the diagnostic classification of dementia with Lewy bodies. *Neurology, 77*(9), 875–882.

Ferman, T., Boeve, B., Smith, G., Silber, M., Kokmen, E., Petersen, R., & Ivnik, R. (1999). REM sleep behavior disorder and dementia: Cognitive differences when compared with AD. *Neurology, 52,* 951–957.

Ferman, T., Boeve, B., Smith, G., Silber, M., Lucas, J., Graff-Radford, N., . . . Ivnik, R. (2002). Dementia with Lewy bodies may present as dementia and REM sleep behavior disorder without parkinsonism or hallucinations. *Journal of the International Neuropsychological Society, 8,* 907–914.

Ferman, T., Dickson, D., Graff-Radford, N., Arvanitakis, Z., DeLucia, M., Boeve, B., . . . Brassler, S. (2003). Early onset of visual hallucinations in dementia distinguishes pathologically-confirmed Lewy body disease from AD. *Neurology, 60*(5), A264.

Ferman, T., Smith, G., Boeve, B., Graff-Radford, N., Lucas, J., Knopman, D., . . . Dickson, D. (2006). Neuropsychological differentiation of dementia with Lewy bodies from normal aging and Alzheimer's disease. *The Clinical Neuropsychologist, 20*(4), 623–636.

Ferman, T., Smith, G., Boeve, B., Ivnik, R., Petersen, R., Knopman, D., . . . Dickson, D. (2004). DLB fluctuations: Specific features that reliably differentiate DLB from AD and normal aging. *Neurology, 62,* 181–187.

Flacker, J., Cummings, V., Mach, J., Jr., Bettin, K., Kiely, D., & Wei, J. (1998). The association of serum anticholinergic activity with delirium in elderly medical patients. *American Journal of Geriatric Psychiatry, 6*(1), 31–41.

Forstl, H., Burns, A., Luthert, P., Ciarns, N., & Levy, R. (1993). The Lewy-body variant of Alzheimer's disease: Clinical and pathological findings. *British Journal of Psychiatry, 162,* 385–392.

Francis, J., Martin, D., & Kapoor, W. (1990). A prospective study of delirium in hospitalized elderly. *Journal of the American Medical Association, 263*(8), 1097–1101.

Fujishiro, H., Ferman, T., Boeve, B., Smith, G., Graff-Radford, N., Uitti, R., . . . Dickson, D. (2008). Validation of the neuropathologic criteria of the third consortium for dementia with Lewy bodies for prospectively diagnosed cases. *Journal of Neuropathology and Experimental Neurology, 67*(7), 649–656.

Gagnon, J., Bedard, M., Fantini, M., Petit, D., Panisset, M., Rompre, S., . . . Montplaisir, J. (2002). REM sleep behavior disorder and REM sleep without atonia in Parkinson's disease. *Neurology, 59*(4), 585–589.

Galasko, D., Hansen, L., Katzman, R., Wiederholt, W., Masliah, E., Terry, R., . . . Thal, L. (1994). Clinical-neuropathological correlations in Alzheimer's disease and related dementias. *Archives of Neurology, 51,* 888–895.

Gnanalingham, K., Byrne, E., Thornton, A., Sambrook, M., & Bannister, P. (1997). Motor and cognitive function in Lewy body dementia: comparison with Alzheimer's and Parkinson's diseases. *Journal of Neurology, Neurosurgery, and Psychiatry*, 62(3), 243–252.

Grace, J., Daniel, S., Stevens, T., Shankar, K., Walker, Z., Byrne, E.,...McKeith, I. (2001). Long term use of rivastigmine in patients with dementia with Lewy bodies: an open-label trial. *International Psychogeriatrics*, 13, 199–205.

Hamilton, J. M., Salmon, D. P., Galasko, D., Raman, R., Emond, J., Hansen, L. A., Masliah, E., & Thal, L. J. (2008). Visuospatial deficits predict rate of cognitive decline in autopsy-verified dementia with Lewy bodies. *Neuropsychology*, 22(6), 729–737.

Hamilton, J. M., Salmon, D. P., Galasko, D., Delis, D. C., Hansen, L. A., Masliah, E., Thomas, R. G., & Thal, L. J. (2004). A comparison of episodic memory deficits in neuropathologically-confirmed Dementia with Lewy bodies and Alzheimer's disease. *Journal of the International Neuropsychological Society*, 10(5), 689–697.

Han, L., McCusker, J., Cole, M., Abrahamowicz, M., Primeau, F., & Elie, M. (2001). Use of medications with anticholinergic effect predicts clinical severity of delirium symptoms in older medical inpatients. *Archives of Internal Medicine*, 161(8), 1099–1105.

Hansen, L., Masliah, E., Galasko, D., & Terry, R. (1993). Plaque-only Alzheimer disease is usually the Lewy body variant, and vice versa. *Journal of Neuropathology and Experimental Neurology*, 52(6), 648–654.

Hansen, L., Salmon, D., Galasko, D., Masliah, E., Katzman, R., DeTeresa, R.,...Alford, M. (1990). The Lewy body variant of Alzheimer's disease: A clinical and pathologic entity. *Neurology*, 40, 1–8.

Harding, A., Broe, G., & Halliday, G. (2002). Visual hallucinations in Lewy body disease relate to Lewy bodies in the temporal lobe. *Brain*, 125(Pt 2), 391–403.

Harding, A., Lakay, B., & Halliday, G. (2002). Selective hippocampal neuron loss in dementia with Lewy bodies. *Annals of Neurology*, 51(1), 125–128.

Haroutunian, V., Serby, M., Purohit, D., Perl, D., Marin, D., Lantz, M.,...Davis, K. (2000). Contribution of Lewy body inclusions to dementia in patients with and without Alzheimer disease neuropathological conditions. *Archives of Neurology*, 57(8), 1145–1150.

Hashimoto, M., Hsu, L., Sisk, A., Zia, Y., Takeda, A., Sundsmo, M., & Masliah, E. (1998). Human recombinant NACP/alpha-synuclein is aggregated and fibrillated in vitro: relevance for Lewy body disease. *Brain Research*, 799, 301–306.

Haupt, M., Karger, A., & Janner, M. (2000). Improvement of agitation and anxiety in demented patients after psychoeducative group intervention with their caregivers. *International Journal of Geriatric Psychiatry, 15,* 1125–1129.

Helmes, E., Bowler, J., Merskey, H., Munoz, D., & Hachinski, V. (2003). Rates of cognitive decline in Alzheimer's disease and dementia with Lewy bodies. *Dementia and Geriatric Cognitive Disorders, 15*(2), 67–71.

Hendricks, J., Morrison, A., & Mann, G. (1982). Different behaviors during paradoxical sleep without atonia depend on pontine lesion site. *Brain Research, 239,* 81–105.

Hope, T., Keene, J., Fairburn, C., Jacoby, R., & McShane, R. (1999). Natural history of behavioural changes and psychiatric symptoms in Alzheimer's disease: A longitudinal study. *British Journal of Psychiatry, 174,* 39–44.

Huber, S., Paulson, G., & Shuttleworth, E. (1988). Relationship of motor symptoms, intellectual impairment, and depression in Parkinson's disease. *Journal of Neurology, Neurosurgery, and Psychiatry, 51*(6), 855–858.

Hulette, C., Mirra, S., Wilkinson, W., Heyman, A., Fillenbaum, G., & Clark, C. (1995). The Consortium to Establish a Registry for Alzheimer's Disease (CERAD). Part IX. A prospective cliniconeuropathologic study of Parkinson's features in Alzheimer's disease. *Neurology, 45*(11), 1991–1995.

Hurtig, H., Trojanowski, J., Galvin, J., Ewbank, D., Schmidt, M., Lee, V.,... Arnold, S. (2000). Alpha-synuclein cortical Lewy bodies correlate with dementia in Parkinson's disease. *Neurology, 54*(10), 1916–1921.

Imamura, T., Ishii, K., Hirono, N., Hashimoto, M., Tanimukai, S., Kazui, H.,... Mori, E. (2001). Occipital glucose metabolism in dementia with Lewy bodies with and without Parkinsonism: a study using positron emission tomography. *Dementia and Geriatric Cognitive Disorders, 12*(3), 194–197.

Inouye, S., van Dyck, C., Alessi, C., Balkin, S., Siegal, A., & Horwitz, R. (1990). Clarifying confusion: the confusion assessment method; A new method for detection of delirium. *Annals of Internal Medicine, 113,* 941–948.

Ishii, K., Imamura, T., Sasaki, M., Yamaji, S., Sakamoto, S., Kitagaki, H.,... Mori, E. (1998). Regional cerebral glucose metabolism in dementia with Lewy bodies and Alzheimer's disease. *Neurology, 51,* 125–130.

Ivnik, R., Malec, J., Smith, G., Tangalos, E., Petersen, R., Kokmen, E., & Kurland, L. (1992). Mayo's Older Americans Normative Studies: Updated AVLT norms for ages 56–97. *The Clinical Neuropsychologist, 6,* 83–104.

Jellinger, K. (2000). Morphological substrates of mental dysfunction in Lewy body disease: an update. *Journal of Neural Transmission. Supplementum, 59,* 185–212.

Jellinger, K., & Attems, J. (2011). Prevalence and pathology of dementia with Lewy bodies in the oldest old: a comparison with other dementing disorders. *Dementia and Geriatric Cognitive Disorders, 31*(4), 309–316.

Joachim, C., Morris, J., & Selkoe, D. (1988). Clinically diagnosed Alzheimer's disease: autopsy results in 150 cases. *Annals of Neurology, 24,* 50–56.

Johnson, D., Morris, J., & Galvin, J. (2005). Verbal and visuospatial deficits in dementia with Lewy bodies. *Neurology, 65,* 1232–1238.

Jouvet, M., & Delorme, F. (1965). [Locus coeruleus et sommeil paradoxal]. *Comptes rendus des séances de la Société de biologie et de ses filiales et associées, 159*(7), 895–899.

Juncos, J., Roberts, V., Evatt, M., Jewart, R., Wood, C., Potter, L., ... Yeung, P. (2004). Quetiapine improves psychotic symptoms and cognition in Parkinson's disease. *Movement Disorders, 19,* 29–35.

Kales, A., Ansel, R., Markham, C., Scharf, M., & Tan, T. (1971). Sleep in patients with Parkinson's disease and normal subjects prior to and following levodopa administration. *Clinical Pharmacology and Therapeutics, 12*(2), 397–406.

Kaplan, E., Goodglass, H., & Weintraub, S. (1983). *The Boston Naming Test* (2nd ed.). Philadelphia: Lea & Febiger.

Katzman, R., Brown, T., Thal, L., Fuld, P., Aronson, M., Butters, N., et al. (1988). Comparison of rate of annual change of mental status score in four independent studies of patients with Alzheimer's disease. *Annals of Neurology, 24*(3), 384–389.

Kaufer, D., Catt, K., Lopez, O., & DeKosky, S. (1998). Dementia with Lewy bodies: response of delirium-like features to donepezil. *Neurology, 51*(5), 1512.

Kim, J., Shim, Y., Song, I., Yoo, J., Kim, H., Kim, Y., & Lee, K. (2009). Cardiac sympathetic denervation and its association with cognitive deficits in Parkinson's disease. *Parkinsonism and Related Disorders, 15,* 706–708.

Klatka, L., Louis, E., & Schiffer, R. (1996). Psychiatric features in diffuse Lewy body disease: a clinicopathologic study using Alzheimer's disease and Parkinson's disease comparison groups. *Neurology, 47*(5), 1148–1152.

Kobayashi, S., Tateno, M., Morii, H., Utsumi, K., & Saito, T. (2009). Decreased cardiac MIBG uptake, its correlation with clinical symptoms in dementia with Lewy bodies. *Psychiatry Research, 174,* 76–80.

Koller, W., Langston, J., Hubble, J., Irwin, I., Zack, M., Golbe, L., et al. (1991). Does a long preclinical period occur in Parkinson's disease? *Geriatrics, 46*(Suppl 1), 8–15.

Kosaka, K. (1990). Diffuse Lewy body disease in Japan. *Journal of Neurology*, *237*(3), 197–204.

Kosaka, K., Yoshimura, M., Ikeda, K., & Budka, H. (1984). Diffuse type of Lewy body disease: progressive dementia with abundant cortical Lewy bodies and senile changes of varying degree—a new disease? *Clinical Neuropathology*, *3*(5), 185–192.

Kulisevsky, J., Garcia-Sanchez, C., Berthier, M., Barbanoj, M., Pascual-Sedano, B., Gironell, A., & Estevez-Gonzalez, A. (2000). Chronic effects of dopaminergic replacement on cognitive function in Parkinson's disease: a two-year follow-up study of previously untreated patients. *Movement Disorders*, *15*, 613–626.

Kuzuhara, S., & Yoshimura, M. (1993). Clinical and neuropathological aspects of diffuse Lewy body disease in the elderly. *Advances in Neurology*, *60*, 464–469.

Lai, Y., & Siegel, J. (2003). Physiological and anatomical link between Parkinson-like disease and REM sleep behavior disorder. *Molecular Neurobiology*, *27*(2), 137–152.

Lebert, F., Pasquier, F., Souliez, L., & Petit, H. (1998). Tacrine efficacy in Lewy body dementia. *International Journal of Geriatric Psychiatry*, *13*(8), 516–519.

Lennox, G., Lowe, J., Landon, M., Byrne, E., Mayer, R., & Godwin-Austen, R. (1989). Diffuse Lewy body disease: correlative neuropathology using anti-ubiquitin immunocytochemistry. *Journal of Neurology, Neurosurgery, and Psychiatry*, *52*(11), 1236–1247.

Levy, R., Eagger, S., Griffiths, M., Perry, E., Honavar, M., Dean, A., & Lantos, P. (1994). Lewy bodies and response to tacrine in Alzheimer's disease. *Lancet*, *343*(8890), 176.

Lippa, C., Pulaski-Salo, D., Dickson, D., & Smith, T. (1997). Alzheimer's disease, Lewy body disease and aging: a comparative study of the perforant pathway. *Journal of the Neurological Sciences*, *147*(2), 161–166.

Lippa, C., Smith, T., & Perry, E. (1999). Dementia with Lewy bodies: choline acetyltransferase parallels nucleus basalis pathology. *Journal of Neural Transmission*, *106*(5–6), 525–535.

Lippa, C., Smith, T., & Swearer, J. (1994). Alzheimer's disease and Lewy body disease: A comparative clinicopathological study. *Annals of Neurology*, *35*, 81–88.

Lobotesis, K., Fenwick, J., Phipps, A., Ryman, A., Swann, A., Ballard, C., . . . O' Brien, J. (2001). Occipital hypoperfusion on SPECT in dementia with Lewy bodies but not AD. *Neurology*, *56*, 643–649.

Maclean, L., Collins, C., & Byrne, E. (2001). Dementia with Lewy bodies treated with rivastigmine: effects on cognition, neuropsychiatric symptoms, and sleep. *International Psychogeriatrics, 13*(3), 277–288.

Marion, M., Qurashi, M., Marshall, G., & Foster, O. (2008). Is REM sleep behavior disorder (RBD) a risk factor of dementia in idiopathic Parkinson's disease? *Journal of Neurology, 255,* 192–196.

Mattis, S. (1988). *Mattis Dementia Rating Scale (MDRS).* Odessa, FL: Psychological Assessment Resources.

Mayeux, R., Stern, Y., & Sano, M. (1985). Heterogeneity and prognosis in dementia of the Alzheimer type. *Bulletin of Clinical Neurosciences, 50,* 7–10.

Mayeux, R., Stern, Y., & Spanton, S. (1985). Heterogeneity in dementia of the Alzheimer type: evidence of subgroups. *Neurology, 35*(4), 453–461.

McKeith, I., Ballard, C., Perry, R., Ince, P., O' Brien, J., Neill, D.,...Perry, E. (2000). Prospective validation of consensus criteria for the diagnosis of dementia with Lewy bodies. *Neurology, 54*(5), 1050–1058.

McKeith, I., Del Ser, T., Spano, P., Emre, M., Wesnes, K., Anand, R.,...Spiegel, R. (2000). Efficacy of rivastigmine in dementia with Lewy bodies: a randomised, double-blind, placebo-controlled international study. *Lancet, 356*(9247), 2031–2036.

McKeith, I., Dickson, D., Lowe, J., Emre, M., O' Brien, J., Feldman, H.,...for the consortium on DLB. (2005). Diagnosis and management of dementia with Lewy bodies: Third report of the DLB Consortium (review). *Neurology, 65*(12), 1863–1872.

McKeith, I., Fairbairn, A., Perry, R., & Thompson, P. (1994). The clinical diagnosis and misdiagnosis of senile dementia of Lewy body type (SDLT). *British Journal of Psychiatry, 165*(3), 324–332.

McKeith, I., Fairbairn, A., Perry, R., Thompson, P., & Perry, E. (1992). Neuroleptic sensitivity in patients with senile dementia of Lewy body type. *BMJ, 205*(6855), 673–678.

McKeith, I., Galasko, D., Kosaka, K., Perry, E., Dickson, D., Hansen, L.,...Perry, R. (1996). Consensus guidelines for the clinical and pathologic diagnosis of dementia with Lewy bodies (DLB): report of the consortium on DLB international workshop. *Neurology, 47*(5), 1113–1124.

McKeith, I., Mintzer, J., Aarsland, D., Burn, D., Chui, H., Cohen-Mansfield, J.,...on behalf of the International Psychogeriatric Association Expert Meeting on DLB. (2004). Dementia with Lewy bodies. *Lancet Neurology, 3,* 19–28.

Mega, M., Masterman, D., Benson, D., Vinters, H., Tomiyasu, U., Craig, A.,... Cummings, J. (1996). Dementia with Lewy bodies: reliability and validity of clinical and pathologic criteria. *Neurology, 47*(6), 1403–1409.

Merdes, A., Hansen, L., Jeste, D., Galasko, D., Hofstetter, C., Ho, G.,... Corey-Bloom, J. (2003). Influence of Alzheimer pathology on clinical diagnostic accuracy in dementia with Lewy bodies. *Neurology, 60,* 1586–1590.

Mesulam, M., Mufson, E., Levey, A., & Wainer, B. (1983). Cholinergic innervation of cortex by the basal forebrain: cytochemistry and cortical connections of the septal area, diagonal band nuclei, nucleus basalis (substantia innominata), and hypothalamus in the rhesus monkey. *Journal of Comparative Neurology, 214,* 170–197.

Miller, C., Mohr, F., Umbricht, D., Woerner, M., Fleischhacker, W., & Lieberman, J. (1998). The prevalence of acute extrapyramidal signs and symptoms in patients treated with clozapine, risperidone, and conventional antipsychotics. *Journal of Clinical Psychiatry, 59*(2), 69–75.

Minett, T., Thomas, A., Wilkinson, L., Daniel, S., Sanders, J., Richardson, J.,... McKeith, I. (2003). What happens when donepezil is suddenly withdrawn? An open label trial in dementia with Lewy bodies and Parkinson's disease with dementia. *International Journal of Geriatric Psychiatry, 18,* 988–993.

Miyamoto, T., Miyamoto, M., Iwanami, M., & Hirata, K. (2009). Three-year follow-up on the accumulation of cardiac (123)I-MIBG scintigraphy in idiopathic REM sleep behavior disorder. *Sleep Medicine, 10,* 1066–1067.

Molano, J., Boeve, B., Ferman, T., Smith, G., Parisi, J., Dickson, D.,... Petersen, R. (2010). Mild cognitive impairment associated with limbic and neocortical Lewy body disease: a clinicopathological study. *Brain, 133*(Pt 2), 540–556.

Molloy, S., McKeith, I., O' Brien, J., & Burn, D. (2005). The role of levodopa in the management of dementia with Lewy bodies. *Journal of Neurology, Neurosurgery, and Psychiatry, 76,* 1200–1203.

Molloy, S., Minett, T., O' Brien, J., McKeith, I., & Burn, D. (2009). Levodopa use and sleep in patients with dementia with Lewy bodies. *Movement Disorders, 24,* 609–612.

Molloy, S., Rowan, E., O' Brien, J., McKeith, I., Wesnes, K., & Burn, D. (2006). Effect of levodopa on cognitive function in Parkinson's disease with and without dementia and dementia with Lewy bodies. *Journal of Neurology, Neurosurgery, and Psychiatry, 77,* 1323–1328.

Molsa, P., Marttila, R., & Rinne, U. (1984). Extrapyramidal signs in Alzheimer's disease. *Neurology, 34*(8), 1114–1116.

Moore, D. (1977). Rapid treatment of delirium in critically ill patients. *American Journal of Psychiatry, 134*(12), 1431–1432.

Mori, E., Shimomura, T., Fujimori, M., Hirono, N., Imamura, T., Hashimoto, M.,...Hanihara, T. (2000). Visuoperceptual impairment in dementia with Lewy bodies. *Archives of Neurology, 57*(4), 489–493.

Morrison, C., Borod, J., Brin, M., Halbig, T., & Olanow, C. (2004). Effects of levodopa on cognitive functioning in moderate-to-severe Parkinson's disease (MSPD). *Journal of Neural Transmission, 111,* 1333–1341.

Mortimer, J., Ebbitt, B., Jun, S., & Finch, M. (1992). Predictors of cognitive and functional progression in patients with probable Alzheimer's disease. *Neurology, 42*(9), 1689–1696.

Mosimann, U., Muri, R., Burn, D., Felblinger, J., O' Brien, J., & McKeith, I. (2005). Saccadic eye movement changes in Parkinson's disease dementia and dementia with Lewy bodies. *Brain, 128,* 1267–1276.

Mulsant, B., Gharabawi, G., Bossie, C., Mao, L., Martinez, R., Tune, L.,...Pollock, B. (2004). Correlates of anticholinergic activity in patients with dementia and psychosis treated with risperidone or olanzepine. *Journal of Clinical Psychiatry, 65,* 1708–1714.

Nagy, Z., Jobst, K., Esiri, M., Morris, J., King, E., MacDonald, B.,...Smith, A. (1996). Hippocampal pathology reflects memory deficit and brain imaging measurements in Alzheimer's disease: clinicopathologic correlations using three sets of pathologic diagnostic criteria. *Dementia, 7*(2), 76–81.

Nelson, P., Jicha, G., Kryscio, R., Schmitt, F., Cooper, G., Xu, L.,...Markesbery, W. (2010). Low sensitivity in clinical diagnosis of dementia with Lewy bodies. *Journal of Neurology, 257*(3), 359–366.

Okazaki, H., Lipkin, L., & Aronson, S. (1961). Diffuse intracytoplasmic inclusions (Lewy type) associated with progressive dementia and quadriparesis in flexion. *Journal of Neuropathology and Experimental Neurology, 20,* 237–244.

Olichney, J., Galasko, D., Salmon, D., Hofstetter, C., Hansen, L., Katzman, R., & Thal, L. (1998). Cognitive decline is faster in Lewy body variant than in Alzheimer's disease. *Neurology, 51*(2), 351–357.

Pearce, J. (1974). The extrapyramidal disorder of Alzheimer's disease. *European Neurology, 12*(2), 94–103.

Perry, E., Haroutunian, V., Davis, K., Levy, R., Lantos, P., & Eagger, S. (1994). Neocortical cholinergic activities differentiate Lewy body dementia from classical Alzheimer's disease. *Neuroreport, 5*(7), 747–749.

Perry, E., Irving, D., Kerwin, J., McKeith, I., Thompson, P., Collerton, D.,...et al. (1993). Cholinergic transmitter and neurotrophic activities in

Lewy body dementia: similarity to Parkinson's and distinction from Alzheimer disease. *Alzheimer Disease and Associated Disorders, 7*(2), 69–79.

Perry, E., Marshall, E., Perry, R., Irving, D., Smith, C., Blessed, G., & Fairbairn, A. (1990). Cholinergic and dopaminergic activities in senile dementia of Lewy body type. *Alzheimer Disease and Associated Disorders, 4*(2), 87–95.

Perry, E., & Perry, R. (1995). Acetylcholine and hallucinations: disease-related compared to drug-induced alterations in human consciousness. *Brain and Cognition, 28*(3), 240–258.

Perry, E., Walker, M., Grace, J., & Perry, R. (1999). Acetylcholine in mind: a neurotransmitter correlate of consciousness? *Trends in Neurosciences, 22*(6), 273–280.

Perry, R., McKeith, I., & Perry, E. (1997). Lewy body dementia—clinical, pathological and neurochemical interconnections. *Journal of Neural Transmission. Supplementum, 51,* 95–109.

Piggott, M., Perry, E., Marshall, E., McKeith, I., Johnson, M., Melrose, H.,...Perry, R. (1998). Nigrostriatal dopaminergic activities in dementia with Lewy bodies in relation to neuroleptic sensitivity: comparisons with Parkinson's disease. *Biological Psychiatry, 44*(8), 765–774.

Plazzi, G., Corsini, R., Provini, F., Pierangeli, G., Martinelli, P., Montagna, P.,...Cortelli, P. (1997). REM sleep behavior disorders in multiple system atrophy. *Neurology, 48*(4), 1094–1097.

Pollanen, M., Dickson, D., & Bergeron, C. (1993). Pathology and biology of the Lewy body. *Journal of Neuropathology and Experimental Neurology, 52*(3), 183–191.

Polymeropoulos, M., Lavedan, C., Leroy, E., Ide, S., Dehejia, A., Dutra, A.,...Nussbaum, R. L. (1997). Mutation in the alpha-synuclein gene identified in families with Parkinson's disease. *Science, 276,* 2045–2047.

Postuma, R., Gagnon, J., Vendette, M., Fantini, M., Massicotte-Marquez, J., & Montplaisir, J. (2009). Quantifying the risk of neurodegenerative disease in idiopathic REM sleep behavior disorder. *Neurology, 72,* 1296–1300.

Ransmayr, G., Cervera, P., Hirsch, E., Berger, W., Fischer, W., & Agid, Y. (1992). Alzheimer's disease: is the decrease of the cholinergic innervation of the hippocampus related to intrinsic hippocampal pathology? *Neuroscience, 47*(4), 843–851.

Rey, A. (1964). *L'examen clinique en psychologie.* Paris: Presses Universitaires de France.

Richards, M., Stern, Y., Marder, K., Cote, L., & Mayeux, R. (1993). Relationships between extrapyramidal signs and cognitive function in a community-dwelling cohort of patients with Parkinson's disease and normal elderly individuals. *Annals of Neurology*, *33*(3), 267–274.

Rinne, U., Laakso, K., & Molsa, P. (1984). Relationship between Parkinson's and Alzheimer's diseases: Involvement of extrapyramidal, dopaminergic, cholinergic, and somatostatin mechanisms in relation to dementia. *Acta Neurologica Scandinavica*, *69*, 59–60.

Rocca, W., McDonnel, S., Strain, K., Bower, J., Ahlskog, J., Elbaz, A., ... Maraganore, D. (2004). Familial aggregation of Parkinson's disease: The Mayo Clinic Family Study. *Annals of Neurology*, *56*, 495–502.

Rockwell, E., Choure, J., Galasko, D., Olichney, J., & Jeste, D. (2000). Psychopathology at initial diagnosis in dementia with Lewy bodies versus Alzheimer disease: comparison of matched groups with autopsy-confirmed diagnoses. *International Journal of Geriatric Psychiatry*, *15*(9), 819–823.

Rosebush, P., & Mazurek, M. (1999). Neurologic side effects in neuroleptic-naive patients treated with haloperidol or risperidone. *Neurology*, *52*(4), 782–785.

Salmon, D., Galasko, D., Hansen, L., Masliah, E., Butters, N., Thal, L., & Katzman, R. (1996). Neuropsychological deficits associated with diffuse Lewy body disease. *Brain and Cognition*, *31*, 148–165.

Samuel, W., Alford, M., Hofstetter, C., & Hansen, L. (1997). Dementia with Lewy bodies versus pure Alzheimer disease: differences in cognition, neuropathology, cholinergic dysfunction, and synapse density. *Journal of Neuropathology and Experimental Neurology*, *56*(5), 499–508.

Samuel, W., Caligiuri, M., Galasko, D., Lacro, J., Marini, M., McClure, F., ... Jeste, D. (2000a). Better cognitive and psychopathologic response to donepezil in patients prospectively diagnosed as dementia with Lewy bodies: a preliminary study. *International Journal of Geriatric Psychiatry*, *15*(9), 794–802.

Samuel, W., Caligiuri, M., Galasko, D., Lacro, J., Marini, M., McClure, F., ... Jeste, D. (2000b). Better cognitive and psychopathologic response to donepezil in patients prospectively diagnosed as dementia with Lewy bodies: a preliminary study. *International Journal of Geriatric Psychiatry*, *15*, 794–802.

Samuel, W., Galasko, D., Masliah, E., & Hansen, L. (1996). Neocortical Lewy body counts correlate with dementia in the Lewy body variant of Alzheimer's disease. *Journal of Neuropathology and Experimental Neurology*, *55*(1), 44–52.

Samuel, W., Henderson, V., & Miller, C. (1991). Severity of dementia in Alzheimer disease and neurofibrillary tangles in multiple brain regions. *Alzheimer Disease and Associated Disorders*, *5*(1), 1–11.

Sanchez-Ramos, J., Ortoll, R., & Paulson, G. (1996). Visual hallucinations associated with Parkinson disease. *Archives of Neurology*, *53*(12), 1265–1268.

Schenck, C., Bundlie, S., & Mahowald, M. (1996). Delayed emergence of a parkinsonian disorder in 38% of 29 older men initially diagnosed with idiopathic rapid eye movement sleep behaviour disorder. *Neurology, 46*(2), 388–393.

Schenck, C., & Mahowald, M. (2002). REM sleep behavior disorder: clinical, developmental, and neuroscience perspectives 16 years after its formal identification in sleep. *Sleep, 25*(120–138).

Schneider, J., Arvanitakis, Z., Leurgans, S., & Bennett, D. (2009). The neuropathology of probable Alzheimer disease and mild cognitive impairment. *Annals of Neurology, 66,* 200–208.

Sechi, G., Agnetti, V., Masuri, R., Deiana, G., Pugliatti, M., Paulus, K., & Rosati, G. (2000). Risperidone, neuroleptic malignant syndrome and probable dementia with Lewy bodies. *Progress in Neuro-psychopharmacology and Biological Psychiatry, 24*(6), 1043–1051.

Shea, C., MacKnight, C., & Rockwood, K. (1998). Donepezil for treatment of dementia with Lewy bodies: a case series of nine patients. *International Psychogeriatrics, 10*(3), 229–238.

Simard, M., van Reekum, R., & Myran, D. (2003). Visuospatial impairment in dementia with Lewy bodies and Alzheimer's disease: a process analysis approach. *International Journal of Geriatric Psychiatry, 18*(5), 387–391.

Stern, Y., Albert, M., Brandt, J., Jacobs, D., Tang, M., Marder, K.,...et al. (1994). Utility of extrapyramidal signs and psychosis as predictors of cognitive and functional decline, nursing home admission, and death in Alzheimer's disease: prospective analyses from the Predictors Study. *Neurology, 44*(12), 2300–2307.

Stern, Y., Brandt, J., Albert, M., Jacobs, D., Liu, X., Bell, K.,...Mayeux, R. (1997). The absence of an apolipoprotein epsilon4 allele is associated with a more aggressive form of Alzheimer's disease. *Annals of Neurology, 41*(5), 615–620.

Stern, Y., Mayeux, R., Sano, M., Hauser, W., & Bush, T. (1987). Predictors of disease course in patients with probable Alzheimer's disease. *Neurology, 37*(10), 1649–1653.

Thaisetthawatkul, P., Boeve, B. F., Benarroch, E. E., Sandroni, P., Ferman, T. J., Petersen, R., & Low, P. A. (2004). Autonomic dysfunction in dementia with Lewy bodies. [Comparative Study Research Support, U.S. Gov't, P.H.S.]. *Neurology, 62*(10), 1804–1809.

Thomas, A., Burn, D., Rowan, E., Littlewood, E., Newby, J., Cousins, D.,...McKeith, I. (2005). A comparison of the efficacy of donepezil in Parkinson's disease with dementia and dementia with Lewy bodies. *International Journal of Geriatric Psychiatry, 20,* 938–944.

Tiraboschi, P., Hansen, L., Alford, M., Merdes, A., Masliah, E., Thal, L., & Corey-Bloom, J. (2002). Early and widespread cholinergic losses differentiate dementia with Lewy bodies from Alzheimer disease. *Archives of General Psychiatry, 59*(10), 946–951.

Tune, L., Damlouji, N., Holland, A., Gardner, T., Folstein, M., & Coyle, J. (1981). Association of postoperative delirium with raised serum levels of anticholinergic drugs. *Lancet, 2*(8248), 651–653.

Tune, L., & Egeli, S. (1999). Acetylcholine and delirium. *Dementia and Geriatric Cognitive Disorders, 10*(5), 342–344.

Turner, R., Chervin, R., Frey, K., Minoshima, S., & Kuhl, D. (1997). Probable diffuse Lewy body disease presenting as REM sleep behavior disorder. *Neurology, 49*(2), 523–527.

Turner, R., D' Amato, C., Chervin, R., & Blaivas, M. (2000). The pathology of REM sleep behavior disorder with comorbid Lewy body dementia. *Neurology, 55*(11), 1730–1732.

Uchiyama, M., Isse, K., Tanaka, K., Yokota, N., Hamamoto, M., Aida, S.,... Okawa, M. (1995). Incidental Lewy body disease in a patient with REM sleep behavior disorder. *Neurology, 45*(4), 709–712.

Vemuri, P., Weigand, S., Knopman, D., Kantarci, K., Boeve, B., Petersen, R., & Jack, C., Jr. (2011). Time-to-event voxel-based techniques to assess regional atrophy associated with MCI risk of progression to AD. *Neuroimage 54*(2), 985–991.

Vendette, M., Gagnon, J., Decary, A., Massicotte-Marquez, J., Postuma, R., Doyon, J.,... Montplaisir, J. (2007). REM sleep behavior disorder predicts cognitive impairment in Parkinson's disease without dementia. *Neurology, 69,* 1843–1849.

Wakabayashi, K., & Takahashi, H. (1997). The intermediolateral nucleus and Clarke's column in Parkinson's disease. *Acta Neuropathologica, 94,* 287–289.

Walker, M., Ayre, G., Perry, E., Wesnes, K., McKeith, I., Tovee, M.,... Ballard, C. (2000). Quantification and characterization of fluctuating cognition in dementia with Lewy bodies and Alzheimer's disease. *Dementia and Geriatric Cognitive Disorders, 11*(6), 327–335.

Wechsler, D. (1987). *Wechsler Memory Scale-Revised.* New York: Psychological Corporation.

Wechsler, D. (1997). *Wechsler Adult Intelligence Scale-III.* New York: Psychological Corporation.

Wengel, S., Roccaforte, W., & Burke, W. (1998). Donepezil improves symptoms of delirium in dementia: implications for future research. *Journal of Geriatric Psychiatry and Neurology, 11*(3), 159–161.

West, M., Coleman, P., Flood, D., & Tronosco, J. (1994). Differences in the pattern of hippocampal neuronal loss in normal ageing and Alzheimer's disease. *Lancet, 344,* 769–772.

Wetter, T., Collado-Seidel, V., Pollmacher, T., Yassouridis, A., & Trenkwalder, C. (2000). Sleep and periodic leg movement patterns in drug-free patients with Parkinson's disease and multiple system atrophy. *Sleep, 23*(3), 361–367.

Whitwell, J., Jack, C., Jr, Parisi, J., Knopman, D., Boeve, B., Petersen, R.,...Josephs, K. (2007). Rates of cerebral atrophy differ in different degenerative pathologies. *Brain, 130*(Pt 4), 1148–1158.

Wilcock, G., & Scott, M. (1994). Tacrine for senile dementia of Alzheimer's or Lewy body type. *Lancet, 344*(8921), 544.

Wilkinson, G. S. (1993). *Wide Range Achievement Test-third edition administration manual.* Wilmington, DE: Wide Range.

Zarit, S., Stephens, M., Townsend, A., & Greene, R. (1998). Stress reduction for family caregivers: effect of adult day care use. *Journal of Gerontology, 53,* S267–S277.

Zimprich, A., Biskup, S., Leitner, P., Lichtner, P., Farrer, M., Lincoln, S.,...Gasser, T. (2004). Mutations in LRRK2 cause autosomal dominant parkinsonism with pleomorphic pathology. *Neuron, 44,* 601–607.

8

■ ■ ■

Frontotemporal Dementias

Case Presentation No. I

The patient was a 73-year-old woman who indicated that she had some problems with naming for example coming up with correct names of individual persons. She noticed this particularly at a recent high school reunion. She thought she read less than she formerly did but otherwise was not aware of any other significant cognitive problems. She still played bridge quite well and did not feel that there were any memory problems. She had been driving and did not get lost. She had some insomnia and consequently took an antihistamine on most nights.

In a separate interview with the patient's husband and two daughters, they indicated that for the past 3 years the patient had been exhibiting a gradual progression of cognitive impairment. She had difficulties coping with new situations, and she had lost interest in other activities besides bridge. She also had significant problems with naming. She frequently referred to objects as "things" rather than their proper names. This naming problem had been getting gradually worse. In addition, she also appeared to have lost the ability to understand the meaning of objects. For example, the husband made popcorn at home, and she said, "Popcorn, what's that?" When asked whether she had a pacemaker before receiving her MRI scan, she asked, "What's a pacemaker?" There had been increasing examples of her loss of some of the meanings of objects in the

(continued)

303

environment. They also indicated that she got lost quite easily. They wondered about her ability to comprehend and problem-solve.

She had a tendency to yell at people and be rude in certain social environments. For example, she had become more irritable and easily lost her temper with store clerks. She exhibited socially inappropriate behavior at a high school basketball game, making rude comments about the players. She made bathroom-oriented comments in a public setting and told her one daughter that she should lose weight. The husband noted a recent event where she exhibited poor judgment by allowing a door-to-door salesman to come in the house and sell her $200 worth of meat. She then allowed the salesman to deliver the meat into the house and wander through the house. The family felt this was quite inappropriate and out of character for her.

They reported some memory difficulties, but these did not appear to be the most prominent feature of her behavioral changes. She had problems remembering who gave her gifts at Christmas recently, and also that she had forgotten details of recent conversations.

Family History

Family history was notable for the mother having some behavioral changes later in life. She died in her early 80s. However there is no obvious other history of dementia in the family.

Neurologic Examination

On the Kokmen short test of mental status, she scored 33/38 (which is within normal limits). Naming was impaired, although her other language testing was normal, and she showed normal repetition, comprehension, and fluency. She had some weakness in her right external rotator. She had a mild voice tremor. Her diagnosis was given as frontotemporal dementia *semantic dementia variant*.

Neuroimaging Findings

The neuroradiologist read the patient's initial MR scan (see Figure 8.1) as:

> MRI of the head obtained using requested dementia protocol
> including axial diffusion weighted images. The study demon-
> strates diffuse cerebral and cerebellar atrophy which is more
> prominent in the anterior temporal lobes, frontal lobes, and
> parahippocampal regions. No evidence for acute ischemia
> on diffusion weighted images. Minimal leukoaraiosis in the

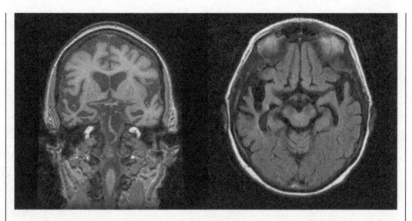

FIGURE 8.1 Coronal and axial MRI scans of a frontotemporal dementia patient at initial evaluation.

periventricular white matter, bilateral basal ganglia, and mid and upper pons.

Course of Illness

At age 78, the patient returned for her fifth annual evaluation. Over the course of the past year, she had declined significantly, according to the family, especially in the progression of her language disorder. She was clearly having more difficulty communicating with family. They were uncertain as to whether she comprehended their communications with her, and she was having difficulty expressing herself. Interestingly, she was also exhibiting features of prosopagnosia. That is, she did not recognize familiar faces such as family members in photographs. In person, she had difficulty recognizing family members at times, including her daughters and, occasionally, even her husband. She was exhibiting more compulsive types of behavior. At times, in restaurants, she would be very impatient and could not wait in line. She would also walk up to persons and inappropriately try to have a discussion with them. One behavior that had become particularly repetitive was her rapping on the windows of the house and waving at cars as they drove by. Since they live on a busy street, she would spend endless periods of time rapping on windows and waving at cars during the rush hour. She had also been exhibiting some delusional behavior such as going into the basement with a flashlight looking for people or children who were hiding. At times, she talked to pictures and dolls as if they were humans.

(continued)

She was quite compulsive about watching the clock. She went to bed at exactly 8:30 every night. She did not exhibit any dream enactment behavior. She was experiencing some urinary incontinence. At times, she had become somewhat belligerent and physical with her husband. She tended to eat everything put in front of her and had gained weight recently. She had even taken to eating dog food, if it was available. She generally dressed herself, but she could not select her own clothes. She needed frequent reminders to bathe.

Her husband was getting some help in the home three days a week, for as much as five hours a day.

Mental status testing was virtually impossible because of her aphasia. The remainder of the exam showed symmetrical reflexes and slightly increased tone in the upper extremities. Six months later, she suffered a left internal capsular stroke. Two and a half years later, she passed away.

Neuropathologic Findings
1. Frontotemporal lobar degeneration (FTLD-U; Mackenzie type 1), characterized by:
    a. Cytoplasmic TDP43 positive inclusions and neurites involving neocortex, amygdala, and cerebellar granular layer.
    b. Gliosis of hypoglossal nucleus, mild.
    c. Marked cortical atrophy, accentuated in the temporal lobe; fixed left hemibrain weight 524 g.
2. Neurodegenerative changes of the Alzheimer type:
    a. Neocortical: frequent diffuse amyloid plaques, sparse neuritic plaques.
    b. Medial temporal: moderate amygdaloid plaques; sparse hippocampal tangles.
    c. Amyloid angiopathy, patchy, involving leptomeningeal vessels.
3. Remote infarct, left medial internal capsule/corona radiata (1.7 × 0.4 × 0.2 cm).
4. Atherosclerosis:
    a. Cranial: Grade 4 (of 4), right vertebral, left posterior communicating; grade 3, right middle cerebral; grade 2 left vertebral, right posterior cerebral; grade 1, left posterior cerebral, left internal carotid arteries.

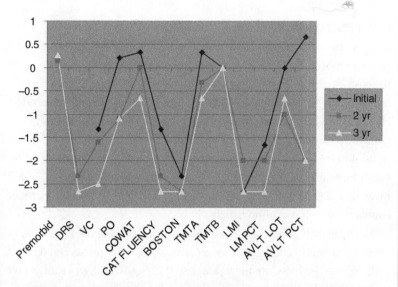

FIGURE 8.2 Neuropsychological findings of case presentation No. 1. (All scores are age adjusted z scores. Premorbid = Wide Range Achievement Test (3rd edition; Wilkinson, 1993); Reading score, DRS = Mattis Dementia Rating Scale (Mattis, 1988); total scores, VC = Verbal comprehension, PO = perceptual organization, WMI = Working Memory Index (all from Wechsler Adult Intelligence Scale-Third edition, 1997; Wechsler, 1997); COWAT = Controlled Oral Word Association Test (Benton & Hamsher, 1978), Cat Fluency = Category Fluency test, LM1 = Wechsler Memory Scale Revised (WMS-R; Wechsler, 1987); Logical Memory Immediate Recall, LMPCT = WMS-R Logical Memory Delay divided by LM1. AVLTLOT = Rey Auditory Verbal Learning Test (AVLT; Rey, 1964) total of trials1–5 minus 5*trial 1 (see Ivnik et al., 1992). AVLTPCT = AVLT 30-minute delay divided by AVLT trial 5. Boston = Boston Naming Test (Kaplan, Goodglass, & Weintraub, 1983). DRS, COWAT, Category Fluency, WMS-R, AVLT. and Boston scores are based on Mayo Older American's Normative Studies (MOANS) norms.

Neuropsychological Findings

As shown in Figure 8.2, the patient presented with a marked discrepancy between verbal comprehension and perceptual organizational skills. She had clear naming and category fluency problems, while lexical fluency was spared. That this was a language rather than speed or memory problem was evident in the dissociation of lexical fluency from category fluency, preservation of Trial Making performances, and the dissociation of Logical Memory and AVLT performance. As the disease progressed, memory became more impaired.

(continued)

Case Presentation No. 2

The patient was a healthy 59-year-old Caucasian man who presented with prominent behavioral symptoms that had been gradually progressing over the past 2 years. Per his wife's report, he had always been very meticulous but had recently left several household projects unfinished and unattended. He failed to clean up one of these projects despite being asked to do so, which was quite out of character. Around the same time he began to show signs of being less "emotionally warm." For example, he had attended his aunt's funeral as well as another family gathering and neglected to ask his wife to accompany him. These actions prompted a visit to a marriage counselor, which was of no benefit.

His hygiene had also steadily declined during this period. He was bathing less frequently and began to wear the same clothes for several days on end. He exercised less, ate more, and had started to indulge in eating large quantities of "junk food." As a result, he gained 20 lbs. over the past two years. He also became easily persuaded by others and was more "moldable to other people's ideas and what they say." In one example he was persuaded by an unknown caller to make a car payment to the caller despite having already paid off the car. He did not exhibit any hypersexual or overt socially inappropriate behaviors, but he had made at least some derogatory comments, about very well regarded neighbors, that were again quite out of character for him.

He had a bachelor's degree and worked for a major telecommunications company until his retirement the year prior to this evaluation. His ability to do complex tasks had been declining prior to his retirement, and his coworkers had noted that he could no longer perform simple wiring jobs. At home, he had been showing a tendency to rush through tasks impatiently and leave them partially or inadequately completed. For example, he overstuffed the washing machine and said that it was broken when it would not work. The quality of his cooking had declined and he had stopped driving due to ongoing confusion about when to stop and go. His wife further indicated that he had been noticeably more forgetful over the past couple of years, such as forgetting items on a shopping list, but that this problem had been stable for some time. His wife indicated that he reported having "seen satan" at night with his eyes closed. He was also exhibiting increased paranoia, thinking that someone was breaking into the house on several occasions during the evening hours.

The patient had been reporting symptoms of depression and anxiety as far back as 6 years ago. He had a history of depression, and 2 years ago he sought psychiatric consultation, complaining of sadness, anhedonia, weight gain, and difficulty concentrating. He was diagnosed with depression and initially treated with Zoloft, 50 mg, but there was no improvement so he was switched to Wellbutrin, 300 mg. His prominent cognitive symptoms prompted neurological and neuropsychological evaluations, as well as neuroimaging.

Family History

The patient's father committed suicide by gunshot in his 50s or 60s. He has a son with a learning disability or possibly autism, and a cousin with Down's syndrome. There is no known family history of Alzheimer's disease, Parkinson's disease, frontotemporal dementia, or amyotrophic lateral sclerosis.

Neurologic Exam

His MMSE score was 29/30. He was mildly disinhibited during the exam, briefly showing inappropriate laughter. He exhibited a mild bilateral postural tremor and a very mild distal sensory loss bilaterally. There were no motor findings, fasciculations, or muscle atrophy. Reflexes were absent except for knee jerks, and toes were flexor bilaterally. His diagnosis was possible frontal dementia versus depression.

Neuroimaging Findings

The neuroradiologist read the patient's initial MR scan as follows:

> Atrophy, which is more pronounced in the frontotemporal regions. Please correlate with clinical evidence of frontotemporal dementia. Minor periventricular T2 hyperintensity is recognized on the flair sequence, which is consistent with minimal small-vessel disease.

Findings from a SPECT scan conducted during the same period indicated the following: "Symmetric, bilateral relative decreased perfusion to the frontal lobes consistent with a frontal process."

(continued)

Course of Illness

Over the first few years following his initial diagnostic assessment, his wife noted continued to decline in his cognitive abilities and ability to perform activities of daily living. He stopped leaving the home and required prompting to perform basic activities, including hygiene, meals, and taking medications. He showed marked lack of motivation and initiative, instead preferring to watch TV, read magazines, and listen to music on the couch all day. He did perform some household chores when prompted, but frequently completed only half of the job. He began to confabulate stories when asked what he did for a living, often telling people that he did research for companies in town. He spent much of his remaining time in an adult day care program. He died a few years later of pneumonia.

Neuropathologic Findings

Grossly atrophic frontal cortex shows severe neuron loss and fibrous gliosis, which in the upper cortical layers has progressed to microcystic rarefaction of neuropil. Many persisting medium sized neurons contain well-defined amphophilic circular intracytoplasmic inclusions, that is, Pick bodies, which peripherally displace neuronal nuclei. Underlying white matter is dramatically rarified and poor in myelin, although some axons remain in dramatically reduced numbers. Neuron loss, gliosis, and microcystic rarefaction are panlaminar in the inferior temporal gyrus. Neurons with Pick bodies are present in the latter, however. Interestingly, while much of the inferior parietal cortical ribbon is comparatively unremarkable, it includes atrophic segments with neuron loss, gliosis, and Pick bodies. The pyramidal cell layer of the hippocampal formation is well populated, but many of its constituent neurons bear Pick bodies. Curiously, neurons with Hirano bodies or granulovacuolar degeneration are also numerous. Pick bodies burden nearly every neuron in the granule cell layer of the hippocampal formation. The entorhinal cortex is nearly as severely atrophic as the frontal and temporal neocortex. The caudate and putamen are essentially unremarkable, while the adjacent insular cortex shows atrophy with Pick bodies. Capillaries are conspicuously congested in the substantia nigra, which shows no significant loss of neuromelanin-bearing neurons, although it does contain scanty focal extraneural neuromelanin. One swollen and chromatolytic neuron in the locus coeruleus has two Pick bodies. Thioflavin S preparations of the neocortex and hippocampus disclose

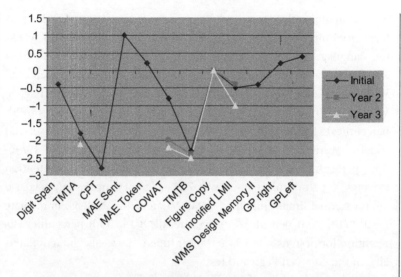

FIGURE 8.3 Neuropsychological findings of case presentation No. 2 across three annual exams depicting the patient's pattern of neuropsychological test performances on the x-axis by percentile rank on the y-axis. Impaired performances include tests of attention and executive function, with all other domains being relatively preserved. (CPT = Continuous Performance Test; MAE Token = Multilingual Aphasia Exam Token Test; MAE Sent = Multilingual Aphasia Exam Sentences; COWAT = Controlled Oral Word Association Test (FAS); LM-II=WMS Logical Memory delay; GP = Grooved Pegboard).

no diffuse plaques, neuritic plaques, neurofibrillary tangles, or amyloid angiopathy. Pick bodies in the hippocampus are faintly stained.

Final Neuropathological Diagnosis:

1. Pick's disease
2. Mild atherosclerosis of the circle of Willis

Neuropsychological Findings

The patient was examined annually for 3 years with partially overlapping batteries. Data from his initial examination is displayed in Figure 8.3. He performed within normal limits on some tests of attention, including one test of simple auditory attention but was impaired on a timed test of visual attention. On a continuous performance Digit Vigilance test, he completed the test very quickly (95th percentile) but

(continued)

---

made a significantly elevated number of errors (1st percentile). He performed within normal limits on several tests of expressive and receptive language ability, including the Aphasia Screening Examination and the Multilingual Aphasia Examination and on the Controlled Oral Word Association Test. Executive function was impaired on Trails B. Visuospatial function was intact on clock and figure copy tests (50th percentiles). Memory ability was normal for immediate and delayed recall of stories (modified WMS story A + B immediate recall, 19/46, 35th percentile; delayed recall, 14/46, 29th percentile). His retention (savings) for story information was 73%. Memory for designs was also within normal limits (modified WMS Memory for Designs, immediate recall 6/14, 20th percentile; delayed recall, 8/14, 35th percentile. His retention for designs was 133%. Motor function was also intact bilaterally on the Grooved Pegboard test.

Overlapping test data from all three annual evaluations are also presented in Figure 8.3. Performance on Trails A remained impaired and further declined after the initial evaluation. On the COWAT his scores rapidly declined from low average to moderately impaired. Executive

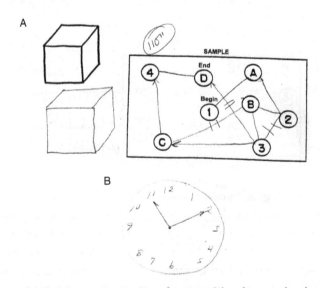

FIGURE 8.4 Case Presentation No. 2's performances (A) on his second evaluation showing the discrepancy between his intact drawing ability (copy-a-cube) and impaired ability to complete the sample portion of the Trailmaking Test Part B, and (B) on the clock drawing test on his third evaluation.

function (Trails B) was initially impaired and remained impaired. Visuospatial ability (figure copy) remained remarkably intact across all three assessments. Memory for stories (WMS Logical Memory delayed recall) was also relatively preserved across the three evaluations, but showed a relative decline by the 3rd year of testing. Initial MMSE was 29 but dropped to 27 at the second evaluation and was down to 19 at the third evaluation. Figure 8.4A illustrates the contrast between his ability to copy a cube and his inability to perform the practice condition of Trails B during his second evaluation. Figure 8.4B displays his copy of a clock in his 3rd and final evaluation, which is intact despite his MMSE score of 19.

Diagnostic Criteria

Pick is credited with providing the original description of frontotemporal dementia (FTD) (Pick, 1892). He described a 71-year-old man with a 3-year history of progressive declines that included a prominent aphasia with many paraphasic errors in his speech and difficulty recognizing objects. Some months later, the autopsy revealed prominent atrophy in a lobar distribution involving the frontal and temporal lobes, and the histologic characteristics of the disease were first described by Alzheimer in 1911.

For much of the next century, there was an effort to split different "diseases" of the frontal and temporal regions. Initially, there was a distinction between Pick's disease and non-Pick's FTD (sometimes referred to as Pick's disease without Pick bodies). Subsequent interest in progressive aphasia syndromes (Josephs & Duffy, 2008; Mesulam, 2003, 2007) led to criteria for primary progressive aphasia (PPA) as distinct from the more behavioral variant of FTD (bvFTD). Moreover, within PPA there were noted to be distinct patterns of fluency, giving rise to progressive nonfluent aphasia—where motor speech may be a primary problem—versus logopenic PPA, where the speech apparatus is intact but word retrieval (e.g., anomia) and grammar are affected. Finally, recognition of a pattern of a loss of word meaning, as opposed to loss of word production, gave rise to the separation of semantic dementia (SD) from PPA.

More recently, there has been a shift back to lumping in the FTD dementia nomenclature to consolidate concepts such as primary progressive aphasia, semantic dementia, frontal dementia (FD), and Pick's disease, into the broader category of frontotemporal lobar degeneration (FTLD) diseases.

This "lumping" has a neuropathological basis, namely that the lobar atrophy associated with PPA, SD, FD, and Pick's disease generally arises from neurofibrillary tangles, that is, a tauopathy, or alternatively from a TAR DNA binding (TDP-43) proteinopathy.

The diagnostic nomenclature in this area remains dynamic, and no real consensus has emerged. We will focus on three clinical variants within the FTLD family: (1) behavioral-variant FTD (bvFTD) characterized by changes in behavior and personality; it is reportedly associated with frontal-predominant cortical degeneration; (2) semantic dementia (SD), which appears to associate with anterior temporal neuronal loss; and (3) progressive nonfluent aphasia (PNFA), the syndrome of effortful language output, loss of grammar, and motor speech deficits, which may reflect predominant left perisylvian cortical atrophy.

The consensus criteria of Neary et al. (1998) remain the most widely used FTD diagnostic criteria, even though some challenges have been noted (Rascovsky et al., 2007; Rascovsky et al., 2011). The Neary et al. (1998) consensus criteria for FTD are shown in Table 8.1.

Recently, new criteria (relative to list 1 in Table 8.1) for behavioral variant FTD have been proposed (Rascovsky, et al., 2011). These criteria adopt the levels of certainty strategy currently in vogue with other dementias (see Table 8.2):

Epidemiology of FTD

A recent study from Italy suggests that the prevalence of FTD in the general population (all ages) is about 0.02%, with rates of 0.02% in the age group 45–64, 0.08% in the age group 65–74 and 0.05% in the age group above 75 (Borroni et al., 2010). In the 50- to 59-year-old onset age group, the incidence of FTD may equal that of AD (Knopman, Petersen, Edland, Cha, & Rocca, 2004), although the data above suggests the prevalence peaks in the 65- to 74-year-old age group. In unselected autopsy series, FTD accounts for about 5% of dementias.

Genetics and Neuropathology of FTD

Josephs and others make the important distinction between dementia syndromes and dementia pathologies (Josephs et al., 2008). Different pathologies can produce similar syndromes and vice versa. This is true across all dementia pathologies (amyloid, synucleinopathy, vascular disease) but is especially true in FTD. Recent neuropathologic and genomic studies have suggested that two main types of pathology underlie the various syndromes aggregated under

Table 8.1 Consensus Criteria for the Diagnosis of Frontotemporal Dementia (Neary et al., 1998)

List 1. The clinical diagnostic features of Behavioral Variant FTD:
Clinical profile

Character change and disordered social conduct are the dominant features initially and throughout the disease course. Instrumental functions of perception, spatial skills, praxis, and memory are intact or relatively well preserved.

I. Core diagnostic features
    A. Insidious onset and gradual progression
    B. Early decline in social interpersonal conduct
    C. Early impairment in regulation of personal conduct
    D. Early emotional blunting
    E. Early loss of insight
II. Supportive diagnostic features
    A. Behavioral disorder
        1. Decline in personal hygiene and grooming
        2. Mental rigidity and inflexibility
        3. Distractibility and impersistence
        4. Hyperorality and dietary changes
        5. Perseverative and stereotyped behavior
        6. Utilization behavior
    B. Speech and language
        1. Altered speech output
            a. Aspontaneity and economy of speech
            b. Press of speech
        2. Stereotype of speech
        3. Echolalia
        4. Perseveration
        5. Mutism
    C. Physical signs
        1. Primitive reflexes
        2. Incontinence
        3. Akinesia, rigidity, and tremor
        4. Low and labile blood pressure
    D. Investigations
        1. Neuropsychology: significant impairment on frontal lobe tests in the absence of severe amnesia, aphasia, or perceptuospatial disorder
        2. Electroencephalography: normal on conventional EEG despite clinically evident dementia
        3. Brain imaging (structural and/or functional): predominant frontal and/or anterior temporal abnormality

(continued)

Table 8.1   (Continued)

List 2. The clinical diagnostic features of Progressive Nonfluent Aphasia:
Clinical profile
Disorder of expressive language is the dominant feature initially and
  throughout the disease course. Other aspects of cognition are intact or
  relatively well preserved.
I. Core diagnostic features
  A. Insidious onset and gradual progression
  B. Nonfluent spontaneous speech with at least one of the following:
  agrammatism, phonemic paraphasias, anomia
II. Supportive diagnostic features
  A. Speech and language
      1. Stuttering or oral apraxia
      2. Impaired repetition
      3. Alexia, agraphia
      4. Early preservation of word meaning
      5. Late mutism
  B. Behavior
      1. Early preservation of social skills
      2. Late behavioral changes similar to FTD
  C. Physical signs: late contralateral primitive reflexes, akinesia, rigidity,
  and tremor
  D. Investigations
      1. Neuropsychology: nonfluent aphasia in the absence of severe
  amnesia or perceptuospatial disorder
      2. Electroencephalography: normal or minor asymmetric slowing
      3. Brain imaging (structural and/or functional): asymmetric
  abnormality predominantly affecting dominant (usually left) hemisphere
List 3. The clinical diagnostic features of Semantic Dementia:
Clinical profile
Semantic disorder (impaired understanding of word meaning and/or object
  identity) is the dominant feature initially and throughout the disease
  course. Other aspects of cognition, including autobiographic memory,
  are intact or relatively well preserved.
I. Core diagnostic features
  A. Insidious onset and gradual progression
  B. Language Disorder characterized by
      1. Progressive, fluent, empty spontaneous speech,
      2. Loss of word meaning, manifested by impaired naming and
  comprehension, and/or
      3. Semantic paraphasias

(continued)

C. Perceptual disorder characterized by
    1. Prosopagnosia: impaired recognition of identity of familiar faces, and/or
    2. Associative agnosia: impaired recognition of object identity
D. Preserved perceptual matching and drawing reproduction
E. Preserved single-word repetition
F. Preserved ability to read aloud and write to dictation orthographically regular words
II. Supportive diagnostic features
  A. Speech and language
    1. Press of speech
    2. Idiosyncratic word usage
    3. Absence of phonemic paraphasias
    4. Surface dyslexia and dysgraphia
    5. Preserved calculation
  B. Behavior
    1. Loss of sympathy and empathy
    2. Narrowed preoccupations
    3. Parsimony
  C. Physical signs
    1. Absent or late primitive reflexes
    2. Akinesia, rigidity, and tremor
III. Investigations
  E. Neuropsychology
    1. Profound semantic loss, manifested in failure of word comprehension and naming and/or face and object recognition
    2. Preserved phonology and syntax, and elementary perceptual processing, spatial skills, and day-to-day memorizing
  F. Electroencephalography: normal

the FTLD rubric. As noted above, these are the tauopathies and the TDP-43 proteinopathies.

The tauopathies are disorders of tau processing leading to neurofibrillary tangles, Pick bodies, and/or argyrophilic grains. For example, Pick's disease, the original FTLD, falls within this family of proteinopathies. This pathology is traced to a variety of mutations (now over 60 have been described) to the MAPT gene on chromosome 17.

TDP-43 proteinopathies are associated with ubiquitinated dystrophic neurites. These pathologies are associated with changes to the progranulin gene on chromosome 17. Four types (labeled Type 0, A, B, and C) of protein misprocessing have been identified. These four genotypes appear to produce

Table 8.2   Newly Proposed Levels of Certainty for Behavioral Variant FTD Proposed by Rascovsky et al. (2011)

I. Neurodegenerative disease

The following symptom must be present to meet criteria for bvFTD

    A. Shows progressive deterioration of behavior and/or cognition by observation or history (as provided by a knowledgeable informant).

II. Possible bvFTD

Three of the following behavioral/cognitive symptoms (A–F) must be present to meet criteria. Ascertainment requires that symptoms be persistent or recurrent, rather than single or rare events.

    A. Early (generally within the first 3 years) behavioral disinhibition [one of the following symptoms (A.1–A.3) must be present]:

        1. Socially inappropriate behavior

        2. Loss of manners or decorum

        3. Impulsive, rash, or careless actions

    B.   Early apathy or inertia [one of the following symptoms (B.1–B.2) must be present]:

        1. Apathy

        2. Inertia

    C. Early loss of sympathy or empathy [one of the following symptoms (C.1–C.2) must be present]:

        1. Diminished response to other people's needs and feelings

        2. Diminished social interest, interrelatedness, or personal warmth

    D. Early perseverative, stereotyped, or compulsive/ritualistic behavior [one of the following symptoms (D.1–D.3) must be present]:

        1. Simple repetitive movements

        2. Complex, compulsive, or ritualistic behaviors

        3. Stereotypy of speech

    E. Hyperorality and dietary changes [one of the following symptoms (E.1–E.3) must be present]:

        1. Altered food preferences

        2. Binge eating, increased consumption of alcohol or cigarettes

        3. Oral exploration or consumption of inedible objects

    F. Neuropsychological profile: executive/generation deficits with relative sparing of memory and visuospatial functions [all of the following symptoms (F.1–F.3) must be present]:

        1. Deficits in executive tasks

        2. Relative sparing of episodic memory

        3. Relative sparing of visuospatial skills

(continued)

III. Probable bvFTD
All of the following symptoms (A–C) must be present to meet criteria.
A. Meets criteria for possible bvFTD
B. Exhibits significant functional decline (by caregiver report or as evidenced by Clinical Dementia Rating Scale or Functional Activities Questionnaire scores)
C. Imaging results consistent with bvFTD [one of the following (C.1–C.2) must be present]:
1. Frontal and/or anterior temporal atrophy on MRI or CT
2. Frontal and/or anterior temporal hypoperfusion or hypometabolism on PET or SPECT
IV. Behavioral variant FTD with definite FTLD Pathology
Criterion A and either criterion B or C must be present to meet criteria.
A. Meets criteria for possible or probable bvFTD
B. Histopathological evidence of FTLD on biopsy or at postmortem autopsy
C. Presence of a known pathogenic mutation
V. Exclusionary criteria for bvFTD
Criteria A and B must be answered negatively for any bvFTD diagnosis. Criterion C can be positive for possible bvFTD but must be negative for probable bvFTD.
A. Pattern of deficits is better accounted for by other nondegenerative nervous system or medical disorders
B. Behavioral disturbance is better accounted for by a psychiatric diagnosis
C. Biomarkers strongly indicative of Alzheimer's disease or other neurodegenerative process

different phenotypes in terms of the distribution of pathology/atrophy and possibly in terms of the clinical presentation. Figure 8.5 illustrates the links between various clinical syndromes to the underlying pathologies. Note also in Figure 8.5, Josephs endeavors to incorporate extrapyramidal and motor neuron disease syndromes into the schema and includes primary supranuclear palsy, cortical basal syndrome, and amyotrophic lateral sclerosis with dementia. We will not deal extensively with those syndromes here but will touch on at least some of them in the next chapter.

Recent findings suggest a need to update Figure 8.5. A new genetic anomaly on chromosome 9, a hexanucleotide repeat has been identified that may explain more cases of FTLD than either of the aforementioned chromosome

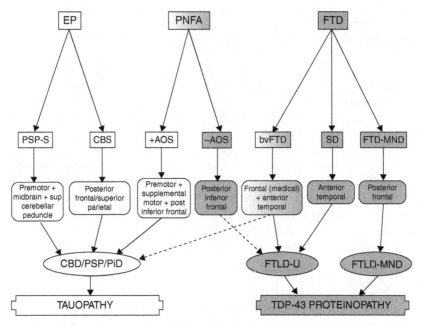

FIGURE 8.5 Schematic plot illustrating the most prominent associations between clinical syndromes, patterns of atrophy, pathological diagnoses, and protein biochemistry for sporadic frontotemporal dementia (FTD). TDP-43 = TAR DNA-binding protein 43. Clinical syndromes: +AOS = apraxia of speech present; –AOS = apraxia of speech absent; bvFTD = behavioral variant FTD; CBS = corticobasal syndrome; EP = extrapyramidal; FTD-MND = FTD with motor neuron disease; PNFA = progressive nonfluent aphasia; PSP-S = progressive supranuclear palsy syndrome; SD = semantic dementia. Pathological diagnoses: CBD = corticobasal degeneration; FTLD-U = frontotemporal lobar degeneration with ubiquitin-only–immunoreactive changes; FTLD-MND = frontotemporal lobar degeneration with motor neuron disease; PiD = Pick's disease; PSP = progressive supranuclear palsy.

From Josephs (2008), reprinted with permission.

17 mutations. Persons carrying an expansion of the GGGGCC hexanucleotide in a noncoding region of a gene on chromosome 9 appear to develop a neurodegenerative syndrome that can take the form of behavioral variant FTD or amyotrophic lateral sclerosis (ALS), but most commonly both, that is, bvFTD with ALS (Dejesus-Hernandez et al., 2011).

The fact that different genetic anomalies can produce similar neuropathologies is not surprising given the complexities of cell biology. However, that specific genetic anomalies can produce such a broad range of clinical phenotypes is beguiling and a reminder against reductionism in neuroscience.

Neuropsychology of FTD

Wittenberg et al. (2008) enumerate five reasons why it is challenging to discuss the neuropsychology of FTD. As previously described, (1) the diagnostic criteria for FTD have evolved and (2) remain confusing. (3) FTD is rare so sample sizes in descriptive studies are small, leading to variable findings; and (4) studies tend to lump bvFTD, SD, and NFPA types to increase sample size. (5) Finally, to compare and contrast within FTLD syndromes and with other dementias, one must equate for severity. This is challenging since severity scales tend to be disease-specific. Given the ever changing nature of the diagnostic criteria it is perhaps difficult to describe "the" neuropsychology of FTD. Rather, we will discuss how the neuropsychological domains are associated with specific FTLD syndromes.

Learning and Memory

FTD syndromes are all contrasted with Alzheimer's disease in the relative sparing of memory early in the illness. This typically refers to better free and cued recall and better recognition than is typically seen in AD. For example, in the Hutchinson and Mathias (2007) meta-analysis of discrimination of lumped FTD syndromes and AD, there are large effect sizes reflecting better performance for FTD on AVLT recognition, Rey Figure delayed recall, and WMS Logical Memory percent retention and smaller but significant effect sizes for AVLT, WMS LM, and VR immediate recall conditions. This pattern reflects both better sparing of immediate recall (i.e., learning efficiency) in AD and also relatively greater problems in learning efficiency, perhaps due to language, attention, and semantic support deficits in FTD syndromes. As dementia worsens, all of the FTLD variants show worse memory performance on standard tests of memory. This highlights the notion that neuropsychological tests may have their greatest value in mild cognitive impairment and early dementia states and lose discriminative value as disease worsens.

Fluency

Whereas AD patients tend to show greater deficits in semantic (category) fluency relative to lexical (letter) fluency (Monsch et al., 1992), FTD patients tend to display impairments in both (Rascovsky, Salmon, Hansen, Thal, & Galasko, 2007) (see Figure 8.6). This finding may be driven especially by the inclusion of PFNA and SD patients in past FTLD samples, but is also observed in bvFTD (Rascovsky, Salmon, et al., 2007). Note that even with the classification of bvFTD, there appears to be variability in the regional atrophy of the disorder (Whitwell et al., 2009). As expected, this is associated with variable

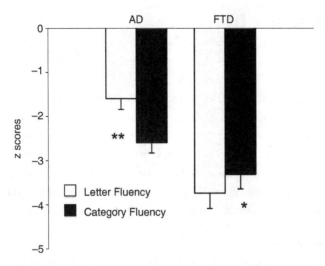

FIGURE 8.6 Mean z-scores of Alzheimer's disease (AD) and frontotemporal dementia (FTD; excluding semantic dementia) patients on letter fluency and semantic category fluency tests. FTD patients were more impaired on the letter fluency than semantic fluency task, whereas AD patients were more impaired on category fluency than letter fluency. *p <.05, **p <.01.
Adapted from Rascovsky et al. (2007), with permission.

patterns of cognitive performance such that more frontal atrophy is associated with greater lexical fluency problems relative to more temporal patterns of atrophy with concomitant greater challenges in naming. Advanced, computer-based algorithms for assessing fluency, and language more generally (cf. Pakhomov, Smith, Chacon, et al., 2010; Pakhomov, Smith, Marino, et al., 2010), may aide in clarity of diagnosis and utility of fluency and language analysis.

Executive Function

One of the consistently annoying findings in the literature is that traditional "frontal" tests are not very good at detecting and distinguishing FTLD syndromes (Miller et al., 2003). In the Hutchinson and Mathias (2007) meta-analysis, for example, there was nearly 80% overlap in the scores of FTLD and AD patients for Trail Making Test Part B and the effect size for differences on the Stroop test was not different from zero. This poor discrimination may arise in part from the problem of mixing different FTD syndromes as described, but also may reflect that fairly early in the AD process there is also involvement of the frontal lobes (Braak & Braak, 1997). However, studies also suggest that executive function tests may not be that good at distinguishing

FTD patients from normally aging samples. FTD patients often score in the normal range on Card Sorting, Stroop, Digits Backwards and Letter-Number Sequencing tasks (Wittenberg, et al., 2008). Thus, traditional "frontal" measures have uneven sensitivity and poor differential specificity for the broad class of FTLD syndromes.

Language/Semantic Knowledge
By definition (i.e., required for the diagnosis), the progressive aphasia variants of FTD have deficits in aspects of language. In addition to fluency problems, PNFA patients have problems with confrontation naming, single word reading, and even comprehension of complex commands or sentences. For example, they may struggle to name a comb, but can demonstrate its use. Semantic dementia patients tend to have preserved repetition and single word reading with fluent output. However, even simple comprehension can be impaired as they lose not only word meaning but also object meaning.

Visuopatial Skills
Visuospatial skills tend to be preserved in FTLD syndromes, given the relative preservation of posterior cortices. For example, Razani et al. (Razani, Boone, Miller, Lee, & Sherman, 2001) observed that visuoconstructional deficits, but not memory deficits, help distinguish AD from FTD. An earlier study from this group had suggested AD and FTD groups differed on the discrepancy between nonverbal memory minus letter fluency. Specifically, AD patients tended to have greater nonverbal memory deficits relative to letter fluency problems, and FTD demonstrated the reverse pattern of greater fluency deficits relative to memory (Pachana, Boone, Miller, Cummings, & Berman, 1996).

Behavioral Scales
Additional research has focused on the use of behavioral scales (e.g. the Frontal Systems Behavior Scale; Grace & Malloy, 2001) that may be better than traditional neuropsychological measures of executive function in distinguishing AD and FTD (Kertesz, Nadkarni, Davidson, & Thomas, 2000). For example, the Frontal Systems Behavior Scale (Grace & Malloy, 2001) was constructed to map onto known basal ganglia thalamocortical circuitry first described by Alexander, DeLong, and Strick (1986) (see also DeLong & Wichmann, 2007; Mega & Cummings, 1994) thought to relate to functions of the orbitofrontal (e.g., disinhibition), medial frontal (e.g., apathy) and

---

dorsolateral (e.g., executive dysfunction) cortices. Ideally, the scale is administered to both patient and informant, and ratings of premorbid and current functioning are obtained.

Clearly, the behavioral disturbances of FTD dwarf those typically seen in AD, and these symptoms can include significant and paradoxical combinations of delusions and hallucinations, depression, anxiety, irritability, elation, disinhibition, apathy, and aberrant motor behavior (see Miller et al., 2003). Historically, the frontal variant of FTD has been more highly associated with behavioral disturbances, whereas the temporal variant of FTD has demonstrated more pronounced deficits in language and semantic knowledge (Perry & Hodges, 2000). However, work by Liu and colleagues (2004) demonstrates that both variants of FTD show many similarities in behavioral disturbances, and both variants show significantly increased behavior disorders when compared to AD patients matched on age and dementia severity (see Liu et al., 2004).

Treatment

As with the other conditions described in this book, treatment of FTD remains symptomatic at this time. This is no small feat in itself because of the range (from apathy to disinhibition) and severity (physical and sexual aggression, mutism) of the various FTD syndromes. Nonpharmacologic treatments remain the first line intervention (Rabinovici & Miller, 2010; see Table 8.3). In Chapter 10, we provide an example of one such intervention in a bvFTD patient that engaged in disruptive yelling behavior. In addition to tailored nonpharmacological treatments, serotonergic and dopaminergic treatments may aid in certain types of behavioral and motor symptoms. Nevertheless, treatment in FTD remains a tremendous challenge.

Conclusion

The nosology of FTD is evolving as new genetic, neuroimaging, and neuropathologic findings drive new efforts to develop a consensus on how to organize these widely varying clinical syndromes. Given the heterogeneity of the pathology, topography, and diagnostic criteria, it is not surprising that there is mixed evidence for the utility of neuropsychological assessment in FTD. Many past studies will need to be reworked as diagnostic schema evolve. Nevertheless, it remains likely that measures of fluency, semantic knowledge, and other language tasks (e.g., repetition, verbal comprehension, etc.) will have high utility in characterizing progressive aphasias and semantic dementia, respectively.

Table 8.3 Symptomatic Therapy in Frontotemporal Lobar Degeneration

SYMPTOM	THERAPY
Behavioral disturbances	Caregiver education
	Environmental, physical, and behavioral modifications
	Antidepressants
	escitalopram, citalopram, sertraline
	bupropion (with parkinsonism)
	venlafaxine (with prominent apathy)
	Antipsychotics[b]
	quetiapine
Aphasia	Speech therapy
	Augmentative communication devices
Parkinsonism	Physical, occupational, and speech therapy
	Levodopa/carbidopa
	Pramipexole, ropinirole
Motor neuron disease	Multidisciplinary treatment
	neurologic
	nutritional
	pulmonary
	physical, occupational, and speech therapy
	Riluzole[c]
Bladder dysfunction	
upper motor neuron	Trospium chloride, darifenacin
lower motor neuron	Intermittent catheterization

[a]Nonpharmacological therapies are paramount, and drug therapy in isolation is unlikely to be successful. All recommendations represent off-label use unless otherwise specified. Medications should always be started at low doses and titrated slowly.
[b]Should be used as last resort and with extreme caution because of increased mortality risk.
[c]US FDA-approved for the treatment of amyotrophic lateral sclerosis.
Reproduced from Rabinovici & Miller (2010), with permission.

Early on, behavioral variant FTD may be better assessed by informant rating scales as opposed to traditional performance measures. However, as described throughout this book, all dementias converge. With progression, dementia cases with presumed SD or PFNA will also have a high likelihood of eventually having behavioral disturbance, and by the same token bvFTD patients will eventually have language problems. Though relatively uncommon, FTD cases are striking not only for the tragic and difficult symptom profiles, but also for the age of onset and tremendous impact on caregivers.

References

Alexander, G., DeLong, M., & Strick, P. (1986). Parallel organization of functionally segregated circuits linking basal ganglia and cortex. *Annual Review of Neuroscience, 9,* 357–381.

Benton, A., & Hamsher, K. (1978). *Multilingual Aphasia Examination: Manual.* Iowa City: University of Iowa.

Borroni, B., Alberici, A., Grassi, M., Turla, M., Zanetti, O., Bianchetti, A.,...Padovani, A. (2010). Is frontotemporal lobar degeneration a rare disorder? Evidence from a preliminary study in Brescia county, Italy. *Journal of Alzheimer's Disease, 19*(1), 111–116.

Braak, H., & Braak, E. (1997). Frequency of stages of Alzheimer-related lesions in different age categories. *Neurobiology of Aging, 18,* 351–357.

Dejesus-Hernandez, M., Mackenzie, I., Boeve, B., Boxer, A., Baker, M., Rutherford, N.,...Rademakers, R. (2011). Expanded GGGGCC hexanucleotide repeat in noncoding region of C9ORF72 causes chromosome 9p-linked FTD and ALS. *Neuron, 72*(2), 245–256.

DeLong, M., & Wichmann, T. (2007). Circuits and circuit disorders of the basal ganglia. *Archives of Neurology, 64*(1), 20–24.

Grace, J., & Malloy, P. (2001). *Frontal Systems Behavior Scale professional manual.* Lutz, FL: Psychological Assessment Resources

Hutchinson, A., & Mathias, J. (2007). Neuropsychological deficits in frontotemporal dementia and Alzheimer's disease: A meta-analytic review. [Meta-Analysis Review]. *Journal of Neurology, Neurosurgery, and Psychiatry, 78*(9), 917–928.

Ivnik, R., Malec, J., Smith, G., Tangalos, E., Petersen, R., Kokmen, E., & Kurland, L. (1992). Mayo's Older Americans Normative Studies: Updated AVLT norms for ages 56–97. *The Clinical Neuropsychologist, 6,* 83–104.

Josephs, K. (2008). Frontotemporal dementia and related disorders: Deciphering the enigma. *Annals of Neurology, 64*(1), 4–14.

Josephs, K., & Duffy, J. (2008). Apraxia of speech and nonfluent aphasia: A new clinical marker for corticobasal degeneration and progressive supranuclear palsy. *Current Opinion in Neurology, 21*(6), 688–692.

Josephs, K., Whitwell, J., Ahmed, Z., Shiung, M., Weigand, S., Knopman, D., . . . Jack, C., Jr. (2008). Beta-amyloid burden is not associated with rates of brain atrophy. *Annals of Neurology, 63*(2), 204–212.

Kaplan, E., Goodglass, H., & Weintraub, S. (1983). *The Boston Naming Test* (2nd ed.). Philadelphia: Lea & Febiger.

Kertesz, A., Nadkarni, N., Davidson, W., & Thomas, A. (2000). The Frontal Behavioral Inventory in the differential diagnosis of frontotemporal dementia. *Journal of the International Neuropsychological Society, 6*(4), 460–468.

Knopman, D. S., Petersen, R. C., Edland, S. D., Cha, R. H., & Rocca, W. A. (2004). The incidence of frontotemporal lobar degeneration in Rochester, Minnesota, 1990 through 1994. *Neurology, 62*(3), 506–508.

Liu, W., Miller, B. L., Kramer, J. H., Rankin, K., Wyss-Coray, C., Gearhart, R., . . . Rosen, H. J. (2004). Behavioral disorders in the frontal and temporal variants of frontotemporal dementia. *Neurology, 62*(5), 742–748.

Mattis, S. (1988). *Mattis Dementia Rating Scale (MDRS).* Odessa, FL: Psychological Assessment Resources.

Mega, M., & Cummings, J. (1994). Frontal-subcortical circuits and neuropsychiatric disorders. *Journal of Neuropsychiatry and Clinical Neuroscience, 6*(4), 358–370.

Mesulam, M. M. (2003). Primary progressive aphasia—A language-based dementia. *New England Journal of Medicine, 349*(16), 1535–1542.

Mesulam, M. M. (2007). Primary progressive aphasia: A 25-year retrospective. *Alzheimer Disease and Associated Disorders, 21*(4), S8–S11.

Miller, B., Diehl, J., Freedman, M., Kertesz, A., Mendez, M., & Rascovsky, K. (2003). International approaches to frontotemporal dementia diagnosis: From social cognition to neuropsychology. [Review]. *Annals of Neurology, 54*(Suppl 5), S7–S10.

Monsch, A. U., Bondi, M. W., Butters, N., Salmon, D. P., Katzman, R., & Thal, L. J. (1992). Comparisons of verbal fluency tasks in the detection of dementia of the Alzheimer type. *Archives of Neurology, 49*(12), 1253–1258.

Neary, D., Snowden, J., Gustafson, L., Passant, U., Stuss, D., Black, S., . . . Benson, D. (1998). Frontotemporal lobar degeneration: A consensus on clinical diagnostic criteria. *Neurology, 51*(6), 1546–1554.

Pachana, N., Boone, K., Miller, B., Cummings, J., & Berman, N. (1996). Comparison of neuropsychological functioning in Alzheimer's disease and frontotemporal dementia. *Journal of the International Neuropsychological Society, 2*(6), 505–510.

Pakhomov, S., Smith, G., Chacon, D., Feliciano, Y., Graff-Radford, N., Caselli, R., & Knopman, D. (2010). Computerized analysis of speech and language to identify psycholinguistic correlates of frontotemporal lobar degeneration. *Cognitive and Behavioral Neurology, 23*(3), 165–177.

Pakhomov, S., Smith, G., Marino, S., Birnbaum, A., Graff-Radford, N., Caselli, R.,... Knopman, D. (2010). A computerized technique to assess language use patterns in patients with frontotemporal dementia. *Journal of Eurolinguistics, 23*(2), 127–144.

Perry, R., & Hodges, J. (2000). Differentiating frontal and temporal variant frontotemporal dementia from Alzheimer's disease. *Neurology, 54*(12), 2277–2284.

Pick, A. (1892). Über die Beziehungen der senilen Hirnatrophie zur Aphasie *Prager medicinische Wochenschrift, 17*, 165–167.

Rabinovici, G., & Miller, B. (2010). Frontotemporal lobar degeneration: Epidemiology, pathophysiology, diagnosis and management. *CNS drugs, 24*(5), 375–398.

Rascovsky, K., Hodges, J., Kipps, C., Johnson, J., Seeley, W., Mendez, M.,... Miller, B. (2007). Diagnostic criteria for the behavioral variant of frontotemporal dementia (bvFTD): Current limitations and future directions. *Alzheimer Disease and Associated Disorders, 21*(4), S14–S18.

Rascovsky, K., Hodges, J., Knopman, D., Mendez, M., Kramer, J., Neuhaus, J.,... Miller, B. (2011). Sensitivity of revised diagnostic criteria for the behavioural variant of frontotemporal dementia. *Brain, 134*(Pt 9), 2456–2477.

Rascovsky, K., Salmon, D., Hansen, L., Thal, L., & Galasko, D. (2007). Disparate letter and semantic category fluency deficits in autopsy-confirmed frontotemporal dementia and Alzheimer's disease. *Neuropsychology, 21*(1), 20–30.

Razani, J., Boone, K., Miller, B., Lee, A., & Sherman, D. (2001). Neuropsychological performance of right- and left-frontotemporal dementia compared to Alzheimer's disease. *Journal of the International Neuropsychological Society, 7*(4), 468–480.

Rey, A. (1964). *L'examen clinique en psychologie.* Paris: Presses Universitaires de France.

Wechsler, D. (1987). *Wechsler Memory Scale-Revised.* New York: Psychological Corporation.

Wechsler, D. (1997). *Wechsler Adult Intelligence Scale-III.* New York: Psychological Corporation.

Whitwell, J., Przybelski, S., Weigand, S., Ivnik, R., Vemuri, P., Gunter, J.,...Josephs, K. (2009). Distinct anatomical subtypes of the behavioural variant of frontotemporal dementia: A cluster analysis study. *Brain*, *132*(11), 2932–2946.

Wilkinson, G. S. (1993). *Wide Range Achievement Test-Third edition administration manual.* Wilmington, DE: Wide Range.

Wittenberg, D., Possin, K., Rascovsky, K., Rankin, K., Miller, B., & Kramer, J. (2008). The early neuropsychological and behavioral characteristics of frontotemporal dementia. *Neuropsychology Review*, *18*(1), 91–102.

9

■ ■ ■

Atypical Dementias

With Guest Author David P. Salmon, PhD

Case Presentation

History of Present Illness

The patient was a 64-year-old retired chairman of a bank who was accompanied by his wife for an evaluation of cognitive impairment. The initial history from the patient indicated that he had been impaired for the past year or so with some progressive irritability and increased ability to lose his temper. He felt that there was something wrong. However, he felt that his cognitive function and other behaviors were largely intact.

His spouse however gave a somewhat different history. She indicated that she and the children had noted for several years that there had been something wrong with the patient's behavior. At first, he looked depressed and tended to be more withdrawn. At present, he tended to watch a great deal of TV and watched the stocks streaming across the bottom of the screen for countless hours. He still read, but the spouse questioned his ability to comprehend. He had been a very high functioning individual in the past and the clinical behaviors had impacted his current function. The patient had continued to work in his banking business in the past two years but his spouse was not convinced that he was very effective at his job. Formerly he was extremely efficient and had a bright business mind, but in the past year or so she doubted if he had made significant contribu-

(continued)

---

tions to the business. The bank asked him to step down as CEO at the end of the year but he remained on the board.

The family had been aware of a personality change. He had always had a quick temper, but that irritability had now increased. He had previously had very good interpersonal skills but now appeared more withdrawn. He was also somewhat more docile than in the past, although he had a tendency to raise his voice.

His spouse felt that her husband's memory was intact. His organizational and calculational skills had changed, however, and she took over the checkbook in the past year. He still drove, but she wondered if this was appropriate. He tended to sleep a bit more and would doze off at 8 p.m. in a chair and get up and go to bed at 10 p.m. He was a minimal snorer. He did not have any daytime hallucinations. He had not had any head trauma or toxin exposure. He had been a casual alcohol drinker over the years but had never misused alcohol. He did not have any HIV or Lyme risk factors. He denied dry eyes or dry mouth. He did not appear depressed and had not had any stroke-like symptoms.

In the past year, the patient was started on Aricept but developed diarrhea. He was then switched to Exelon. He was tolerating it well and he felt it was helping him, but his spouse was not convinced.

Current Medications
Exelon 6.0 mg. in a.m. and 4.5 mg. in p.m.
Centrum Silver vitamin
Extra Strength Tylenol in the evening
Occasional medication for fever blisters

Social History
The patient graduated from the university with a bachelor's degree and did graduate banking work. He was on the faculty there for several years and was involved in long-range planning.

Family History
The patient's father died in his 60s of lung cancer.
The patient's mother died at age 75 of complications of rheumatoid arthritis. Both of them were cognitively intact.
The patient lost one brother at age 36 to malignant melanoma and had four living brothers who are alive and well.

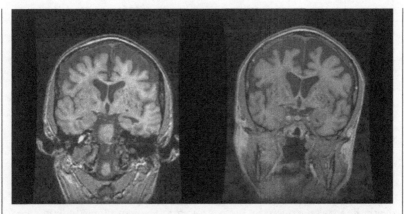

(a) Year of diagnosis   (b) 2-years later.

FIGURE 9.1 Coronal MRI scans of a patient with corticobasal degeneration at (a) initial evaluation and (b) 2 years later.

Neurological Examination

On the Kokmen short test of mental status, the patient scored 32/38. He lost three points on attention and two points on calculation. Memory was intact. Otherwise, on the examination, he was hyperreflexic in a symmetrical fashion. Plantar responses were flexor bilaterally. The remainder of the exam was unremarkable.

Neuroimaging Studies

He underwent MRI scans as part of a research imaging project. His initial diagnostic MRI scan (see Figure 9.1a) was read as:

> Moderate to severe cortical volume loss, given patient's age, involving the frontal and temporal lobes. Posterior fossa arachnoid cyst. Prominent perivascular spaces at both cerebral hemispheres on an ex vacuo basis. Hippocampal fissure cyst on right. Scattered foci of T2 signal hyperintensity in the periventricular and subcortical white matter of both cerebral hemispheres, and at the central pons, consistent with moderate small vessel ischemic/degenerative changes.

Two years later, follow-up scanning (Figure 9.1b) showed the amount of periventricular T2 hyperintensity has moderately increased around the anterior horns of both lateral ventricles, left more prominent than right. In addition, the scattered centrum semiovale T2 hyperintensity and pontine

(continued)

Atypical Dementias

T2 hyperintensity has minimally increased. Furthermore, there has been moderate progression of the frontal atrophy in the interval between the exams, and there may be minimal progression of the parietal atrophy as well. No other change. Old lacunar infarcts versus prominent perivascular spaces within the basal ganglia. Moderate generalized cerebral and cerebellar atrophy.

Course of Illness

The patient returned for a series of follow-up visits after the initial consult. He was seen by Neurology, Psychiatry, and Neuropsychology over time. Twenty-five months after initial evaluation and 17 months prior to his death, he was seen again by his neurologist. The neurologist documented the patient had moved into assisted living and adapted to that facility well. The patient seemed to be contented in the new environment. He did not interact a great deal with the other residents, who were many years his senior, but on occasion if they happened to get in his way he may get slightly physical with them. He spent a good deal of the day pacing and there was a large area for him to continuously move around. He generally was compliant.

The patient developed prominent echolalia. He repeated virtually everything said him. His comprehension skills were surprisingly good. He followed instructions well.

The family indicated that he showed very little emotion or emotional attachment. When he was in the presence of family members such as grandchildren he would let them hug him and be with him but he did not display a great deal of emotion toward them. He also wanted to leave that situation quickly. At the same time he was generally not belligerent nor did he cause a great deal of difficulty. For example, on a trip he sat in the airplane quite readily and did not want to get out of the seat and pace.

The patient was essentially untestable from a mental status standpoint due to his echolalia during the neurological exam. He was cooperative for the remainder of the examination. He had bilateral hyperreflexia with flexor plantar responses. He had some rigidity in his upper extremities. Eye movements were difficult to determine completely because of uncooperation, and upgaze was uncertain. The remainder of the examination was unchanged.

Autopsy Findings
1. Corticobasal ganglionic degeneration (CBGD/CBD), characterized by:
   a. neocortical neuronal loss and gliosis with superficial spongiosis, predominately subpial and gray-white junction, predominately superior parietal, superior frontal, and precentral.
   b. White matter rarefaction, myelin loss, and gliosis, with numerous tau-immunoreactive thread-like deposits and oligodendroglial "coiled" bodies.
   c. Widespread neocortical and subcortical "ballooned" neurons, predominately superior parietal, superior frontal, precentral, anterior cingulate, amygdala, insular cortex, and claustrum.
   d. Widespread neocortical and subcortical pleomorphic tau-immunoreactive deposits, including pretangles and threads, periaqueductal gray, thalamus, and subthalamic nucleus, and nigral corticobasal bodies with profound gross pallor of substantia nigra.
   e. Widespread neocortical and subcortical tau-immunoreactive astrocytic plaques, predominately frontal and parietal neocortex.
2. Argyrophilic grain (Braak) disease, with medial temporal pretangles, grains, tau-positive astrocytes and coiled bodies, and ballooned neurons in amygdala and limbic cortices.
3. Cerebral atrophy, moderate, generalized, marked frontal; left hemibrain weight 634.
4. Cranial arteriolosclerosis, marked with prominent cribriform change, and white matter rarefaction and gliosis.
5. Ischemic microinfarcts and foci of ischemic microgliosis, left basal ganglia.
6. Cranial atherosclerosis: Right and left vertebral, left internal carotid, left middle cerebral (M1), grade 1 (of 4).
7. No evidence of amyloid angiopathy, diffuse or neuritic plaques, hippocampal, dentate fascia ubiquitin-immunoreactive inclusions, or alpha-synuclein immunoreactive deposits.

Neuropsychological Studies
The patient had three neuropsychological studies in all (see Figure 9.2). Initial neuropsychological test results were significant for moderate to severe

(continued)

impairment of complex attention and moderate to severe impairment of other executive and higher-order cognitive abilities involved in reasoning and problem-solving. He could not complete the Wisconsin Card Sorting Test, his score on the color-word interference trial of the Stroop test fell in the moderately impaired range. Most likely secondary to these primary impairments, language, visuospatial abilities, new learning, and access to remotely acquired information were unreliable. The ability to retain new information once it has been learned appeared relatively preserved. Follows-ups occurred on an annual basis. First follow-up was remarkable for the progression of attention and visual spatial problems but also a nonfluent aphasia pattern of language deficits with preserved naming, comprehension, and verbal memory but prominent dysfluency. By the 2-year follow-up his Dementia Rating Scale score was 43 and he was essentially untestable but could still score within normal limits for naming and word recognition reading.

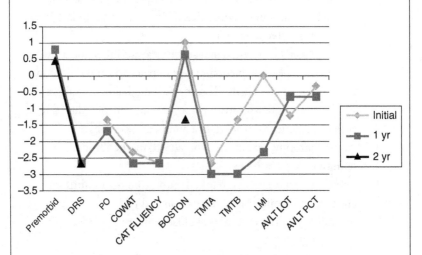

FIGURE 9.2 Neuropsychological profile. All scores are age adjusted z scores. Premorbid = Wide Range Achievement Test (3rd edition; Wilkinson, 1993); Reading score, DRS = Mattis Dementia Rating Scale (Mattis, 1988); total scores, PO = perceptual organization (from Wechsler Adult Intelligence Scale-Third edition (Wechsler, 1997), COWAT = Controlled Oral Word Association Test (Benton & Hamsher, 1978), Cat Fluency = Category Fluency test, LM1 = Wechsler Memory Scale Revised (WMS-R; Wechsler, 1987), Logical Memory Immediate Recall. AVLTLOT = Rey Auditory Verbal Learning Test (AVLT; Rey, 1964), total of trials1–5 minus 5*trial 1 (see Ivnik et al., 1992). AVLTPCT = AVLT 30-minute delay divided by AVLT trial 5. Boston = Boston Naming Test (Kaplan, Goodglass, & Weintraub, 1983). DRS, COWAT, Category Fluency, WMS-R, AVLT, and Boston scores are based on Mayo Older American's Normative Studies (MOANS) norms.

Introduction

There are a number of relatively rare neurodegenerative diseases that produce a dementia syndrome. Several of these diseases share histopathological features with more common causes of dementia, but differ from them in the distribution of pathology throughout the brain. The specific brain structures and neuroanatomical networks affected determine the unique clinical features and neuropsychological deficits associated with each disease. Neuropsychological research that has taken a comparative approach to the study of cognitive disorders has shown that these etiologically and neuropathologically distinct neurodegenerative diseases produce different patterns of relatively preserved and impaired cognitive abilities. At a broad level, these patterns can be classified as those arising primarily from pathology in frontosubcortical brain circuits (similar to Parkinson's disease) and those that primarily involve regions of the cerebral cortex (similar to Alzheimer's disease). Although it is well known that pathological changes in these various disorders are not limited to either cortical or subcortical brain regions, the cortical-subcortical dementia distinction serves as a heuristically useful model for describing the pattern of neuropsychological deficits that are observed in the various patient groups (See Table 6.2).

Atypical dementia syndromes associated with predominant pathology in frontosubcortical brain circuits often are preceded or accompanied by a parkinsonian movement disorder, and are characterized by slowness of thought, impaired attention, deficits in executive functions, and personality changes such as depression and apathy. They often have only mild or moderate memory and language disturbances that are quantitatively and qualitatively different from those of patients with cortical/limbic neurodegenerative diseases such as Alzheimer's disease (AD). Three relatively uncommon diseases that fit this profile are progressive supranuclear palsy (PSP), corticobasal degeneration (CBD), and multiple systems atrophy (MSA). Progressive supranuclear palsy and CBD are histopathologically associated by the presence of tau-positive neuronal inclusions similar to those in AD. In contrast, MSA is associated with synuclein-positive neuronal inclusions similar to those in PD. An atypical subcortical dementia syndrome may also be present in disorders without prominent histopathology, as in normal pressure hydrocephalus (NPH), a condition that arises from increased intracranial pressure due to abnormal accumulation of cerebrospinal fluid (CSF).

Other atypical dementia syndromes derive from focal cortical pathology. Posterior cortical atrophy (PCA) and Creutzfelt-Jakob disease (CJD) both primarily affect distinct regions of the neocortex, but the relatively circum-scribed nature of the distribution of pathology in these disorders produces patterns of neuropsychological deficits distinct from the prototypical global cortical dementia of AD. In the case of PCA, this distinction occurs despite the fact that in most cases the histopathological basis of the disorder is the same as in AD (i.e., abnormal tau-positive neurofibrillary tangles and extracellular amyloid plaques). The specific neuropsychological deficits that characterize these various atypical dementia syndromes are described below. To facilitate the ability to appreciate the distinct pattern of deficits associated with each disorder, the syndromes are in some cases compared to each other or to the typical cognitive deficit profile of AD.

Progressive Supranuclear Palsy (PSP)

Progressive supranuclear palsy is a neurodegenerative disease characterized by supranuclear vertical gaze palsy and parkinsonian features of symmetri-cal akinetic rigidity, bradykinesia, and prominent postural instability caus-ing falls (Steele et al., 1964). There may also be early pseudobulbar features such as dysphagia and dysarthria. Bower et al. (1997) reported an average annual incidence rate of 5.3 per 100,000 people per year, which increased steeply with age from 1.7 at 50–59 years to 14.7 at 80–99 years. It was also consistently higher in men. Median survival time from symptom onset was 5.3 years.

The pathology of PSP includes widespread tau-positive neuropathology and neuronal loss in brainstem nuclei (e.g., red nucleus, subthalamic nucleus, locus ceruleus, midbrain reticular formation, superior colliculus, vestibular and den-tate nuclei) and basal ganglia, with relative sparing of limbic and most neocortical regions (Hauw et al., 1994; Gröschel et al., 2004; Soliveri et al., 1999; Taki et al., 2004). Atrophy may occur in frontal cortices, but is less severe than in AD or in CBD (Dickson, 1999; Soliveri et al., 1999; Taki et al., 2004). Hypoperfusion has been noted in medial premotor cortex with SPECT (Okuda et al., 2000).

Cognitive impairment is an early and prominent feature of PSP and was initially described as the prototypical subcortical dementia syndrome (Albert et al., 1974). Consistent with frontostriatal dysfunction, the dementia syn-drome of PSP includes significant cognitive slowing (Pillon et al., 1986) and disproportionate executive dysfunction (Rosser & Hodges, 1994; Lange et al., 2003; Grafman et al., 1990; Pillon et al., 1991). Executive dysfunction in PSP is evident on tests that require cognitive set shifting, such as the Wisconsin Card Sorting Test, Stroop Test, Hayling Test, and Part B of the Trail-Making

Test (Grafman et al., 1990; Lange et al., 2003; Millar et al., 2006; Pillon et al., 1991), on tests that require conceptual thinking such as the WAIS-R Similarities Test (Cambier et al., 1985; Grafman et al., 1990; Maher et al., 1985; Pillon et al., 1986), and on tests that require generation of words or designs (Grafman et al., 1990; Lange et al., 2003; Litvan, 1994; Rosser & Hodges, 1994; Soliveri et al., 2005). Patients with PSP also have severely impaired sustained and divided attention (Esmonde et al., 1996). Semantic memory is relatively preserved in patients with PSP, and their performance on tests of language is often characterized by normal or near normal confrontation naming in the face of severe deficits in verbal fluency. The ability to rapidly generate words that begin with the same letter (i.e., phonemic or letter fluency) may be equally or more impaired than the ability to rapidly generate words that are exemplars from a particular semantic category (semantic or category fluency), presumably due to the more effortful retrieval required by the phonemic fluency task. This pattern stands in contrast to the semantically based language deficit in AD, which is characterized by markedly impaired confrontation naming and a greater deficit on tests of semantic fluency than phonemic fluency (Milberg & Albert, 1989). It should be noted, however, that semantic deficits as severe as those in patients with AD have been observed in some studies that directly compared PSP and AD patients on tests of naming, synonym judgments, and semantic associations (van der Hurk & Hodges, 1995).

Episodic memory is usually only mildly impaired in patients with PSP and characterized by poor learning in a free recall format with normal or near normal recognition. This pattern of performance is consistent with a significant deficit in effortful retrieval processes rather than a true amnesia associated with poor consolidation (Aarsland et al., 2003; Litvan et al., 1989; Milberg & Albert, 1989; van der Hurk et al., 1995). Patients with PSP performed better than patients with AD on short-delay and long-delay free recall measures from the California Verbal Learning Test (CVLT), and on immediate free recall and total recall measures of a selective reminding test with controlled encoding (Pillon et al., 1995). Immediate memory measured by Digit Span or the Sternberg paradigm (i.e., memory for the presence of a digit in a previously presented digit string) is normal in patients with PSP (Litvan et al., 1989).

A recent study (Zarei et al., 2010) examined retrograde memory loss in patients with PSP using the Autobiographical Memory Inventory (AMI). The AMI is a standardized test of remote memory that assesses autobiographical and personal semantic memories from childhood, early adulthood, and the recent past. In the autobiographical condition, the patient is asked to generate details of three personally experienced episodes from each of the three time periods. In the personal semantic condition, they are asked to produce factual information from these same time periods (e.g., names of friends, teachers, or schools). The results showed mild retrograde memory impairment in patients with PSP for both autobiographical and personal semantic information. The deficit was similar for each of the three time periods. This pattern of performance differs from the severe and temporally graded remote memory deficit that occurs in AD, where newer memories are more impaired than memories from the distant past. The mild impairment and lack of a temporal gradient in PSP patients is consistent with a retrieval deficit that equally affects all time periods, whereas the severe, temporally graded deficit in AD suggests an inability to consolidate memories over time (Beatty et al., 1988).

Corticobasal Degeneration

Corticobasal degeneration (CBD) is a slowly progressive neurodegenerative disorder characterized by an asymmetric presentation of Parkinsonism (e.g., rigidity), ideomotor apraxia, cortical sensory loss, asymmetric limb dystonia, alien limb syndrome, myoclonus, gaze palsy, and cognitive dysfunction. Neuropathological features of CBD include asymmetric focal atrophy in frontoparietal cortex (particularly in motor and sensory areas) with sparing of temporal and occipital cortex (Gröschel et al., 2004; Taki et al., 2004), and depigmentation and neuronal loss in the substantia nigra (Dickson, 1999). Abnormal tau-positive filamentous inclusions accumulate in neurons and glia in the areas affected, a histopathological feature CBD shares with PSP. Consistent with the distribution of pathology, neuroimaging studies reveal asymmetric frontoparietal cortical atrophy without significant midbrain atrophy in most patients with CBD, and the opposite pattern in patients with PSP (Soliveri et al., 1999). Asymmetric hypoperfusion in frontoparietal cortex has also been noted in patients with CBD (Okuda et al., 2000). CBD is a rare disorder with an estimated incidence of less than 1 in 100,000 people per year. It accounts for about 4% to 6% of all cases of parkinsonism (for review, see Mahapatra et al., 2004).

The dementia syndrome of CBD entails prominent ideomotor apraxia that is often asymmetric, nonfluent aphasia with severely impaired verbal fluency (Graham et al., 2003), prominent executive dysfunction (Pillon et al., 1995), deficits in visuospatial abilities (Bak et al., 2006), and a mild episodic memory deficit (Pillon et al., 1995; Massman et al., 1996). Semantic memory is relatively spared. A deficit in number representation, simple arithmetic, and magnitude judgment may be associated with atrophy of right parietal cortex in patients with CBD (Gibb et al., 1989; Halpern et al., 2004).

The nonfluent aphasia associated with CBD is characterized by deficits in object naming (i.e., anomia) and expressive language with relative preservation of receptive language functions and single word comprehension (Kertesz & McMonagle, 2010). It involves dysfunction in motor aspects of language production and agrammatism with sparing of semantics. As in patients with PSP, those with CBD have severe deficits in phonemic fluency. The fluency deficit may not only reflect a language deficit, but also executive dysfunction that has been demonstrated in patients with CBD using tasks such as the Wisconsin Card Sorting Test (Pillon et al., Mathew et al., 2011).

Visuospatial deficits are commonly observed in patients with CBD and often entail impairments in drawing and copying figures (constructional apraxia) or performing tests of block design. These deficits are presumably related to pathology in the parietal cortex and may help to distinguish patients with CBD from those with PSP who do not have these deficits (Bak et al., 2006). There is some concern that the visuoconstructive deficits in patients with CBD may be attributable to dystonia affecting the limbs, but patients with CBD are also impaired on visuoperceptual tasks from the Visual Object and Space Perception Battery that do not have motor requirements (Bak et al., 2006). It is interesting to note that visuoperceptual impairment may affect the ability of patients with CBD to learn new perceptual categories using similarity-based processing that involves the mental comparison of a to-be-categorized visual stimulus with previously encountered exemplars or prototypes. While patients with AD acquire this type of categorization normally, patients with CBD are impaired (Koenig et al., 2007).

The episodic memory deficit associated with CBD is milder than that of AD and presents in a different pattern. When compared on the WMS-R Logical Memory and Paired Associates tests, patients with CBD performed significantly better than equally demented patients with AD in the immediate condition of both tasks and in the delayed recall condition of Logical Memory (Massman et al., 1996). Patients with AD exhibited rapid forgetting on Logical Memory, only retaining about 23% of the information they had learned over the delay period. Patients with CBD, in contrast, retained approximately 62% of the information they had learned. A similar result was obtained with the CVLT (Pillon et al., 1995). Patients with CBD performed better than patients with AD, and at about the same level as patients with PSP, on short-delay and long-delay free recall measures of the CVLT. Patients with CBD also performed better than patients with AD on immediate free recall and total recall measures of a selective reminding test with controlled encoding. Notably, they did not differ significantly from normal elderly individuals or patients with PSP on these measures (Pillon et al., 1995).

Multiple System Atrophy (MSA)
Multiple system atrophy is a sporadic neurodegenerative disease characterized by parkinsonism, autonomic dysfunction (Shy-Drager syndrome), and cerebellar and pyramidal signs (e.g., cerebellar ataxia). Autonomic dysfunction can include orthostatic hypertension, syncope, sleep disordered breathing, and urinary incontinence. Behavioral changes such as depression may also occur. MSA is clinically divided into parkinsonism-predominant (MSA-P) and cerebellar-predominant (MSA-C) subtypes, although symptoms of both syndromes may overlap in a particular patient. As shown in Figure 9.3, the pathology of MSA includes atrophy and alpha-synuclein positive neuronal inclusions in the basal ganglia, substantia nigra, and supplementary and primary motor cortices (MSA-P), and in the reticular formation and olivopontocerebellar system (MSA-C). Mild atrophy of the frontal cortex can be observed on MRI, and decreased prefrontal cortex perfusion is evident on SPECT. MSA is a relatively rare disease with a prevalence of about 4.4 per 100,000 people. Bower et al. (1997) reported an average annual incidence rate of 3.0 per 100,000 people per year, and median survival time from symptom onset was 8.5 years.

Cognitive deficits associated with MSA can be quite subtle and were initially considered a reason for exclusion from the diagnosis. Recent research has shown, however, that significant cognitive decline occurs in about 20% of MSA patients and is more common in MSA-P than MSA-C. The cognitive deficits that occur in MSA include frontal dysfunction (e.g., deficits in attentional set shifting, rule shifting, spatial working memory), impaired verbal fluency, and visuospatial and constructional deficits. Memory and language are relatively preserved (Kawai et al., 2008; Robbins et al., 1992).

This general profile of cognitive deficits was observed in one of the earliest studies of cognition in MSA that used subtests from the CANTAB, a computer-based neuropsychological test battery (Robbins et al., 1992). Patients with MSA-P were impaired compared to healthy individuals on subtests that engaged frontostriatal functions, including spatial working memory, intradimensional and extradimensional shifts of attention, and simultaneous

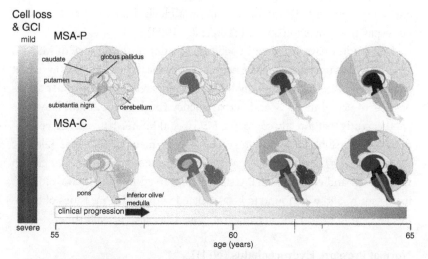

Cell loss
& GCI
mild MSA-P

caudate   globus pallidus

putamen

substantia nigra   cerebellum

MSA-C

pons   inferior olive/
medulla

clinical progression

severe
55   60   65
              age (years)

FIGURE 9.3 Schematic diagram of the amounts and progression of glial cytoplasmic inclusion (GCI) pathology in parkinsonism-predominant (MSA-P) and cerebellar-predominant (MSA-C) subtypes of multisystem atrophy.
Reprinted from Halliday et al. (2011), with permission.

matching-to-sample. In contrast, impairments were not observed on subtests that assessed visual learning and memory, visuospatial processing, or general intellectual abilities. Subsequent studies confirmed this frontostriatal profile of cognitive deficits by demonstrating deficits on tests of attention (Testa et al., 1993), the Similarities subtest (Balas et al., 2010; Testa et al., 1993), Part B of the Trail-Making Test (Chang et al., 2009; Meco et al., 1996), the Stroop Color-Word Interference test (Chang et al., 2009; Meco et al., 1996), and tests of verbal fluency (Bak et al., 2005; Balas et al., 2010; Berent et al., 2002; Brown et al., 2010 [on the Mattis DRS Initiation/Perseveration subtest]; Kao et al., 2009; Soliveri et al., 2000). In several of these studies, patients with MSA-P were significantly more impaired than patients with Parkinson's disease (PD) on a number of these tests of frontostriatal function (Kao et al., 2009 ; Meco et al., 1996; Soliveri et al., 2000).

In contrast to executive function deficits, most studies have failed to find significant deficits in patients with MSA-P on tests of global mental status (Bak et al., 2005), language (other than verbal fluency; Chang et al., 2009; Kao et al., 2009), or episodic memory (Chang et al., 2009; Kao et al., 2009; Meco et al., 1996; Soliveri et al., 2000; but see Balas et al., 2010). Visuospatial function has not been extensively examined in patients with MSA-P, although

Atypical Dementias   *343*

one study observed significant deficits on a block design test and a test of visuospatial organization ability (Testa et al., 1993).

Few studies have examined cognitive function in patients with MSA-C. One study that used an extensive neuropsychological test battery showed that patients with MSA-C were mildly impaired compared to healthy older adults on tests of verbal memory and verbal fluency (Burk et al., 2006). However, another study that directly compared MSA-P and MSA-C patients showed significantly worse performance on verbal episodic memory (Buschke Selective Reminding Test) and verbal fluency tests in those with MCA-P. Deficits on visuospatial and constructional tests were observed in patients with MSA-C in one study, and were found to be associated with SPECT measures of hypometabolism in frontal and cerebellar regions (Kawai et al., 2008).

Normal Pressure Hydrocephalus (NPH)

Idiopathic NPH is a condition of increased intracranial pressure due to abnormal accumulation of cerebrospinal fluid (CSF). The cause of NPH is unknown, but is related to impaired drainage, circulation, or reabsorption of CSF. NPH is clinically characterized by disturbed gait (usually the most prominent feature), urinary incontinence, and cognitive dysfunction that can sometimes predate the other symptoms (Hakin & Adams, 1965). The symptoms of NPH occur in the context of enlargement of the ventricular system (see Figure 9.4). Ideopathic NPH may account for up to 5% of all cases of dementia (Vanneste, 2000), a portion of which may have comorbidity with other neurodegenerative disorders such as AD. However, Klassen and Ahlskog (2011) suggest that studies likely overestimate NPH prevalence on the basis of screening for the compatible clinical and neuroimaging features, and that many patients originally suspected of having NIH do not respond to a CSF removal trial. The incidence rate for shunting is quite low at 1.19 per 100,000 people, often with modest or transient improvements and complications in about one-third who receive shunting (see Klassen & Ahlskog, 2011).

Fife (2003) contends that the difficulties in diagnosis, combined with some of the complications associated with shunting, have led many in the neurologic community to hold a rather pessimistic view of NPH treatment. He also comments that myths about NPH abound and include the following: (1) NPH can be diagnosed only when patients exhibit the full triad of incontinence, dementia, and gait apraxia; (2) ventricular size strongly correlates with the degree of gait disturbance; (3) shunting is seldom worthwhile because of its high rate of complications; and (4) if patients are unresponsive to a CSF

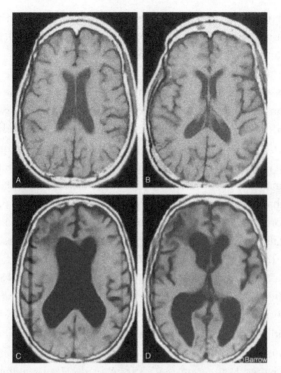

FIGURE 9.4 Increased intracranial pressure due to abnormal accumulation of cerebrospinal fluid and its effects on ventricular size in a patient with normal pressure hydrocephalus (C, D) relative to a normal individual (A, B).
Reprinted from Fife (2003), with permission.

removal trial, then they will not respond to shunting. Safer and more effective shunt methods should reinvigorate efforts to identify patients most likely to benefit from CSF shunting, as will detailed cognitive characterization of the patient with suspected NPH.

The cognitive features of NPH appear to be driven by frontal systems dysfunction and include "executive" dysfunction, impaired learning and memory, and reduced information processing speed. A study comparing the performance of patients with NPH to that of healthy elderly individuals on the CANTAB neuropsychological test battery revealed deficits on subtests of spatial recognition memory and intradimensional and extradimensional shifts of attention (Iddon et al., 1999). On the latter subtest, patients with NPH were more impaired than patients with AD. Improvement in these executive function deficits was observed following shunting to reduce intracranial pressure in demented, but not in nondemented, patients with NPH. A study that compared patients with NPH to those with Binswanger's disease (i.e., vascular encephalopathy characterized by subcortical arteriolopathy, demyelination of the centrum semiovale, and deep infarcts) showed that both groups were impaired on all measures of a battery of tests that assessed executive functions and episodic memory, and that those with NPH were significantly more impaired than those with Binswanger's disease on a test of phrase construction, spatial memory span, and delayed recall on the Rey Auditory Verbal Learning Test (Gallassi et al., 1991). The disproportionately severe executive function deficits associated with NPH were shown in another study that compared their performance on the Wechsler Memory Scale-Revised (WMS-R) and the WAIS-R to that of patients with AD (Ogino et al., 2006). While patients with AD were more impaired than those with NPH on the General Memory and Delayed Recall measures of the WMS-R, patients with NPH performed significantly worse than AD patients on the WMS-R Attention/Concentration subtest and the Digit Span, Arithmetic, Block Design, and Digit Symbol Substitution subtests of the WAIS-R. A similar study that included more severely demented patients with idiopathic NPH showed that, when their memory deficit is as severe as patients with AD, they have significantly greater deficits than the AD patients on tests of executive function (e.g., phonemic fluency, Frontal Assessment Battery), attention (e.g., Part A of the Trail-Making Test), and visuospatial abilities (e.g., discrimination of complex forms and visual counting) (Saito et al., 2011). In an earlier study it was shown that the severity of the executive function deficit in patients with NPH was correlated with the severity of their gait disturbance (Miyoshi et al., 2005).

Despite circumspection over the value of shunting (Klassen & Ahlskog, 2011), several studies have shown that there can be significant recovery of cognitive abilities following CSF shunting. In one study, 40% to 60% of patients with NPH showed significant postshunt improvement on the Stroop Color-Word Interference Test, Part B of the Trail-Making Test, total learning on the RVALT, and delayed recall on the RAVLT and the Wechsler Memory Scale (Thomas et al., 2005). This finding replicated a study that compared preshunt performance of patients with NPH with their performance 6 to 12 months postshunt (Duinkerke et al., 2004). Several additional studies showed similar significant postshunt improvement on tests of executive function (e.g., Part B of the Trail-Making Test, Symbol-Digit Substitution Test), phonemic fluency (Backward Digit Span Test), attention (Part A of the Trail-Making Test), learning (total recalled on the learning trials of the RAVLT), and psychomotor performance (Perdue Pegboard test) (Gleichgerrcht et al., 2009;

Katzen et al., 2011; Mataro et al., 2003). Importantly, a methodological study that examined the effects of repeated cognitive testing in patients with NPH prior to CSF shunting showed that there were little or no practice effects on tests widely used to assesses the cognitive effects of shunting, validating the beneficial effects of the procedure (Solana et al., 2010). It should be noted, however, that AD comorbidity is high in elderly patients with NPH and may preclude cognitive improvement postshunt (Cabral et al., 2011).

Posterior Cortical Atrophy

Although deficits in visuospatial abilities and constructional praxis are usually not apparent in the very earliest stages of AD, there are somewhat rare instances when the disease initially presents with relatively circumscribed posterior cortical atrophy with dementia dominated by higher-order visual dysfunction (Caine, 2004; Mendez et al., 2002; Tang-Wai et al., 2004). This clinical syndrome of posterior cortical atrophy (PCA) is usually associated with AD pathology (i.e., neuritic plaques and neurofibrillary tangles), but may also occur in the presence of neuropathological changes of dementia with Lewy bodies or Creutzfeld-Jakob disease (described below) (Renner et al., 2004).

Neuropathologically, PCA is characterized by disproportionate atrophy and pathologic lesions in the occipital cortex and posterior parietal cortex relative to other cortical association areas (Hof et al., 1997; Renner et al., 2004). Posterior cortical dysfunction in patients with PCA has also been shown with PET, with particular involvement of the dorsal visual stream (Nestor et al., 2003). In the case of PCA due to AD, the neurofibrillary tangles and neuritic plaques in the posterior cortical regions are qualitatively identical to those in typical AD and have the same laminar distribution in the cortex (Hof et al., 1997). The disproportionately posterior cortical distribution of AD pathology in PCA has recently been demonstrated in vivo using PET imaging with Pittsburgh compound-B ($[^{11}C]$-PIB), an agent that binds to β amyloid (the main constituent of the plaque) in the brain (Tenovuo et al., 2008). The cause of the focal presentation of PCA is unknown.

Despite relatively preserved memory functions, intact language, and preserved judgment and insight, patients with PCA usually have prominent visual agnosia (sometimes including prosopagnosia) and constructional apraxia, and exhibit many or all of the features of Balint's syndrome including optic ataxia, gaze apraxia, and simultanagnosia (i.e., can detect visual details of an object but cannot organize them into a meaningful whole). They may also exhibit many or all of the components of Gerstmann's syndrome including acalculia, right-left disorientation, finger agnosia, and agraphia (Caine, 2004; Mendez et al., 2002; Renner et al., 2004; Tang-Wai et al., 2004). A visual field defect, decreased visual attention, impaired color perception, or decreased contrast sensitivity may also occur (Della Sala et al., 1996). As shown in Table 9.1, Mendez et al. (2002) summarized many of the above findings in the literature and suggested tentative criteria for the clinical diagnosis of PCA.

Creutzfelt-Jakob Disease

Creutzfelt-Jakob disease (CJD) is a neurodegenerative disease that produces rapidly progressive dementia with features of cortical dysfunction. The disease is transmissible through a virus-like proteinaceous infectious particle (prion) and produces a noninflammatory spongiform encephalopathy that is most apparent in the cortex and basal ganglia. Symptoms of CJD include gradual onset of dementia, anxiety, fatigue, dizziness, headache, impaired judgment, and abnormal behavior. Neurologic signs and symptoms that may occur include extrapyramidal signs (e.g., tremor, rigidity, dysarthria), limb weakness and deterioration of reflexes (due to pyramidal tract disease), cortical blindness, seizures, and EEG abnormalities (e.g., periodic sharp waves). CJD is rapidly progressive with the interval between initial symptoms and death usually only a few months to one year. The disease may occur sporadically or due to infection. There are also familial forms of the disease associated with a point mutation in the prion protein gene. CJD is rare with a prevalence of about 1 in one million people. Only about 10 to 15% of all cases are of the familial type.

Because of its rarity and the rapid course of the disease, there are few systematic studies of the neuropsychological deficits associated with CJD. There are, however, a number of case reports that support the idea that CJD produces a cortical dementia syndrome. These reports show that the cognitive presentation of CJD is highly variable but often includes one or more focal deficits such as primary visual loss, attention deficits with susceptibility to distraction from visual surroundings, aphasia characterized by anomia and paraphasic errors, difficulties in writing or spelling, and impaired memory with frank amnesia in some cases (Snowden et al., 2002; Zarei et al., 2002). Ataxia, occulomotor deficits (e.g., slow saccades), and cortical deafness have also been reported. These cortical neuropsychological deficits are consistent with diffusion-weighted MRI findings of diffuse asymmetric cortical abnormalities with minimal subcortical grey matter involvement (usually in the basal ganglia) (Bahn et al., 1997).

Table 9.1 Clinical Diagnostic Criteria for Posterior Cortical Atrophy Proposed by Mendez et al. (2002)

1. *Core Diagnostic Features* (all must be present)
   A. Insidious onset and gradual progression
   B. Presentation with visual complaints with intact primary visual functions
   C. Evidence of predominant complex visual disorder on examination
      Elements of Balint's syndrome
      Visual agnosia
      Dressing apraxia
      Environmental disorientation
   D. Proportionally less impaired deficits in memory and verbal fluency
   E. Relatively preserved insight with or without depression
2. *Supportive Diagnostic Features*
   A. Presenile onset
   B. Alexia
   C. Elements of Gerstmann's syndrome
   D. Ideomotor apraxia
   E. Physical examination within normal limits
   F. Investigations
   Neuropsychology: predominantly impaired perceptual deficits
   Brain imaging: predominantly occipitoparietal abnormality (especially on functional neuroimaging) with relative sparing of frontal and mesiotemporal regions

Recent studies of healthy presymptomatic individuals who carry the gene mutation for CJD suggest that cortical neuropsychological deficits are probably an early manifestation of the disease (Gigi et al., 2005). Gigi and colleagues (2005), for example, showed that gene carriers performed significantly worse than age-matched noncarriers from affected families on tests of visual perception, visual memory and attention, verbal learning, and object naming. This poor cognitive performance was accompanied by increased anxiety and was most evident in older presymptomatic gene carriers.

The neuropsychological impairment associated with a newly identified variant of CJD (vCJD) that is caused by the same prion strain that produces bovine spongiform encephalopathy in cattle has been described (Cordery et al., 2005; Kapur et al., 2003). Like the sporadic and genetic forms of the disease, vCJD leads to very rapid cognitive decline characterized by deficits in verbal and visual memory, attention, executive functions, and some aspects of language (e.g., verbal fluency). Perceptual deficits are less apparent than in the standard form of CJD. These cognitive deficits are an early manifestation of vCJD and may precede the development of psychiatric and behavioral symptoms in some cases.

Conclusion

Although the neurodegenerative diseases described above are rare, the ability to accurately identify the atypical dementia syndromes they engender, and to distinguish them from the typical dementia syndromes associated with more common disorders such as AD or PD, is important for treatment and prognosis. As progress is made with respect to treatments for the major forms of dementias, differential diagnosis from the more atypical dementias will assume increasing importance also. Careful description of the differences in patterns of impaired and relatively spared cognitive abilities associated with each disorder also allows inferences to be drawn about the role various brain structures and circuits play in supporting specific aspects of cognition. This knowledge can enhance the development of better methods of neuropsychological assessment and increase understanding of the functional architecture of the brain.

References

Aarsland, D., Litvan, I., Salmon, D., Galasko, D., Wentzel-Larsen, T., &Larsen, J. P. (2003). Performance on the Dementia Rating Scale in Parkinson's disease with dementia and dementia with Lewy bodies: Comparison with progressive supranuclear palsy and Alzheimer's disease. *Journal of Neurology, Neurosurgery, and Psychiatry, 74*, 1215–1220.

Albert, M. L., Feldman, R. G., &Willis, A. L. (1974). The "subcortical dementia" of progressive supranuclear palsy. *Journal of Neurology, Neurosurgery and Psychiatry, 37*, 121–130.

Bahn, M. M., Kido, D. K., Lin, W., &Perlman, A. L. (1997). Brain magnetic diffusion abnormalities in Creutzfeldt-Jakob disease. *Archives of Neurology, 54*, 1411–1415.

Bak, T., Caine, D., Hearn, V. C., &Hodges, J. R. (2006). Visuospatial functions in atypical parkinsonian syndromes. *Journal of Neurology, Neurosurgery, and Psychiatry*, 77, 454–456.

Bak, T. H., Crawford, L. M., Hearn, V. C., Mathuranath, P. S., &Hodges, J. R. (2005). Subcortical dementia revisited: Similarities and differences in cognitive function between progressive supranuclear palsy (PSP), corticobasal degeneration (CBD) and multiple system atrophy. *Neurocase*, 11, 268–273.

Balas, M., Balash, Y., Giladi, N., &Gurevich, T. (2010). Cognition in multiple system atrophy: Neuropsychological profile and interaction with mood. *Journal of Neural Transmission*, 117, 369–375.

Beatty, W. W., Salmon, D. P., Butters, N., Heindel, W. C., & Granholm, E. L. (1988). Retrograde amnesia in patients with Alzheimer's disease or Huntington's disease. *Neurobiology of Aging*, 9(2), 181–186.

Benton, A., & Hamsher, K. (1978). *Multilingual Aphasia Examination: Manual.* Iowa City: University of Iowa.

Berent, S., Giordani, B., Gilman, S., Trask, C. L., Little, R. J. A., Johanns, J. R., ... Koeppe, R. A. (2002). Patterns of neuropsychological performance in multiple system atrophy compared to sporadic and hereditary olivopontocerebellar atrophy. *Brain and Cognition*, 50, 194–206.

Bower, J. H., Maraganore, D. M., McDonnell, S. K., & Rocca, W. A. (1997). Incidence of progressive supranuclear palsy and multiple system atrophy in Olmsted county, Minnesota, 1976 to 1990. *Neurology*, 49, 1284–1288.

Brown, R. G., Lacomblez, L., Landwehrmeyer, B. G., Bak, T., Uttner, I., Dubois, B., ... Leigh, N. (2010). Cognitive impairment in patients with multiple system atrophy and progressive supranuclear palsy. *Brain*, 133, 2382–2393.

Burk, K., Daum, I., &Rub, U. (2006). Cognitive function in multiple system atrophy of the cerebellar type. *Movement Disorders*, 21, 772–776.

Cabral, D., Beach, T. G., Vedders, L., Sue, L. I., Jacobson, S., Myers, K., &Sabbagh, M. N. (2011). Frequency of Alzheimer's disease pathology at autopsy in patients with clinical normal pressure hydrocephalus. *Alzheimer's and Dementia*, 7, 509–513.

Caine, D. (2004). Posterior cortical atrophy: A review of the literature. *Neurocase*, 10, 382–385.

Cambier, J., Masson, M., Viader, F., Limodin, J., &Strube, A. (1985). Frontal syndrome of progressive supranuclear palsy. *Revue Neurologique*, 141, 528–536.

Chang, C. C., Chang, Y. Y., Chang, W. N., Lee, Y. C., Lui, C. C., Huang, C. W., &Liu, W. L. (2009). Cognitive deficits in multiple system atrophy correlate with frontal atrophy and disease duration. *European Journal of Neurology, 16,* 1144–1150.

Cordery, R. J., Alner, K., Cipolotti, L., Kennedy, A., Collinge, J., &Rossor, M. N. (2005). The neuropsychology of variant CJD: a comparative study with inherited and sporadic forms of prion disease. *Journal of Neurology, Neurosurgery, and Psychiatry, 76,* 330–336.

Della Sala, S., Spinnler, H., &Trivelli, C. (1996). Slowly progressive impairment of spatial exploration and visual perception. *Neurocase, 2,* 299–323.

Dickson, D.W. (1999). Neuropathologic differentiation of progressive supranuclear palsy and corticobasal degeneration. *Journal of Neurology, 246,* 6–15.

Duinkerke, A., Williams, M. A., Rigamonti, D., &Hillis, A. E. (2004). Cognitive recovery in normal pressure hydrocephalus after shunt. *Cognitive and Behavioral Neurology, 17,* 179–184.

Esmonde, T., Giles, E., Gibson, M., &Hodges, J. R. (1996). Neuropsychological performance, disease severity, and depression in progressive supranuclear palsy. *Journal of Neurology, 243,* 638–643.

Fife, T. D. (2003). Clinical features of normal pressure hydrocephalus. *Barrow Quarterly, 19*(2).

Gallassi, R., Morreale, A., Montagna, P., Sacquegna, T., Di Sarro, R., &Lugaresi, E. (1991). Binswanger's disease and normal pressure hydrocephalus: Clinical and neuropsychological comparison. *Archives of Neurology, 48,* 1156–1159.

Gibb, W. R., Luthert, P. J., &Marsden, C.D. (1989). Corticobasal degeneration. *Brain, 112,* 1171–1192.

Gigi, A., Vakil, E., Kahana, E., &Hadar, U. (2005). Presymptomatic signs in healthy CJD mutation carriers. *Dementia and Geriatric Cognitive Disorders, 19,* 246–255.

Gleichgerrcht, E., Cervio, A., Salvat, J., Loffredo, A. R., Vita, L., Roca, M.,... Manes, F. (2009). Executive function improvement in normal pressure hydrocephalus following shunt surgery. *Behavioral Neurology, 21,* 181–185.

Grafman, J., Litvan, I., Gomez, C., &Chase, T. N. (1990). Frontal lobe function in progressive supranuclear palsy. *Archives of Neurology, 47,* 553–558.

Graham, N. L., Bak, T., Patterson, K., &Hodges, J. R. (2003). Language function and dysfunction in corticobasal degeneration. *Neurology, 61,* 493–499.

Gröschel, K., Hauser, T. K., Luft, A., Patronas, N., Dichgans, J., Litvan, I., &Schulz, J. B. (2004). Magnetic resonance imaging-based volumetry differentiates progressive supranuclear palsy from corticobasal degeneration. *Neuroimage*, *21*, 714–724.

Hakin, S., &Adams, R. D. (1965). The special clinical problem of symptomatic hydrocephalus with normal cerebrospinal fluid pressure observations on cerebrospinal fluid hydrodynamics. *Journal of Neurological Science*, *2*, 307–327.

Halliday, G. M., Holton, J. L., Revesz, T., &Dickson, D. W. (2011). Neuropathology underlying clinical variability in patients with synucleinopathies. *Acta Neuropathologica, 122*, 187–204.

Halpern, C., Clark, R., Moore, P., Antani, S., Colcher, A., &Grossman, M. (2004). Verbal mediation of number knowledge: evidence from semantic dementia and corticobasal degeneration. *Brain and Cognition*, *56*, 107–15.

Hauw, J. J., Daniel, S. E., Dickson, D., Horoupian, D. S., Jellinger, K., Lantos, P. L.,…Litvan, I. (1994). Preliminary NINDS neuropathologic criteria for Steele-Richardson-Olszewski syndrome (progressive supranuclear palsy). *Neurology*, *44*, 2015–2019.

Hof, P. R., Vogt, B. A., Bouras, C., &Morrison, J. H. (1997). Atypical form of Alzheimer's disease with prominent posterior cortical atrophy: a review of lesion distribution and circuit disconnection in cortical visual pathways. *Vision Research*, *37*, 3609–3625.

Iddon, J. L., Pickard, J. D., Cross, J. J. L., Griffiths, P. D., Czosnyka, M., &Sahakian, B. J. (1999). Specific patterns of cognitive impairment in patients with idiopathic normal pressure hydrocephalus and Alzheimer's disease: A pilot study. *Journal of Neurology, Neurosurgery, and Psychiatry*, *67*, 723–732.

Ivnik, R., Malec, J., Smith, G., Tangalos, E., Petersen, R., Kokmen, E., & Kurland, L. (1992). Mayo's Older Americans Normative Studies: Updated AVLT norms for ages 56–97. *The Clinical Neuropsychologist*, *6*, 83–104.

Kao, A. W., Racine, C. A., Quitania, L. C., Kramer, J. H., Christine, C. W., &Miller, B. L. (2009). Cognitive and neuropsychiatric profile of the synucleinopathies: Parkinson's disease, dementia with Lewy bodies and multiple system atrophy. *Alzheimer's Disease and Associated Disorders*, *23*, 365–370.

Kaplan, E., Goodglass, H., & Weintraub, S. (1983). *The Boston Naming Test* (2nd ed.). Philadelphia: Lea & Febiger.

Kapur, N., Abbott, P., Lowman, A., &Will, R. G. (2003). The neuropsychological profile associated with variant Creutzfeldt-Jakob disease. *Brain*, *126*, 2693–2702.

Katzen, H., Ravdin, L. D., Assuras, S., Heros, R., Kaplitt, M., Schwartz, T. H.,…Relkin, N. R. (2011). Postshunt cognitive and functional improvement in idiopathic normal pressure hydrocephalus. *Neurosurgery*, *68*, 416–419.

Kawai, Y., Suenaga, M., Takeda, A., Ito, M., Watanabe, H., Tanaka, F., ... Sobue, G. (2008). Cognitive impairments in multiple system atrophy: MAS-C vs MSA-P. *Neurology, 70,* 1390–1396.

Kertesz, A., &McMonagle, P. (2010). Behavior and cognition in corticobasal degeneration and progressive supranuclear palsy. *Journal of Neurological Sciences, 289,* 138–143.

Klassen, B. T., & Ahlskog, J. E. (2011). Normal pressure hydrocephalus: How often does the diagnosis hold water? *Neurology, 77,* 1111–1125.

Koenig, P., Smith, E. E., Moore, P., Glosser, G., &Grossman, M. (2007). Categorization of novel animals by patients with Alzheimer's disease and corticobasal degeneration. *Neuropsychology, 21,* 193–206.

Lange, K. W., Tucha, O., Alders, G. L., Preier, M., Csoti, I., Merz, B., ... Naumann, M. (2003). Differentiation of parkinsonian syndromes according to differences in executive functions. *Journal of Neural Transmission, 110,* 983–995.

Litvan, I. (1994). Cognitive disturbances in progressive supranuclear palsy. *Journal of Neural Transmission, 42,* 69–78.

Litvan, I., Grafman, J., Gomez, C., &Chase, T. N. (1989). Memory impairment in patients with progressive supranuclear palsy. *Archives of Neurology, 46,* 765–767.

Mahapatra, R. K., Edwards, M. J., Schott, J. M., &Bhatia, K. P. (2004). Corticobasal degeneration. *Lancet Neurology, 3,* 736–743.

Maher, E. R., Smith, E. M., &Lees, A. J. (1985). Cognitive deficits in the Steele-Richardson-Olszewski syndrome (progressive supranuclear palsy). *Journal of Neurology, Neurosurgery and Psychiatry, 48,* 1234–1239.

Massman, P. J., Kreiter, K. T., Jankovic, J., &Doody, R. S. (1996). Neuropsychological functioning in cortical-basal ganglionic degeneration: Differentiation from Alzheimer's disease. *Neurology, 46,* 720–726.

Mataro, M., Poca, M. A., Matarin, M., Catalan, R., Sahuquillo, J., &Galard, R. (2003). CSF galanin and cognition after shunt surgery in normal pressure hydrocephalus. *Journal of Neurology, Neurosurgery, and Psychiatry, 74,* 1272–1277.

Mathew, R., Bak, T., &Hodges, J. R. (2011). Screening for cognitive dysfunction in corticobasal syndrome: Utility of Addenbrooke's cognitive examination. *Dementia and Geriatric Cognitive Disorders, 31,* 254–258.

Mattis, S. (1988). *Dementia Rating Scale: Professional Manual.* Odessa, FL: Psychological Assessment Resources Inc.

McHugh, P. R., & Folstein, M. F. (1975). Psychiatric symptoms of Huntington's chorea: A clinical and phenomenologic study. In D. F. Benson & D. Blumer

---

(Eds.), *Psychiatric aspects of neurological disease* (pp. 267–285). New York: Raven Press.

Meco, G., Gasparini, M., &Doricchi, F. (1996). Attentional functions in multiple system atrophy and Parkinson's disease. *Journal of Neurology, Neurosurgery, and Psychiatry*, *60*, 393–398.

Mendez, M. F., Ghajarania, M., Perryman & K. M. (2002). Posterior cortical atrophy: Clinical characteristics and differences compared to Alzheimer's disease. *Dementia and Geriatric Cognitive Disorders*, *14*, 33–40.

Milberg, W., &Albert, M. (1989). Cognitive differences between patients with progressive supranuclear palsy and Alzheimer's disease. *Journal of Clinical and Experimental Neuropsychology*, *11*, 605–614.

Millar, D., Griffiths, P., Zermansky, A. J., &Burn, D.J. (2006). Characterizing behavioral and cognitive dysexecutive changes in progressive supranuclear palsy. *Movement Disorders*, *21*, 199–207.

Miyoshi, N., Kazui, H., Ogino, A., Ishikawa, M., Miyake, H., Tokunaga, H., Ikejiri, Y., & Takeda, M. (2005). Association between cognitive impairment and gait disturbance in patients with idiopathic normal pressure hydrocephalus. *Dementia and Geriatric Cognitive Disorders*, *20*(2–3), 71–76.

Nestor, P. J., Caine, D., Fryer, T. D., Clarke, J., &Hodges, J. R. (2003). The topography of metabolic deficits in posterior cortical atrophy (the visual variant of Alzheimer's disease) with FDG-PET. *Journal of Neurology, Neurosurgery, and Psychiatry*, *74*, 1521–1529.

Ogino, A., Kazui, H., Miyoshi, N., Hashimoto, M., Ohkawa, S., Tokunaga, H.,...Takeda, M. (2006). Cognitive impairment in patients with idiopathic normal pressure hydrocephalus. *Dementia and Geriatric Cognitive Disorders*, *21*, 113–119.

Okuda, B., Tachibana, H., Kawabata, K., Takeda, M., &Sugita, M. (2000). Cerebral blood flow in corticobasal degeneration and progressive supranuclear palsy. *Alzheimer's Disease and Associated Disorders*, *14*, 46–52.

Pillon, B., Blin, J., Vidailhet, M., Deweer, B., Sirigu, A., Dubois, B., &Agid, Y. (1995). The neuropsychological pattern of corticobasal degeneration: Comparison with progressive supranuclear palsy and Alzheimer's disease. *Neurology*, *45*, 1477–1483.

Pillon, B., Dubois, B., Lhermitte, F., &Agid, Y. (1986). Heterogeneity of cognitive impairment in progressive supranuclear palsy, Parkinson's disease, and Alzheimer's disease. *Neurology*, *36*, 1179–85.

Pillon, B., Dubois, B., Ploska, A., &Agid, Y. (1991). Severity and specificity of cognitive impairment in Alzheimer's, Huntington's, and Parkinson's diseases and progressive supranuclear palsy. *Neurology*, *41*, 634–43.

Renner, J. A., Burns, J. M., Hou, C. E., McKeel, D. W., Storandt, M., &Morris, J. C. (2004). Progressive posterior cortical dysfunction: A clinicopathologic series. *Neurology, 63*, 1175–1180.

Rey, A. (1964). *L'examen clinique en psychologie.* Paris: Presses Universitaires de France.

Robbins, T. W., James, M., Lange, K. W., Owen, A. M., Quinn, N. P., &Marsden, C. D. (1992). Cognitive performance in multiple system atrophy. *Brain, 115*, 271–291.

Rosser, A., &Hodges, J. R. (1994). Initial letter and semantic category fluency in Alzheimer's disease, Huntington's disease, and progressive supranuclear palsy. *Journal of Neurology, Neurosurgery and Psychiatry, 57*, 1389–1394.

Saito, M., Nishio, Y., Kanno, S., Uchiyama, M., Hayashi, A., Takagi, M., … Mori, E. (2011). Cognitive profile of idiopathic normal pressure hydrocephalus. *Dementia and Geriatric Cognitive Disorders, 1*, 202–211.

Snowden, J. S., Mann, D. M. A., & Neary, D. (2002). Distinct neuropsychological characteristics in Creutzfeldt-Jakob disease. *Journal of Neurology, Neurosurgery, and Psychiatry, 73*, 686–694.

Solana, E., Poca, M. A., Sahuquillo, J., Benejam, B., Junque, C., & Dronavalli, M. (2010). Cognitive and motor improvement after retesting in normal pressure hydrocephalus: A real change or merely a learning effect? *Journal of Neurosurgery, 112*, 399–409.

Soliveri, P., Monza, D., Paridi, D., Carella, F., Genitrini, S., Testa, D., &Girotti, F. (2000). Neuropsychological follow up in patients with Parkinson's disease, striatonigral degeneration-type multisystem atrophy, and progressive supranuclear palsy. *Journal of Neurology, Neurosurgery and Psychiatry, 69*, 313–318.

Soliveri, P., Monza, D., Paridi, D., Radice, D., Grisoli, M., Testa, D., … Girotti, F. (1999). Cognitive and magnetic resonance imaging aspects of corticobasal degeneration and progressive supranuclear palsy. *Neurology, 53*, 502–507.

Soliveri, P., Piacentini, S., &Girotti, F. (2005). Limb apraxia and cognitive impairment in progressive supranuclear palsy. *Neurocase, 11*, 263–267.

Steele, J. C., Richardson, J. C., &Olszewski, J. (1964). Progressive supranuclear palsy: A heterogeneous degeneration involving the brain stem, basal ganglia and cerebellum with vertical gaze and pseudobulbar palsy, nuchal dystonia and dementia. *Archives of Neurology, 10*, 333–59.

Taki, M., Ishii, K., Fukuda, T., Kojima, Y., & Mori. E. (2004). Evaluation of cortical atrophy between progressive supranuclear palsy and corticobasal degeneration by hemispheric surface display of MR images. *American Journal of Neuroradiology, 25*, 1709–14.

Tang-Wai, D. F., Graff-Radford, N. R., Boeve, B. F., Dickson, D. W., Parisi, J. E., Crook, R.,... Petersen, R.C. (2004). Clinical, genetic, and neuropathologic characteristics of posterior cortical atrophy. *Neurology, 63,* 1168–1174.

Tenovuo, O., Kemppainen, N., Aalto, S., Nagren, K., &Rinne, J.O. (2008). Posterior cortical atrophy: A rare form of dementia with in vivo evidence of amyloid-B accumulation. *Journal of Alzheimer's Disease, 15,* 351–355.

Testa, D., Fetoni, V., Soliveri, P., Musicco, M., Palazzini, E., &Girotti, F. (1993). Cognitive and motor performance in multiple system atrophy and Parkinson's disease compared. *Neuropsychologia, 31,* 207–210.

Thomas, G., McGirt, M. J., Woodworth, G. F., Heidler, J., Rigamonti, D., Hillis, A. E., &Williams, M. A. (2005). Baseline neuropsychological profile and cognitive response to cerebrospinal fluid shunting for idiopathic normal pressure hydrocephalus. *Dementia and Geriatric Cognitive Disorders, 20,* 163–168.

Wechsler, D. (1987). *Wechsler Memory Scale-Revised.* New York: Psychological Corporation.

Wechsler, D. (1997). *Wechsler Adult Intelligence Scale-III.* New York: Psychological Corporation.

Wilkinson, G. S. (1993). *Wide Range Achievement Test-Third edition administration manual* Wilmington, DE: Wide Range.

Van der Hurk, P. R., &Hodges, J. R. (1995). Episodic and semantic memory in Alzheimer's disease and progressive supranuclear palsy: A comparative study. *Journal of Clinical and Experimental Neuropsychology, 17,* 459–471.

Vanneste, J. A. (2000). Diagnosis and management of normal-pressure hydrocephalus. *Journal of Neurology, 247,* 5–14.

Zarei, M., Nouraei, S. A. R., Caine, D., Hodges, J. R., &Carpenter, R. H. S. (2002). Neuropsychological and quantitative oculometric study of a case of sporadic Creutzfeldt-Jakob disease at predementia stage. *Journal of Neurology, Neurosurgery, and Psychiatry, 73,* 56–58.

Zarei, M., Pouretemad, H. R., Bak, T., &Hodges, J. R. (2010). Autobiographical memory in progressive supranuclear palsy. *European Journal of Neurology, 17,* 238–241.

10

■ ■ ■

Interventions for the Behavioral Disturbances of Dementia

Case Presentation No. I

Chief Complaint/Reason for Visit

A regional assisted living facility requested consultation on a fairly new male resident. The patient's daughters and nurses, nurse aides, and activities director from the facility were present for the consult. The consulting team included a medical psychiatrist, an internal medicine resident, and a clinical neuropsychologist. Behaviors of concern included: wandering and wanting to go home, constantly looking for reassurance and asking that his daughter be contacted. He at times had made sexual comments during personal cares but not recently, and he had been involved in sexual touching with female staff when personal cares were involved.

The evaluation was conducted via 2-way fully interactive video (Skype) technology.

History of Present Illness

The patient was an 86-year-old man with a progressive dementia who had been in independent living prior to moving to the memory unit four months earlier. He had been having gradually progressive memory difficulties; but after a significant illness with a bladder infection or perhaps

(continued)

---

a CVA (he was not completely assessed given his age and cognitive status), his cognition and behaviors worsened.

The staff had tried several behavioral interventions that had been somewhat successful. He was sleeping reasonably well. His weight was stable. He occasionally became tearful when he believed his wife had just passed away (she had actually been dead for several years), but generally he was calm and pleasant. He could at times be engaged in activities and enjoy these things. He was not seen by the staff or the family as being overtly depressed or anxious on a consistent basis.

He had recently been started on a low dose of Zoloft as well as Seroquel. Initially, he was thought to be somewhat unsteady on his feet with the addition of the Seroquel in conjunction with Ativan, so the Ativan was discontinued. He appeared to be tolerating the medication well, with perhaps some improvement in his behaviors. He had no known history of any kind of psychiatric disturbance prior to the onset of his dementia.

Mental Status Examination
The mental status examination was conducted via video technology. The patient had difficulty with hearing, so nursing staff and the patient's daughter helped by repeating nearly all of the questions. The patient was generally cooperative during the exam. He was not oriented to aspects of date except for day and season. He was oriented to town and state, but not the fact that he was in a care facility. He could register only two of three items adequately, and was not able to retrieve any of this information after delay. Language was spared for naming, and generally for repetition. Mini mental status score was 14 out of 30. Mood seemed generally euthymic. He was able to joke and showed no evidence of irritability or anxiousness.

Impression/Report/Plan
The patient had a progressive dementia of at least moderate severity. His daughter seemed to serve as an "anchor" or presence to reassure him in his confusion and disorientation. We recommended the following:

1. Use "surrogates" of the daughter in order to provide regular reassurance. This was accomplished by having the daughter create short videos and 10 to 15 little cards or letters that provide simple, reassuring messages like, "Dad-I'm thinking of you. I know you are doing your best there. Stay put and keep it up.

Love, Liz." The video and/or cards were to be provided to the staff. Periodically throughout the day, staff were to redirect him to watch the video or provide the card to the patient, saying, "Here, your daughter Liz sent this to you." Later, the staff would retrieve the video/cards from the patient's room and use them over again.

2. Create an activities bag for the patient that might have blocks of wood and sand paper, quilting patches, parts of a milking machine, and so forth. Staff could pull something out as they walked by and ask Lyle's help in sanding, sorting, polishing, and so on.

3. Emphasize the use of the first two strategies in the afternoons, or at that time when the patient was most likely to start searching for his daughter and wanting to leave.

4. We reemphasized good communication practices when approaching for cares, for example, staff should identify themselves and their purpose ("I am your nursing assistant Kelly, I am here to give you your shower"). Staff should also understand that sexual comments reflect the disinhibition of dementia, and to respond in a matter-of-fact but clear fashion ("No, that is not why we are here. Let's finish changing you").

Case Presentation No. 2
Chief Complaint/Reason for Visit
A local dementia care facility requested consultation on a 64-year-old new resident. Behaviors of concern included her being verbally very loud and repetitive, causing agitation in other residents in her facility, which led to verbally abusive interchanges between the patient and other residents.

History of Present Illness
The patient was a generally pleasant 64-year-old woman who just moved from out of state to a local dementia care facility to be near her son. He had power of attorney. The patient was a poor historian. Most of the time, she just repeated the questions asked of her. Twenty-four years earlier she had a grand mal seizure. She was started on Dilantin and was found to have a meningioma. Twenty-two years ago, she had her left-sided meningioma removed. After that, she had another grand mal seizure, but for the last 12 years she had

(continued)

no seizures. At the time of evaluation, she was on Dilantin and stable with this medication regimen. According to her son she had displayed some forgetfulness for about 4 to 5 years, and was unable to manage her money. She also was in a minor motor vehicle accident. For the last 3 years, after she lost her husband, her memory impairment was getting worse, and she had stopped communicating. She was more forgetful. She was completely unable to manage financial issues. She started to have some urinary incontinence and sometimes bowel incontinence. She had a couple of psychiatric evaluations, and a psychiatric admission a year ago. At that time, she had stopped taking all of her medications, and she had an episode of paranoid ideations and thought that someone was going to kill her. After the admission and restarting all her medications, her paranoid thinking abated. Per her son, she had an MRI scan in 2007 that showed some decrease in the frontal lobe size. At the time of her evaluation, at the dementia care facility she was generally calm but sometimes got angry when they wanted to give her a bath or shower. She sometimes yelled at the TV. She had some auditory hallucinations and thought that her dead husband talked to her, but she denied any significant visual hallucinations. She denied any acting out dreams, nor was she observed to have any such acting out dreams. She and her son denied any tremors or falls or gait problems. She was cooperative with taking her medications, but she could not manage her medications by herself.

Social History
She was a smoker until 1986 and quit. She denied significant alcohol use. At the time of the evaluation, she was residing in an assisted living facility.

Family History
Her father died of leukemia. Her mother had coronary artery disease and Alzheimer's disease diagnosed in her mid-60s. One of her older sisters had dementia at about age 60. One of her younger sisters also started to have dementia symptoms around the time of this consult.

Medications
Prilosec 20 mg one tablet by mouth daily.
Phenytoin EX 100 mg one tablet by mouth three times daily.
Aricept 10 mg one tablet by mouth daily.
Risperdal 0.5 mg one tablet by mouth three times daily.

Cymbalta 60 mg one tablet by mouth daily.
Seroquel 25 mg one to two tablets by mouth daily.

Mental Status Examination
The patient was seated in a common area, waiting for her scheduled trip to Wal-Mart when approached for mental status examination. When told we were going to relocate to another room to do the mental status examination, she said "NO" very loudly, but then got up and started walking to the next room. This was apparently typical of her to engage in these impulsive "no" responses to any requests, but she was generally compliant and cooperative. The patient would repeat every question asked of her and every statement made by others and was thus obviously quite echolalic. She was grossly oriented to place and time and could register three objects in a single trial. She had difficulty with serial subtraction and backward spelling, suggesting prominent concentration and sequencing problems. She had trouble with retrieval and recognition. She was unable to recall three previously presented objects. This may have overestimated her memory deficits, because her attention and concentration deficits, as well as perseverative behaviors, complicated assessment. The patient was clearly able to learn the names of the staff who provided care for her and was exquisitely attentive in prospective memory, such as knowing about her scheduled trip to Wal-Mart. Language was generally preserved, in spite of the echolalia. For example, after repeating the question, she could name two objects. She had no difficulty repeating a saying. After repeating a written statement aloud several times, she was finally able to be cued to comply with the written statement and was able to follow two steps of the three-step command. Overall, she obtained a score of approximately 20 out of 30 on the mini mental status examination. Her deficits were not so much in the areas of language and memory and reasoning, but rather centered on problems with impulsivity, perseveration, initiation, and sequencing. For example, she was not able to initiate counting down from 20 to 1; however, she could comply when prompted with 20, 19, 18, and so on. She made it down to 13, lost her place and when cued, started counting up rather than down.

Impression/Recommendations
The patient had a fairly classic pattern of behavioral variant frontotemporal dementia with prominent perseveration and impulsivity. This

(continued)

impulsivity led her to blurt out responses like "no," even though she readily complied with such requests, and to be repetitious or echolalic (she repeated exactly what she had heard). The patient showed concomitant problems with being drawn to stimuli, which is a mild utilization-type or stimulus bound phenomenon. So, for example, when given the full book of songs at music time, she could not keep herself from flipping to the next song and the next song and getting ahead of the group. The same impulsiveness is probably what led to her poor modulation of her loudness, as well as her inability to suppress repeating what she just heard.

Given this constellation of symptoms, we made the following recommendations:

1. Use her perseverative repetition to try and increase the likelihood that she is blurting out acceptable comments rather than her inappropriate comments. For example, start regularly cueing her throughout the day by saying to her, "I love this place." Then try and get her to repeat that with some frequency. Or try, "We love you," as an alternate statement. These kinds of statements could also be posted on banners around her room or the facility, since she impulsively tends to read things.

2. Build on her need for order and routine and her tendency to perseverate by tightly scheduling her day in a way that keeps her busy and away from the overstimulating and unstructured milieu. Have a time of day for her to do "paperwork"; have a time of day where she listens to music in her room; have a specific time of day where she watches some routine television programs; and, provide to her a checklist of her day so she can go through and check off those activities.

3. She had a characteristic chair that she sat in and got agitated when others tried to use it. We suggested moving that chair to a less busy area to reduce the frequency with which other people ended up sitting in that chair.

4. We encouraged her son to participate in one of the Department of Neurology's frontotemporal dementia education programs.

Introduction

Cases such as the two above are often referred to geriatric psychiatry inpatient units or other similar settings. A common pattern emerges. The patient is admitted from the nursing home through the emergency room, described as "uncontrollable" by the care facility. On interview they are docile and pleasant and have no recollection of any recent events of behavioral disturbance. This person is nevertheless admitted for observation. During the course of the 24–72 hours, there are no episodes of behavioral disturbance. Just in case, a tranquilizing medication (anxiolytic or atypical anti-psychotic agent) is started as a matter of prophylaxis, but the ability to assess efficacy is limited by the absence of any target behaviors observed on the unit. The facility is contacted regarding return but is resistant, saying they lack the capacity to care for the patient. Another facility is contacted but resistant to accept the patient because of his or her history of agitation. The family is distressed that no one will provide care for their loved one. Ultimately, social work "strong arms" the original facility into taking the patient back with threat of turning the case over to state regulators. Within 24–48 hours the facility is seeking readmission stating that the patient is no better. Ultimately this is a clear A-B-A behavioral design demonstrating that environmental factors, rather than patient factors, are mediating the disruptive behavior.

In the mid-1990s, this exact experience led to the creation of the Dementia Behavioral Assessment and Response Team (DBART) at Mayo Clinic in Rochester. This team provides outreach into regional facilities (now using Skype-like technologies) to assess dementia-related disruptive behavior in the environment in which it is occurring, and to emphasize environmental adaptation as an alternative or augmentation to medication as a solution to these challenging behaviors. This chapter provides a cursory description of some of the lessons learned from this experience.

Philosophy

Over the course of 15 years of service provision, the DBART team has recognized and been guided by five key axioms and their corollaries.

- Understand the dementia syndrome
- Behavior is communication
  - o Identify environmental, physical, psychological, and social mediators of behavior

- Manage antecedents not consequences
  - o This means be proactive not reactive
- Use what the dementia "gives"
- Do not create a behavioral vacuum
  - o Focus on activity-based care

Throughout this book, we have discussed the clinical syndromes associated with various common dementia subtypes. We have discussed, for example, that it is not uncommon to encounter visual hallucinations early in Lewy Body disease but only later in Alzheimer's disease. Thus, seeing visual hallucinations would raise concern about another process such as an emerging delirium early in AD, whereas these symptoms would be an expected part of the disorder in early DLB. Or, disrobing might be understood as simple disinhibition in an early FTD, versus a need to use the bathroom in advanced AD. Understanding the nature and extent of the dementia can help provide the context for understanding what behavior may be communicating.

Understand the Dementia Syndrome

The book has reviewed how different behavioral profiles associate with dementia etiologies, for example, fully formed visual hallucinations are common early in Lewy Body Dementia, impulsive behavior is a symptom of FTD, and an inability to learn (often without awareness of one's own deficit) is a hallmark of AD. Understanding these patterns facilitates appropriate intervention plans. Helping caregivers understand these patterns aids their adherence to intervention plans.

For example, understanding the new learning deficits in AD helps caregivers understand why frequent reorientation is an exercise in futility and may well be agitating to the person with Alzheimer's disease (and their caregiver!). Understanding this cognitive deficit can also clarify behaviors that otherwise get mislabeled. A person with AD will often forget where she placed valuables, like a purse. Being unaware of her forgetfulness she will assume others are stealing from her. So she will begin a vicious cycle of hiding her purse, again forgetting where it is, and thereby reconfirming to herself that someone is stealing from her. This behavior risks being labeled as "paranoia." Unfortunately, then, some health providers will hear family describe the patient as paranoid and prescribe antipsychotic medications without carefully assessing the situation. Likely the most appropriate intervention here is to have caregivers unobtrusively search living quarters for the purse.

Often, patients in care facilities have a generic dementia diagnosis without benefit of evaluation of the etiology of the dementia. By establishing etiology, the DBART team has had several positive outcomes in patients who were clearly oversedated after aggressive behavior resulted in use of antipsychotic medications. In these patients, we identified a remote history of REM sleep behavior disorder, fluctuating levels of arousal, hallucinations, and a poor ability to distinguish dream content from reality. We were able to clarify for caregivers the presence of Lewy Body disease, caution about the risks of neuroleptic sensitivity, and in a few cases add cholinesterase inhibitor therapies with significant benefit.

Behavior: A Key Form of Communication

Communication is adaptive for all people, generally a means toward need fulfillment. When language and reasoning are limited, communication is likely to be more overtly behavioral. In a young child, crying as a means of communicating hunger, pain, or fear is not considered a "behavior problem." In patients with dementia, as reasoning and language skills are lost, overt behavior will increasingly become a primary form of communication. Even when speech is intact, verbal communication is often limited by difficulties in expressing desired thoughts correctly. The behavior of patients with advanced dementia often represents an attempt to express feelings and needs that cannot be verbalized adequately. Labeling of unwanted behaviors as "bad" or "difficult" negates the adaptation that may be inherent in the behavior. Such labeling can foster a sense of futility or resignation. Patients with dementia typically lack the cognitive skill to be manipulative with their behaviors. Rather, behavioral problems arise from the disease process, resulting in primitive coping and communication styles (German, Rovner, Burton, Brant, & Clark, 1992).

Identifying Environmental, Physical, Psychological and Social Mediators

Patients with dementia present a wide array of challenging behaviors that can cause physical and emotional burdens for both caregivers and the patients themselves. To develop a plan for reducing these behaviors, caregivers and clinicians must thoroughly assess for mediators. The same calling out, wandering, restlessness, aggression, and other difficult behaviors might be the expression of an inner emotional state in one patient, a long-standing behavioral pattern in another, an unrecognized physical need in a third patient, and a reaction to an external stimulus in a fourth. If clinicians observe only the behavior itself and ignore the complex and interrelated components, intervention is likely to be ineffective.

Environment

The DBART team was called to consult on a nursing home resident who placed himself and others at risk by spending a significant amount of time on the dementia care unit sitting in front of an inward opening door. He would become agitated when people entering the unit swung the door into his wheelchair. The facility wanted advice on how to teach him not to sit there. Our recommendation was to reverse the hinges on the door so that it opened out. This is an example of how it is sometimes easier to adapt the environment, than to expect a dementia patient to adapt.

Because environmental factors can cause or exacerbate behavioral disturbances, patients with dementia should be evaluated in their typical living environments when possible. Depending on a person's level of impairment, nursing home patients may be at risk for understimulation or overstimulation, often leading to the development of undesirable behaviors. If bored, a patient may become restless and wander, attempt to escape, or become involved in self-stimulating behaviors, such as repeatedly calling out to caregivers (Hellen, 1992). As described below activities-based care can reduce understimulation.

Conversely, multiple simultaneous, or unnecessary stimuli may be difficult for the patient to interpret or may be overwhelming. Loud and repeated noise may lead to agitation (Robinson, Spencer, & White, 1988). Extraneous stimuli, such as television shows, may be misunderstood or mistaken for reality and cause patients with dementia to be frightened or angry. "Disembodied" voices from radios or overhead paging systems, or that result from whispering or laughing out of view, can similarly contribute to confusion, misperceptions, suspiciousness, and agitation. "Old-fashioned" music may be soothing to the patient, but modern music preferred by the young-adult care provider may be agitating. As a patient's language skills degenerate, they may become distressed in situations where there is high demand for language, such as congregate dining.

Familiar cues or personal belongings in the environment may reduce confusion, fear, and agitation. To compensate for sensory losses, environmental modifications such as reducing glare, increasing lighting, and using contrasting colors may enhance appropriate behavior (Whall et al., 1997). At later stages, dementia patients may need to take meals and engage in activities in social settings with smaller groups and less talking. A simple, consistent, and predictable environment will provide familiarity and comfort for the patient. Conversely, an environment poorly adapted to cognitive losses may cause the patient to misinterpret surroundings and events and either behave in socially inappropriate ways or withdraw (Dawson, Kline, Wiancko, & Wells, 1986).

Physical Factors

The DBART team was consulted on an advanced dementia patient with end-stage renal disease. He was combative before, during, and after his regular dialysis treatment. The behavior was "communicating" that he could not tolerate this process any longer. The challenge was that his (second) wife did not feel comfortable stopping dialysis without approval from the children of his first marriage. By convening the entire family and engaging in a palliative care discussion a consensus was reached that the patient would have wanted to discontinue therapy under these circumstances. He died about 2 weeks later.

This is an extreme example of the role of physical health factors in behavioral disturbance. It also illustrates that one of the most useful aspects of consultation is simply to get all the care stakeholders together to facilitate communications. In fact, our program evaluation data suggests that consumers value this as much as any other component of the process (see Figure 10.1).

More commonly, it is issues of unrecognized infection (e.g., urinary tract infection) or pain that are the physical health mediators of behavior. Dementia patients are often unable to describe the pain or physical symptoms that alert the care team to these factors. However, standard nursing home practices generally provide better support for assessing these issues, compared to the environmental and social factors described above and below. Generally, but not universally, physical factors have been assessed by the time the DBART team is recruited.

Some of the physical mediators of disruptive behavior are iatrogenic and reflect a failure to consider palliative approaches in advanced dementia care. It is not uncommon for the team to encounter a patient on diuretics whose sleep is disrupted due to the need to be changed at night secondary to incontinence and risk for skin break-down; or, to encounter a diabetic who is resistant to twice-daily blood testing. The pros and cons of tight hypertension or diabetes control in these patients should be reviewed with the appropriate medical decision makers.

Most Important Factors

FIGURE 10.1 Program evaluation data (N = 50) compiled from the Dementia Behavioral Assessment and Response Team (DBART) at the Mayo Clinic (Rochester, MN).

Psychological Factors

Estimates are that 40% of Alzheimer's disease patients will meet criteria for major depression at some point during the course of their illness. Ascertaining depression can be difficult, even in MCI stages, because patients may not be able to reliably respond to questions like "how has your mood been the past 2 weeks?" Of course, as the disease progresses, the patient's ability to understand concepts like "feeling blue" or "having low self-esteem" also diminishes. Informant reports on depression may be reliable, but since the informant must infer the patient's subjective state, informant report can be of dubious validity. A clinician is wise to consider the full range of self- and informant-report and behavioral observations when assessing for mood disorder in dementia.

Depression

The criteria for depression are well known and involve depressed mood and vegetative changes in sleep, appetite, and activity level. There is a tendency to interpret the term "depression" narrowly as depression, that is, sad mood. However, the term could encompass bad mood, or irritability, as well, and DSM-V proposes this accommodation for children and adolescents, but not for patients with cognitive impairment. The DBART team's experience is that

Mild Cognitive Impairment and Dementia

a significant proportion of the cases of "agitation" are cases where irritability is present along with vegetative changes. These patients have often responded well to antidepressant medication in combination with behavioral activation.

Anxiety

Imagine living in a condition where you are not sure of what has recently happened or what is going to happen. In this condition, it would be reasonable to be in a heightened state of anxiety. Such is the condition of many persons with memory impairment. The DBART team hypothesized with Case 1 above that his behavior was communicating anxiety, or at least a need for reassurance. Since family serves a powerful role in providing reassurance in dementia, but cannot be continually present, the team regularly suggests methods for creating family reassurance "surrogates."

Social Factors

A dementia care facility requested assistance with a resident that frequently tried to elope. Assessment revealed this behavior to occur primarily in the afternoon, especially between 3 and 4 p.m. Staff felt it might indicate "sundowning." Assessment of social history revealed the patient had worked in the post office, 7:00–4:00 for 20+ years. We noted that change of shift in the facility, with staff putting on coats to leave might be serving as a cue to the patient that it was time to go home from work to her family. We recommended the resident be provided a late afternoon activity in her room, and staff were encouraged to leave from obscured exits. The elopement efforts decreased substantially. We describe this as a social mediator, as it reflects on the patient's life history, overlearned behavior, and affiliation with family.

Social factors include the life experience of patients, their values, culture, family structure, history of preferences, and so forth. Despite progressive cognitive loss, older adults with dementia retain basic human needs, including the need to belong, to be loved, to be touched, to follow their values and to feel useful. Activities based care, as described below, can help address the need for patients to feel useful. Unfortunately, meaningful relationships and appropriate social groups can be unavailable or insufficiently matched to the functional level of such patients. The case of John O'Connor, husband of former Supreme Court Justice Sandra Day O'Connor, provides a poignant example of social mediators. While in a care facility he began to "court" another resident there. They would sit and hold hands. It is not clear whether he mistook this woman for Sandra, whether he had regressed to the point that he did not remember being married, or whether he was so impaired this was all moot. In any event, his need for affiliation persisted. Fortunately, rather than expect the facility to limit this behavior, Ms. O'Connor said, "If it makes him happy then I am happy."

Manage Antecedents Not Consequences

Applied behavioral analysis reminds us that all behavior occurs in a context. This has been described as the ABCs of behavior management: antecedent, behavior, consequence. For each behavior, there are antecedent conditions that provide a setting for the behavior and, in many cases, may increase the probability of the behavior occurring. Then there is the behavior itself, followed by the consequences of behavior. Much of traditional behavior management has focused on controlling the consequences in order to shape behavior. The classic example is of course placing a child in time-out for bad behavior and providing rewards for good behavior. However, the ability of an event happening after a behavior to influence the future probability of that behavior requires the event to form a new association with the prior behavior. Another name for that association is learning or recent memory. There must be a new trace formed to connect behavior and consequence. In dementia, the ability to form that association is increasingly suspect as the dementia progresses (and the probability of behavioral disturbance increases). For this reason, managing antecedents as opposed to applying consequences becomes increasingly important.

Managing antecedents means being proactive, not reactive. It means providing cues to desired behavior, rather than punishing unwanted behavior, or rewarding wanted behavior for that matter. In her extraordinary book, *Your Name Is Hughes Hannibal Shanks, A Caregivers Guide,* Lela Knox Shanks describes how her husband would urinate in the heat registers in the floor of their home. Sensing a hole in the ground might be a cue for this behavior, she proceeded to cover all the registers with cookie sheets while providing a commode in his vicinity. By managing the cues (i.e., antecedents), she was able to reduce this disruptive incontinence.

Use What the Dementia "Gives"

Managing disruptive behavior in dementia is challenging, and even the best intervention plans are unlikely to entirely eliminate disruptive behavior. However, management is made even more difficult if the proclivities and deficits created by the condition are not put to good use. In Case 2 above, rather than try to eliminate the echolalia and impulsivity of the FTD, the team encouraged the facility to modify the behavior to a more acceptable form.

Redirection is the most commonly used method of behavior management in most facilities. Simply put, it involves directing patients engaged in an undesired behavior to a more desirable behavior. Among the myriad situations in which redirection is used are when patients enter restricted areas, attempt to elope, or engage in problematic interpersonal exchanges. Redirection is often an antecedent to agitated or aggressive behavior, possibly because the behavior of patients with dementia is often goal-directed or purposeful. The patient may be unable to communicate the goal, or the goal may be nonsensical in our reality; however, in the patient's subjective reality, the goal is often important. Because redirection represents a thwarting of the goal-directed behavior, frustration and agitation should not be surprising. Mitigating this agitation may be possible, but redirection should be approached routinely as a multistep process. First, caregivers can validate the apparent emotional state of the patient (e.g., "You look worried"); this helps to establish rapport. Next and critically, the caregiver should join in the patient's behavior. For example, "You're looking for your parents? Well, I am trying to find something too. Let's look together." Once a common goal is established, distraction is easier ("Let's look over there where people are having coffee"). Distraction works best with patients who have severe memory or attention problems. Most patients with dementia have such problems. Finally, redirection ("That coffee smells good; do you want a cup?") may now be possible without directly thwarting the now-forgotten goal. This strategy may seem to require more time than simple redirection. However, facile caregivers can perform all steps quickly and ultimately save time because agitated behavior does not need to be managed.

Do Not Create a Behavioral Vacuum
Focus on Activity-Based Care

Adapting "chores" to patients' level of ability can address their desire to feel useful (Hellen, 1992). Planned activities should be "failure free," promoting a sense of success by accommodating the ability level of the patient. Meaningful activities should correspond to individual life history, current abilities, and attention spans when possible. Exercising existing abilities in a failure-free manner will provide reassurance and contribute to a sense of competence.

Caregivers can unintentionally contribute to a patient's disability in excess of that dictated by the disease. By reinforcing problematic behavior with attention and ignoring independent behavior, caregivers may foster patient disability or aggressive behavior. A patient with mild dementia who can still perform hygiene measures may be agitated by caregivers who insist on intervening to accelerate the process. When patients with dementia do not engage in certain common tasks, such as brushing their teeth or dressing themselves, these abilities can be lost prematurely. Thus, a patient's dependence on others may be increased, and a sense of helplessness and failure may be reinforced.

Examples of Behavior Problems
Wandering
Wandering is defined as moving about in an apparently aimless or disoriented manner. Yet from the perspective of the patient, wandering is not really aimless. He or she may need to find the bathroom, may be looking for a person or lost object, or may believe they need to go home or to work. Wandering may serve to communicate boredom, the need to exit a stressful situation, or a search for something familiar and comforting, as the primary problem (Hellen, 1992). Wandering may reflect lifelong patterns of coping with stress, the need to keep busy, or a search for security. Fortunately, many care providers no longer view wandering as a behavior problem as long as the person is not intruding into others' space. In fact, wandering provides a form of exercise and helps prevent social isolation (Snyder, Rupprecht, Pyrek, Brekhus, & Moss, 1978).

When intrusiveness is a problem, behavioral interventions should be the primary management approach for wandering. Interventions for wandering should be guided by what the behavior may be communicating about past patterns or current needs. For some patients, answers may differ from day to day, and their general mood may produce the key to interpreting the behavior. Sometimes, however, no answer is apparent. Caregivers might attempt to reduce wandering by providing meaningful activities and familiar objects or by planning regular exercise. When wandering becomes a safety issue, more restrictive environmental adaptations may be needed. In institutional settings, alarm systems, stop signs, concealed or camouflaged doors and doorknobs, and locks placed in unfamiliar places can be useful. A secured indoor or outdoor circular path can reduce concerns about escape or intrusiveness, although an identification bracelet or necklace and an updated photograph of the patient are recommended.

Agitation

Agitation is reported to occur in more than half of community-dwelling patients with dementia and affects up to 70% of nursing home residents (Folstein, Anthony, Parhad, Duffy, & Gruenberg, 1985). Agitation may be a behavioral manifestation of anxiety. It is a final common pathway for the expression of numerous symptoms, as patients with dementia experience progressively limited responses (Loebel & Leibovici, 1994). Common agitated behaviors can be classified as aggressive (kicking, pushing, grabbing, biting, scratching, spitting, and cursing), repetitious (repeating sentences, questions, words, or sounds), or socially objectionable actions (sexual disinhibition, screaming, and undressing or voiding in inappropriate places) (Cohen-Mansfield & Billig, 1986).

Behavioral management of agitation typically focuses on reducing the frequency and intensity of the behavior. If agitation is occurring during the provision of care to the patient, an effort to reduce the number of care interactions, and the risk of overstimulation, may help. Maximizing patients' sense of control in their environment may also reduce agitation. Providing reassuring objects such as written, audio, or video messages from family members can be helpful.

Sexual Behavior

The story of John O'Connor described above, focused a great deal of public attention on intimacy and sexuality issues as they pertain to dementia. The Chief Justice was lauded for accepting and permitting her husband's behavior, since it seemed to contribute to his (and the other woman's) contentment. On the other hand, DBART team has been consulted in many cases where residents were making sexually suggestive comments and/or attempting to touch other residents or professional care providers in unwanted and sexual ways.

An important assessment framework is to focus on level of risk. The Shalom Village Long Term Care Home, Hamilton, Ontario, Canada, has articulated one of best frameworks for managing sexual behavior in congregate dementia care settings (see www.rgpc.ca/rgpc_resource_library/sexualitypra cticeguidelinesllgdraft_17.pdf). This group describes five levels of risk and response as summarized in Table 10.1. This framework acknowledges that sexuality is a normal part of human behavior, and only constitutes a problem when it violates the dignity of the person with dementia, or the wishes of another. Lichtenberg and Strzepek (1990) provide one framework for assessing ability to consent.

Table 10.1 Sexual Behavior and Associated Levels of Risk in Dementia Patients

LEVEL	BEHAVIOR	RISK	POSSIBLE INTERVENTION
1	Intimacy/Courtship behaviors	Low (if both parties are consenting)	Reassure staff, families
2	Verbal sexual talk/ language directed to care providers	Low	Avoid punitive response Redirect
3	Self-directed sexual behaviors	Low	Protect privacy
4	Physical sexual behaviors directed toward coresident with agreement	Moderate	Assess ability of both parties to consent* Watch for signs of distress indicating nonconsent
5	Unwanted, overt physical sexual behaviors directed toward others	High	Direct intervention to protect "other" and resident.

As noted in Table 10.1 (level 5), there are instances where sexual behavior must be curtailed. This can be very challenging. Facilities often use a medication solution, but there are no well-controlled clinical trials regarding medical management of sexual behavior (Tucker, 2010). For behavior management strategies, it can be helpful to try to discern the extent to which the behavior reflects intimacy seeking versus disinhibition (de Medeiros, Rosenberg, Baker, & Onyike, 2008). Intimacy-seeking can often be addressed by increasing access to appropriate types of touch (e.g., shaking and/or holding hands; providing hand, arm, and shoulder massage; pet therapy, etc.). Disinhibited sexual behavior more typically requires redirection (e.g., providing privacy and cues for masturbation as an alternative to sexual behaviors directed to other residents).

Empirical Base

Unfortunately, there is not a vast empirical literature to support the types of recommendations described in this chapter. Though, frankly, there is little empirical basis for the usual kinds of treatments that are utilized on the aforementioned geriatric psychiatry units. In fact, recent meta-analyses have shown limited benefit of using neuroleptic medications in dementia patients, whereas their uses are associated with increased mortality (see Chapter 5). Unfortunately, tailored behavioral interventions for disruptive behaviors in dementia are not prioritized for clinical trials. Moreover, these behavioral interventions are not especially amenable to clinical trials—as the interventions recommended in this practice are highly individualized to each clinical situation. In fact, one of the great mistakes in dementia-related behavior management is to treat "agitation" as a unitary construct and therefore apply the same strategies of medication and redirection in each case.

Our own evaluation data of our outreach team is open-label and without a control group. It nevertheless suggests findings supporting those of Cohen-Mansfield et al. (2007). Before our intervention, we asked facilities and families to rate frequency of disruptive behaviors (generically defined). At 8-week follow-up, we asked the same groups to rerate. Figure 10.2 provides data for 50 consecutive cases. As is clear from the figure, a couple of cases continued to worsen, and in eight cases there was no change. But in 80% of the cases, there was a decreased frequency of problems behaviors. Figure 10.3 provides the aggregated data for these cases.

Nevertheless a few leaders in this area have provided empirical support for tailored behavioral interventions in dementia-related behavioral disturbance. Cohen-Mansfield and colleagues (J. Cohen-Mansfield, Libin, & Marx, 2007) conducted one of the best studies. By randomizing facilities, as opposed to patients to treatment arms, they were able to reflect the fact that behavioral interventions impact the entire environment and have the potential to be

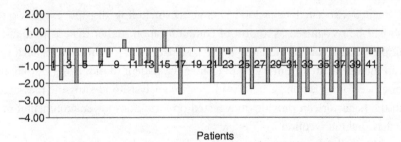

FIGURE 10.2 Change in frequency of problem behaviors following intervention of outreach team. 0 = a few times a month, 1 = 1–2 times/week, 2 = 3–4 times per week, 3 = daily

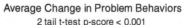

Average Change in Problem Behaviors
2 tail t-test p-score < 0.001

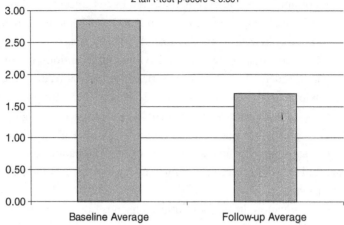

Baseline Average   Follow-up Average

<small>FIGURE 10.3 Average change in frequency of problem behaviors following intervention of outreach team. N = 50. 0 = a few times a month, 1 = 1–2 times/week, 2 = 3–4 times per week, 3 = daily</small>

generalized across patients. These investigators found that implementation of personalized, nonpharmacological interventions resulted in statistically significant decreases in overall agitation in the intervention group relative to the control group. In addition, implementation of individualized interventions for agitation resulted in statistically significant increases in pleasure and interest. Their findings emphasize the importance of searching for underlying reasons for agitated behaviors and support the use of individualized, nonpharmacological interventions for agitation in dementia.

Conclusion

Dementia-associated behavioral alterations, including disruptive behavior, should be recognized as a form of communication, rather than as random, unpredictable, or meaningless events. Management of problem behaviors can then be shifted from trying to change the patient to modifying causative or exacerbating factors. Careful and creative analysis to identify the message in the behavior can provide unexpected opportunities for environmental or behavioral intervention.

When clinicians are unfamiliar or fail to consider environmental, physical, psychological, or social mediators of behavior, and thus do not develop an integrated care plan, the goal of reducing unwanted behaviors is unlikely to be achieved. Since only death creates a true behavioral vacuum, reducing unwanted behaviors necessitates increasing wanted behaviors. Understanding of the patient's life history, combined with consideration of their presumed underlying dementia etiology and functional capacity, can point the direction to meaningful activities to promote with the patient. With complete integration of these approaches to patient assessment and management, difficult behavior problems can be reduced, and the quality of life for patients with dementia improved. Caregivers who learn what to expect as the disease progresses can anticipate cognitive and functional limitations and the expected behavioral effects as the dementia progresses.

References

Cohen-Mansfield, J., & Billig, N . (1986). Agitated behaviors in the elderly, I: A conceptual review. *Journal of the American Geriatrics Society*, *34*, 711–721.

Cohen-Mansfield, J., Libin, A., & Marx, M. S . (2007). Nonpharmacological treatment of agitation: A controlled trial of systematic individualized intervention. *The Journals of Gerontology. Series A, Biological Sciences and Medical Sciences*, *62*(8), 908–916.

Dawson, P., Kline, K., Wiancko, D., & Wells, D . (1986). Preventing excess disability in patients with Alzheimer's disease. *Geriatric Nursing*, *7*, 298–301.

de Medeiros, K., Rosenberg, P. B., Baker, A. S., & Onyike, C. U . (2008). Improper sexual behaviors in elders with dementia living in residential care. *Dementia and Geriatric Cognitive Disorders*, *26*(4), 370–377.

Folstein, M., Anthony, J., Parhad, I., Duffy, B., & Gruenberg, E . (1985). The meaning of cognitive impairment in the elderly. *Journal of the American Geriatrics Society*, *33*, 228–235.

German, P., Rovner, B., Burton, L., Brant, L., & Clark, R . (1992). The role of mental morbidity in the nursing home experience. *Gerontologist*, *32*, 152–158.

Hellen, C . (1992). *Alzheimer's disease: Activity-focused care*. Boston, MA: Andover Medical Publishers.

Lichtenberg, P. A., & Strzepek, D. M . (1990). Assessments of institutionalized dementia patients' competencies to participate in intimate relationships. *Gerontologist*, *30*(1), 117–120.

Loebel, J., & Leibovici, A . (1994). The management of other psychiatric states: Hallucinations, delusions, and other disturbances. *Medical Clinics of North America*, *78*, 841–859.

Robinson, A., Spencer, B., & White, L . (1988). *Understanding difficult behaviors: Some practical suggestions for coping with Alzheimer's disease and related illnesses*. Ypsilanti: Geriatric Education Center of Michigan, Michigan State University.

Snyder, L., Rupprecht, P., Pyrek, J., Brekhus, S., & Moss, T . (1978). Wandering. *Gerontologist, 18*, 272–280.

Tucker, I . (2010). Management of inappropriate sexual behaviors in dementia: A literature review. *International Psychogeriatrics, 22*(5), 683–692.

Whall, A., Black, M., Groh, C., Yankou, D., Kupferschmid, B., & Foster, N . (1997). The effect of natural environments upon agitation and aggression in late stage dementia patients. *American Journal of Alzheimer's Disease and Other Dementias, 12*, 216–220.

Index

VH and, 273
visual asymmetries and, 174–175
visual variant, 173–174
visuospatial abilities and, 172–174
Alzheimer's Disease Centers, 226
Alzheimer's Disease Neuroimaging
    Initiative (ADNI), 7, 15
    IADL assessments and, 94
    MCI criteria and, 73–74
    PIB uptake and, 112f
    summary of, 161t–162t
    Uniform Data Set, 217
Alzheimer's Disease Patient Registry, 138
Alzheimer's Disease Research Center, 21
aMCI. *See* amnestic mild cognitive
    impairment
American Heart Association/American
    Stroke Association (AHA/ASA),
    210–211
American Psychiatric Association (APA),
    96–97
AMI. *See* Autobiographical Memory
    Inventory
amnestic mild cognitive impairment
    (aMCI), 25
    characterizations of, 220
    executive functions and, 171
    neuropathology of, 100t
    prevalence of, 90, 99f
    procedural memory and, 27
    reversion rates of, 87
    single-domain, 159
    stability of, 88f
    studies, 82–83
    subtypes, 89–90
amygdala
    LB density in, 267
    spongiosis in, 264
amyloids. *See also* beta amyloid
    angiopathy, 137
    binding, 174
    diffuse, 58
    immunization trials, 151
    processing, 153
amyloid cascade hypothesis, 7,
    148–149, 148f

critique of, 149–151
amyloid imaging, 51, 95
    ligands, 47
    positive, 49
    studies, 110–113
Amyloid Precursor Protein (APP) gene,
    153
amyotrophic lateral sclerosis (ALS), 320
angiopathy, 137
angiotensin-converting-enzyme
    inhibitors, 237
annual conversion rate (ACR), 77t–80t
antecedent management, 366, 372
antiamyloid therapies, 110–111
antihypertensive medications, 237–238
anxiety
    as AD behavioral disturbance, 177
    agitation and, 375
    as psychological factor, 371
APA. *See* American Psychiatric
    Association
aphasia. *See also* primary progressive
    aphasia; progressive nonfluent
    aphasia
    CBD and, 340–341
    FTD and, 227
    nonfluent, 197, 340–341
Aphasia Screening Examination, 312
Apnea/Hypopnea index, 256
APOE. *See* apolipoprotein E
APOE ε4. *See* apolipoprotein E, epsilon
    variant
apolipoprotein E (APOE), 45–47, 74,
    154–156
    genotype, 155
    isomers, 154
    VaD risk factors and, 203
apolipoprotein E, epsilon variant (APOE
    ε4), 146–147, 154
    allele status, 159
    BBB and, 147–148
    cardiovascular disease and, 206
    Cox proportional hazards analyses
        of, 160t
    diabetes and, 139
apparent diffusion coefficient (ADC), 105

amyloid cascade hypothesis and,
148–149, 148f
deposits, 110–112
PCA and, 347
plaque burden, 51
toxicity of, 150–151
beta-blockers, 237
BIN1, 154
Binswanger's disease, 208, 346
biomarkers, 21–22
AD, 48
AD diagnostic criteria and, 144t–145t
cognitive function and, 26f
DLB and, 22
dynamic, 23f
possible AD dementia and, 142
preclinical AD, 139
probable AD dementia and, 142
reliance on, 95–96
timing dynamics of, 163f
bipolar cells, 271
blood-brain barrier (BBB)
APOE ε4 and, 147–148
cerebral infarctions and, 204
blood oxygen level dependent (BOLD)
signal, 51–52
fMRI, 53–54, 107–108
blood pressure (BP), 234–237
BNT. *See* Boston Naming Test
BOLD signal. *See* blood oxygen level
dependent signal
boredom, 374
Boston Diagnostic Aphasia Exam, 201
Boston Naming Test (BNT), 84, 86t,
139, 200f, 260f, 336f
VaD and, 228–229
boundary conditions overlap, 4f
bovine spongiform encephalopathy, 350
BP. *See* blood pressure
Braak staging system, 54, 149
DLB and, 265
bradykinesia, 276, 338
brain
atrophy, 50–51
atrophy rates, 101–102
autopsy, 39

fitness, 116
microbleeds, 147, 205
brain injury. *See also* traumatic brain
injury
disease-related, 205–206
prior, 155
vascular cognitive impairment and,
205
brainstem
microbleeds in, 205
neuronal loss in, 338
brain structures
atrophy rates, 101–102, 102f
atrophy with DLB, 274
atypical dementia and, 337
hemorrhages in, 205
British Association for
Psychopharmacology, 114
Broca's area, 198
bvFTD. *See* behavioral variant of
frontotemporal dementia

CAA. *See* cerebral amyloid angiopathy
CADASIL. *See* cerebral autosomal
dominant arteriopathy with
subcortical infarcts and
leukoencephalopathy
calcium channel blockers, 237
California Verbal Learning Test (CVLT),
86t, 200f
CBD and, 341–342
Cox proportional hazards analyses
of, 160t
DLB and, 272
episodic memory and, 159
PSP and, 339
sensitivity of, 92
Canadian Study of Health and Aging
(CSHA), 5–6
CANTAB, 342, 345
CARASIL. *See* cerebral autosomal
recessive arteriopathy with
subcortical infarcts and
leukoencephalopathy
carbon-labeled Pittsburgh Compound B
(^{11}C-PiB), 110

cardiovascular disease
  APOE ε4 and, 206
  VCI prevention and, 211
Cardiovascular Health Study (CHS),
    97–98
carotid pulsatility index, 236
carotid sinus sensitivity, 279–280
category fluency, 226, 321–322
  lateral temporal lobe and, 228
  semantic memory deterioration and,
    158
Category Fluency test, 260*f*, 306*f*, 336*f*
CATIE-AD. *See* Clinical Antipsychotic
    Trials of Intervention Effectiveness-
    Alzheimer's Disease
CBD. *See* corticobasal degeneration
CBF. *See* cerebral blood flow
CBGD. *See* corticobasal ganglionic
    degeneration
CD2AP, 154
CD33, 154
CDR-SB. *See* Clinical Dementia Rating
    Scale Sum of Boxes
CDR scale. *See* Clinical Dementia Rating
    scale
central nervous system (CNS)
  demyelination, 103
  insulin and, 149
CERAD learning test, 92, 98
cerebellum
  microbleeds in, 205
  structural changes in, 50
cerebral amyloid angiopathy (CAA),
    147, 204–205, 210
cerebral atrophy, 335
cerebral autosomal dominant
    arteriopathy with subcortical
    infarcts and leukoencephalopathy
    (CADASIL), 206
cerebral autosomal recessive arteriopathy
    with subcortical infarcts and
    leukoencephalopathy (CARASIL),
    207
cerebral blood flow (CBF), 52–53
  age-related patterns in, 53
  BOLD fMRI and, 54

BP and, 236–237
cerebral infarctions, 204
cerebrospinal fluid (CSF)
  accumulation, 337
  assays, 15, 95
  entorhinal cortex and, 101
  NPH and, 344
  shunting, 346–347
  tau levels of, 21
cerebrovascular accident (CVA), 197
cerebrovascular disease (CVD), 147–148
  AD and, 202
  AD *versus*, 223*f*
  aging and, 203
  cognitive impairment and, 223
ChEIs. *See* cholinesterase inhibitors
choline, 103–104
  depletion, 268–269
choline acetyltransferase, 264
cholinergic hypothesis
  of AD, 146–147
  of DLB, 268–269
cholinesterase, 146–147
cholinesterase inhibitors (ChEIs)
  in AD interventions, 176
  in DLB interventions, 282
  in MCI interventions, 113–114
  VH and, 269
CHS. *See* Cardiovascular Health Study
CIND. *See* cognitive impairment no
    dementia
circle of Willis, 197, 311
CJD. *See* Creutzfeldt-Jakob disease
Clinical Antipsychotic Trials of Intervention
    Effectiveness-Alzheimer's Disease
    (CATIE-AD), 177
Clinical Dementia Rating (CDR) scale, 4,
    94, 217, 270
  false positive errors and, 16
  IADL assessments and, 94
Clinical Dementia Rating Scale Sum of
    Boxes (CDR-SB), 102*f*
clinical judgment, 217
clinicopathologic correlates in DLB and
    AD, 267–268
clock drawing tests, 173, 312*f*

diastolic blood pressure (DBP), 234–235
differential diagnosis
    of AD, 157
    of dementia, 219–220
    with DLB and AD, 273
diffuse hypoxia, 204
diffusion imaging, 50–51
diffusion tensor imaging, 105
diffusion weighted MR imaging (DWI),
    105–106
Digit Span, 339
Digit Vigilance test, 311–312
disclosure interaction effects, 48*f*
disease burden, 25–26
disease trajectory, 25–26
distraction, 373
diuretics, 237
D-KEFS. *See* Delis-Kaplan Executive
    Function System
DLB. *See* dementia with Lewy bodies
DMN. *See* default mode networks
donepezil, 73, 176, 282
DRS. *See* Dementia Rating Scale
DSM-5. *See* Diagnostic and Statistical
    Manual of Mental Disorders, fifth
    edition
DWI. *See* diffusion weighted MR
    imaging
dysautonomia, 279–280

echolalia, 334
educational programming, 116
elastin, 234
encoding
    immediate recall and, 91
    semantic, 158
entorhinal cortex
    CSF and, 101
    structural changes in, 50
environment, 368–370
EPHA1, 154
epidemiology
    of AD, 143–146
    of cognitive aging, 49–50
    of DLB, 261
    of FTD, 314

of MCI, 97–98
of VaD, 203–204
episodic memory, 90
    AD neuropsychology and, 158–165
    CBD and, 341
    composite scores, 225–226
    CVLT and, 159
    decline models, 164*f*
    differential diagnosis of AD and, 157
    DLB and, 271–273
    impairment, 95–96
    mean z-scores of, 168*f*
    models, 164–165
    MSA and, 343–344
    MTL and, 158
    preclinical AD and, 160, 164
    PSP and, 339
    tasks, 168
    VaD and, 220–228
    verbal, 224
EPS. *See* extrapyramidal symptoms
executive functions
    AD and, 169–172
    AD dementia and, 142
    aMCI and, 171
    CBD and, 340
    composite scores, 225–226
    definitions of, 225–226
    differential diagnosis of AD and, 157
    frontal lobe and, 168
    FTD and, 322–323
    high, 171*f*
    low, 171*f*
    MCI and, 169–170
    mean z-scores of, 168*f*
    measures, 170–171
    NPH and, 346
    PSP and, 338
    small vessel ischemic VaD and, 221
    tasks, 168
    VaD and, 220–228
Exelon. *See* rivastigmine
extraneous stimuli, 368
extrapyramidal symptoms (EPS), 177,
    224, 319, 348
    CJD and, 348

FA. *See* fractional anisotropy
face-encoding tasks, 107
false positive errors
   AD biomarkers and, 48
   CDR and, 16
   sensitivity and, 219–220
   VE and, 232
FCSR. *See* free and cued selective
   reminding
FDA. *See* Food and Drug Administration
FDG. *See* fluorodeoxyglucose
FDG-PET. *See* fluorodeoxyglucose
   positron emission tomography
fibrous gliosis, 310
finite trajectories for MCI, 74*f*
flash electroretinography, 271
florbetapir F18, 110
Florida Alzheimer's Disease Initiative
   (ADI), 280
Fluctuations Score, 277–278
fluency
   category, 158, 226, 321–322
   FTD and, 321–322
   letter, 226, 228, 321–322
   phonemic, 339
   semantic, 339
   verbal, 167–169, 343–344
fluorine 19, florbetapir, 47
fluorodeoxyglucose (FDG), 53
fluorodeoxyglucose positron emission
   tomography (FDG-PET), 109–110
   hypometabolism and, 139
fMRI. *See* functional magnetic resonance
   imaging
Food and Drug Administration (FDA)
   neuroleptics and, 178
   VCI prevention and, 211
forgetting, rate of, 225
fractional anisotropy (FA), 105–106,
   106*f*
Framingham Stroke Risk Profile, 106*f*
free and cued selective reminding
   (FCSR), 91–92
FreeSurfer, 103
frontal cortex atrophy, 310
frontal lobe

accumulation of NFTs in, 156–157
   executive functions and, 168
Frontal Systems Behavior Scale,
   323–324
frontoparietal cortex atrophy, 340
frontotemporal dementia (FTD), 7, 111
   AD *versus*, 111, 322*f*
   age of onset, 326
   aphasia and, 227
   behavioral scales for, 323–324
   behavior disturbances with,
   323–324
   course of, 305–306, 310
   diagnostic criteria for, 313–314,
   315*t*–317*t*
   epidemiology of, 314
   executive functions and, 322–323
   fluency and, 321–322
   genetics of, 314–320
   Kokmen Short Test of Mental Status
   and, 304
   language and, 323
   learning and, 321
   memory and, 321
   mixed-cause dementia and, 209
   MMSE and, 309
   MRI of, 304–305, 305*f*
   neuropathology of, 306, 310–311,
   314–320
   neuropsychological assessments of,
   307, 307*f*, 311–313, 311*f*
   neuropsychology of, 321–324
   non-Pick's, 313
   protein biochemistry for, 320*f*
   semantic dementia variant, 304
   semantic memory and, 323
   SPECT and, 309
   visuospatial abilities and, 323
   WMS and, 321
frontotemporal lobar degeneration
   (FTLD), 306, 313–314
   symptomatic therapy in, 325*t*
   syndromes, 321
FTD. *See* frontotemporal dementia
FTLD. *See* frontotemporal lobar
   degeneration

in medial premotor cortex, 338
hypothalamus
    atrophy of, 274
    subcortical LB in, 264
hypoxia, 149, 204

IADL. *See* instrumental activities of daily
    living
IL6. *See* interleukin 6
IL10. *See* interleukin 10
immediate recall, 321
    encoding and, 91
    measures, 17
immunostaining techniques, 261
impulsivity, 363–364
Independent Living Scales, 93
infections, 369
inferior temporal cortex, 267
inflammation, 204
instrumental activities of daily living
    (IADL)
    assessments, 93–95, 217
    cortical surface maps and, 95*f*
insulin, 149
integrated care plans, 378–379
intelligence quotient (IQ), 16
    memory and, 85
interleukin 6 (IL6), 45
interleukin 10 (IL10), 45
International Psychogeriatric
    Association, 5
interventions
    AD, 175–178
    for agitation, 375
    antihypertensive pharmacological,
        237–238
    behavioral, 376–378, 377*f*, 378*f*
    for delusions, 282
    for DLB, 281–283
    for FTD, 324
    for MCI, 113–116
    multicomponent, 115–116
    neuropsychological assessments and,
        27–28
    nonpharmacological, for AD,
        175–177

nonpharmacological, for DLB,
    282–283
nonpharmacological, for MCI,
    114–116
for normal cognitive aging, 56–58
pharmacological, for AD, 176–178
pharmacological, for DLB, 281–282
pharmacological, for MCI,
    113–114
physical activity, 115–116
psychoeducation, 283
for sexual behavior, 376*t*
for VaD, 232–238
for VH, 282
for wandering, 374
intimacy seeking, 376
intracranial pressure, 345*f*
intraindividual change, 97
intrusion errors, 159, 220
    CVLT sensitivity and, 92
    VaD and, 225–227
intrusiveness, 374
IQ. *See* intelligence quotient

*Journal of the American Medical
    Association*, 16

Kokmen Short Test of Mental Status, 70,
    304, 333
Kral, V. A., 1

lacunar infarcts, 206
    in basal ganglia, 334
    VaD neuropathology and, 203
language
    AD and, 165–167
    FTD and, 323
    later stage AD and, 175
    MSA and, 343
    VaD and, 228–229
late life forgetfulness (LLF), 3–4
lateral temporal lobe
    category fluency and, 228
    damage to, 166
    semantic memory and, 168
LB. *See* Lewy bodies

MOAANS. *See* Mayo Older African
      American Normative Studies
MOANS. *See* Mayo Older American
      Norms
Money Road Map Test, 172
morphometry, 50–51
motor cortex, 342
motor skills
   DLB and, 276
   PDD and, 276
   VaD and, 231–232
MRI. *See* magnetic resonance imaging
MS4A4/MS4A6E, 154
MSA. *See* Mayo Study of Aging; multiple
      system atrophy
MTL. *See* medial temporal lobe
Multilingual Aphasia Exam (MAE)
      Token Test, 200–201, 311*f*, 312
multiple system atrophy (MSA), 279,
      337, 342–344, 343*f*
myoclonus, 340
myo-inositol (MI), 103–105

N-acetyl aspartate (NAA), 103–104
naMCI. *See* nonamnestic mild cognitive
      impairment
Namenda. *See* memantine
naming errors
   AD and, 166–167
   asymmetric cognitive decline and, 174
   semantic memory deterioration and,
      158
National Institute of Aging-Alzheimer's
      Association (NIA-AA)
   AD criteria for, 7
   AD diagnostic criteria and, 139
   dementia criteria of, 16
   MCI diagnostic criteria and, 96–97
   reliance on biomarkers and, 96
National Institute on Aging-Reagan, 98
National Institutes of Health (NIH), 21
neuritic plaques, 54, 137
   AD-type pathology in DLB and, 264
   PCA and, 347
neurocognitive disorders
   major, 8

minor, 9–10
   proposed DSM-5 criteria for, 8–10
neurodegenerative etiology of MCI, 140
neurofibrillary tangles (NFTs), 58, 137,
      149
   accumulation of, 156–157
   AD-type pathology in DLB and,
      264–265
   density of, 267
   distribution of, 150*f*
   PCA and, 347
   Pick's disease and, 314
   tauopathies and, 317
neuroimaging, 15, 50–54. *See also*
      specific imaging techniques
   functional change, 51–54
   structural change, 50–51
   studies of AD, 136–137
   studies of DLB, 273–274
   studies of MCI, 100–113
   of VaD, 196, 198–199, 205–206
neuroleptics, 178, 276, 281
neurological measures
   construct validity of, 17
   countervailing influences on disease
      trajectory and, 25–26
   democratically corrected norms in,
      19–21
   factor structure of, 18*f*
   functional deficits and, 27
   practice effects in, 19*f*
   as predictors of AD, 22–23
   as predictors of dementia, 22–23
   test stability of, 17–19
neuronal integrity, 103
neuropathology
   of aMCI, 100*t*
   of CDB, 340
   of DLB, 261–273
   of FTD, 306, 310–311, 314–320
   of MCI, 98–100
   of naMCI, 100*t*
   of VaD, 203–204
neurophysiology of cognitive aging,
      54–56
neuropsychological assessments, 16–17

of AD, 138–139, 138f
AD *versus* CVD, 223f
AD *versus* VaD, 222–224
bedside, 216
as biomarkers, 21–22
of CBD, 335–336, 336f
composite, 224–225
distinctions between, 157
for DLB, 259–260, 260f
of FTD, 307, 307f, 311–313, 311f
interventions and, 27–28
of MCI, 71–72
multiple, 83–89, 218–219
with older adults, 41–44
optimizing, 17–21
rating forms, 217
sensitivity of, 91–92, 218
statistically defined MCI subtypes
and, 90–91
of VaD, 196, 197f, 199–201, 200f
neuropsychological profile, 40f
of DLB, 270–273
of MCI, 72f
of VaD, 211–232
neuropsychology
of AD, 156–175
clinical, 219–220
of cognitive aging, 44–45
of FTD, 321–324
NFTs. *See* neurofibrillary tangles
NIA-AA. *See* National Institute of Aging-
Alzheimer's Association
NIH. *See* National Institutes of Health
nonamnestic mild cognitive impairment
(naMCI)
neuropathology of, 100t
prevalence of, 99f
reversion rates of, 87
stability of, 88f
noninflammatory spongiform
encephalopathy, 348
nonspecific cognitive stimulation, 57
normal pressure hydrocephalus (NPH),
337, 344–347, 345f
normative studies, 45
Notch3 gene, 206

NPH. *See* normal pressure
hydrocephalus
nucleus basalis of Meynert, 146, 268
nutritional status, 155

obesity, 233
occipital lobe
aging and, 53
atrophy in, 173–174
CAA and, 205
DLB and, 271
PCA and, 347
O'Connor, John, 371–372, 375
olanzapine, 177, 281
older adults
neuropsychological assessments with,
41–44
physical disabilities in, 42
olivopontocerebellar system, 342
operational research criteria for
preclinical AD, 139–140
orthostatic hypotension, 279–280
outcome studies, 219
oxidative stress, 204
oxygen consumption, 54

parahippocampal gyrus, 107
parahippocampus
CBF in, 52
LB density in, 267
volume, 5
paralimbic cortex, 109–110
paranoia, 366
paraoxonase 1 (PON1), 45
parietal lobe
accumulation of NFTs in, 156–157
LB in, 267
parkinsonism
AD and, 273
CBD and, 340
DLB and, 260
MSA and, 342
spontaneous motor features of, 276
Parkinson's disease (PD)
genetics of, 269
Lewy bodies and, 264

Razadyne. *See* galantamine
RBD. *See* REM sleep behavior disorder
RCI. *See* reliable change indices
recall. *See also* delayed recall; immediate
    recall
    composite neuropsychological
        assessments and, 224–225
    recognition memory *versus*, 218
    testing, 218
recognition memory
    composite neuropsychological
        assessments and, 224–225
    Memory Assessment Scale and, 224
    recall *versus*, 218
    testing, 158, 218
Record of Independent Living (ROIL),
    29t–30t
redirection, 372–373
relative risk (RR), 23, 24f
reliable change indices (RCI), 10
Remember Everything Test (RET), 165f
REM sleep. *See* rapid eye movement
    sleep
REM sleep behavior disorder (RBD), 256
    dementia and, 278
    DLB and, 268, 274, 278–279
    idiopathic, 279
Repeatable Battery for the Assessment of
    Neurophysiological Status, 57–58
RET. *See* Remember Everything Test
retention
    cortical surface maps and, 104f
    MRI studies and, 103
    MTL and, 103
reticular formation
    alpha-synuclein inclusions in, 342
    midbrain, 338
    pontine-medullary, 278
Rey Auditory Verbal Learning Test
    (AVLT), 22, 38, 103, 163, 260f,
    307f, 336f, 346
    RR and, 23, 24f
Rey-Osterrieth Complex Figure Test
    (ROCF), 231
right-left disorientation, 174, 348
risk factors. *See also* relative risk

cerebrovascular, 88
diabetes as, 203, 238
genetic, 46–49
for MCI progression to dementia, 75f
nongenetic, 155–156
VaD, 203
vascular, 233
for VCI, 210–211
risperidone, 177
rivastigmine, 176
robust norms, 45
ROC curve analysis, 107
ROCF. *See* Rey-Osterrieth Complex
    Figure Test
ROIL. *See* Record of Independent Living
RR. *See* relative risk

saccadic eye movements, 271
SBI. *See* silent brain infarction
SBP. *See* systolic blood pressure
semantic dementia (SD), 314
    clinical features of, 316t–317t
semantic memory, 90
    AD and, 165–167
    CBD and, 340–341
    deterioration, 158
    differential diagnosis of AD and, 157
    FTD and, 323
    lateral temporal lobe and, 168
    mean z-scores of, 168f
    PSP and, 339
    tasks, 168
    VaD and, 228–229
senescing, 40–41
sensitivity, 19, 85
    carotid sinus, 279–280
    of CVLT, 92
    false positive errors and, 219–220
    of neuropsychological assessments,
        91–92, 218
serial position effect, 158
sexual behavior, 375–376, 376t
Shalom Village Long Term Care Home,
    375
Shanks, Lela Knox, 372
shunting, 346–347

About the Authors

Glenn E. Smith, Ph.D., ABPP/CN, is a board-certified clinical neuropsychologist and professor of psychology at Mayo Clinic in Rochester, MN. He has served as principal investigator of the Mayo Alzheimer's Disease Research Center Education Core and is associate director of Mayo's Clinical and Translational Science Education Resource. Dr. Smith has had continuous research funding since 1994 and has authored or co-authored more than 180 original articles on normal aging, mild cognitive impairment, and dementia. He was the past president of both the American Board of Clinical Neuropsychology and Division of Clinical Neuropsychology of the American Psychological Association. In addition to supervising postdoctoral fellows, he maintains an active diagnostic neuropsychology practice. He led the development of and directs Mayo's Dementia Behavior Assessment and Response Team and Healthy Action to Benefit Independence and Thinking (HABIT) program for persons with mild cognitive impairment.

Mark W. Bondi, Ph.D., ABPP/CN, is a board-certified clinical neuropsychologist, professor of psychiatry at the University of California San Diego, and director of the Neuropsychological Assessment Unit at the VA San Diego Healthcare System. He is recipient of a Mid-Career Investigator Award in Patient-Oriented Research from the National Institute on Aging. His NIH-funded research centers on the cognitive and brain changes of individuals at risk for dementia, and he has published more than 120 articles, books, and book chapters. Dr. Bondi is a Fellow of the American Psychological Association and National Academy of Neuropsychology, former secretary of the Division of Clinical Neuropsychology of the American Psychological Association, and member of the board of directors of the American Board of Clinical Neuropsychology and board of governors of the International Neuropsychological Society. Dr. Bondi maintains a clinical practice in neuropsychology, and he is an active teacher and a supervisor for his institution's doctoral training, predoctoral internship, and postdoctoral fellowship programs.